The Long Shadow of Antiquity

The Long Shadow of Antiquity

What Have the Greeks and Romans Done for Us?

Gregory S. Aldrete and Alicia Aldrete

continuum

Continuum International Publishing Group

The Tower Building
11 York Road
London
SE1 7NX

80 Maiden Lane
Suite 704
New York
NY 10038

www.continuumbooks.com

First published 2012

British Library Cataloguing in Publication Data
A catalogue record for this book is available from the British Library.

ISBN: HB: 978–1–4411–6247–2

Library of Congress Cataloging-in-Publication Data
A catalog record for this book is available from the Library of Congress.

Typeset by Fakenham Prepress Solutions, Fakenham, Norfolk NR21 8NN
Printed and bound in India

Contents

Introduction: Knowing yourself

One of the longest-running institutions in human history was the Delphic Oracle, which operated continuously for over 1,000 years from the seventh century B.C. up until the end of the fourth century A.D. Located in a spectacular natural setting, the sanctuary clings dramatically to the slopes of Mt. Parnassus, and from it one has a dazzling view stretching down to the Gulf of Corinth far below. The centerpiece of the sanctuary was the Temple to Apollo, within whose marble walls the representative of the god, a priestess known as the Pythia, was believed to speak with the god's voice to human beings. The façade of this temple was allegedly inscribed with several aphorisms, one of which was the phrase "Know Yourself." Just as the sanctuary of Delphi was of central and communal importance to all the Greek city-states, so too its motto of self-knowledge is an appropriate thesis and inspiration for this book.

It is impossible to understand who you are without knowing where you came from. This is equally true of both individuals and civilizations. Just as one's character and personality are inevitably shaped by one's parents, family, and friends, the environments one grows up in, and the experiences that one has, a culture is made up of many strands and influences. It is impossible to meaningfully comprehend the complex culture that we live in today without having at least some knowledge of how those individual strands that comprise our culture were formed. This book is intended to help you to better "Know Yourself" by taking you on an entertaining journey through the institutions, artifacts, rituals, and structures that make up our modern culture, and to point out some of the myriad ways in which the civilizations of ancient Greece and Rome have fundamentally influenced and shaped the world that we live in today. You will discover that everything from how we measure time, build our cities, get married, and organize our governments, to what we do for fun and how we worship, has origins in the classical world.

In this study, we have especially focused on the effects that classical civilization has had on European-based Western civilization for the obvious reason that this has been the area in which ancient Greece and Rome have had the most direct and profound cultural impact. Because of the way in which the era of colonization has spread the Western cultural heritage around the globe (and whether or not one views this as a positive development), the classical world has ended up exerting a wide-ranging influence far beyond the borders of Europe, and its presence can be detected in nearly every modern society. This is not intended as a scholarly book, but rather it is for the general reader who is curious about the world that he or she lives in and would like to know a little more about how that world came to be. Accordingly, it does not presuppose any prior knowledge of classical history, so all ancient terms will be explained and all quotations from Greek and Roman authors will be translated into English.

Tracing one's genealogy has become a popular pursuit, with numerous websites and how-to books offering advice about how best to go about it, and handsome books and family trees available for recording the information you uncover. All over the world, people are trying to find their "roots"—the roots of their family trees. Curiously, at the same time that the genealogy craze continues to thrive, history languishes as a subject in schools because people perceive it as being boring and irrelevant to today's world. We seem able to separate our obsession with our families' particular histories from the grand sweep of history with a capital H. But if we are concerned with our families' origins, shouldn't we also question where we come from in a more general way?

Obviously, our families have shaped who we are, but, on a broader scale, so have the cultures and societies that have come before us. In the United States, we still speak of the "Founding Fathers," a term which stresses the significant role they played in forming our way of life; they were the "parents" of America's new-born government. But we can extend that analogy back even further. On a broader historical timeline, the ancient Greeks and Romans were the parents of the world we live in today, by providing us with all sorts of cultural touchstones, ideas, and inspirations that we now often have either forgotten about or else take for granted. Indeed, the "Founding Fathers" of the United States were very aware of their own indebtedness to the Greeks and Romans, as we will see, and would find our current relative indifference to them hard to fathom. When George Washington was sculpted wearing a toga, he was not just playing dress-up but rather was making a statement about values and ideals.

The past usually determines the future, and we cannot fully "know ourselves" and where we come from until we understand how the past has shaped us, in matters both great and small. In this book, let us consider some of the ways in which our Greek and Roman "parents" gave birth to the world we live in today.

Acknowledgment

Most of this book was written while Greg Aldrete held a Solmsen Postdoctoral Fellowship at the Institute for Research in the Humanities at the University of Wisconsin at Madison. The authors would like to thank the staff and fellows of the Institute for providing a pleasant, stimulating, and supportive environment for both of us to work in while writing this book.

Abbreviations

CIL, which stands for *Corpus Inscriptionum Latinarum*, is an extensive, much-cited collection of ancient Latin inscriptions.

ILS stands for *Inscriptiones Latinae Selectae*, a standard collection of Latin inscriptions.

SHA stands for *Scriptores Historiae Augustae*, a collection of ancient biographies of emperors by various unknown authors.

1

The bare necessities: Food and shelter

A few basic needs shape our everyday lives just as much today as they did 2,000 years ago, and, of these, the two most crucial are food and shelter. This chapter will explore how the ancient Greeks and Romans met these essential requirements of daily life, and the manner in which their solutions continue to influence and shape the structures of daily life in the contemporary world. We will end the chapter with a brief look at a modern necessity—money—and how this too has its roots in antiquity.

You are what you eat: Food and drink

The phrase "You are what you eat" would have resonated with the ancients. Just as there are stereotypes today of what types of food the people of certain regions like to eat, your choice of cuisine in the ancient world said a great deal about who you were culturally. A major way in which the Romans distinguished themselves from people whom they regarded as barbarians, especially the tribes living in Northern Europe, was through their differing diets. Those who lived around the shores of the Mediterranean ate primarily three basic staples. Today these three foods form the core of one of the currently trendy diets recommended by doctors and health gurus as a way both to stay healthy and to lose weight. The ancient "Mediterranean triad" of foods comprised probably more than 80 percent of the caloric intake of more than 80 percent of the people who lived in the ancient Mediterranean world. The three foods that made it up were: wheat, olives (largely in the form of oil), and wine. One of the most common meals in the classical world would have been a chunk of bread dipped in olive oil washed down with wine, although wheat was also frequently cooked into a sort of porridge or gruel. The next time you dip a piece of bread into a dish of olive oil and take a sip of wine at a fancy Italian restaurant, remember that you are eating what the poorest Greek and Roman peasants ate three times a day every day.

Olives are the quintessential Mediterranean food. In fact, if you superimpose a map of the Roman Empire at its height over a map of the geographic zone where it is possible to grow olives, the two are nearly identical. Olive oil was used for many purposes in addition to food—it was the basis of perfumes; it provided light when burnt in clay lamps; and it was rubbed over the body and then scraped off as a kind of soap or cleanser. The Roman author Pliny states that "There are two liquids that are specially agreeable to the human body, wine inside and oil outside" (*Natural History* 14.29.150). The importance of the olive in Mediterranean life is suggested by the foundation myth of how the Greek goddess Athena became the patroness of Athens, beating out her uncle Poseidon by offering the Athenians the gift of an olive tree.

Grain was a crucial element in the ancient Mediterranean diet. The Greeks ate primarily two kinds of bread, a bread made of wheat and a bread made of barley flour; as barley was more common than wheat, wheat bread was more expensive and mainly for the wealthy. Whereas today we have begun to view bread made from tough grains such as barley as good and healthy, to the Romans it was inferior to wheat, and was often given to slaves. Since special ovens were needed to bake bread, the majority of Romans probably purchased their bread from bakeries rather than making their own. Carbonized loaves buried in Pompeian bakeries by the eruption of Mount Vesuvius reveal that the concept of pre-sliced bread is not a new one. The round loaves offered on sale whose imprints are preserved in the volcanic ash were shaped so that convenient pie-shaped wedges could be torn off individually. Grain was also cooked into porridges and gruels, and pulses of dried beans and legumes, particularly chickpeas, peas, and lentils, supplied a relatively cheap source of protein for the majority of Romans who could not afford meat.

Figure 1.1 *Scenes of Roman breadmaking from the tomb of the baker, Eurysaces. In the top panel, mules are being used to turn hourglass-shaped mills, grinding grain into flour. In the middle, workers are kneading dough at long tables, and at the bottom, a baker inserts loaves into a large oven.*

Another specialized diet focusing on grains that already existed in the ancient world was a concentrated high-carbohydrate regime for certain athletes. Recent studies of the remains of gladiators suggest that they ate an exclusively high-carb diet in order to bulk up and develop layers of muscle and fat. The goal was to possess a thick padding of tissue to cover and protect their vulnerable internal organs. A gladiator could survive a gory but superficial slash to this bulky layer of muscles and fat, but a sword that penetrated his chest or abdominal cavity was almost always fatal due to infection. This special gladiator diet seems to have consisted largely of cooked barley. Thus, just as modern athletes follow strict dietary regimes so as to develop speed, flexibility, endurance, or strength, ancient athletic performers had already learned to exploit the link between certain types of food and desired physical characteristics.

The third core component in the Mediterranean diet was wine. In the classical world, wine was more than just a luxury alcoholic drink imbibed on special occasions; it was a basic staple of life. Studies of twentieth-century Greek peasants who still lived a traditional lifestyle similar to that in antiquity suggest that the average inhabitant of the ancient world may have drunk more than a liter and a half of wine per day. Wines existed in a wide range of types and qualities, from the rough vintages consumed by farmers and the poor to varieties from coveted regions or even specific fields, which sold for vast sums. The entire apparatus of wine appreciation was fully developed in the ancient world, with critics and tasters who rated the numerous vintages and argued vehemently over which wines were the best. In words that would resonate with any wine snob today, Pliny the Elder wrote that "Every person fancies himself judge of the competition regarding which wine tops the list" (*Natural History* 14.8). Nevertheless, just as today certain vineyards and specific harvest years are widely believed to have produced the finest (and most expensive) wines, there were regions, farms, and eras that were renowned in the ancient world for the consistently superlative quality of their vintages. Thus in Italy, wines that originated from the Falernian district were regarded as a by-word for quality, while in Greece, wines from the island of Chios boasted a formidable reputation as early as the time of Homer. Some hint of the complexity of ancient wine appreciation can be obtained by noting that Pliny devoted dozens of pages in his encyclopedic *Natural History* to delineating and ranking wines from different regions, and in his *Epigrams*, the poet Martial casually mentioned no fewer than 19 distinct varieties. One major difference between Greek and Roman wine-drinking and current practices is that the ancients always mixed their wine with water before drinking it. While people today still drink wine mulled with spices or honey and served hot, particularly during the winter holiday season, such beverages were far more common in the ancient world.

Wheat, olive oil, and wine composed the classic Mediterranean triad and served as the foundation of many people's diets, but outsiders were also defined by what they ate. Thus, while in the United States today we might be tempted to stereotype and identify a Southerner by his or her love of barbecue, a Midwesterner by a predilection for meat and potatoes, and a Californian by a fondness for avocados and sprouts on a sandwich, the people of the ancient Mediterranean also defined others by their foods of choice. The sharpest contrast was with the northern barbarian tribes, who were mainly cattle-herders. They, too, had their own triad of staples that formed the majority of their diet, but in their case it was red meat, cheese, and beer. Instead of olive oil, their fat of choice was butter. To ancient Mediterranean people, this menu was a highly unappetizing prospect, and carried pejorative connotations of being uncivilized. One Greek senator who was serving in the Roman administration had the misfortune to be posted far to the north along the Danube river. Homesick and tormented by having to subsist on the "barbarian diet," he wrote a letter home in which he lamented his culinary woes: "The inhabitants here … lead the most miserable existence of all mankind … for they cultivate no olives and they drink no wine" (quoted in Peter Brown, *The World of Late Antiquity AD 150–750*, London: Thames and Hudson, 1971, p. 11). If an ancient Roman were somehow transported to modern Germany or butter- and cheese-producing Wisconsin and saw everyone eating bratwurst and drinking beer, he would have immediately known that he was among "barbarians."

In Homer's *Odyssey*, we see both the centrality of bread for the Greeks and how diet defines character and nationality. Homer depicts bread-eating as, in and of itself, a sign of humanity. Odysseus sends out scouts looking for "Men, eaters of bread" (*The Odyssey* 9.l.89), but they only find the Lotus-Eaters, drugged by their diet of sweet fruit into a state of oblivious lassitude. They next encounter the monstrous Cyclops, described as wild and unaware of civilized culture and the laws of men. His savagery is reflected in what he eats, for he devours Odysseus' men, whole and raw. He then caps off his barbaric feast by drinking milk rather than watered wine, as a Greek would have. Although the ancient Greeks did, like the Cyclops, herd goats and make cheese, they tended not to drink milk—another sign of the Cyclops' uncivilized nature, and again a reflection of the Mediterranean person's association of dairy products with "barbarians." When he does drink wine, he becomes so inebriated that he passes out and Odysseus' men blind him—perhaps a warning to those who do not mix their wine with water, as the Greeks habitually did, that drinking yourself "blind" would incapacitate you.

If elites both ancient and modern share a connoisseurship of rare and fine wines and would probably feel quite at home at one another's exclusive wine-tastings, at the opposite end of the spectrum of food consumption, where we find mass-produced, cheaply-priced food intended to be eaten on the run, there are also more than a few similarities between ancient and modern practices. Contrary to popular opinion, the fast-food restaurant is not a creation of modern society, and ancient Rome had a thriving "fast-food industry" that would seem quite familiar to us today. In addition to street vendors hawking every possible type of edible treat, there were bars on nearly every street corner that seem to have served as the ancient equivalent of McDonald's. Some of these were called a *popina* (in Latin) or a *thermopolium*, from the Greek for "selling hot things."

Figure 1.2 *Exterior and interior of a Roman bar and restaurant. The street-side counters usually contained clay pots filled with drinks and snacks. The painting on the interior depicts some of the food offerings available and may have served as a kind of visual menu, such as those found in fast-food restaurants today.*

Today, tourists can see ample evidence of these at Pompeii and Herculaneum, where their counters, inset with large pottery containers called *dolia*, still remain. Busy customers could stop in for a quick bite or drink consumed either standing or perhaps sitting at a handful of tables and chairs. Much of the food sold here likely consisted of variants on the basic combination of wine, bread, and olive oil, with perhaps some meat or fish bits thrown in to liven things up. On the walls, there were sometimes paintings of the basic sorts of food and drink available, in much the same way that fast-food restaurants today display large glossy photographs or a wall of lit-up pictures of plates of food and meal combos. Then, as now, this meant that even if you couldn't speak the language you could just point at what you wanted—always a handy feature in large, cosmopolitan cities full of travelers.

While many bars were probably reputable, these sorts of establishment often earned a shady reputation from their representation by upper-class authors, who described them as hotbeds of gambling, prostitution, and, of course, drunkenness and rowdy behavior. Like at wine bars today, different amounts of money could purchase different levels of quality, as suggested by this inscription by the entrance of a Pompeian bar: "Hedone says: One *as* (a type of coin) for a drink; 2 *asses* for a better one; and 4 *asses* get you Falernian wine" (*CIL* IV 1679).

If we turn to attitudes towards eating, the origins of many of our ideas regarding indulgence and overindulgence have their seeds in the ancient world. Whereas we tend to speak of the two categories of "food" and "drink," the ancient Greeks had three: staple (*sitos*), relish (*opson*), and drink. The *sitos* was made of grain, typically in the form of bread or porridge, whereas the *opson* was pretty much anything else, eaten as an accompaniment to the *sitos*—whether olives, cheese, fish, or a meat stew, for example. What mattered most was the ratio of *sitos* to *opson*; in keeping with the idealized Greek idea of moderation, you were supposed to eat mostly *sitos* and very little *opson*. Otherwise, you might risk being seen as gluttonous or overly luxurious in your tastes.

In *The Republic*, for instance, Plato condemns the unseemliness of excessive *opson*-eating (*opsophagia*) by initially leaving them entirely out of the diet prescribed for the inhabitants of his ideal state, where the people are allowed to eat only bread at their feasts. "No relishes!", exclaims Glaucon, one of his shocked listeners. In response, Socrates (Plato's mouthpiece in the dialogue) then allows olives, cheese, beans, and vegetables. Still troubled, Glaucon refers to this *opson* as "fodder" for "a city of pigs." "Where are the fish and meat?", he asks. But Socrates sarcastically points out that Glaucon is thinking of a "luxurious city" rather than a "healthy state" (*Republic* 2.13, 372D–E).

Socrates then outlines a process whereby fancy *opson* directly leads to all sorts of material and moral excesses.

Nowadays, gluttony is regarded as one of the seven deadly sins, but for the ancient Greeks, or at least for Greek philosophers engaged in moralizing discussions, overly enjoying any food other than bread led down the slippery slope to immorality. When Socrates observes that a man at dinner "had ceased to take bread, and ate the meat by itself," he begins talking about how greedy such behavior is until the guilty party picks up some bread as well. Socrates then admonishes, "Watch the fellow, you who are near him, and see whether he treats the bread as his meat or the meat as his bread" (Xenophon, *Memorabilia* 3.14.2–4). We have to take such texts with, as it were, a grain of salt. This is, after all, a philosopher being quoted, and in practice, people no doubt took a great deal of pleasure in their *opson*. Nevertheless, in these dialogues, we find the basic attitude that overindulgence in food is a moral failure, which was a part of later Christian sermons and is still sometimes expressed today.

Come to my banquet: The social experience of dining

One of the most important aspects of food is the rituals that we develop to accompany the act of eating. Today, we still place great social importance on various types of meals, ranging from elaborately staged and planned banquets to which a host invites a set of guests to the simple idea that families should gather together at the end of the day for a communal meal. All of these dining occasions, from the most stiffly formal to the most relaxed, tend to feature certain rituals and behaviors that give them shape and meaning. Let us consider a few of these, and see how many of these patterns extend back to the dining tables of antiquity.

Imagine a formal dinner party today. After receiving an invitation, you dress nicely in order to attend a meal that is served as a series of distinct courses. If the recipes are fancy or complex, chances are that the hosts are out to impress their guests. Such a scenario originated in the ancient world, where entertaining played a significant role in both social life and status enhancement. The Greeks are famous for the *symposium*, which, although now thought of primarily as a conference convened to discuss a particular topic, originally meant a type of dinner party featuring drinking—albeit one where conversation about intellectual subjects was often engaged in. The Roman *convivium* (Latin for "dinner party," "banquet," or "feast") gives us the root of our word "convivial": festive, social, or jovial. Let us look at each in turn.

The *symposium*, literally meaning "drinking together," was a highly important social ritual in ancient Greek society. It was for men only, as can be gathered from the fact that it took place in the *andron* (the "men's room") in Greek homes, and respectable women did not attend *symposia*. Only after dinner was over and the dining tables had been removed did the drinking begin in earnest. Couches were arranged to accommodate the guests, who drank while reclining. Despite the fact that the outcome might be drunkenness, licentious behavior, and hangovers, certain rules did govern the proceedings. Wine-drinking possessed a religious dimension that was reflected throughout the different stages of the *symposium*. Libations and hymns to the gods came first, the party concluded with a paean to Apollo and a hymn to Hygieia (the goddess of health, who gives us the word "hygiene"), and purification rites both preceded and followed the drinking.

A master of drinking (*symposiarch*) was appointed to ensure that things went smoothly; he could penalize someone for misbehavior and even have him kicked out. The *symposiarch*'s first task was to choose the ratio of wine to water, since the Greeks always drank their wine diluted. This was a crucial decision, since it would determine the tone of the ensuing party. He then decided how many cups would be drunk, as guests were expected to all drink the same amount so that everyone would reach a similar state of intoxication. (In fact, at certain public functions, officials called *oinoptai*, or "wine-watchers," ensured that everyone drank the same.) The *symposiarch* also suggested what entertainment there should be. The guests might amuse themselves by telling stories, posing riddles, singing drinking songs, playing drinking games, or, for those of a more intellectual bent, engaging in learned conversation and philosophical debates like those described in some of Plato's dialogues, one of which is even called *The Symposium* because of its setting.

Hired entertainers might include dancing girls, musicians, acrobats, tumblers, and jugglers. Cultured, educated courtesans, known as *hetairae*, often served as flute-players and dancers. The *symposium* might be seen as an important form of social networking that was encouraged among and expected of male citizens, as, for example, in the modern world, Japanese "salarymen" have traditionally been expected to drink together after work.

Although singing as an accompaniment to drinking still resonates with us today, the topics of some of the ancient Greeks' drinking songs might surprise us. The Greeks, the inventors of democracy, were highly political beings, and even their drinking songs dealt with politics. A particularly popular one was about how two men, the lovers Harmodios and Aristogeiton, killed Hipparchos, one of the members of the family of tyrants then ruling over Athens. This slaying was in revenge for Hipparchos having sexually harassed one of them. This incident led to a popular uprising against the tyrants and the establishment of the first democracy at Athens. The lyrics of the song commemorate the deed:

> I shall carry my sword hidden in a branch of myrtle like Harmodios and Aristogeiton when they slew the tyrants and established Athenian democracy. Dearest Harmodios, you are not dead, but they say you live in the Isles of the Blest, where swift-footed Achilles lives and godlike Diomedes, the son of Tydeus.
>
> I shall carry my sword hidden in a branch of myrtle like Harmodios and Aristogeiton, when they slew the tyrant Hipparchos at the festival of Athena. Your fame shall live on the earth forever, dearest Harmodios and Aristogeiton, since you slew the tyrant and established Athenian democracy.
> *(quoted in Robert Garland, "Daily Life of the Ancient Greeks," Westport, CT: Greenwood Press, 1998, p. 101.)*

In bars and taverns today, there are popular games that often accompany drinking, ranging from darts and billiards to games whose purpose is to encourage further drinking, such as beer pong. It is really not surprising that such activities were common in ancient Greece as well. The Greeks loved playing various drinking games at *symposia*, which ran the gamut from intellectual challenges to rowdy fun. The "capping game" required a good knowledge of poetry; either the first player would recite a line of poetry to which the next player would have to add the following line, or else the first player would recite from memory an entire passage which the next player would then have to follow up with another passage on the same theme but from a different poet. Indeed, a number of Greek poets, such as Anacreon, were renowned for the poetry that they wrote to be recited at *symposia*. A less intellectually demanding and more popular game was *kottabos*. This seems to have had a number of variants, but all involved flicking the dregs at the bottom of one's wine cup at a target.

Today, particularly enthusiastic drinkers will often go bar-hopping, wandering in an ever-drunker state from one establishment to another, and frequently engaging in rowdy behavior in the streets. This, too, is nothing new; in ancient Greece, if the guests grew drunk enough, when they left the *symposium*, they might *komazein*, a verb meaning to roam the streets in an unruly gang—challenging passers-by, fighting, and crashing parties. The fact that a gathering ostensibly governed by rules sometimes ended in disorder and brawling indicates the gap between the ideal and the reality of *symposia*. Similar in meaning to the commonly-heard contemporary saying "What happens in Vegas stays in Vegas," a popular Greek saying was "I hate a drinker with a good memory"—or, in other words, "What happens at the *symposium* stays at the *symposium*."

When we turn to the Roman world, the parallels to a modern formal dinner party are even more evident. An invitation to a Roman *convivium* would often be proffered several days or weeks in advance, and an RSVP would be expected. However, last-minute invitations often occurred if guests cancelled; some people hung around hoping for a spur-of-the-moment dinner invitation, as the poet Martial describes: "You see ... how Selius wears a cloudy brow; how he paces up and down the colonnade late; how his heavy countenance silently bespeaks some melancholy thought ... how with his right hand he beats his breast and plucks his hair. Yet he is not lamenting the death of a friend or of a brother ... His sorrow then—what is the cause of it? He dines at home!" (*Epigrams* 2.11) In another epigram (2.14), he lists at least 10 different places where the hungry Selius goes, one after another, desperately seeking dinner invitations. The urgent need to replace a canceling guest was due to seating arrangements, as a typical dining room had three couches, known as *triclinia*, arranged in a U shape with three people per couch, and ideally all the seats needed to be filled. A couch could be brought in or left empty, but multiples of three were preferable. Thus, the writer Varro said that the Nine Muses would form a nice large party and the Three Graces a nice small one (Aulus Gellius, *The Attic Nights* 13.11.1).

Figure 1.3 *Banquet scene from a Roman relief. The male diners recline on a pillow-laden bench called a triclinium.*

In Rome, unlike in Greece, both women and men attended dinner parties, evidently a hold-over from Etruscan practices. Guests took off their outdoor shoes upon arrival and wore slippers to the table. Dinner was usually served in three courses: the appetizer course (the *gustatio* or *promulsis*); the main course, where a selection of dishes was presented in successive services; and the dessert. However, additional courses could be served at a more elaborate feast.

Raw vegetables and fish and egg dishes were common appetizers; indeed, eggs were so regularly part of the *gustatio* that the Latin phrase *ab ovo usque ad mala* ("from the egg to the apples") was equivalent to our phrase "from soup to nuts." Eggs were served boiled, fried, poached, scrambled, and in omelettes; a square-shaped pan with a handle and four circular depressions, on display at the National Archaeological Museum at Naples, was used for frying eggs. Serving dishes with egg-shaped indentations in them, resembling deviled egg platters, suggest that attractive presentation was a concern when entertaining. A dish of olives was usually set out among the appetizers. Salads served with dressing were, like today, a popular starter. Pliny recommends lettuce in the summer for its cooling properties and as an appetite stimulant, while the cookbook-writer Apicius suggests that, in winter, endive can take the place of lettuce, "with a dressing or with honey and strong vinegar." Columella's basic salad recipe included "savory, mint, rue, coriander, parsley, chives or green onion, lettuce leaves, colewort, thyme or catmint, and green flea-bane." Cucumbers were known to the Greeks and Romans, and were eaten cooked, raw, and as dressed salads. The emperor Tiberius evidently liked cucumbers so much that he had them grown on movable frames so that he could eat them wherever he went. Tomatoes, so crucial to today's Italian cuisine, were a New World plant unknown to the ancient Romans.

Class distinctions came into play when choosing what vegetables to eat. Although they were closely related, leeks were a popular starter vegetable whereas onions were relegated to garnishes and dressings among the wealthy; the onion was seen more as a "poor man's" food. Similarly, while radishes were widely grown in Italy, Pliny criticizes them as a "vulgar article of diet" due to their believed tendency to cause flatulence and belching. Greens such as cabbage, chard, and mustard leaves were eaten, though spinach, originating in Persia, was unknown to the Greeks and Romans. The famous upholder of tradition, Cato the Elder, adored cabbage, which he saw as a sort of cure-all for a huge variety of ailments. To Cato, cabbage was a miracle substance. Eating it could cure ulcers, headaches, tumors, arthritis, heart disease, and hangovers. If you fried it, it cured insomnia, and if you dried it, crushed it into a powder, and inhaled it, it would cure respiratory ailments. If boiled, it cured ear problems (Cato, *On Agriculture* 157). Perhaps he was on to something, given the cabbage family's, and especially broccoli's, current healthful reputation as being chock-full of anti-cancer compounds. The poet Martial offers a recipe for improving a pale cabbage's appearance: "In order that pale sprouts may not move your disgust, let the cabbage become green in water and soda" (*Epigrams* XIII.XVII). Mushrooms were beloved by the wealthy, so much so that special cooking pots known as *boletaria* were used in their preparation, and poisoned mushrooms were rumored to have been the death of the emperor Claudius, who could not resist eating the specimens offered to him by his wife Agrippina—though he probably should have known better.

Martial's dinner invitation to a friend (*Epigrams* 11.52) includes a description of the appetizers that he will serve, which comprise a fairly standard assortment: "The first course will be lettuce (a useful digestive aid), and tender shoots cut from leek plants, and then a pickled young tuna ... garnished with eggs and rue leaves. And there will be more eggs, these cooked over a low flame, and cheese from Velabrum Street, and olives which have felt the Picene cold." Elsewhere, he shows an awareness that leeks, though tasty, can have negative effects: "As often as you have eaten the strong-smelling shoots of Tarentine leeks, give kisses with shut mouth" (*Epigrams* 13.18).

The second course usually consisted of meats and cooked vegetables. Game, such as wild boar, venison, and rabbit, was popular; domesticated animals commonly eaten included pigs, sheep, goats, and fowl, although the only animal raised solely for meat was the pig. Stuffed dormice were considered a particular delicacy, and the Romans devised a specialized type of urn in which they were fed and fattened up. Meat was often served in the form of stews, cutlets, meatballs, sausages, forcemeats, minced meats, meat puddings, and croquettes. Indeed, sausages and blood puddings could be purchased by the average Roman from street vendors and at bars. Apicius records recipes for seafood croquettes made of crab, lobster, cuttlefish, scallops, and oysters as well.

We should not assume that aquaculture and farmed fish are modern phenomena, since the Romans' fondness for seafood led them to oyster-culturing (using long ropes suspended from horizontal wooden beams) and the construction of fish ponds, called *piscinae* (Varro, *On Agriculture* 3.17). Aristocratic Romans avidly competed with one another to see who could produce the most impressive specimens of fish in their private ponds. Land snails were also cultivated, in special "snail-beds" that restricted their movement so that they would grow plump. The use of organ meats, brains, and sweetbreads in French cookery today would have been familiar to the Romans; the Roman gourmand, Apicius, provides recipes for lungs, livers, kidneys, brains, sow's belly, sow's womb, skin, crackling, tails, and feet.

Figure 1.4 *Roman fish mosaic. The variety of fish and other marine animals depicted in a highly realistic manner gives a sense of the many edible creatures that were transferred from the sea to Roman tables.*

As one might expect from civilizations based around a sea, marine life also played an important role in ancient diets and ideas about food. The Greek colonies of Sicily were evidently a hotbed of culinary activity, especially in regards to sea-life. The first cookbooks were written there; a famous chef named Mithaecus, described as an exemplary cook by Plato (*Gorgias* 518B), offers what is perhaps one of the oldest recipes ever published: "Cut off the head of the ribbon fish. Wash it and cut into slices. Pour cheese and oil over it" (Athenaeus, *Deipnosophists* 7.325a). Another Greek colony in southern Italy, Sybaris, was so renowned for its luxurious lifestyle that it has given us the word "sybaritic." The Sybarites' obsession with food is suggested by claims that new recipes there were given a year's copyright; that eel-sellers and eel-fishers were allowed a special tax exemption; and that a Sybarite named Smindyrides reportedly brought along one thousand fishermen, bird-catchers, and cooks when he moved to mainland Greece because he feared it might not be up to snuff gastronomically.

The Mediterranean Sea was full of all sorts of edible creatures. A popular genre of Roman mosaics depicting sea-life reveals a familiarity with many different species, represented naturalistically and in great detail (for example, eels, octopus, shrimp, lobster, squid, and many identifiable types of fish). The literature dedicated to aquatic life was also extensive, including a five-book hexameter epic about fishing (*The Halieutica* by Oppian from Cilicia) that referred to more than 120 different types of sea creature. The Sicilian writer Epicharmus in his play "Earth and Sea" even describes an argument between farmers and fishermen as to which realm supplies better food for the table. While today fish are generally regarded as low in intelligence, the Greeks and Romans considered them wily and hard to catch; it was a challenge for the fisherman to trick sea creatures, who were themselves cunning, capable of deceit, and often able to escape the traps set for them.

Perhaps their elusiveness added to their allure, for seafood was much loved by the ancients. Pliny describes how wrasse were so popular that some were brought from the Carpathian Sea and released along the Campanian coast; for the first five years, any which were caught were released again, perhaps the earliest recorded case of fish management. Fish were seen as inspiring a kind of lust akin to a sexual one, as in this paean to the fisherman's skill in Anaxandrides' play "Odysseus": "What other craft gets youthful lips burning, gets their fingers fumbling, has their lungs gasping for air, in their haste to swallow? … when it comes to seducing a real beauty, with what magic words, with what chat-up lines would you overcome his defences if you take away the fisherman's art?" (cited in Davidson, 1997: p. 9) Fish as a gift to aid in seduction sometimes appear in Greek vase paintings, as in one where a prostitute is offered an octopus by her prospective suitor. Flute-girls and prostitutes often had fishy nicknames, like "Sand-smelt," Red Mullet," and "Cuttlefish," and two sisters were evidently known as "the Anchovies" because of their pale skin, long fingers, and large eyes. It should be noted that their physical resemblance to fish was seen as attractive—perhaps only possible in a culture where sea-food was so well-loved.

While the ancient Greeks obviously did enjoy meat and fish, these were more expensive foodstuffs and thus more rare in the average person's diet. Oxen were used for farm work; goats and sheep supplied hair or wool, skins, and cheese. Only pigs were raised primarily as a source of meat. A sacrifice to the gods was significant from a culinary standpoint as well as a religious one because such an occasion offered one of the few opportunities for a poor person to eat meat. The Greek gods enjoyed the odor of animal thighs wrapped in fat burning on their altars and rising up through the air to Mount Olympus, not the actual meat itself, as they traditionally dined on ambrosia and nectar rather than human food. Therefore, the meat was left to the hungry worshippers, who lined up to collect portions of cooked meat after the sacrifice was over. Indeed, except for the religious overtones, an ancient Greek sacrifice rather closely resembled an antecedent of the modern barbecue, or perhaps a tailgating party at a sporting event. The Homeric heroes, after offering a hecatomb (the sacrifice of one hundred cows), stuff themselves with grilled meat, guzzle wine, and sing drinking songs in praise of the gods. They honor the Olympian gods, who love to feast while listening to the singing of Apollo and the Muses, by imitating them through engaging in their favorite activity.

At Rome, the presence of butchers and butcher-shops suggests that meat was more readily available, but probably still restricted in its consumption by its expense. Unlike in Greece, Roman sacrificial meat was generally eaten by priests or sold to market vendors. Distribution of meat to citizens was associated with other public events, such as triumphs, games, and gladiator shows. Some historians even suggest that the many animals killed in the arena, including the exotic ones, may have provided a welcome source of meat for the populace. In a modern analogy, meat from bulls killed in bullfights was sometimes given to the poor, although this practice no longer seems common. Further confirming the idea that public spectacles sometimes resulted in a rare taste of meat for ordinary Romans, the author Apuleius tells a story of how the people of Rome stripped meat from the carcasses of some wild bears that had been left lying in the street, and archaeologists have unearthed a giraffe bone in the area of a butcher's shop. On occasion, the spectators at wild beast hunts might become participants, and procure their own meat; at a triumph in A.D. 281, the Circus Maximus was reportedly rigged out as a forest containing 1,000 ostriches, 1,000 stags, 1,000 wild boars, deer, ibexes, and wild sheep, and "The populace was then let in, and each man seized what he wished" (*SHA*, *Life of Probus* 19.2–5). Perhaps the well-known phrase "bread and circuses" might thus be more aptly rendered as "meat and circuses," given that bread was a necessity of life versus the treat-like, holiday connotations of meat.

When it came time for the dessert course, chocolate, which figures so prominently in modern sweets, was unknown in the ancient Mediterranean, since the cocoa bean is a New World crop. Instead, fruits and nuts were served in a typical dessert course. Apples were well-established in the ancient world; orchards are attested in Homeric times, and by Pliny's era, about 36 types of apple were known. Figs, both fresh and dried, were popular among all classes, and grapes were served fresh as well as dried into raisins and turned into wine. Dates were imported from the East. Fruit of all sorts was dried in order to last through the winter. The Romans seem to have been fond of referring to nuts by their place of origin; they called the almond the "Greek Nut," the walnut the "Persian nut," and the hazelnut the "Pontic nut" (Pliny, *Natural History* 15.24.90; 15.24.88; 15.24.87). Peanuts and cashews, also New World crops, were not yet available. The Roman gourmand Apicius offers recipes for a sweet custard of eggs, milk, honey, and chopped nuts, and a boiled pudding of farina, nuts, and raisins.

Since sugar was unknown in the classical world, honey served as the primary sweetener. Bee-keeping, already mentioned by Hesiod in the eighth century B.C., was a well-developed industry by the time of the Romans, who frequently wrote about it in their treatises on agriculture. Like wine, honey was seen as having different qualities depending upon its region; Aristotle rated the honeys of Greece on a scale, with Attic at the top, followed by honey from Salamis, Leros, Calymna, and Hybla. The Romans liked thyme honey best, and used it to preserve food as well as in cakes and desserts. Clearly, varietal honeys are not just a recent development. The status of honey in the classical world is attested by its privileged role in Greek mythology, where it is worthy of the gods and supernatural beings; nymphs feed the infant Zeus milk and honey and the vicious three-headed dog Cerberus is appeased with drugged honey-cakes.

The abundance of food at dinner parties ensured that there were leftovers. Just as today, frugal diners did not want to abandon the excess and so guests often made up doggy bags for later consumption. Guests brought along their own napkins, and these were typically pressed into service to hold the extra food for transportation home. Martial vividly describes a host's frustration at having an excessively greedy guest at dinner: "Anything that is placed on the table, you sweep off of it. Whether sow's udder or pork-ribs, a bird meant to feed two, half a mullet and an entire bass, a cutlet of moray and the leg of a chicken, even a whole pigeon dripping with white sauce. Every one of them is concealed in your sodden napkin and handed to your servant to take home. If you have any decency, I beg you to return our dinner" (Martial, *Epigrams* 2.37). Another guest is even worse: "He demands triple helpings of boar, four of pork loin, the haunches and shoulders of the rabbit. Without a blush he steals thrushes and snatches the oysters right out of their shells. Within his dirty napkin are stashed mouthfuls of cake, jelly, apple cores … a dripping fig and a mass of mushroom. When his napkin is full to bursting … he conceals half-chewed bones and the body of a turtle dove in the folds of his toga" (Martial, *Epigrams* 7.20).

In terms of spicing and flavor preferences, the Romans were pioneers of what we now call "fusion cuisine." They imported herbs such as cumin, which they used in their cooking extensively, from the Middle East. Certain flavors which we now often associate with Asian cuisines, such as sweet and sour sauces and pungent, salty fish sauces, were well-loved by the Romans. Vinegar and honey were often used in conjunction, and raisins and raisin wine and date wine were also sometimes added, to achieve a sweet and sour effect. Garum, a fermented fish paste, was used both in cooking and as an extremely popular condiment in its own right. To make it, fish skin, entrails, heads, and fins were put in a vat with oil and seasonings, and then left in the sun to rot. The resultant paste was strained and then used as a dip, a sauce, or an added flavoring.

The ability to eat expensive or rare foods and elaborate concoctions has always been appealing to those who wish to boast of their wealth or display their status. A restaurant recently advertised a $5,000 hamburger made with Kobe beef and adorned with truffles and foie gras. Fancy desserts are even sometimes adorned with flakes of real gold, which, although they don't add to the taste, certainly increase the sense of luxury—and the expense. Such literal conspicuous consumption was a staple of competition among ancient Greeks and Romans. Unlike the vast majority of inhabitants of the ancient world, whose diet was largely restricted to the three staples plus occasional supplements of other foods, the wealthy could and did eat exotic foodstuffs that were often transported to their tables over great distances. Certain rarefied items in particular have become notorious symbols of Roman culinary decadence: pies made entirely of flamingos' tongues, for example, or a whole boiled peacock. Recipes for these are actually attested in ancient cookbooks.

Like today, the procurement of certain extremely expensive foods (and their display at dinner parties) could add to one's prestige. Pepper, for instance, was a costly spice that the wealthy gastronome Apicius frequently employed in his recipes (often sprinkled on sweet dishes), although the thriftier Pliny considered it a luxury. One of today's gourmet delicacies, foie gras, was already known to the Romans; Horace mentions servants bringing in to dinner "the liver of a white goose fattened on rich figs" (*Satires* 2.8.88). This ancient Roman practice of fattening geese on figs is preserved in the Italian word for liver, *fegato*, derived from the Latin word *ficus*, fig.

Perhaps because the Romans lacked anything akin to fancy, sit-down restaurants, dinner parties were not only the occasion for gourmet experimentation and indulgence but also for a luxurious atmosphere. An elaborate dinner would probably remind us of what we would today call dinner theater, since entertainment was often provided: there might be musicians, dancers, acrobats, or the recitation of poetry or speeches. Food might even be made into part of the entertainment, as in one over-the-top dinner party described in Petronius' novel *The Satyricon*, at which the guests expect to see a cook gutting a huge pig and instead are treated to the spectacle of sausages and blood puddings tumbling forth when it is cut open.

We can get a sense of the Roman aristocrats' love of food and elaborate meal preparations from both the prosaic and decorative elements of their homes. As well as pots and pans of various shapes and sizes, a range of specialized kitchen utensils existed. The profusion of gadgets that graced a wealthy Roman's kitchen suggests that this is not just a tendency among today's would-be home chefs (though of course the ancient Roman had those gadgets to be used by slaves, not by himself). At the National Archaeological Museum in Naples, one can view copper strainers and colanders, a large mold with round depressions in it, and a rabbit-shaped mold. Beautiful colored glassware was no doubt intended to be admired by guests at feasts. Mosaics and wall paintings often depicted wildlife and produce that would eventually reach the table, such as braces of ducks and fish hanging (illusionistically) on the wall and still-life images of bowls of fruit and nuts. Even the aftermath of a feast might be memorialized in the decor. Floor mosaics of food debris have been found that depict bones, fish skeletons, crustacean legs, snail shells, and shrimp carapaces, as if they have been scattered there by ravenous diners; one mosaic shows a mouse nibbling a half-walnut as if it's been accidentally dropped.

Figure 1.5 *An assortment of bronze pans, dishes, ladles, ewers, and other items found at Pompeii, which illustrate the variety of kitchen paraphernalia used by Roman cooks.*

Not surprisingly, the Roman dinner party reached its apex of luxury (and weirdness) with the emperors. Nero's fabulous palace, known as "The Golden House," contained "dining rooms with fretted ceilings of ivory, whose panels could turn and shower down flowers and were fitted with pipes for sprinkling the guests with perfumes," and "The main banquet hall was circular and constantly revolved day and night, like the heavens" (Suetonius, *Nero* 31.2). At what was perhaps the cruelest-themed dinner party ever, the influential men whom the emperor Domitian invited to his infamous "Black Feast" dined in an entirely black room upon black foods in black dishes surrounded by naked boys painted black, offerings to the dead, and gravestones inscribed with their own names, while the emperor talked about death. The terrified guests naturally spent the entire evening imagining that they were about to be killed (especially in light of Domitian's murderous reputation), but the emperor spared them and sent them gifts the next day, content merely to have enjoyed their fear (Cassius Dio 67.9).

Combine these ingredients: Cookbooks

As has already been mentioned, the first cookbooks were probably written in the food-loving Greek colonies in Sicily, such as Sybaris, where new recipes allegedly enjoyed a year's copyright. However, the only actual cookbook that has survived from the ancient world—*De Re Coquinaria*, "The Art of Cooking" (written down in the late fourth century A.D.)—has been attributed at least in part to a Roman named Apicius, who lived during the first century A.D., when Rome was renowned for its gourmets—and its gluttons. With the many exotic foods and spices being imported from all over the Roman empire, it was possible to concoct expensive and esoteric recipes, some of which are found in this cookbook, in addition to many earlier (and simpler) Greek recipes.

Rather like a modern cookbook, it was arranged in 10 sections divided among vegetables, poultry, fish, seafood, meat, etc. The meat section ("The Quadruped") included recipes for boar, venison, goat, sheep, beef and veal, lamb, suckling pig, hare, and dormice. We may believe that modern cooks work with a creative array of ingredients, but elite Roman chefs were just as experimental. The cookbook tells us how to prepare cucumbers, asparagus, mushrooms, artichokes, squash, many varieties of sausage and fish, and all sorts of sauces. There are simple recipes, like roast meat, barley soup with lentils and chick-peas, dressed salads, and deviled eggs (this version is topped with pine-nuts). However, there are also recipes for flamingo (which begins, "Pluck the flamingo, wash, truss, and put it in a saucepan"), sauce for a boiled ostrich (consisting of pepper, mint, toasted cumin, celery-seed, dates, honey, vinegar, fish-sauce, and a little oil, thickened with flour), and pork-stuffed dormice that were cooked on a hot tile in an oven. The recipes named after Apicius are particularly elaborate; Soufflé à la Apicius calls for sow's udder, fish fillets, chicken, turtle-dove breasts, fig-peckers (a type of bird), "and whatever other good things you can think of," chopped, cooked with eggs and spices, and then layered with pancakes, and Fricassée à la Apicius requires small fish, tiny meat-balls, suckling pig sweetbreads, and capons' testicles. Just as a comprehensive cookbook today might include sections on different ethnic cuisines such as French, Indian, and Chinese, this ancient cookbook aspires to cover the known world, with recipes like "Squash Alexandrian Style," "Chicken Parthian Style," and "Chicken Numidian Style." Recipes are also named after famous individuals, like "Peas à la Vitellius." Some recipes sound like they could have emerged from a trendy modern restaurant: skewered, grilled truffles; seafood croquettes; pork shoulder with sweet-wine cake; carrots with cumin sauce; custard pine-nut turnover. Others, such as "Grilled Sow's Womb" and "Pig's Stomach," might appeal to dedicated carnivores.

The first chapter offers useful general tips for the cook, which evince a careful frugality and pragmatism not evident in some of the fancier recipes: "how to keep meat fresh"; "how to preserve oysters"; "how to make bad honey good"; "how to keep grapes fresh"; "how to preserve fresh figs, apples, plums, pears, and cherries"; "how to make white wine out of red wine"; and "how to make one ounce of *silphium* (an expensive spice) last indefinitely." On the other hand, many of these directions could be viewed as ways to stretch expensive ingredients or to conceal poorer quality ones. It also includes recipes for "Spiced Wine Surprise" (a spiced, sweetened, boiled-down wine drink that calls for 15 lbs. of honey) and for a spiced honey-wine for travelers "which keeps forever."

One of the reasons why the Romans have become so associated with gluttony and overindulgence is no doubt at least partially due to the reputation of Apicius, whose celebrity status probably caused his name to be attached to this cookbook. Later authors made him a byword for excess. It was rumored that he ate expensive prawns that were bigger than lobsters, sailed to Libya just to see if they grew larger there, and turned back immediately when he found that they didn't (Athenaeus, *Deipnosophists* 1.7); and that, when he had literally eaten away his vast fortune down to ten million sesterces (still an enormous sum), he committed suicide because he felt this would amount to "starvation" compared to the diet he was used to (Seneca, *To Helvia on*

Consolation 10.10). The crazy emperor Elagabalus cited Apicius as one of his role models (*SHA*, *Elagabalus* 18.4), and, in imitation of him, allegedly ate such rarefied fare as camels' heels, cocks-combs (cut off live birds), and peacocks' and nightingales' tongues; gave his servants at the palace flamingo-brains, mullets' viscera, and the heads of parrots and peacocks to eat; fed his dogs goose-livers; and had pieces of gold put in his peas, onyx in his lentils, amber in his beans, and pearls on his fish instead of pepper (*SHA*, *Elagabalus* 20.5–21.5). However, not all the ancients were so extravagant in their tastes; in words that echo the advice of many master chefs today, the Greek gourmet Archestratus emphasized fresh ingredients and simplicity: "... for a good-quality fish, with naturally tender flesh, it is enough to merely sprinkle with a little salt and baste with oil. For it contains within its unvarnished nature the reward of joy" (Athenaeus, *Deipnosophists* 7.321).

A roof over your head I: Apartments

After food, the next most important necessity of life is shelter. From primitive man cowering in a crude hut or a cave to modern millionaires constructing vast mansions, human beings have always sought to make their dwellings as comfortable as possible. While the conditions of life on a small family farm remained the same for thousands of years, one way in which large cities of the ancient world (and especially the great city of Rome) were perhaps unexpectedly modern was the sort of housing in which the majority of the population lived.

Rapidly growing megacities where people live crammed densely into towering high-rise concrete apartment complexes are not just a feature of modern life. The Romans led the way in housing much of Rome's huge population in multi-story apartment buildings called *insulae*, or "islands," because they divided up city blocks into self-contained structures floating alone like individual islets. At its height around the first century A.D., ancient Rome had a population of around one million inhabitants. This was an enormous number—far larger than any other ancient city, and larger than any city in the western hemisphere all the way up until the nineteenth century, when London and Paris became the first cities since antiquity to exceed one million people. All those Romans were crammed into a relatively small area, however, and this meant that the only way to house them was in multi-story apartment complexes.

Figure 1.6 *Model of the city of Rome as it appeared in the fourth century A.D., showing the density of the city's urban fabric. The huge entertainment complexes, the Flavian Amphitheater (The Colosseum) and the Circus Maximus (for chariot racing), are clearly visible.*

Imagine ancient Rome as being like the center portion of a large, compact city, such as New York or Chicago, in which the major public buildings, monuments, and both rich and poor housing are closely clustered. As in a place like Manhattan, the number of private homes was very small, and these were owned by a tiny number of elites representing the very wealthiest strata of society, whereas the overwhelming majority of residents, rich, poor, and middle-class, lived in apartments. We actually have an ancient Roman document surviving from the fourth century A.D. that purports to list statistics about the sorts of residence available in ancient Rome. According to the document, there were only 1,782 private homes in the city. On the other hand, it claims that there were 43,580 apartment complexes. Since some of these apartment complexes might have housed hundreds or even thousands of tenants, we have a situation very much like middle and lower Manhattan, where a few houses of the exceptionally wealthy are scattered around a city overwhelmingly made up of apartment buildings.

As for the nature of these apartment complexes, there seems to have been great variety in terms of both size and luxuriousness. The largest were towering structures that sprawled across entire city blocks. In Roman law, we find frequent measures attempting to limit the height of apartment buildings. These usually specify a maximum height of around 75 feet, indicating a structure of at least seven or eight stories. The fact that such laws repeatedly had to be enacted suggests that they were routinely being broken by builders who exceeded these heights. The poet Martial mentions one apartment tenant who had to trudge up 200 steps in order to reach his garret apartment, suggesting a building that was at least ten stories in height. None of the apartment buildings of Rome survive intact today, but of the half dozen or so whose remains can be examined by archaeologists, three had at least four stories, and one at least five.

Like today, slum-lords extracted rents from poor tenants who were in danger of having their shoddily constructed buildings collapse on their heads—an alarmingly common occurrence. As the satirist Juvenal described it: “We dwell in a city which is, for the most part, held up only by feeble props. For your apartment manager stands there in the tottering building, and while he patches up a yawning crack in the decrepit walls, he urges you to sleep securely, while the whole ruin above you threatens to collapse” (*Satire* 3 lines 193–8). The philosopher Seneca even mentions the existence of a guild of construction workers whose specialty was installing supports to hold up crumbling buildings. While the famous Roman politician Cicero is nowadays known to many as a great orator, in reality he was also a slum-lord who, in one of his letters, expresses the hope that one of his *insulae* will fall down so that he can build a new one and charge even higher rents. These rents could be a major source of income for the building owners. Just one of Cicero’s properties is recorded as having yielded an annual income of 100,000 sesterces, or more than the yearly wages of over 100 Roman legionaries.

Figure 1.7 *Reconstruction of an insulae, a typical Roman apartment building. The overwhelming majority of inhabitants of large cities like Rome lived in such structures, which would not look out of place in a modern city.*

And, as in modern big cities, the rents and cost of living were much higher to begin with than they were in the countryside and in smaller towns, since people were willing to pay more for the thrill of urban life: "You could buy a fine mansion in Sora, Fabrateria, or Frusino (rural towns) for the same price you pay to rent a single dark and squalid room in Rome," Juvenal warns (*Satire* 3 lines 224–6). If you left the family farm seeking the excitement of the big city, you might be aided in your search for a wildly overpriced apartment by reading the "For Rent" advertisements painted on the fronts of rental properties, much as prospective renters seek "For Rent" signs nowadays. One such ad, found on a wall in the ritzier seaside resort of Pompeii, was clearly aimed at a somewhat wealthier clientele, but with the same goal: "The Arrius Pollio Apartment Complex owned by Gnaeus Allius Nigidius Maius FOR RENT from July 1 street-front shops with counter space, luxurious second-story apartments, and a penthouse. Prospective tenants, see Primus, slave of Gnaeus Allius Nigidius Maius, for negotiations" (*CIL* 4.138; *ILS* 6035).

Whereas, today, there are many luxury apartments in which penthouses are coveted for their lofty height above the ground and expansive views, this was not the case in the ancient world. (Note how the "luxurious" apartments for rent in Pompeii were second-story ones.) The more luxurious apartments were usually those on the lower floors, while the higher up your apartment was, the less desirable it became. This arrangement created a different pattern of class division than in most modern cities. Today, neighborhoods tend to be separated by wealth, with one area, for example, containing apartments catering to rich tenants, whereas another section of the city might be inhabited only by the poor. In Rome, wealth distribution was vertical rather than horizontal. Thus, the same building might have apartments of rich people on the bottom couple of floors, middle-class apartment dwellers above them, and impoverished tenants residing in the upper stories.

In an era before elevators, this was a logical arrangement, but there were serious risks to living on an upper storey, not just inconveniences. If a fire broke out, you would be far more likely to perish on one of the upper floors, which turned into death traps. The topmost floors were often rickety constructs of wood tacked onto the building proper so that the landlord could squeeze a few more tenants into these precarious garret rooms. Juvenal again vividly expresses the hazards of apartment life: "It is better to live away from here, where there are not fires every night, where there are not terrified alarms every night. Other apartment dwellers shout for water, and drag out what little they own. Meanwhile, the third floor where you live is ablaze and smoke pours out, but you don't realize it. While the people on the ground floor have panicked at the first alarm, upstairs, you, who live where the pigeons nest and only tiles protect you from the rain, will be the last to burn" (*Satire* 3 lines 197–202). Walking (and hauling things) up and down steep flights of steps was onerous. Since there was no running water, you would have had to go to the nearest public fountain out in the streets, fill a pot, and lug it back up the stairs every time you needed water.

When a fire broke out, this would also be your only means of extinguishing it—which is why fires proved so deadly, and arson was considered an especially heinous crime in the ancient world. Some Romans even had fire insurance; another satirist, Martial, accuses a man of burning down his own house in order to collect an inflated insurance pay-out (*Epigrams* 3.52). However, only the wealthy had such insurance. For the less fortunate who lacked insurance, when you lost everything, you truly lost everything.

A roof over your head II: Private homes

There were some private residences in Rome. The Roman word for an individual house or home, *domus*, has left its imprint in the English language, and its traces are evident in many familiar words, but also in some unlikely places. First, the more logical connections: "Domain" comes from *dominium*, right of ownership, which comes from *dominus*, master of the household, lord, or sovereign. The parallels, commonly drawn throughout history, between a king/father ruling over a country/household of subjects/children can thus be traced back to Roman roots. The suffix "dom," attached to so many English words (e.g., kingdom, officialdom, wisdom), derives from *domus* in the sense of domain of, dominion of, or the seat of an activity. The words "domicile," "domestic," and "domesticate," all emphasizing connections with the home, come from *domus* as well. The Latin adjective *domabilis* means tamable, and the verb *domo* means to tame, domesticate, or break in an animal. Therefore, bachelors who fear being "domesticated" by marriage (literally brought into the *domus*/home to live) are perhaps not wrong to identify with "wild" animals being tamed and taught more docile habits. There are less obvious derivations from *domus* as well. The game of dominoes, for example, traces its name back to *dominus*. The domino was a hooded cloak, usually black, worn by cathedral canons, who were addressed as "dominus," sir. From there, it was extended to mean the hooded black cloak, and then also the black mask, worn at masquerades. The domino tile, so named because of its blackness, perhaps also reminded people of the mask divided into two halves, one over each eye.

But back to the Roman *domus* as an actual physical dwelling rather than a linguistic root. While Roman houses were different from ours in many ways (no windows opening on the outside world, little furniture, and less strict notions of privacy, for instance), some modern terms originated in their floor plan. All *domus* roughly conformed to a basic design—something still found today despite the proliferation of custom home plans. The Romans entered their *domus* through the *vestibulum*, an area just in front of the main entrance. Today, we enter a building through the vestibule, a lobby or passage connecting the outer door to the building's interior. The formal entrance hall and main reception area of the *domus*, the *atrium*, was a central, open courtyard. Today, many buildings still feature a large open space called an atrium, and most larger homes still have a main doorway that opens onto a vestibule or entry hall.

Figure 1.8 *The central atrium of a Roman house preserved at Herculaneum by the eruption of Mt. Vesuvius in A.D. 79.*

While those of us who work in small office cubicles might assume that the word refers to its size and shape, since it sounds like "small cube," the reality is more complex. "Cubicle" began its life as the Latin word *cubiculum*, which referred to the tiny bedrooms in the Roman *domus*. In turn, *cubiculum* derives from *cubo*, "to lie down" or "to recline." In 1967, an office furniture system called Action Office II, designed by Robert Propst (the originator of some 120 inventions, including a "vertical timber harvester" and an "electronic tagging system for livestock") was first sold; it evolved into the cubicle system now so ubiquitous in offices. So when office workers succumb to late afternoon drowsiness and sprawl forward on their desks for a quick nap, they are actually using their *cubiculum* for its original purpose—to lie down and sleep—a notion that would not be welcome among office managers. In late antiquity, *cubiculum* also came to refer to the mortuary chapels in Christian catacombs, which is perhaps metaphorically fitting for those people who feel that their job is boring them to death.

A worker frequently encountered in our public buildings, the janitor, also had his start in the ancient Roman *domus*, but in a very different capacity. Rather than cleaning, the janitor's job was to guard the entrance to a *domus*. Rome was full of thieves and robbers, so one's home needed to be shut up like a fortress, with access carefully controlled. This is probably at least partly why Roman homes did not have windows on their outer walls opening onto the outside world, and instead focused inward, on the family courtyard. The term janitor took a while to morph from security guard to building cleaner. In the 1580s, it denoted "an usher in a school or a doorkeeper," and was first used in the sense of a building's caretaker in 1708. Obviously the job description expanded from simply guarding a building to generally taking care of it.

In his task, the janitor was often assisted by a guard dog, and ancient Roman floor mosaics depict alert-looking dogs (sometimes on leashes) along with the phrase "*Cave Canem*" ("Beware of Dog"). Like today's "Beware of Dog" signs, these were displayed in the entryways of Roman houses as a warning to discourage thieves. You can still see a particularly fine example in the entryway of a house at Pompeii. Roman guard dogs were typically chained in the entryway, and a cast made from the hollow left in the volcanic ash after the eruption at Pompeii vividly preserves the contorted body of one such unfortunate animal whose chain prevented him from escaping his post when disaster overtook the city.

The janitor's name came from his duty post, the door (*ianua*), which is linked linguistically to the ancient Roman god Janus. The god of doorways and the guardian of gates, Janus was often depicted as having two faces gazing in opposite directions. In his manifestation as Janus Patulcius, he was the god that opens doors, and as Janus Clusivus, the god that closes doors. Janus was also the god of beginnings, so that the first month of the Roman calendar, January, was named after him, and January 1st, New Year's Day, was dedicated to him. As the god of beginnings, he was the first deity to be named in any list

Figure 1.9 *Mosaic of a guard dog. Such animals were often chained in the entryways of private homes. A similar mosaic from Pompeii bears the inscription Cave Canem ("Beware of Dog").*

of gods being prayed to, and also the first to be offered a portion of a sacrifice. Thus, even though the janitor was only a humble slave, his duty was connected to a powerful and important god. So when you celebrate New Year's, show your appreciation and respect to the janitors you meet.

We can also look to the ancient Romans as early believers in the notion of "exclusive" neighborhoods. The wealthy liked to live on the tops of Rome's hills, which kept them safe and dry above the periodic devastating floods of the Tiber River. The Esquiline and Viminal hills were the location of some of the largest and most elaborate *domus* in the city. Houses on the Palatine hill were also very expensive, and, under the empire, the residence of the emperor dominated the Palatine hill. Hence the English word "palace" (and the adjective "palatial") come from the Latin word for Palatine, *palatium*.

There are entire television programs devoted to taking their viewers on tours of the homes of rich and famous people. Their lavish residences are often regarded as extensions or embodiments of their status, or sometimes, even of their personalities. The Romans pioneered the concept that one's home is a reflection of one's character and social and economic standing. Roman politicians adorned their houses with works of art (often looted from other countries, such as Greece) and decorated their walls with expensive and eye-catching wall paintings.

It makes the world go round: Money

While food and shelter are basic necessities for almost all living creatures, human beings spend a great deal of their lives thinking about, and attempting to acquire, another item: money. Given the amount of time and effort that we spend in the pursuit of money, and the way in which, no matter how much they have, people always seem to want more of it, money is certainly one of the basic preoccupations that shapes almost every aspect of most people's lives. For better or worse, a great many people are utterly obsessed with the acquisition and spending of money. Certainly from the dawn of time, humans must have been exchanging valuable items for goods and services, but have you ever wondered where the specific form of money as we know and use it today came from? As with so much else, we have the ancient Greeks and Romans to thank (or blame) for the basic form of our money and for many of our attitudes towards it. So, the next time you pull out your wallet to pay for something, reflect on how the custom of exchanging small metal disks for goods began. While the use of money arose in a number of ancient societies throughout Europe and Asia, it was the Greeks and Romans who left a particularly strong imprint on our ideas about coinage, how to produce it, how to use it, and how to talk about it.

A society can vigorously engage in buying, selling, and trading without a system of coinage. The ancient Egyptians and Sumerians did not use coins, and even peoples particularly renowned as traders did not always use them; the Phoenicians, for instance, seldom did. Barter was common, and animals often functioned as a popular form of "living" currency. Indeed, one early attempt at producing money reflects its strong association with livestock; large metal slabs in the shape of a stylized cow-hide, dating to sixteenth–fourteenth century B.C. Mycenae, were probably employed as money. The role of ancient money as a stand-in for cattle can be traced in words we still commonly use today: "capital" and "capitalism" derive from the Latin *caput* (head), which designated heads of cattle (or other grazing animals) as well as the human head. The English word "pecuniary" also reveals the cow connection, as it derives from the Latin word *pecunia* (wealth or money), which is related to the word *pecus* (livestock, especially sheep and cattle). Whereas wealthy people in the past measured their wealth in livestock, we have now replaced animals with money. Instead of driving a herd of cows to the market, we carry a "herd" of tiny cow markers in our pockets—a much more compact and portable way of denoting wealth.

Although it is possible to exchange goods and services without using money, a standardized currency is necessary to the development of a more sophisticated economy. Barter does not allow for the concepts of credit and loans, and makes large-scale transactions much harder to execute than small-scale ones. The fact that the Greeks and Romans developed standardized currencies facilitated the growth and spread of their trade networks. Modern economies would not have evolved as they have had the ancients not thought of striking pictures onto small metal disks. The phrase "striking" coins comes from the method of producing coins employed by the ancients—putting metal disks between a pair of dies and hitting them with a hammer— which continued until the seventeenth century, when machines took over. The origins of our modern word "coin" refer to this centuries-old process. Its ancestor, the Old French word "coin," a wedge, stamp, or die, evolved from the Latin word *cuneus*, a tapering bar of metal, or a wedge.

While it has been debated where the very first coins were produced, coinage became a part of Greek culture and expanded throughout the ancient world wherever the Greeks did. As different currencies are employed in different countries today, the ancient Greek city-states developed coinages that reflected their civic identities. Thus, coins might bear images alluding to a city's major source of wealth or fame, its patron god, or its mythological associations. For instance, the Greek colony of Metapontum in southern Italy placed an ear of wheat on its coins, Cyzicus incorporated the tuna into its coin designs, and Naxos included a bunch of grapes; Athens usually featured its patron goddess, Athena, on its money, while Ephesus referred to its patron goddess, Artemis, by including a deer (the huntress' special animal) next to a palm tree (under which the goddess was famously born); and Corinth chose to picture the winged horse Pegasus, who was tamed by a Corinthian hero, Bellerophon, while Taras depicted a man riding a dolphin, because that city's founder was said to have been saved by one of these friendly sea creatures. Coins sometimes even made puns on their city's names; Panticapeum bore the head of the god Pan, while Rhodes' coin had its patron god, Helios, on one side and a rose (Rhodos in Greek) on the other. One is reminded of how, in the modern world, countries have often continued to decorate their money with symbols of their culture or heritage, such as Canadian pennies sporting a maple leaf and American quarters featuring an eagle.

Figure 1.10 *Greek coins. The one on the left bears a rose, the emblem of the city-state of Rhodes, while the one on the right depicts the winged horse Pegasus, which was used as a symbol by Corinth.*

Long before the Deutschmark, the euro, and the dollar, international currencies were a phenomenon in the ancient world. While the Greek city-states all produced their own money, a few currencies came to be commonly accepted throughout the Mediterranean world. Perhaps the most famous of all ancient coins were silver ones minted by Athens, which constitute an early example of this phenomenon. Popularly known as Athenian Owls, these coins referenced Athens' foundation myth of how the goddess Athena (on the obverse) became its patron by giving them the superior gift of the olive tree (a sprig of which, next to Athena's special animal, the owl, graces the reverse). For nearly five centuries, the Athenian Owl circulated widely. Other internationally accepted coins were Aegina's turtle (named for the reptile depicted on it) and Corinth's foal (thus called for its winged horse, Pegasus). The Owl was so respected that other cities even began to issue imitation Owls, some inscribed in their native languages instead of Greek. Uniform coinage was established under Alexander the Great, but collapsed after his death. The Romans also produced longstanding currency trusted for its dependability. The *solidus*, a gold coin introduced at the time of Diocletian's monetary reforms (A.D. 284–305), was known for the purity of its metal; our word "solid" derives from the Latin word, which refers both to the coin and to the state of being composed "of the same material throughout." Fixed at a weight of 4.5 g during the reign of Constantine (c. A.D. 310), the *solidus* reportedly maintained this purity, uncontaminated, until the eleventh century A.D.

Another significant innovation that the Greeks and Romans pioneered was using multiple denominations to pay for different-scale transactions. Coins of assorted sizes and composed of several types of metals varied in their worth and purchasing power. In ancient Athens, the following monetary gradations operated: one *talent* = 60 *minae*; one *mina* = 100 *drachms*; one *drachm* = six *obols*; one *obol* = eight *chalkoi*. There were also numerous coins that represented multiples or fractions of these basic units. For example, a large silver coin known as a *tetradrachm* was equivalent to four drachms, and the *triobol*, as the name implies, was worth three *obols*. The larger the coin or the higher its weight or percentage of silver, the more it was worth. Less valuable coins were often of silver-bronze alloy, or just bronze. Indeed, the eight *chalkoi* per *obol* take their name from the word *chalkos*, Greek for copper; perhaps this is reflected in the later custom of calling small denomination coins of copper or bronze "coppers."

One can easily observe the parallel with modern currencies. In the United States, four quarters comprise a dollar in the same way that four drachms equal a tetradrachm, and originally the quarter was meant to contain some silver, the nickel was named for the less valuable metal it was made of, and the penny or cent, the least valuable coin, was just copper. The dram (1/8 oz.), a modern unit of weight used by apothecaries, is derived from *drachm*, and today the term has also taken on the meanings of a small drink or quantity.

The Romans, following the model of the Greek colonies in southern Italy, also devised a coinage with gradations of value: the *denarius*, a silver coin which functioned as the primary denomination for five centuries; the *sestertius*, four of which equaled one *denarius*, which was suitable for small transactions; and the *aureus*, a gold coin equivalent to 25 *denarii*. The *denarius* left its mark both in Spain, where the word for money, "dinero," clearly echoes it, and in England, where the symbol for British pence (d) derives from its initial letter. The gradated coinages currently being used in the United States and Canada owe their names to ancient Rome as well: the quarter can be traced back to the Latin *quartarius*, meaning a fourth part; the dime derives, through the Middle English and Old French *disme*, to the Latin *decimus*, a tenth; and cent comes from the Latin *centum*, a hundred.

The Romans even gave us the word money itself; the story of its derivation is an interesting one involving Juno, the queen of the gods, a group of barbarian Gauls, and some sacred birds. In 390 B.C., the Gauls were besieging Rome, and one night a group of them attempted to scale the cliffs of the Capitoline hill upon which the Roman defenders were holding out. Atop this hill was a temple to Juno at which was kept a flock of geese, birds considered sacred to the goddess. These sacred geese were awakened by the climbing Gauls, and the birds began to hiss and cackle loudly. This commotion roused the Roman watchmen, who then defeated the assault. The term Moneta (derived from the Latin verb *monere*, meaning "to warn" or "to admonish") was then bestowed upon Juno because it was her geese that had given the warning that saved the city. Accordingly, her temple became known as the Temple of Juno Moneta, and later, when the Romans began to coin money, the mint was located either in or next to her temple. From this, the word *moneta* took on the general meaning of "mint," and our modern words "money" and "monetary" are directly derived from this Latin term. Therefore, the next time you think about or spend some money, you should think of cackling geese.

The Roman system of weights proved influential as well. Its principal unit, the *libra*, also formed the basis for the Roman monetary system. The *libra* spread with soldiers and settlers to Rome's provinces, where it developed into the standard for weighing gold and silver. Quite recently, the Roman *libra* was still echoed in the name of its descendent, the Italian lira, until Italy switched to the Euro. But the *libra* remains enshrined in England's monetary system, where the former Roman province abbreviates the pound as lb., which stands for *libra*. Similarly, the English ounce is derived from the Roman *uncia*, a weight equal to one-twelfth of a *libra*. Pound comes from the Latin *pondus*, weight, although *libra* was also one of the sub-definitions of *pondus*. As well as referring to a measure of weight, the Latin word *libra* also meant a pair of scales (the way to determine a weight) and the constellation and sign of the Zodiac Libra, which the Romans envisioned as a pair of scales in the night sky—as Ovid called it, *pendula caelestis Libra*, "the Balance hung in the heavens" (*Fasti* IV.386).

It has already been mentioned how Greek cities used coinage to assert civic identity, by depicting their famous products, symbols, legends, and patron gods. Eventually, the profiles of famous people—not just gods—began to show up on coins. The first significant embodiment of this trend was Alexander the Great, who played an important role in spreading Greek coinage throughout the many lands he conquered. Alexander continued this process, striking coinage in Persian cities such as Babylon and Susa. His eastern conquests had long-lasting monetary ramifications as well as cultural ones, since Bactrian Greeks took up the practice of minting Greek coins in western India. Greek coinage was also adopted by the Kushans in northern central India and Afghanistan, by the Parthians, and eventually by the Sassanians. Even far to the north in Celtic lands, coins were produced in imitation of Macedonian coinage, all the way from the Danube River to Britain. After Alexander's death, his former generals put his head on their coins in a bid to add to their own legitimacy as his potential successors. As veterans returned home from Alexander's campaigns, they spread coins bearing his image throughout their home countries. The coins stamped with Alexander's head embodied his power; on them, he is identified with demi-gods such as Hercules (by wearing his lion-skin) and gods such as Ammon (by exhibiting his rams' horns). This forcefully demonstrates how coins function as a symbol of a ruler's (or a country's) might—a strategy that has echoed down through the ages, as rulers repeatedly put themselves on their coins, often emphasizing their almost superhuman power or their divine favor in the images they created and circulated. Later, the Roman emperors eagerly embraced this idea as a useful means of propaganda and self-promotion.

Over the centuries, European rulers have frequently appeared on money, as do American presidents (George Washington on the $1 bill and the quarter, Thomas Jefferson on the nickel, Andrew Jackson on the $20 bill, Ulysses S. Grant on the $50 bill, Franklin D. Roosevelt on the dime, and Abe Lincoln on the $5 bill and the penny). Money also reflects the might of empires; just as Roman money emblazoned with the emperor's head spread throughout the territory they governed, the British empire asserted its dominion by putting Queen Victoria not just on British money, but on denominations used throughout its empire. For example, the memory of empire is still preserved on the current Canadian quarter, with its portrait of Queen Elizabeth II. The connection of money to national identity and power is perhaps also reflected in how we speak of a "strong" dollar or euro; a currency, like a country, exhibits weakness or strength in relation to other currencies and countries in the economic pecking order.

The tradition of depicting important buildings on coins is also an ancient one. Putting famous buildings and monuments on the reverse of coins was a common practice in classical times. For example, coins struck at Ephesus, even under the Roman emperors, often bore their world-renowned Temple of Artemis (her cult statue looming at its center), considered one of the Seven Wonders of the Ancient World. Indeed, the Seven Wonders of the Ancient World, such as the Temple of Apollo at Didyma and the Pharos (lighthouse) of Alexandria, frequently showed up on coins. Rulers also liked to mint coins that portrayed what they had built, in order to remind people that they had made an impact. For example, the Roman emperor Titus, under whose rule the Flavian Amphitheater (better known as the Colosseum) was dedicated, put that famous entertainment complex on some of his coins, and the emperor Trajan struck coins with images of his harbor of Portus as well as of his famous column. On American money, we have the Lincoln Memorial on the back of the penny, Monticello on the back of the nickel, the White House on the back of the $20 bill, and the U.S. Capitol on the back of the $50 bill.

Finally, if you have a dollar bill handy, take it out and have a look at it. Familiar to people around the world, the U.S. dollar is loaded with ancient imagery. To begin with, the back of the dollar boasts no fewer than three slogans in Latin: *Annuit coeptis*, meaning "He (God) favors our endeavor";

Novus ordo seclorum, meaning "A new order of the ages"; and *e pluribus unum*, meaning "from many, one." In addition, there are depictions of both sides of the Great Seal of the United States, which features on one side an eagle, the same bird that the Romans used to represent their state, and on the other a pyramid similar in appearance to Egyptian pyramids. The eagle clutches arrows in one claw, symbolizing war, and an olive branch symbolizing peace in the other. The olive branch was used as an emblem of peace by both the Greeks and the Romans, and appears on Roman coins in this capacity. On the other side, in addition to the portrait of George Washington, itself an echo of the rulers' portraits on ancient coins, there is a set of scales, the ancient Greek and Roman symbol for justice. Finally, Washington's portrait rests atop a bed of laurel leaves, which in the classical world represented victory and great achievement.

For many people today, closely intertwined with the concept of money is the experience of shopping. What better apparent symbol of the modern consumer culture is there than the ubiquitous and often gigantic shopping mall where the contemporary shopper can browse among multiple levels and hundreds of specialized shops? As it turns out, even this quintessentially modern experience was anticipated by the ancients. In the Greek world, the *agora*, or town square, was typically lined on at least two sides by a structure known as a *stoa*. This consisted of a long, roofed, colonnaded building with the front that faced the *agora* consisting of open columns and the back divided up into multiple small rooms. *Stoas* were multi-purpose venues, and it was common to find things such as government offices in the rooms, but probably their most common use was for shops. Greeks could stroll along under the shaded colonnades with their friends, perusing the merchandise on display, gossiping and socializing, seeing and being seen, and occasionally buying snacks from the many food vendors who also set up their establishments here. In other words, it was just like an afternoon at the mall.

The Romans emulated these Greek buildings with their own, often multi-story, porticoes, but one emperor took it further by erecting a structure that looks even more overtly like a modern shopping mall. This was the emperor Trajan, who, as part of his general reconstruction of the area behind the Roman Forum, built an edifice known today as Trajan's Markets. Reaching four stories high in some sections, this structure consists of more than 170

Figure 1.11 *Reconstruction of the Stoa of Attalos in the agora at Athens. Stoas such as this were multi-purpose structures used to house (among other things) shops, government offices, art displays, food stalls, and schools.*

small shops opening onto streets, covered colonnades, and promenades, and connected by numerous stairways. Trajan's Markets are solidly built out of brick and concrete, but the gracefully curving façade and the spacious,

Figure 1.12 *Part of Trajan's Markets at Rome. Each of the doorways would have led into a separate shop or office.*

well-lit, vaulted passageways make it an attractive space to stroll through. It is easy to imagine Romans wandering through the Markets and perusing the shops filled with an array of foods and merchandise, both practical and exotic. While there is debate as to whether some of the shops were actually offices, the entire complex is strongly reminiscent of modern shopping centers, and at the very least, the lower levels must have served this purpose.

Food, shelter, and money are some of the most basic necessities of modern urban life, but throughout history, they have come to represent and to make statements about much more than just subsistence and survival. From the little rituals that accompany our meals to the manner in which we use our homes to express our personalities, many of the ways in which these fundamental items continue to shape our lives have their origins in the world of classical antiquity.

2

From the cradle to the grave: The family and the journey of life

The core and central focus of most people's lives is their family. We are nurtured as children within the family structure, form important bonds within the family, often receive emotional and financial support from the family, raise our own children within the family, and in old age are often tended by, and once again supported by, family members. While the basic family structure is near-universal in human societies, many of the specific family structures, customs, and rituals that we employ today, such as many of those involving marriage, have their origins or predecessors in classical antiquity. One of the main preoccupations of families in all eras is raising children and preparing them for adult life. Often this includes some type of formal education, and here, too, much of modern practice is rooted in antiquity. In this chapter, we will examine life from the cradle to the grave, with an emphasis on those activities and behaviors that center around or are supervised by the family. We'll end by considering the formal ways in which the classical world marked out time, including the ancient calendar and its modern echoes.

Before embarking upon our topic, one fundamental difference between the modern Western world and the classical Mediterranean one that affects every aspect of family life needs to be emphasized. Ancient Greece and Rome were unabashedly male-dominated societies in which women, on the whole, were regarded as legal, social, and intellectual inferiors. In none of these societies did they have equal rights or could they vote, and they very often possessed the same status as a piece of property. As unpalatable as this might seem from a modern perspective, it is simply a historical fact. Women were revered and honored for certain skills and abilities that were regarded as appropriately feminine, such as childbearing, weaving, and running the household. While some women achieved high public status as queens, priestesses, or poets, and no doubt many more wielded significant behind-the-scenes power, they were on the whole, at least officially, second-class citizens—indeed, they weren't actually citizens at all.

Figure 2.1 *A family consisting of husband, wife, and two daughters depicted on a Greek gravestone.*

In ancient Rome, the male head of a family was known as the *paterfamilias* ("father of the family"). The Greek and Roman terms for father and mother, *pater* and *mater*, are obviously from the same original Sanskrit root as the Germanic-derived English words "father" and "mother." Far more than modern fathers, the Roman *paterfamilas* held near-total legal power over all the members of his extended family. He could even put his own children to death and sell members of the family into slavery. Naturally, he arranged the marriages for his children and could also order them to divorce.

First steps: Childhood

For a child born in the ancient world, there were at first some major hurdles to overcome. First of all, childbirth was risky for both the mother and the baby, so that survival of this initial ordeal was in itself a major accomplishment. A further test was the father's decision whether or not an infant should be accepted into the family and raised. In ancient Rome, the newborn baby was laid on the floor before its father. If it was a boy, he picked it up to acknowledge his acceptance; if a girl, rather than picking it up, he told one of the household's women to feed it. If he left it lying there, it would be put outside and abandoned. In ancient Greece, the father also decided whether to keep a baby or leave it exposed outside to die. In Sparta, a committee of male elders came to inspect a newborn child to make sure that it was physically sound and healthy; if it seemed sickly or handicapped in any way, they condemned it to abandonment. Whereas today we would call this infanticide, it was standard practice in the ancient world, seen as neither criminal nor morally culpable. Families could not always afford another child. Girls in particular seem to have been discarded. Any infants left exposed to the elements could be "rescued" by slave-traders and raised to be slaves or prostitutes.

If a baby was accepted into the family, the next major obstacle was disease, which carried off many in the first few years of life. This has led some people to question how deeply attached to their children parents allowed themselves to become, and whether they were so hardened to infant mortality that they were not intensely affected by it. However, heartfelt epitaphs inscribed on Roman children's tombstones, Greek funerary reliefs of little girls cuddling birds, and burials of even the youngest of infants suggest that we should not hastily jump to conclusions.

Interestingly, in Latin, there is no word that translates exactly as "baby." *Infans* (the source of our word "infant"), literally meaning "not speaking," is used in legal texts to refer to children under seven. Other terms for children included *progenii* (offspring), from which our word "progeny" comes; *filii* (sons and daughters), from which the adjective "filial" derives; and *pueri* (young children both male and female). *Puer* (Latin for "boy") is the source of our word "puerile," meaning juvenile or childish. *Puer* technically meant a boy before puberty, who could not yet have children of his own or fight for the state.

Parents today can seek guidance about caring for their newborns from a bewildering array of books, websites, and experts. While there may have been fewer outlets offering advice to ancient parents, there were plenty of popular notions regarding the proper way to raise children, including written advice. The Roman philosopher Seneca offers this take on how to rear children, and much of his advice would easily fit into any contemporary child-care manual:

> Care must be taken that we not allow children to indulge in anger tantrums, but at the same time we should be careful not to stifle their individual personalities … Unlimited freedom creates a willful child, complete repression leads to a sullen personality. Praise inspires children and gives them confidence, but excessive praise makes him lazy and obstinate. When raising a child, we should strive to follow a middle course, sometimes holding him back, and sometimes pushing him forward … Do not allow him to whine and badger you for rewards, bestow them only as merited rewards for good deeds, whether actual or promised. When the child enters into competition with his peers, do not allow him to become sullen or angry … If he is successful, give praise, but do not allow him to be too pleased with himself, because this leads to boastfulness, and produces an egotism and an overly inflated self-image … a child who always gets what he wants, whose tears have always been wiped away by a hovering mother, will not be able to deal with the harsh realities of life.
>
> *(Seneca the Younger, "An Essay about Anger" 2.21.1–6)*

Another timeless piece of wisdom comes from the Roman writer Pliny the Younger, who offers this advice to a friend with a rambunctious son: "Remember that he is just a boy, as you too were once, and act towards him as a father, keeping always in your mind that you are a human, and are the father of another who is human" (Pliny the Younger, *Letters* 9.12).

Nevertheless, both the ancient Romans and the Spartans of ancient Greece believed that babies should not be excessively babied. Roman infants were given cold baths in order to toughen them up, and children were not allowed to bathe in warm water or get too much sleep because this might make them weak and decadent. Both Greek and Roman babies were swaddled, or kept tightly bound up in pieces of cloth, to restrict their movements. A Roman infant's limbs were kept rigid against sticks. Eventually, the right arm would be released, but not the left; this was to discourage left-handedness, which was considered unlucky. This association is still with us today, since the Latin word "sinister" meant "left" or "on the left side," while the English word now means "ominous" or "suggestive of evil." But in the ancient world, the left side *was* negative and evil. In Greek augury, a bird coming from the right was a good omen, while a bird coming from the left was bad news. Therefore, you did not want your child to be affiliated with the ill-omened left side. Indeed, even into the twentieth century, left-handed children were sometimes still being forced to use only their right hands, due to a lingering sense of the left side denoting evil.

The Spartans went even further than cold baths, however. In order to make boys into hardened warriors, they sent them out to find their own food, barefoot and practically naked even in the winter. They had to hunt and steal food in order to survive; those who could not feed themselves would starve to death. A famous Spartan story tells of a boy who caught a fox and was sneaking it back to his barracks under his tunic when he encountered one of his teachers. While the teacher questioned him, the concealed fox began to gnaw away at the boy, but he betrayed no sign of pain or discomfort. It was later found that he had bled to death on his cot. He became a hero and an example to other boys for his courage and stoic refusal to complain. Our word "laconic," expressing oneself in few words, derives from Laconian, an inhabitant of the Greek region of which Sparta was the capital, as the Spartans were known for the terseness of their speech.

Spartan boys were educated away from home, living in group barracks from the age of seven (and even into adulthood). The emphasis was on toughening them up, discipline, and vigorous exercise. The boys lived and ate together, the food was plain and scarce, and they fought one another (with their teachers' approval) to hone their survival skills. If you have read about (or experienced)

British boarding schools of a certain era, perhaps the Spartan educational system will not seem entirely foreign and strange to you. Incidentally, when we speak of a "Spartan" lifestyle or accommodation, we are recalling these aspects of how the ancient Spartans lived—although our notion of Spartan is actually much less Spartan than theirs was.

These practices might lead us to assume that childhood in the ancient world was entirely different from its current state, yet some things would seem familiar. Vase paintings show Greek mothers rocking their babies in cradles made of wood or wicker, and they used a special type of flat-topped, footed pottery bottle with a spout on its side to feed their infants; these ancient baby-bottles were sometimes included in the burials of young children. Like today, anxious parents sought cures for the common tribulations of infancy. For example, one Roman cure for pain caused by teething was to rub sheep's brains on the gums or have the baby wear an amulet that contained the sandy substance supposedly found in the horns of snails. Modern parents might seek an alternate balm to soothe their children, but some things never change: the favorite word of the young grandson of the Roman statesman Fronto was 'Da!,' meaning "Give me!"

And while some aspects of ancient childhood were undoubtedly harsh, children nevertheless still felt the impulse to play. There is rich evidence for toys and games, many of which would not seem out of place in today's nurseries and playgrounds. Babies entertained themselves by shaking pottery rattles—for instance, a hollow animal filled with pebbles—and little bells with clappers. Girls played with dolls made of various materials, such as wood, bone, clay, and rags, sometimes even with jointed arms and legs. They also had dollhouses with miniature furniture, and used child-sized utensils to mimic their mothers' tasks and chores. Miniature carts and chariots accompanied by horses were probably a boy's equivalent of toy cars and trucks. One source tells of an interesting variant on this in which boys harnessed live mice to miniature wagons as if they were tiny oxen (Horace, *Satires* 2.3.247). They had yo-yos, spun tops, and rolled dice (*kuboi* in ancient Greek; *kubos* also meant cube), and tourists can still see board games carved into the steps of Greek and Roman public buildings, where both children and adults could stop for a game.

Figure 2.2 *An ancient clay toy horse with wheels.*

In art, we observe people on swings and see-saws, rolling hoops, and playing various ball games (ball was *sphairai*—sphere—in ancient Greek) reminiscent of handball, basketball, and field hockey. The Greeks played a ball game in which a designated player threw a ball at the others, and those who were hit were eliminated—a sort of ancient forerunner of modern dodgeball. Roman writers reminiscing about childhood recall skipping stones on the water and building sandcastles, and there is evidence that they played leapfrog, blind man's bluff, and guessing games. The idea of educational toys also existed; the Church Father Jerome recommended ivory bricks with the letters of the alphabet on them, which sound rather like the wooden blocks our children still build with, and the Roman writer Fronto gave his grandson writing paper and tablets to encourage him to learn how to write. In a symbolic ritual that might strike us as poignant, girls about to marry and boys attaining adolescence put aside their toys by dedicating them to the gods—a sign that they were ready to embark upon adulthood.

One issue that all societies must determine is when childhood ends. The poet Horace focused on behavior, characterizing children as prone to mood swings, not yet able to control themselves, liable to change their mind a lot, and easily overwhelmed by their desires. With adulthood came self-control and consistency in behavior. Focusing on physical changes, the famous and influential Greek physician Galen stated that puberty began at age 14 for boys and lasted until age 25. The Alexandrian scientist Ptolemy memorably characterized puberty as an eight-year stage running from 14 to 22 during which people experience turbulent, unbridled sexual impulses, a definition that many worried parents of teenagers today might agree with wholeheartedly. The Roman author Varro methodically divided a lifetime into five stages of 15 years each: childhood (*puerita)* until 15; from 15 until 30, adolescence (*adulescentia)*; from 30 to 45, young adulthood (*juventus; juvenis*, young man, is the source of the word "juvenile"*)*; from 45 to 60, maturity (*seniorus,* echoed in our terms "senior" and "senior citizen"*)*; and from 60 until death, old age (*senectus)*. Legally, however, puberty was set at 12 for a girl and 14 for a boy among the Romans (Gaius, *Institutes* 1.196).

Learning your lessons: Education

Words such as "academy," to denote a place of learning, and "pedagogy," meaning "the art of teaching," have their origins in the ancient world. While the idea of universal education for all children is a relatively recent phenomenon, the wealthy parents of antiquity were every bit as concerned that their children should get the best possible education as today's anxious parents who worry over what college their child will get admitted to.

In Greece and Rome, much of education was originally conducted relatively informally, within the household. The father would typically give his sons, and occasionally daughters, whatever teaching he thought was appropriate. The classic example of this sort of old-style home-schooling was the traditionally-minded Roman aristocrat Cato, who personally instructed his son in reading, writing, and military training. This was all that he deemed necessary or desirable. Others took a more sophisticated approach, particularly in the Greek world, where there was a longer tradition of valuing intellectual achievements. Once Rome had conquered Greece, the Romans absorbed many Greek attitudes, and they too became interested in more formal and elaborate types of education. Many Greeks who were enslaved by Rome ended up becoming teachers and instructing the children of their conquerors in the niceties of Greek literature, art, and philosophy. When that generation grew up, they valued Greek intellectual culture and passed it on to their children. This offers a nice parable about the power of education, since one could argue that, in terms of culture at least, the conquered Greeks ended up conquering the Romans. Much of ancient education was also directed towards teaching the oratorical skills that would be useful in both the Greek assembly and the Roman Forum.

Even when parents were not directly involved, the very first stage of instruction still usually took place within the household, and the key figure entrusted with this task was often an educated slave. In Rome, such a person was known as the *paedogogus*, from which our word "pedagogy" is derived. He was a kind of combination nurse, protector, and first teacher, who replaced the nurse as the child grew out of infancy. One description of the *paedogogus* states that he should "… speak well, teach charges how to walk correctly, sit properly, how to wear their clothes and how to eat" (Plutarch, *Moralia* 439F–440A). His job was to generally look after the child in all regards, and one aspect of his duty was to give him his basic instruction in languages.

Once they reached the age of about six, roughly when today's children embark upon first grade, Roman boys would also begin attending their first formal school. This consisted of classes given by a man known as a *litterator*, who taught reading, writing, and arithmetic. Slightly more advanced levels of classes of the same type were taught by another teacher called a *grammaticus* ("someone who knows about grammar")—perhaps preserved in our term "grammar school." (Actually, in England, a grammar school was originally one where Latin was taught.) Unless the child was very wealthy and had a private instructor, these classes were held outside the home, and the experience of ancient schoolboys had much in common with that of modern ones.

School started early, usually at dawn, so, like today, grumpy children had to be rousted out of bed and sent on their way to school, usually still accompanied by their faithful *paedogogus*. Incidentally, *paedogogus*, derived from Greek roots, literally means "to lead a child," referring to this basic task of walking his young charge to school. Those practicing pedagogy today would perhaps prefer to interpret this in a more figurative sense, as guiding a child towards knowledge. There were no true, designated school buildings in the modern sense, so classes were simply held wherever the instructor could find space. This might be a public area, such as an arcade or park, or a private room. Except in a few special cases, such as Sparta, there were no state-run or organized institutions of learning, so teachers were private contractors who negotiated with parents to instruct their offspring for a fee. Some teachers had only a handful of students, but there were also larger classes. The philosopher Seneca reports having attended a school with over 200 students in the class when he was a boy. Teachers of such big classes employed apprentice teachers to help them manage the throngs of students, in a system reminiscent of that in place at many universities today, whereby professors make use of graduate students to assist them in grading and teaching large classes.

The basic equipment of the student was a writing implement and something to write on; in the ancient world, this most likely meant a pointed metal cylinder called a *stilus* with which the student scratched marks into a small, wax-covered wooden tablet. These marks could then be wiped away with the other end of the *stilus,* which was flared. Some classroom exercises of ancient students survive, such as practicing verb conjugations and learning to form and write the letters of the alphabet. For some assignments, wealthier students might have been allowed to write upon papyrus using ink. To learn the alphabet, students were given small letters made out of wood or ivory which they had to learn to identify, copy, and place in the correct order. For mathematical calculations, students utilized an abacus. Much instruction consisted of rote memorization and repetition.

Teachers used both threats and rewards to motivate their students. Students who misbehaved or who simply gave the wrong answer were subjected to corporal punishment, usually meted out with a stick. Some teachers were known to flagellate their students towards achievement using more exotic items, such as the eel skin employed by one. The frequency of such punishments is revealed in the nicknames that ancient students gave their teachers, including "The Whacker" and "Old Leather-Arm." Caning the palms of a slow learner was a common form of discipline, and the poet Ovid describes

Figure 2.3 *Reconstructions of ancient writing implements. The scrolls would have been made out of the Egyptian plant, papyrus. The wooden tablets would have held wax panels into which temporary messages could be inscribed with the bronze stylus, and then erased for re-use.*

children holding out their swollen hands to be chastised. (While the beatings administered at British boarding schools—at times in retaliation for students' lax standards in Greek and Latin—have achieved legendary status, corporal punishment in many American public schools lasted well into the twentieth century, and the caning of one's palms will be painfully remembered by Catholic School students of a certain era.) A graffito at Pompeii, obviously inscribed by a frequent miscreant, states that he had been given three beatings, presumably all in the same day. On another wall at Pompeii, a painting depicts an even worse punishment. It shows a student stripped to his loincloth being held suspended over the back of another, while the teacher flogs him with a multi-thonged whip. This was a ritual known as the *catomus*, inflicted for particularly egregious offenses.

Current pedagogical theory emphasizes encouraging students to achieve by using positive reinforcement rather than coercive punishments, and some ancient teachers took this approach as well. The students were often required to give public performances displaying what they had learned, and those who excelled at this were awarded prizes. In order to motivate his pupils to learn the letters of the alphabet, one teacher rewarded success with a cookie. A particularly clever Roman teacher, who had been ordered to teach Latin to the sons of barbarian chiefs whom the Romans were cultivating, realized that the best way to engage them was to give them awards that were meaningful in their own culture. Since barbarian warriors were rewarded for bravery by their lords with golden bands known as torques that were worn around the arms or neck, this teacher bestowed miniature versions of torques upon his star students.

Once the basics of literacy had been mastered, instruction focused on literature, particularly a set of classic epic poems such as Homer's *Iliad* and Virgil's *Aeneid*. This phase of education lasted until the age of approximately 12 or 13. Due to the rarity and high cost of texts, often only the teacher possessed them, so much of class time was spent reading aloud from these to the students. They in turn were required to commit long passages to memory.

Roman weeks had 8 days, with the last being market day. Classes were usually held every day except market day, and there were only three breaks during the course of the year. One was in late December for the festival of Saturnalia, which corresponded roughly in its timing to our modern Christmas break; another was in the spring; and the last and longest was summer recess. Thus, the rhythm of their school life was quite similar to ours, with classes held every day during the week followed by a "weekend," and with the major holidays being in December, spring break, and summer vacation.

One surviving ancient source offers a first-hand account of what must have been a typical routine for many schoolboys: "I woke before dawn, rose from bed, put on my socks and shoes. Asking for water, I washed first my hands, then my face, and dried them off. I put on my tunic, and combed my hair … and left home. Arriving at school, I said "Hello, Teacher" and he kissed and greeted me. My slave who carries my books gave me my wax writing tablets and writing implements. I sat down at my spot and rubbed the tablets smooth. I then copied a sentence and, when finished, displayed it to Teacher. He fixed my errors, and had me read it out loud. I then recited to another student, and was recited to by another ... Teacher interrogated me about grammar ... asking 'What are the parts of speech?' I declined nouns and analyzed sentence structures. After this, Teacher sent us home for lunch" (*Corpus Glossariorum Latinorum* III).

The ancient world did not have formal colleges or universities that provided a generalized education as modern ones do, but the equivalent of a course of higher learning was to study with a renowned orator or philosopher. Public speaking was a highly useful practical skill for aspiring aristocrats and politicians, and there were instructors who taught advanced oratory. Such a man was called a *rhetor*, literally a specialist in rhetoric. Rhetoric supposedly originated in Sicily in the mid-fifth century B.C., and a man named Isocrates had established a specialized school of rhetoric and philosophy in Athens by 392 B.C.

Figure 2.4 *A Roman boy clad in a toga and perhaps practicing his oratorical skills. Such training was thought to be good preparation for a public life.*

Oratorical training included a number of exercises, such as practicing the composition, memorization, and delivery of speeches. Students were given assignments to write descriptions based on mythological topics, to draft comparative essays, and to create hypothetical speeches that might have been given by famous historical or mythical figures. This phase of instruction also taught students logic and formal argumentation.

To hone these skills, one common strategy was to pose a difficult moral or legal question and then ask the student to compose a short speech arguing one side of the case. The philosopher Seneca recorded a number of these sorts of assignment. A rather colorful example of one such controversy went as follows: "The law requires that a priestess must be chaste and pure. A young woman was captured by pirates and sold by them as a slave. She was bought by a pimp for use as a prostitute. She was able to persuade all her customers to give her money without sex, until a soldier came who could not be persuaded. He tried to rape her, but she fought back and killed him. She was put on trial, acquitted, and returned to her family. She then tried to become a priestess, but her petition was opposed" (Seneca, *Controversiae* 1.2). The student then had to argue either that she was still pure and chaste and should be allowed to be a priestess, or why she was not and should not be.

Perhaps the pinnacle of education was to study with a famous philosopher. The great Greek thinker Plato established a school for students that was known as the Academy. It got this name because they habitually met at a grove of trees just outside of Athens that was dedicated to the hero Academus, and, from that point on, the word "academy" has meant a place of intellectual learning. One of the students at Plato's Academy was Aristotle, who grew up to be just as famous an intellectual as his mentor. Aristotle also founded an institution of learning, which he called the Lyceum. It was in another grove of trees, this one sacred to the deities Apollo, Lyceius, and the Muses. It was very much a forerunner of today's universities, since it was explicitly intended to serve as a place that would add to and preserve knowledge. "Lyceum" continues to be used, especially in Europe, to refer to a place offering public lectures, concerts, and other forms of educational and cultural enrichment, while in France, "lycée" still denotes a public secondary school.

One of the common finishing touches to a college education often consists of spending a semester or a year abroad in a foreign country. Parents hope that such an experience will impart a degree of worldly sophistication to their offspring as well as giving them the opportunity to absorb a foreign culture and learn another language. For many students, however, such trips are viewed as opportunities to indulge in drinking and partying in an exotic locale. All too often, this results in an exchange of texts or phone calls in which parents urge their children to restrain themselves and take their studies more seriously, while students hasten to reassure their parents that great intellectual and cultural gains are being made. Frequently at the center of such dialogues is the subject of the student's allowance, with the exasperated parents threatening to cut off funds if the student does not shape up, and the student perennially complaining that life abroad is expensive and that he or she needs additional money sent from home.

While this situation may seem modern, in reality this exact same family drama has been played out for thousands of years. In the Greek and Roman world, it was common for the offspring of the wealthy to cap off their education by spending time overseas studying at one of the famous centers of learning in the ancient Mediterranean, such as Athens or Alexandria. Some students were sent by their parents to the cities of specific philosophers with whom they wished to study, and traveled to the site of their "schools" to become disciples at the feet of the master.

A uniquely personal perspective on the experience of one such ancient student sent abroad by his father to polish his education can be found in the letters of Cicero, the famous Roman orator, politician, and philosopher. Cicero had grand intellectual ambitions for his son, Marcus, and took an active role in directing every stage of the boy's education, personally selecting the finest tutors and constantly hounding the boy to apply himself diligently to his studies. (The scenario of a parent pressuring a child to achieve or to follow in his footsteps, and of living vicariously through his offspring, is evidently an ageless and universal one.) This cannot have been a pleasant experience for poor Marcus, but he seems to have worked doggedly, following the dictates of his father. As a final step in his education, Cicero dispatched Marcus to Athens, the home city of many of the most famous philosophers, and provided the boy with a generous allowance. Finally freed from his father's direct supervision, Marcus immediately threw himself into a boisterous lifestyle of drinking, carousing, and enjoying the delights of life in Athens. In these pleasures of the body, he actually seems to have been led and encouraged by one of the philosophers hired to provide his mind with advanced instruction. In surviving letters, we can trace Cicero's steadily growing suspicions that his son is not being as abstemious and studious as he would like. There is also a constant flurry of requests from Marcus for ever more money, which Cicero continues to indulge, even against the counsel of his friends. Finally, the truth is revealed, and an outraged Cicero demands that the pleasure-seeking philosopher be fired and that Marcus dedicate himself to his studies. A chastened Marcus complies, and writes that he deeply regrets the "errors of his youth," but ends the letter on a less humble note by asking to be given a secretary so as to free him from the burden of writing down lecture notes himself. Thwarting his father's plans that he become a philosopher, young Marcus soon afterwards embarked upon a military career. While the setting may be the Roman world, the elements of this tale—including the overbearing father, the reluctant scholar, the youthful partying abroad, and the struggles over allowance—should be fully familiar to many parents and teens today.

Teenagers have always exasperated and tested the patience of their parents. Particularly the later teen years, marked by raging hormones, are often viewed with trepidation and anxiety by fathers and mothers. The words of the Greek moralist Plutarch could have been uttered by any such parent today: "The impetuosity of youth rages unrestrained … the vices of late adolescence are often irresistible and depraved—rampant gluttony, stealing money from parents, gambling, partying, drinking contests, promiscuity … The impulses of young men absolutely must be kept in check and restrained by constant vigilance" (Plutarch, *De Moralia: The Education of Children* 12).

It seems to be basic human nature for the older generation always to view the younger one with disapproval, and to believe that they are less virtuous and more morally degenerate. Today's media is filled with condemnations of the supposedly degraded music, habits, and clothing of youth culture, but if we look back 2,000 years we find numerous ancient authors expressing exactly the same sentiments. Thus, Seneca lamented that the young men of his time were lazy and spent too much time on fancy hairstyles, while Columella contrasted the allegedly tough, vigorous, hard-working, industrious, farm-bred youths of his day with the current generation of city-born children who drank too much, ate too much, gambled too much, slept too much, and were weak and flabby.

Tying the knot: Marriage

Historically, perhaps the most important of all family rituals has been the marriage ceremony. It marks one's passage from one's own family and the creation of a new one. If you had attended an ancient Greek or Roman wedding, you would have experienced a combination of the familiar and the unexpected. At times, you would have known exactly how to react; but other customs might have puzzled or surprised you.

The Greeks and the Romans married at younger ages than we allow today. While Greek men were typically in their mid-to-late twenties when they married, Greek girls were only around 14 or 15. In ancient Rome, 12 was considered legally old enough for a girl, and 14 for a boy, although in practice they were occasionally younger and often older than this. Whereas laws today mandate only a minimum age for marriage, the Roman emperor Augustus actually enacted legislation requiring that men marry by the age of 25 and women by the age of 20 because he was worried about birth rates. Among the Roman upper classes, arranged marriages were common, and children were on occasion betrothed in infancy, though it was preferred that they be old enough to comprehend what was being promised. The first aspect of Roman marriage rituals that would seem wholly familiar today is that, as a symbol of their engagement, the man (or boy) placed an engagement ring made of iron on the third finger of the woman's (or girl's) left hand, since doctors believed that a nerve ran directly from this finger to the heart. Many of today's brides-to-be might be disappointed by an engagement ring made of iron, given the often stratospheric costs of the jewel-studded versions relentlessly hawked in ads as the only fitting symbol of a serious commitment; but in the ancient world, it was usually the bride's side of the family (rather than the groom) which ended up having to spend a great deal of money on marriage in the form of a dowry. Perhaps the longstanding tradition of the bride's family paying for the wedding represents a hold-over from the provision of a substantial dowry.

Today, popular locations for weddings are often reserved months or even years in advance by anxious couples eager to secure the perfect setting, and dates perceived as possessing lucky qualities due to the repetition of certain numbers—for example, July 7, 2007 (7/7/07)—are especially coveted. In ancient Rome, there were a number of superstitions regarding wedding dates, and one had to be careful when choosing the day for a wedding. Interestingly, the Romans seem to have been more concerned with avoiding days that were seen as unlucky rather than picking days that promised good fortune. For instance, the month of May was bad because that was when Romans sacrificed to the dead. (A common saying ran, "Wed in May and rue the day.") The first half of June was also inopportune. It was necessary to wait until after the thorough cleaning of the Temple of Vesta had been completed, on June 15th. (Vesta, the goddess of the hearth, was guardian of the home and domestic life but also of the wider community, and the fire in her temple hearth had to be kept perpetually burning to ensure the state's welfare; so perhaps the state hearth had to be put in order before domestic hearths could bring married couples luck.) The second half of June was the best time for a wedding—a time of fruitfulness and abundance in nature that would hopefully be reflected in the marriage. Perhaps the popularity of June for weddings today recalls this old connection and sense of an optimistic start.

The most elaborate Greek weddings took three days: on the first, the bride dedicated her childhood toys to the virgin goddess Artemis as a sign of her changing role and status; on the second, a wedding banquet was held by the bride's father; and on the third, the bride left her childhood home for her new one. An older woman, the *nympheutria* (often translated as "bridesmaid"), escorted the bride to help her out in following the nuptial rituals.

The most important part of a Greek wedding was the procession, by chariot, from the bride's home to the groom's—traditionally at night by the light of torches. The bride lit her own torch at her family's hearth, and ultimately used it to light the hearth of her new home. Relatives carrying wedding gifts followed the chariot, in which the veiled bride rode, seated between her new husband and the *paranymphos* (the best man). Finally, there was a custom of the bride eating a many-seeded fruit before consummating the marriage in order to increase her fertility. Similarly, during the wedding banquet, instead of slices of a wedding cake, the guests ate little individual sesame seed-covered cakes, since the seeds were believed to enhance a woman's fertility.

Technically, a Roman marriage did not require a ceremony in order to be valid; a man and woman had only to state that they were married. None the less, many observed the traditional rites. As among the Greeks, a girl first dedicated her childhood toys and clothes—in this case, to the household gods—as a sign that she was about to acquire an adult role. Then she prepared for her wedding by donning a white, tunic-like dress (that would be worn only on this one occasion), a wreath of marjoram, and a transparent veil with matching shoes. The veil, not the dress, was regarded as the distinctive and symbolic wedding garment, but, unlike a modern wedding veil, the Roman bride's veil was flame-colored and shaped more like a scarf, covering her head but not her face. Her hair was also prepared in a special fashion to suggest her transition to adulthood. As a child, she wore it in a ponytail, but now it was parted into 6 strands and braided into a cone on top of her head (a style worn only on her wedding day). An iron spearhead (preferably one that had killed a gladiator) was used to part the hair; the reasons for this ritual are debated, but it may have been intended either to scare off evil spirits or to promote fertility, since gladiators were renowned for their virility. Although weapons are no longer used to arrange a bride's coiffure, the custom of sporting a special one-time gown and hairstyle is still familiar.

The Roman marriage vow was restricted to the woman, who said to the groom, "To whatever family you belong, I also belong." After this, a bridesmaid joined her hand with that of her husband, and a formal marriage contract might be signed in front of witnesses. The crowd then shouted "Feliciter!", meaning "Happiness" or good luck for the couple. As in the Greek marriage ceremony, a wedding meal was served, and the torch-lit procession from the bride's house to the groom's later that evening was also a significant part of the ritual.

The parade of relatives and friends sang wedding songs to encourage the begetting of children, and shouted risqué jokes. The lyrics of one wedding song preserved by the poet Catullus include the lines: "Come forward, new bride. Be willing, and hear our words. Look how our torches flicker like golden hair. Come forward, new bride. Just as the supple grapevine embraces the nearby tree, so will your husband be entwined in your embrace … What joys are coming to your new lord, what pleasures he will know during the shadowy night, or even at mid-day … Raise up your torches, boys! I see her wedding veil … And you, bride, be sure not to deny what your husband wants lest he seek it elsewhere. O Hymen Hymenaeus, O Hymen Hymenaeus!"

(Poem 61, lines 91–146). The god Hymen Hymenaeus invoked at the end of this song was the deity who presided over weddings.

Another wedding ritual that might seem familiar is that the guests in the procession traditionally threw nuts (the rice we now use for this purpose had not yet found its way to the Mediterranean world). Three young boys accompanied the bride, two holding her hands and the third leading her and carrying a special wedding torch which had been lit at her parental home (echoing the Greek custom). This torch was the focal point of another ritual that has modern parallels, since, upon reaching her new home, she would fling the torch into the crowd. There would be a struggle to see who could catch it, because doing so was believed to confer long life.

The modern throwing of the bridal bouquet may preserve some echo of this gesture, although the modern version is certainly a far safer ritual since people are trying to catch a bunch of flowers rather than a flaming torch. Note, too, how the torch-boy at some point seems to have turned into a flower girl. It is not surprising that longevity rather than marriage was believed to be the reward bestowed upon the lucky torch-catcher, given the many threats of mortality in the ancient world. Upon reaching the house that they would live in, the parade ended with another ceremonial act that remains unaltered today. The bride was lifted by the groom and carried by him over the threshold and into their new mutual home.

The significance of the bride's torch in both Greek and Roman wedding ceremonies may well have provided the inspiration for the "torch song" (usually sung by a woman about unrequited love) and "carrying a torch" for someone. The notion of love as a flame or a fire no doubt contributed to the popularity of these phrases, but the specific image of carrying a wedding torch that you can never use to light your beloved's hearth-fire (either in marriage or even just in a sexual sense) possesses a special poignancy.

The game of love: Sexuality

Sexuality is one of the areas in which the inhabitants of the ancient world had very different ideas from current ones. The most fundamental of these differences is that the majority of people today regard sexual orientation as consisting of two well-defined polar opposites, homosexual and heterosexual, with a small scattering of those who are bisexual in between, whereas most ancient Mediterranean civilizations regarded sexual orientation in a wholly different way. They considered sexuality as more of a continuum in which some people might gravitate towards one end of the spectrum and be exclusively attracted to members of either the same or the opposite sex, but most were somewhere in the middle. Thus, it was not regarded as odd that, for example, a man would be sexually active primarily with women, but might occasionally engage in sex with other men. This did not make him homosexual, since such a term and concept did not even exist. Just as the ancients were not hung up on sexual orientation, they did not attach much moral significance to the types of sexual acts that people practiced. There were distinct verbs to describe different sexual acts, and the three main ones were for what we would now term vaginal sex, oral sex, and anal sex. Once again, it was regarded as normal to engage in all of these.

It should be mentioned that the entire topic of ancient sexuality is a much-debated area among scholars, who are not entirely in agreement regarding these issues. However, many currently believe that there was one specific aspect of sexuality that was viewed as much more significant in the ancient world and that carried strong moral overtones of appropriate (or inappropriate) behavior. This was the specific role that you played in any given sexual encounter. In the classical world, passivity or submission was equivalent to inferiority, and males in particular were expected to always be active rather than passive. How this translated to sex was that the ancients seem to have had strong feelings regarding who was doing the penetrating during a sex act. If you were the penetrator, you were superior, and there was nothing shameful about what you were doing. Who or what you penetrated did not matter nearly as much as the fact that you were the active partner. On the other hand, if you were penetrated, it implied that you were like a woman, and thus were regarded as inferior, submissive, and morally bad.

Thus, to accuse a man of being effeminate was an insult, but it was not necessarily a comment on his demeanor—rather, it was an accusation that he took on the passive role in sex acts. For example, Julius Caesar, who was notorious for having an active sex life, was criticized because rumors spread that he had at times played the "inferior" role. A ditty about his activities that made the rounds included the accusation that he was "every woman's man and every man's woman" (Suetonius, *Julius Caesar* 52). The first half only meant that he was promiscuous, but the second part was a serious slander because it accused him of playing the passive role. As stated, this entire topic is fraught with disagreement among scholars, and there are those who maintain that sexual orientation and the role one played were both less significant than how much one was in control of one's own sexual urges and whether or not one practiced them in moderation.

Figure 2.5 *Drinking vessel with an erotic scene. Such subjects were often illustrated on everyday household items, such as cups and lamps.*

Despite all of these potential differences regarding categorization, much of the actual sexual activity and the rituals surrounding it that took place in the classical world are familiar ones. Ancient Greece and Rome certainly had their fair share of seduction, adultery, prostitution, promiscuity, and idealized chastity, and ancient lovers experienced the full rollercoaster of emotions that flirtation, courtship, infatuation, romantic rivalry, break-up, and loss can provoke.

One of the best sources for such emotions is love poetry. One poet who wrote a number of works on seduction and love affairs was Publius Ovidius Naso, better known as Ovid. A typical passage records the thoughts of a man who is carrying on an affair with a married woman and finds himself in the awkward situation of having to attend the same banquet as his lover and her husband. Consumed with jealousy, he inwardly rages, "Must I watch while another man enjoys the pleasure of your caresses, as you snuggle against him and warm his chest, as he places a proprietary arm around you? … Don't allow your husband to lean against you so. Don't allow your lovely head to rest up against his ugly chest. Don't allow him to lay his fingers on your soft breasts." He then progresses to tortured visions of what will happen "after the banquet is over and you go to your home and your husband will take his pleasure of your kisses, and of much more than just your kisses … May he not enjoy his lovemaking with you, or at least may you not enjoy it. But no matter what takes place between you in the night, when I see you tomorrow, tell me in a convincing tone that nothing at all happened" (Ovid, *Amores* 1.4.2–70).

Today, one can go to any bookstore and find a shelf-full of books about dating, finding a perfect mate, and how to appeal to the opposite sex. Ovid's most famous work was an ancient forerunner to all of these, and its advice in many respects seems surprisingly contemporary. This was the *Art of Love*, much of which is devoted to giving practical recommendations about how to seduce women—making it perhaps one of the earliest how-to manuals. To Ovid, love was a game, and the winner was the one who got the girl by any means necessary. The *Art of Love* is filled with pragmatic advice outlining every phase of seduction and amorous conquest. One perennial concern of the lothario is where to go to find attractive and potentially amenable women. Ovid suggests attending the law courts (a popular form of entertainment at that time) or hanging around public spaces such as gardens or the Forum. When preparing oneself to go out to pick up women, Ovid stresses the importance of personal grooming, including wearing clean, well-fitting clothes, combing one's hair so it is not unruly, washing one's hands, trimming one's nostril hair, and taking pains to prevent bad breath and body odor.

A central concern of modern guidebooks for dating aimed at men is how to talk to a woman, and Ovid offers plenty of advice on this topic. He recommends that, above all, when wooing a woman, you should constantly praise her appearance and flatter her ego. Ovid notes that such fulsome words need not actually conform to reality, but that they will help you to win your way to her heart. Ovid is not one to give up easily, and if a woman initially rejects you, he advises that you be patient and persistent, and you will eventually wear down her defenses. If you are becoming impatient with the pace of your seduction, his suggested solution is to ply her with alcohol, and finally, if all else fails, he notes that women are unable to resist tears, and if real tears are not forthcoming, you should simply induce them artificially. Once you have obtained the object of your desires, if you and she have an argument, he advises that a bout of lovemaking can restore the relationship.

One of the more entertaining passages in the *Art of Love* concerns where to take a woman on a date. Ancient Rome had no movie theaters, but perhaps the equivalent was the Circus Maximus, where chariot races were held. According to Ovid, this setting provided many good opportunities for hopeful lovers to gain their dates' affections. To begin with, the prospective seducer should buy a woman tasty sweets from the food vendors to whet her appetite. He should purchase a soft cushion for her to sit on in the stands. He should ascertain what horses or team she is rooting for, and then cheer enthusiastically for them, regardless of his own preferences. Best of all, the densely packed crowd will give him an excuse to press up against her body, and when the inevitable dust kicked up by the chariots settles onto her tunic, he can hope to fondle her breasts under the guise of helpfully brushing it off her clothes. Ovid's practical (yet rather cynical) advice for lovers was too much for the more traditionally-minded among the Romans, and, in consequence, the emperor Augustus banished him to a remote corner of the empire. There Ovid lived out the rest of his days in misery, far from the bustle and excitement of the great metropolis. Such actions became something of a habit with Augustus, who exiled his own daughter to a small island for her promiscuity and adultery.

Less poetic but more concise expressions of ancient love and lust that will be completely familiar to anyone who has visited certain public or college bathrooms can be found in the graffiti scratched or painted on the walls of Pompeii. Much of this body of material consists of variations on the timeless statement that "so-and-so loves so-and-so," or, as one actual graffito reads, "Marcus loves Spendusa" (*CIL* 4.7086). Some record the boasts of successful seducers, such as one blunt message that reads "I have screwed many girls here," and another that proclaims, "May I always be as potent with women as I was here" (*CIL* 4.2175). A rather astonishingly literal-minded variant on this theme states, "I came here. I screwed. I returned home" (*CIL* 4.2246). On the other hand, perhaps this was intended as a witty play on Julius Caesar's famous line about Pontus in Asia Minor: "I came, I saw, I conquered."

A range of universal emotions is revealed in these scribblings. One lonely traveler expressed his feelings in a graffito, written on the walls of an inn, that reads: "Vibius Restitutus slept here alone with his heart filled with longing for his Urbana" (*CIL* 4.2146)—certainly a sentiment shared by many devoted spouses while separated from their beloveds while on a business trip. Angry or frustrated ancient lovers left messages such as "Thyas, don't give your love to Fortunatus" (*CIL* 4.4498) and "Atimetus got me pregnant" (*CIL* 4.10231). One interesting series of graffiti scratched on the doorposts of a tavern seems to record an exchange of messages between the members of a love triangle. The first declares: "Successus the weaver loves Iris, the slave of the innkeeper's wife. She doesn't return his affections, but he tries to make her pity him. So says his rival. Farewell." It is signed by a man named Severus. Successus then apparently wrote his reply next to the first message: "You are envious and angry, but don't try to steal from someone who is better-looking than you are, who knows what to do in bed, and who is better endowed than you are." Severus then added: "Severus to Successus—I have said it and written it: you love Iris, but she does not love you" (*CIL* 4.1928).

Finally, the extremes of emotion provoked by love, from ecstasy to despair, are exemplified by the poet Catullus. He was an intense young pleasure-seeker living during the time of the Late Roman Republic who fell head-over-heels in love with a married woman named Clodia. He ended up writing a sequence of poems relating the ups and downs of his attempts to court her, which veer wildly from verses in which some favorable sign from Clodia transports him to the heights of euphoria to others where an apparent rejection causes him to crash down to the bitter depths of loathing and self-pity. A famous opening line of one of his poems succinctly captures both conditions: "I hate you and I love you" (Poem 85). Catullus could not sustain such intensity for long, and he died at age 33, broke and ultimately rejected by Clodia.

While today there is a common stereotype of the Greeks and (perhaps especially) the Romans as being promiscuous and decadent, at times these societies could be rather sternly moralistic. For example, in the old Roman Republic, even public displays of affection were frowned upon. On one occasion, a senator was expelled from the senate for committing the unacceptably immoral act of giving his wife a kiss in public. Nevertheless, there were also occasions when individuals, especially the more mentally unbalanced emperors, engaged in the sort of debauched orgies that are often associated with the Romans. This sort of behavior does represent an atypical extreme, however.

Turning to practical aspects of sex there was, like today, considerable interest in finding a means of contraception. Unfortunately, the ancients did not have our modern understanding of biology, so many of their solutions were ineffective. One common method of attempting to prevent pregnancy was to resort to various charms and spells. An example cited in an encyclopedia written by Pliny the Elder instructs women to locate a certain large hairy spider, cut open its head, remove the two worms supposedly contained there, and then wear these worms on their bodies (*Natural History* 29.27.85). This was believed to provide reliable contraception for up to one year. Rather more effective were condoms fashioned out of sheep's intestines. While reasonably good at stopping pregnancy, this remedy may have helped to spread venereal diseases, since such condoms were intended to be reusable and were often shared by several people.

Respect your elders: Old age

While seniors today look forward to retirement as a time when labor is exchanged for leisure and a pension or Social Security payments, the ancient world did not have a similar social safety net for its elderly. In ancient Rome, the concept of old age was not entirely based on chronological years, but instead also considered the degree of one's physical and mental wellbeing. The category of *seniores* or *senex* (*senex* meaning "old" and *seniores* "older ones," the sources of our words "senior," "seniority," "senescence," and "senile") could begin anywhere between the ages of 46 and 60. Your class or status determined what old age would mean for you; if you were wealthy enough, you could devote yourself to activities intended to exercise your brain, and many ancient philosophical treatises deal with issues of aging because it was primarily the elderly who had the time and inclination to pursue the study of philosophy.

Figure 2.6 *Portrait bust of an aged Roman. The realistic style of Roman portraiture accurately records the ravages of age, down to the smallest wrinkle, in such sculptures.*

Adult life was burdened with political and public responsibilities and duties, such as serving in the army, voting in the various citizen assemblies, and marrying and having children. At the age of 60, much of this changed; men could no longer serve in the army or vote, and under the empire they could relinquish the duties of senator and judge without giving up the titles, and Augustus' marriage laws declared that they were no longer required to be married or produce offspring to serve the state. An ancient Roman adage, "Sixty years and over the bridge," referred to an elderly man's banishment from voting, since "bridges" was the slang term used for the narrow pathways through which voters were funneled into voting pens. While our phrase "over the hill" (first recorded in 1950) is unrelated, it is obviously similar in sentiment. Basically, an ancient Roman man's status followed an arc: as a child, he lacked rights, power, and a role in public life; as an adult, he gained these; and in old age, he lost them again and reverted to a kind of second childhood in which he was dependent on others and lost much of the independence and many of the rights he had previously enjoyed (or been burdened by).

The Roman virtue of *pietas*, respect for one's parents and the responsibility of caring for them in old age, acted as a counterweight to this view of the elderly. This sense of duty is vividly illustrated by Virgil's image in *The Aeneid* of "pious Aeneas" carrying his enfeebled father, Anchises, on his back as they flee from the burning city of Troy. The emperor Antoninus reputedly had "Pius" attached to his name because he helped to support his weak, elderly father-in-law.

In memoriam: Burial

This sense of piety extended to the grave. For those wealthy enough to afford them, funerals were important rituals upon which much money could be expended. Because one often literally worshipped and prayed to one's ancestors, guaranteeing that the deceased received a proper burial was a major concern. The entire plot of the famous Greek play, the *Antigone*, for example, revolves around the powerful obligation that the protagonist Antigone feels to ensure that her brother gets a proper burial, even if this means defying a direct order of the king. The Romans also felt intense reverence for their ancestors, and many great families kept a cabinet containing the wax death masks of family members of the previous generations, which were taken out for and played a key role in important family rituals.

The Greeks practiced a three-part process in their funerary rites. First, the female family members of the deceased prepared the body by washing it, rubbing it with oil, clothing it, and crowning it with flowers, so that it was ready to be displayed. The next day, a viewing (*prothesis*) of the body occurred at which family and friends could come pay their respects, as still commonly happens today. Women wore black and cut their hair short as tokens of mourning, and publicly showed their grief by beating their breasts, wailing, and tearing out their hair. If you were wealthy, you could pay professional mourners to further augment the lamentations. The funeral procession (*ekphora*) took place on the third day, when, before dawn, the shroud-encased corpse was transported to the place of burial, interred, and given offerings of food, drink, and jars called *lekythoi*, which were used to store olive oil and were commonly included in tombs because of the anointing of the dead with oil. A feast was held after the ceremony, similar to the way in which people still congregate at the home of the deceased to share food after a funeral.

Incidentally, the phrase "pay the ferryman" originates from another funerary custom of the Greeks and Romans. One step in the preparation of the body was to place a coin under its tongue, as payment for Charon, the ferryman who carried the spirits of the dead in his boat across the River Styx from the land of the living to the Underworld. If he was not paid, Charon left the spirit stranded, unable to enter the land of the dead, so that it would be forced to wander as a ghost among the living. The long-lived custom of covering a corpse's eyelids with coins no doubt preserves a memory of this myth, although a pragmatic reason—weighing down the eyelids so that they would not unnervingly pop open—has been cited as another inspiration for the practice.

Roman funeral rites (*funus*, the source of our word "funeral") also followed a typical pattern. Family and friends often sat by a person's deathbed to offer comfort. The closest relative would give him or her a final kiss in order to capture the soul, which was released in one's dying breath, and would then shut the corpse's eyes. The family repeatedly cried out the name of the deceased (a rite known as the *conclamatio*) as an expression of their grief. Like the Greeks, the Romans washed, oiled, clothed, and crowned the body (a male citizen was buried in his toga, the sign of his status). The body was placed on a special funeral bed with its feet pointed towards the front door of the house; the long-lasting superstition that a corpse must be carried out of a home "feet first" in order to prevent its ghost from returning to haunt it allegedly originated with this custom. The door was marked with a bough of cypress, a tree associated with death in the ancient world, perhaps because of its unique combination of being an evergreen whose branches refuse to grow back if they are pruned too harshly. In fact, the cypress tree endured as a symbol of mourning well into modern times, frequently appearing as sprigs carved on tombstones and as the most common tree planted in cemeteries in both the European and the Muslim worlds.

The Romans, like the Greeks (and like us), allowed bodies to lie in state (the *collocatio*) for viewing by family and friends, although the Romans evidently did this for up to seven days. One detailed marble relief depicting a *collocatio* includes two incense burners and several garlands of flowers, which no doubt helped to counteract any signs of decay. The profession of undertaker (*libitinarius*) existed among the Romans to make funeral arrangements for those wealthy enough to afford it, and grave-diggers (*fossores*, literally "diggers") dug out graves and catacombs.

Naturally, one of the most important of these rituals was the funeral ceremony. In its fullest form, this featured a eulogy by a family member, a procession to the place of burial, and the actual cremation or burial of the body. Roman funeral processions typically took place at night, accompanied by torchlight. Close friends and family members of the deceased would carry the body on its funeral bed, in the same way that the pallbearers who carry a coffin today are still often chosen for their closeness to the deceased. The procession was accompanied by hired musicians playing flutes and horns, and, at times, even by choruses and dancers. Sometimes actors or young members of the family wore the wax death masks of the ancestors, so that they would seem to come to life again to witness a new inductee into their ranks. Family members dressed in special black garments, and this association may have formed the basis for the somber garb still traditionally worn at funerals today. The body of the deceased, on the other hand, was attired in the finest, costliest, most elaborate clothing. It was surrounded with expensive incense and spices and carried on a bier to the place of cremation outside the city. During the procession, female members of the family might scream, scratch and beat themselves, and tear out their hair in a display of grief. Sometimes additional professional "mourners" were hired to shriek and wail in a dramatic fashion alongside the body. The pyre could be a luxurious construct replete with gold, paint, and more precious incenses, and the favorite possessions of the deceased might also be placed on it to burn along with him. We know of at least one man whose funeral cost over one million sesterces, equivalent to the minimum net wealth required to be a senator.

After cremation, the ashes would be gathered and stored in some sort of container, often a little chest or an urn. These could be buried, placed in a house-like family tomb, or slid into a niche in a *columbarium* (literally a dovecote), a specialized sort of tomb thus named because it resembled the structures used to house doves, which were full of little compartments. The tombs themselves could be quite elaborate. The wealthiest Romans built large marble funerary monuments that could hold the remains of multiple family members. In order to insure that their heirs built a suitably impressive edifice, many wills contained detailed instructions for the type of tomb the person wanted. Often, it was even stipulated that the heir could not receive his inheritance until he had buried the deceased in the specified manner.

Some sense of the degree of detail that such directions could attain is indicated by one man's will, which stipulated: "I desire that my tomb be built according to these specifications: The shrine must feature an area containing a seated statue of myself made from the best quality imported marble (or fine bronze), and it must be at least five feet in height. In this area must be a bench and two seats on each side, all made of fine imported marble. When the shrine is open, this area must be provided with pillows, two rugs, two cushions, two cloaks, and a tunic. Every year, my descendants, freed slaves, and all their descendants must hold a feast at my tomb and stay there until all the food and drink is consumed … [Around the tomb are to be gardens] tended by no fewer than three gardeners and their apprentices. No one shall be buried nearby ever. These rules are to be enforced for all time." No doubt many heirs resented having to expend such effort and money on funerary monuments, and to gain a small measure of revenge they would place their own names on the monument as well. Perhaps understandably, in quite a few instances, the name of the builder is larger and more prominent than that of the deceased.

Families often gathered at tombs in later years to hold memorial feasts for the deceased. To observe the festival of Parentalia, Romans decorated their family graves with flowers, perhaps the origin of this custom today. Whereas today we leave flowers and plants at graves as tokens of remembrance and affection, the Romans left offerings of food and wine, and gathered to eat meals at the graves and in the tombs of the deceased on their birthdays and during festivals honoring the dead. Both the Greeks and the Romans planted walled funerary gardens sacred to the dead, which were replete with fruit trees, flowers, climbing vines, and pools of water, as a tranquil retreat where visitors could commune with the dead and as a reflection of the Elysian Fields, that perfect landscape where heroes aspired to go after death. The manicured green, tree-shaded expanses of cemeteries today, decorated with mourners' gifts of flowers and plants, reflect a similar impulse.

Figure 2.7 *Tombstone of Lucius Vibius, his wife, Vecilia Hila, and their son, Lucius Vibius Felicio Felix. Note how her posture emphasizes her wedding ring.*

Finally, there were the inscriptions chiseled on the tombs. Today, it has become customary that tombstones bear very simple epitaphs that usually list only the deceased person's name, dates of birth and death, and perhaps a brief formulaic phrase such as "Rest in Peace." This is a bit disappointing, since a tombstone represents both one's final chance to make a statement to the people of the present and the possibility of speaking to the people of the future. Fortunately, ancient tombstones were far more descriptive. Sometimes the text was chosen by a person before he or she died, while at other times, it was selected by the person who put up the monument; but in either case, these often lengthy epitaphs typically record details of the deceased person's life, his or her achievements and/or personality, and even bits of his or her personal philosophy or a message for posterity.

Some inscriptions succinctly summarize the entire life story of the deceased, which at times can be quite dramatic: "Gaius Julius Mygdonius, born a free man in Parthia, was captured in his youth and sold as a slave in Roman territory. Once I became a freedman and a Roman citizen, thanks to kind Fate, I saved up a nest egg for when I reached 50. Ever since my youth I have been traveling toward old age, so now, O gravestone, receive me willingly. In your care I will be released from my worries" (*CIL* 11.137). In a few brief sentences, this man's colorful life, during which he passed from freedom to slavery to freedom and ultimately to prosperity, is memorialized.

An aspect of life that these tombstones bring to light is the strong emotions that tied together spouses, family members, and friends. One grave marker records a husband's grief for his young wife: "To the eternal memory of Blandina Martiola, a most blameless girl, who lived eighteen years, nine months, five days. Pompeius Catussa, a Sequanian citizen and a plasterer, dedicates this monument to his wife, who was incomparable and very kind to him. She lived with him five years, six months, eighteen days without any shadow of a fault. You who read this, go bathe in the baths of Apollo as I used to do with my wife. I wish I still could" (*CIL* 1.1983).

The affection that some parents felt for their children is also reflected in these inscriptions: "Spirits who live in the underworld, lead innocent Magnilla through the groves and the Elysian Fields directly to your places of rest. She was snatched away in her eighth year by cruel fate while she was still enjoying the tender time of childhood. She was beautiful and sensitive, clever, elegant, sweet, and charming beyond her years. This poor child who was deprived of her life so quickly must be mourned with perpetual lament and tears" (*CIL* 6.21846).

Some Romans seemed more concerned with ensuring that their bodies would lie undisturbed after death than with recording their accomplishments while alive. An inscription of this type states: "Gaius Tullius Hesper had this tomb built for himself, as a place where his bones might be laid. If anyone damages them or removes them from here, may he live in great physical pain for a long time, and when he dies, may the gods of the underworld deny entrance to his spirit" (*CIL* 6.36467).

Some tombstones offer comments that perhaps preserve something of their authors' temperaments. One terse inscription observes: "I was not. I was. I am not. I care not" (*CIL* 5.2893). Finally, a man who clearly enjoyed life left a tombstone that included the statement: "Baths, wine, and sex ruin our bodies. But what makes life worth living except baths, wine, and sex?" (*CIL* 6.15258).

Perhaps one of the greatest values of these tombstones is the manner in which they record the actual feelings of individuals, and demonstrate the universality across time, cultures, and geography of basic emotions such as love, hate, jealousy, and pride. They also preserve one of the most complicated yet subtle characteristics of human beings—our enjoyment of humor. Many of the messages were plainly drafted to amuse and entertain the reader, and the fact that some of them can still do so after 2,000 years is one of the best testimonials to the humanity shared by the people of the ancient and the modern worlds.

Counting out time: The calendar

This chapter has been about tracing the arc of one's life through the dimension of time, from birth to the grave. The divisions used have been descriptive ones that identify clearly defined stages of life such as childhood or old age. These stages are given meaning with reference to a specific person's life, but as a concluding segment to this chapter, we will extend this idea a bit further to consider how societies divide and measure out the fundamental dimension of time itself.

Almost all societies tend to measure time in several basic units, all of which are based on the movement of the earth in relation to the sun and the physical effects that this produces. Thus the most basic unit of time, which is caused by one complete revolution of the earth, has as its physical manifestation a single iteration of one night and one day. A second natural unit is the time it takes the moon to pass through a full lunar cycle, beginning with a full moon, which wanes, waxes, and again becomes full. The third great natural cycle is the year, defined in physical terms by the rotation of the seasons. Nearly all societies recognize some version of these three basic units of time, and use them to create a calendar. Such calendars function as a way to bring order to time and to organize our lives. They help us keep track of where we are in the progression of the seasons and allow us to anticipate important days and make schedules so that existence seems less chaotic and arbitrary. Calendars also help bring a sense of social cohesion, since they help people follow the same time scheme, celebrate the same festivals, and coordinate their plans. Let us look at how the Greeks and Romans organized time, and investigate how their calendar developed into the one that we now use. Finally, to conclude this chapter, we will examine some of the major holidays that function as significant points in our year's progress, and we will see how these celebrations also often had their origins in antiquity.

Nowadays, public noticeboards and calendars in prominent meeting places inform people of communal happenings. In ancient Rome, they inscribed calendars called *Fasti* in public places and on the sides of public buildings listing all the days of the year, pointing out which were festivals, and marking the days with letters as symbols to indicate their nature and any restrictions on one's activities. Thus, everyone could consult the big public calendar and see where they all were in the year's progress.

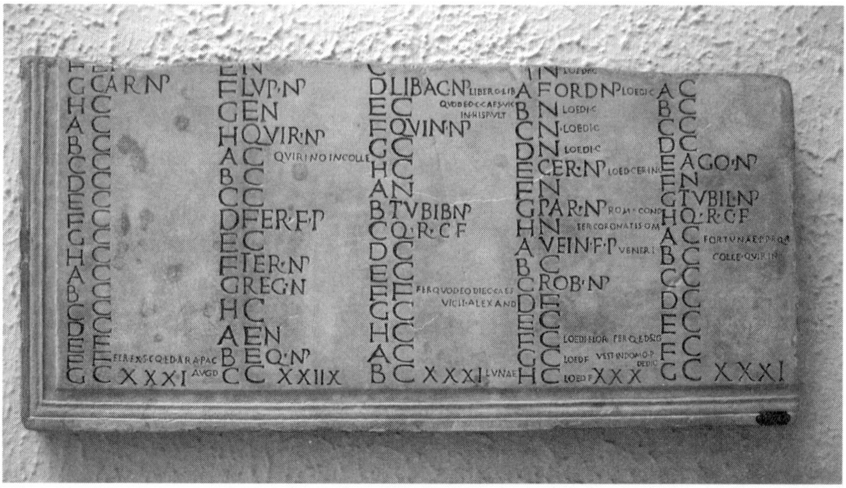

Figure 2.8 *A reconstruction of a Roman calendar. The various notations indicate market days, holidays, and days when it is forbidden to conduct business.*

Timekeeping ordered the cycle of the day as well as the cycle of the year. Jibes are sometimes made about Mediterranean concepts of time, but a certain flexibility in figuring time has of necessity long been part of the mental landscape. Like us, the Romans had a 24-hour day, but, unlike us, instead of dividing the day into 24 equal hours, they split it into 12 hours of night and 12 hours of day. Without a widely available accurate device for measuring the hours, such as today's ubiquitous wristwatch, this was a logical way to arrange things, although it meant that the lengths of day hours and night hours were never the same except at the equinoxes, and day hours were much longer in summer than they were in winter. It also meant that when people arranged appointments and meeting times, these could only be approximate, for "the first hour" (the hour after sunrise) or "the twelfth hour" (noon), for example. Noon, *meridies*, divided the morning hours, called *ante meridiem* ("before midday"), from the afternoon ones, called *post meridiem* ("after midday")—a distinction we still make by adding A.M. and P.M. to our hours.

Why is our calendar year 365 days long and divided into 12 months? We have Julius Caesar, who reformed the Roman calendar, to thank. But why did the most powerful man in Rome expend effort on fiddling with the calendar? The Romans initially divided their year into 10 months, but very early on they switched from a 10-month to a 12-month calendar. The effects of the original 10-month system are preserved in the anomalous names of some of our months: their 10 month-year started in March (reflecting an agricultural society), so they called their seventh month September (from Latin *septem*, seven), their eighth month October (from Latin *octo*, eight), their ninth month November (from Latin *novem*, nine), and their tenth month December (from Latin *decem*, ten). Therefore, we are inaccurately referring to our ninth month as "month seven," our tenth month as "month eight," our eleventh month as "month nine," and our twelfth month as "month ten." By at least 153 B.C., the beginning of the civil year had been shifted from March 1 to January 1, as in our current reckoning.

However, an important difference was that the Roman year originally consisted of 355 days. Obviously, over time, this led to the calendar months becoming misaligned with the seasons, which reflect the earth's movement around the sun. Every now and then, the priests would add what was called an intercalary month (a nameless month inserted between two existing months) to fix the discrepancy, but they occasionally neglected to do this, with confusing effects. When Julius Caesar finally defeated his rivals to become the sole ruler of Rome, the calendar was out of whack by six months, so one of Caesar's first actions was to add six intercalary months in a row, resulting in a year that was actually 1½ years long. Starting in January 1, 45 B.C., the Julian Calendar took effect; 46 B.C. was known as *ultimus annus confusionis*, "the last year of confusion." In order to prevent such "confusion" occurring again, Caesar did away with intercalary months and instead increased the number of days in a year to 365. This kept the calendar pretty much in sync with the seasons, but because the solar year is 365¼ days long, Caesar declared that an extra day would be added to February every 4 years (what we now call a leap year). The Julian Calendar, devised by and named after Julius Caesar, remained in use over the centuries and (with a few minuscule adjustments made by Pope Gregory the Great in 1582) is basically the same one that we still use today.

Why is it called a calendar in the first place? The word "calendar" in the sense of a system for dividing the year first occurred around 1200, and, as a table drawn up to show these divisions, in the mid-fourteenth century. "Calendar" can be traced back through the Old French "calendier," a list or register, to the Latin word *calendarium*, an account book, which derives from the Latin word *Kalends*, the first day of the month—the day on which accounts fell due. Thus, whenever we look at a calendar, it should immediately remind us of all our bills that are due on the first of the month.

We've already considered the origins of the months September through December. How about the others? These largely stem from the names of gods—or humans later declared to be divine—and religious observances. January (Latin *Ianuarius*), the first month of the year, is named after Janus (or Ianus), the Roman god of doorways, gates, beginnings, and transitions. He was typically depicted with two faces gazing in opposite directions, just as a door (Latin *ianua*) swings two ways. Logically, the month that begins the year is thus named after the god of beginnings, and, like a threshold, January 1 is a time of transition from one year to the next.

February (Latin *Februarius*) is named after *februa*, "expiatory offerings" or "a means of purification." The early Romans saw February (the last month of the year in the old calendar) as a turning point in the year, when winter was about to change into spring (a time of new growth and new beginnings), so this was a good time to propitiate the gods of fertility and the spirits of dead ancestors, purify and clean everything, and start with a blank slate, so to speak. Ovid said that the early Romans also called "instruments of purification" *februa*, and cites the practice of sweeping out a house with a broom; this was usually done after a death, to purify the house and to "sweep out" the ghost of the deceased so it would not return, but the association with February is reminiscent of our practice of Spring cleaning to eliminate the grunge accumulated over the winter.

March (Latin *Martius*) was named after Mars, the god of war; March 1, the original start of the New Year, was the day of a major festival of the god. Some Roman authors thought that *Aprilis* (our month April) was derived from Aphrodite, the Greek goddess of love and sexuality, although most thought that it was connected with *aperire*, "to open," because it was the month when buds and flowers began to open—and, whether or not it was named for her, April was under Venus' protection. So perhaps our association of spring with romance has ancient roots. May (Latin *Maia*) was probably named after Maia, a Roman goddess of growth and increase. June (Latin *Iunius*) may have been named after Juno, queen of the gods, or may derive from *iuvenis* (used to refer to a young person of either sex). July (Latin *Iulius*) was originally called *Quintilis*, "the fifth month" (of the old calendar) before its name was changed to honor Julius Caesar, and August (Latin *Augustus*) was *Sextilis*, "the sixth month," before it was renamed *Augustus* after the first Roman emperor. Most of the Roman months were either 29 or 30 days long, except for February, which was 28 days. Perhaps that is why February is our only 28-day month.

In the ancient world, different cultures employed weeks of varying lengths. The seven-day week was prevalent in the East, especially among Hellenistic astrologers, who assigned to the days of the week, the names of planets, which were believed to be governed by particular Greek gods. The Romans originally observed an eight-day week, but the seven-day week first appeared at Rome under the reign of Augustus. When the Romans adopted the seven-day week, they changed the names of the days so that Roman gods replaced the Greek ones: *dies solis* (our Sunday), literally "the day of the Sun"; *dies lunae* (our Monday), "the day of the moon"; *dies Martis* (our Tuesday), "the day of Mars"; *dies Mercurii* (our Wednesday), "the day of Mercury"; *dies Jovis* (our Thursday), "the day of Jupiter," who was also known as Jove; *dies Veneris* (our Friday), "the day of Venus"; and *dies Saturni* (our Saturday), "the day of Saturn."

These Latin days are still echoed in many of the Romance languages—to take French as an example, Monday is *lundi* ("Moon-day"), Tuesday is *mardi* (Mars' day), Wednesday is *mercredi* (Mercury's day), Thursday is *jeudi* (Jove's day), and Friday is *vendredi* (Venus' day)—but the correspondences don't extend to the weekend, where Saturday generally becomes "Sabbath-day" (*sabato* in Italian, *sabado* in Spanish) and Sunday becomes "the Lord's day" (*domingo* in Spanish, *domenica* in Italian, from the ecclesiastical Latin *dies Dominica*). In English, we can clearly see "Saturn's day" in Saturday, "Sun's day" in Sunday, and "Moon's day" in Monday, but what about the others? What happened is that the Roman gods were run through a Germanic filter, so that Mars was turned into the Germanic god of combat, Tiw (Norse Tyr), giving us Tiw's day (Tuesday); Mercury was changed into Wodan (Norse Odin), giving us Wodan's day (Wednesday); Jove, the wielder of the thunderbolt, turned into the Germanic/Nordic god of thunder now commonly known as Thor, giving us Thor's day (Thursday); and Venus' day became "Frigg's day," named after the queen of the Germanic gods, although because there were a lot of similarities between her and Freyja, the Germanic love goddess, some scholars think that both goddesses had a common origin, so perhaps Friday still belongs to the goddess of love.

Interestingly, English also keeps the pagan names for Saturday and Sunday instead of Christianizing them into the Sabbath and the Lord's day the way that the Romance languages do. Therefore, our English days of the week remain especially pagan. There were no weekends in the pagan world; the idea of the Sabbath originated with the Jews, and obviously the pagans considered every day to be devoted to a god rather than thinking of one day as *the* day to worship the *only* god. The eight-day week and the seven-day week coexisted in the Roman empire until Constantine, the first Roman emperor, officially adopted the seven-day week in A.D. 321.

Fun for all: Holidays and festivals

Perhaps partly because there were no weekends to function as days of rest in the pre-Christian world, festivals were even more important as an opportunity to take time off and have some fun. Christianity absorbed and transformed some of the more popular pagan holidays into Christian ones, since it would have been hard to eliminate them; it also sometimes turned days devoted to the celebration of pagan gods into saints' feast days. For instance, the Roman festival of Caristia or Cara Cognatio ("Dear Relation"), aimed at resolving a family's quarrels and strengthening its ties, was changed into the Feast Day of St. Peter on February 22. In fact, the concept of the "moveable feast," the term for Christian religious days which are set according to the occurrence of Easter, originated in ancient Rome, where, each year, the priests or magistrates set the date for when certain festivals (a category known as *feriae conceptivae*) should be held. The ancient world was full of festivals, so much so that the Emperor Marcus Aurelius felt compelled to place an upper limit of 135 on the number of festival days in a year. Some ancient festivals influenced the holidays we still celebrate. Let's consider a few of the more important ones.

One of the most important Christian holidays, Christmas, occurs every year on December 25. However, the Bible nowhere says exactly what time of year Jesus was born. What led to the adoption of December 25 for this important birthday?

Sol Invictus ("the Unconquered Sun") was a god of Syrian origin whose cult was enthusiastically promoted at Rome by the nutty emperor Elagabalus (who came from Syria). In fact, it has been suggested that he sought to suppress all other religions and make Sol Invictus the supreme god. After Elagabalus' death, the cult waned in influence somewhat, but the emperor Aurelian revived interest in it by building a temple to Sol Invictus at Rome and founding a priesthood dedicated to him in A.D. 273, and he established the sun god as one of the major deities in the Empire. As a young man, the emperor Constantine appears to have worshiped Sol Invictus with particular fervor, often minting coins bearing Sol's image and the inscription *Soli Invicto Comiti*, "Sol Invictus, Companion of the Emperor"; some gold coins and medallions portray Sol Invictus and Constantine together, with the inscription *Invictus Constantinus*. This sense of a special relationship with the sun god seems to have continued to some extent even after his conversion to Christianity in A.D. 312, for he continued to mint coins stamped with Sol Invictus' image until at least A.D. 324; the Arch of Constantine, erected in A.D. 315, depicted three statues of Sol Invictus being carried, and was placed in such a way that, when one approached the arch, it would perfectly frame a colossal statue of Sol Invictus that stood next to the Colosseum; and, when Constantine dedicated the city of Constantinople in A.D. 330, he wore a diadem crowned with sun-rays.

In A.D. 321, Constantine decreed the *dies Solis*, the day of the sun, to be a day of rest for both pagans and Christians alike, when work should cease and government offices should close. During his conversion experience, Constantine looked up at the sun and saw the chi-rho symbol there, so perhaps he even associated Sol Invictus with Christ. Indeed, in the Bible, Christ is compared to the Sun and described using solar imagery. It has long been held that the cult of Sol Invictus had its major yearly festival on December 25, the day of the midwinter solstice (as established by the Julian Calendar), although the first definitive evidence for this appears in the *Chronography of 354 AD* in a section known as the Philocalian Calendar, which places the festival of *Natalis Invicti* (the Sun's Birthday) on December 25, and also first mentions Christ's birthday being December 25. It has generally been accepted by scholars that Christianity adopted December 25 as Christ's birthday as part of a campaign to diminish the hold of this pagan cult, which had been its direct rival in Constantine's affections and was still followed by enough people to cause Augustine to preach against it. While there is currently some debate about the exact reason for the Church's choice of December 25, there certainly is evidence for a possible connection with pagan beliefs.

Regardless of whether or not Sol Invictus and Christ shared the same birthday, the customs of Christmas have been influenced by an older and even more central Roman festival: the Saturnalia, celebrated December 17–23, near the time of the winter solstice, in honor of the god Saturn, described in Latin literature as having reigned over a prosperous Golden Age of humankind. Everyone went on vacation; shops, schools, and law-courts shut down. There was a big feast, and public gambling (technically against the law) was permitted. In addition to being a religious festival, it was also a time of merry-making for everyone, when the usual rules were relaxed and even overturned. For instance, slaves would be served meals by their masters, and could playfully order them around without being punished. People wore casual clothes and a pointy felt cap called a *pilleus* (also known as a Liberty Cap or Freedman's Cap because it was worn by slaves at the ceremony during which they were freed), perhaps reflecting their freedom from rules and restrictions. Families would choose a "Saturnalian king" to preside over the revelries.

These practices were echoed in medieval England's Twelfth Night festivities, held between Christmas and January 5, the eve of Epiphany (the 12 days of Christmas), a time when the social hierarchy was turned upside down, with peasants and nobles switching roles. At the start of the festival, a cake with a bean hidden in it was eaten, and whoever found the bean became the "Bean King" or the "Lord of Misrule." This custom, in turn, is still reflected in the King Cake with a little trinket, often a baby, baked into it that is still served in many European countries at Christmas-time (although in Louisiana the tradition has shifted to Mardi Gras). The Romans exchanged gifts during the Saturnalia, especially wax candles called *cerei* and pottery dolls for children; perhaps that is partly why we still light candles at Christmas, why lit candles used to be placed on Christmas trees, and why we exchange gifts.

The Lupercalia (February 15) was one of the longest enduring Roman festivals, from Rome's earliest times until its suppression by Pope Gelasius I, who waged a campaign against it for several years, wrote a diatribe against it, and, in A.D. 496, established the Feast of Purification of the Virgin Mary on February 15 and the Feast of St. Valentine on February 14 in an attempt to replace it. There were actually several saints named Valentine, one of whom was a Roman priest imprisoned for aiding persecuted Christians. There was also a long-lived notion that Feb. 14 was the day when birds paired off (as, literally, "love-birds"), mentioned by both Chaucer and Shakespeare, though it is unclear when this superstition started.

Why was Pope Gelasius so disturbed by this particular pagan holiday? The ritual went like this: priests called *Luperci* ("wolfmen") met at the sacred cave (the Lupercal) where the she-wolf had nursed Romulus and Remus (the founders of Rome), sacrificed goats and a dog, and made an offering of sacred cakes baked by the Vestal Virgins. The *Luperci* smeared blood from the sacrificial knife onto the foreheads of aristocratic youths, cut up the goatskins into strips, and then the young men ran naked through the streets of Rome, hitting people (especially women) with the goat strips. It was believed that this induced fertility, so women who wanted to become pregnant no doubt tried to get whipped. The origins of the festival were so old that it was no longer clear what exactly was being symbolized or who exactly was being worshiped, but by the Late Republic it had become a huge spectacle that drew massive crowds.

The sexual overtones of the festival, with its streaking men, whipping of women, and connection to fertility, did not mesh well with Christianity, so it was sanitized into a celebration of Christian love and the purification of the Virgin—purity and virginity both being the complete opposite of what the pagan festival represented (although it is thought that the Lupercalia was actually a ritual of purification as well as one of fertility). But popular culture transformed St. Valentine's Day (which was actually dropped from the official Church Calendar of saints' feasts in 1969), dropping the "Saint" and switching the emphasis from Christian to romantic love.

On January 1, the Romans celebrated New Year's Day. "Why on the first day of the year do we wish one another cheerfully a happy and prosperous New Year?", Pliny the Elder asked (*Natural History* 28.5.22), revealing that the Romans did the same sort of well-wishing that we still do today. The day began with the equivalent of our New Year's Day parade. Groups of senators, friends, and clients met at the homes of the two Consuls, and joined them as they marched through the streets to meet one another. The two groups then formed an even larger procession and continued up the Capitoline hill, with crowds of people gathering to watch. In front of the Temple of Jupiter Optimus Maximus, the Consuls sacrificed two bulls to pay for vows for Rome's safety made by the Consuls the previous year, and then made new vows (*vota publica*) to protect the state. One is reminded of our practice of starting afresh by making New Year's resolutions. January 1 was also the festival of Aesculapius (the god of health), held at his Temple on Tiber Island, which was perhaps linked to the idea of seeking good health for the year to come.

March 17, designated St. Patrick's Day in the Church Calendar of saints, is traditionally the day of Patrick's death. On this day, the restrictions of Lent placed on eating meat and drinking alcohol were lifted, so in addition to being a holy day, it was also an opportunity to celebrate. Nowadays, especially in the United States, it has become more of a secular holiday observed by drinking lots of beer. In an interesting coincidence, March 17 in ancient Rome was the Liberalia, the feast dedicated to Liber Pater ("Free Father"), an ancient god of fertility, wine, and freedom who became identified with Dionysus/Bacchus. His festival was a time for letting loose, with lots of drinking and a freer attitude towards sex. It is odd to think that we now drink copious amounts of alcohol on the same day that the Romans did, as part of a purportedly religious feast day. Incidentally, Patrick started life as a pagan, was enslaved and then freed, converted to Christianity, and is known for the legend of having chased all the snakes out of Ireland. Since no snakes are indigenous to that island, this has often been interpreted as an allegory for driving out paganism; given the association of paganism with sacred snakes, this is certainly a potential reading.

April 1, known to us as All Fool's Day or April Fool's Day and a time for tricking people, was for the Romans the Veneralia, a festival of Venus, the goddess of love and sex. A note on the Praenestine calendar says that, at the Veneralia, "Women in crowds supplicate Fortuna Virilis, and women of humbler rank do this even in the baths, because in them men exposed that part of the body by which the favor of women is sought." Fortuna was likely a goddess of fertility as well as of luck or fortune. Women of higher rank were said to worship Venus. Ovid mentioned that women offered incense to Fortuna Virilis when entering the baths so that, if the goddess saw any blemishes on them, she would conceal these from the men. Also worshipped on April 1 was Venus Verticordia, the "Changer of Hearts," an aspect of the goddess. While today, April 1 is about fooling people in general, the Roman holiday seems to have been about fooling men in particular into falling in love with or having sex with women, whose flaws were hidden by goddesses.

Like us, the Romans had a Mother's Day. On March 1, husbands prayed for their wives' health and gave them gifts. The Romans also celebrated an independence day called *Regifugium* ("the flight of the king") on February 24, in commemoration of having driven the last Etruscan king, Tarquin the Proud, out of Rome and establishing the Roman Republic. Given the Founding Fathers' familiarity with and emulation of Roman history, it would not be surprising if they were aware of this earlier Independence Day that recognized the replacement of a tyrannical monarch with a new Republican form of government. Although not made an official holiday for some time, the anniversary of July 4 was already being celebrated the year following the signing of the Declaration of Independence. And, as is discussed in the section on superstitions, the Romans had days when, like Halloween or the Day of the Dead, it was thought that the entrance to the Underworld opened, allowing ghosts to emerge and haunt our world.

"Good fences make good neighbors," a seventeenth-century proverb famously quoted in Robert Frost's poem "Mending Wall," is an apt description for the Terminalia, a festival honoring Terminus, the god of boundaries and boundary-stones, on February 23. Neighbors living on adjacent plots would walk towards one another, meeting at the boundary-stone, where they would place offerings of a wreath or garland and a cake. They would sacrifice a piglet or a lamb and, afterwards, feast on it together, so that the religious ritual helped to promote and cement a friendly relationship through a shared meal. An early Roman law said that anyone who removed boundary stones would be cursed. This ritual offered a way to promote "neighborliness," peaceful coexistence, and the sorts of bonds that allow a society to run smoothly and follow the rule of law.

To a surprising extent, the rhythms of our lives today reflect patterns established in antiquity, in how we divide and measure the progress both of our lives and of the year. Greek astrologers shaped the days of our week, while the Romans gave us our calendar and influenced some of the holidays we celebrate. The classical world has also left its imprint on the ceremonies that we use to mark important transitions, such as marriage and death, and on how we envision the various stages of human life. We can observe similarities in how we conduct some of our most significant relationships, and how certain behaviors and emotional bonds—whether it is children playing, parents interacting with their offspring, or relations between the sexes—have persisted over the centuries. Our perceptions of time and of how we should chart our journey through it owe much to the ancients.

3

Living the good life: Entertainments and leisure activities

Beyond acquiring the basic necessities for survival and creating kinship bonds, human beings have always had an enormous capacity for play. We love to indulge in games and sports, and to witness spectacles and entertainments. Such amusements are not just idle pastimes, but rather often embody or reflect our cultural attitudes about ourselves, our bodies, and our values. Many of the attitudes prevalent today, as well as many of the games that we play, can be directly traced back to the ancient world.

Looking good: Athleticism and the perfect body

Everywhere we go or look today, we are bombarded with images of young, muscular, idealized bodies. Long, slender legs strut across billboards, "washboard abs" leap at us from the pages of magazines, an endless parade of impossibly gorgeous models sells us products in commercials, the rippling muscles of athletes are on display in close up and slow motion at sporting events, and the television programs we watch are improbably populated almost exclusively by young and beautiful people with "hard bodies." Goaded by the vain hope of emulating these images of the idealized, thin, muscular body, millions of ordinary people flock to their local gym and spend countless grim hours pounding away on a treadmill, feverishly lifting weights, obsessively counting calories, experimenting with various "miracle diets," and even filling their bodies with possibly dangerous supplements and drugs. This fascination with the perfect body and the methods by which it might be achieved is nothing new, however. Many of the inhabitants of the ancient world were every bit as obsessed with the body and looking good as the most ardent modern workout fanatic or body-builder, and images of the ideal body were equally pervasive.

An ancient Greek walking through the center of his city in the fourth century B.C. would have been confronted everywhere he looked with gleaming bronze and marble statues, almost every one of which depicted a naked, trim, muscular male body. Whether the face was that of a god, a mythological hero, a famous athlete, or an honored citizen, all these statues would have shared a similar body, and that body was always an expression of perfection. The Greeks regarded the naked, young, athletic male body as the highest aesthetic ideal, and much of Greek sculpture can be interpreted as a quest to identify the exact proportions of the perfect male body. Many scholars believe that a statue known as the Doryphoros, "the Spear-Bearer," represents the attainment of these idealized proportions, and certainly museums today are filled with statue after statue that closely emulate this one.

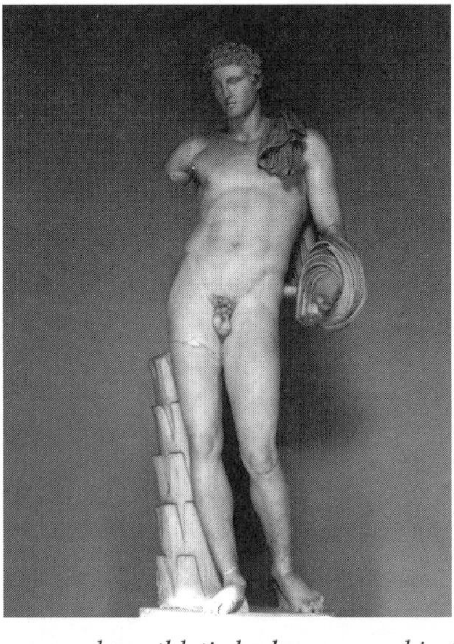

Figure 3.1 *The young, muscular, athletic body was an object of particular veneration by the ancient Greeks, who regarded it as the height of aesthetic beauty.*

In addition to this forest of statues, every surface of the monumental public buildings through which our notional ancient Greek was striding would have been covered with carved reliefs and paintings that similarly depicted perfect, naked male bodies. On the pediments and rooftops looming overhead, yet more statues and carvings would have flexed their muscles in poses carefully crafted to show them off to maximum effect. If our Greek stopped for a moment at a stall to refresh himself with some wine, the cup he drank from and the pitcher from which it was poured might well be painted with yet more images of flawless bodies. Once he reached home, more perfect bodies would likely have stared back at him from his own plates, bowls, and containers, and even the humble olive oil lamps that flickeringly illuminated his dwelling might have borne the stamped image of an athlete.

Given the pervasiveness of the image of the athletic male body in ancient Greek society, it is no surprise that Greek men expended a great deal of effort attempting to mold their own bodies toward this ideal. As today, the primary way to accomplish this was through regular and vigorous exercise, and the place to do this was at the local gymnasium. In classical times, the Greek gymnasium, which has given us our modern word for a place where one exercises, comprised an open space surrounded by covered tracks for running and colonnades forming a large rectangle. A major difference from today is, of course, that the ancient Greeks exercised naked; "gymnasium" literally means "the naked place." Like today, the first room that ancient Greeks seeking a workout entered was the locker room, but in ancient Greece this room was called the "undressing room" rather than the dressing room. The practice of exercise was limited to men; women did not exercise in public, except in the special case of Sparta, where it was thought that physically fit mothers would give birth to stronger warriors. Outside Sparta, this was seen as odd, as evidenced by one ancient writer who called Spartan girls "unchaste, indecorous thigh-flashers."

At the gymnasium, popular activities included running, wrestling, ball games, boxing, and weight-lifting. The weights might consist of lead weights, or simply large rocks with handholds carved into them. Today, the blare from boom boxes or mp3 players is a common part of the gym experience, but even working out to music at the gym may have had some ancient precedents. The

Figure 3.2 *Sculptural relief of athletes. They are engaged in playing some sort of ball game using sticks, perhaps akin to modern field hockey, in front of a crowd of onlookers.*

long jump was originally performed while swinging 4 to 8-pound lead weights in one's hands. Aristotle claimed that these weights helped one to jump further. Since the Greeks considered it the most difficult athletic event, a flute player offered accompaniment, presumably as assistance in coordinating the movement of arms and legs. Athletes were encouraged to carry these weights while swinging their arms, and it was seen as a good exercise in general, not just for those practicing for the long jump.

Before exercise, athletes anointed their bodies with olive oil; indeed, the one crucial item required by competitors at athletic festivals was good quality olive oil. Wrestling was the most popular sport among ancient Greek men. They would typically join a *palaestra*, a wrestling school, and hang out there with friends, engaging in pick-up wrestling bouts. Before wrestling, they powdered themselves with dust to allow for a better grip. Two types of ring were available, a dry one of sand and a wet one of mud, to prepare for matches after a rainstorm. A proverb, "Out of the sand and into the mud," equivalent to our "Out of the frying pan and into the fire," developed from this two-ring training approach. Evidence that wrestlers kept their hair short to avoid its being pulled is suggested by lines from Euripides' play *The Bacchae*: "Your curls are long. You do not wrestle, I take it" (line 455).

Faster, higher, stronger: Sports and athletic competitions

Sporting events were ever-present in the ancient world. Every little town staged competitions of one kind or another, and there were great contests to which athletes would journey from all over to take part in. There was also a wide variety of popular sports, most of which still have their modern counterparts. The Greeks were especially fond of foot races, and running was an important activity at the gymnasium. In athletic competitions such as the Olympics, the most prestigious event was the 200-yard dash, an event known as the "stade," the source for our word "stadium." The running track was a 200-meter strip. Unlike modern oval-shaped racetracks, for ancient races that covered longer distances runners had to turn 180 degrees around posts positioned at each end of the track.

The ancient pentathlon, which consisted of the long jump, the discus, the javelin, a race (probably a stade), and wrestling, is first mentioned as occurring at the Olympic Games in 708 B.C. Unlike today, only running and wrestling were also contested as separate events; the long jump, discus, and javelin were just part of the pentathlon. The javelin throw differs from our current practice in that the Greeks used a thong looped over the first finger or first two fingers of the throwing hand when hurling it, which steadied its flight.

Boxing matches were not divided into rounds; they went on uninterrupted until one of the fighters either gave up by raising a hand or else was knocked out. Punching bags were used in training. Boxers wrapped their hands and fingers with leather thongs in order to protect them, not to spare their opponents; indeed, a heavy leather knuckle pad was eventually added which provided a hard edge to cut an opponent's face. Statues of disfigured fighters depicting their broken, flattened noses and cauliflower ears attest to the viciousness of fighting contests. Similarly, a nickname for boxers' hand wrappings, *myrmex* (ant), alludes to an ant's tendency to inflict many painful bites, and vase paintings show blood flowing down boxers' faces from cuts and smashed noses. Some later models evidently sported a sheepskin band that was used to wipe sweat off the brow and out of one's eyes.

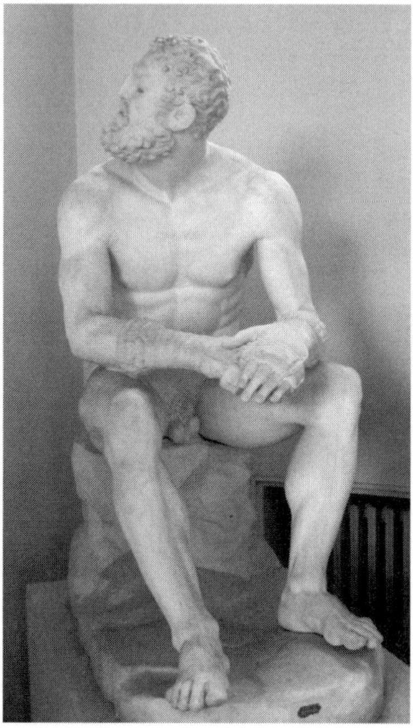

Figure 3.3 *Sculpture of a veteran boxer. Note the leather straps wrapped around his fists, which served as gloves, and his battered nose, reflecting the many bouts that he has fought in.*

Today, combat sports such as "ultimate fighting" and Mixed Martial Arts are gaining in popularity, but these, too, are nothing new. The Greeks had a sport known as the *pankration*, a word meaning "complete strength," which was a kind of combination of boxing and wrestling fought with minimal rules. Indeed, only two maneuvers were prohibited: biting and eye-gouging. Referees stood nearby holding rods to beat anyone who disobeyed. That this rule was none the less broken is suggested by vase paintings of eye-gouging and the satirist Lucian's quip that "Lions" was a good nickname for *pankratiasts* because of all the biting they did. Kicking was a common strategy, and low blows were expected; a satire on athletes awards top prize in the *pankration* to the donkey because of its fine kicking. The contest ended only when one of the fighters either surrendered or was physically incapacitated. There are mentions of *pankratiasts* dying during the event, which is not surprising considering Pindar's advice that "One must wipe out his rival by doing everything" (*Isthmian Odes* 4.48). Punching, boxing, wrestling, and choking were all permitted, and one famous *pankratiast* was known for breaking his opponents' fingers. It is said that another *pankratiast* actually died winning his bout, so that the victor's crown had to be placed on his dead body. Perhaps it is not surprising that our word "agony" is derived from the Greek word for athletic contest, *agon*.

Because there were no weight classes in the ancient world, the larger you were, the better your chances at boxing, wrestling, and the *pankration*, and the Greeks called these "the heavy events" due to the athletes' size being such an important factor. Just as today, this led to many athletes eating special diets to "bulk up." The wrestler Milo purportedly consumed twenty pounds of meat, a similar amount of bread, and nine quarts of wine every day, and once carried a bull around the stadium at Olympia as he ate it over the course of a day. In the constant quest to gain an edge over their opponents, modern athletes try many exotic training routines, but they have nothing on their ancient predecessors. The wrestler Amesinas was said to hone his skills by wrestling with a bull. He even took this bull with him when he went to compete at the Olympics, and since he won, the strategy seems to have paid off, perhaps thanks to his bovine training partner.

The Olympic Games, founded in 776 B.C., occurred every four years, as they do today, until they were banned by the Roman emperor Theodosius I in A.D. 393 due to their pagan associations. The athletic portion of the ancient Olympics lasted only two to three days, unlike the modern version. Additional days were devoted to religious rites and sacrifices, a crucial component of the Games, which honored the god Zeus, whose temple dominated the site of Olympia. During the four-year gaps between competitions, the stadium would lapse into an overgrown, neglected state, and the competing athletes were expected, by tradition, to pick up garbage and pull out weeds in order to make it ready for the Games.

Today, the Olympic truce is often cited as a call for wars to cease for the duration of the Games, but while the truce originated in ancient Greece, its meaning was different. Rather, it simply called for safe conduct for athletes and spectators traveling to and from the Olympics, and forbade fighting between attendees at the Games whose cities were at war. Before the competition began, the judges were required to take an oath that they would judge

Figure 3.4 *The stadium at Olympia. This was the setting for many of the original Olympic events, including the 200-meter race known as the stade, from which the word "stadium" is derived.*

fairly and accept no bribes, and the athletes also took an oath to "do nothing evil." As all athletes except for charioteers and jockeys were required to compete in the nude, there was no place for them to display endorsements, as is so common in sports today.

The current popularity of NASCAR and Formula One motor racing finds its parallel in ancient Rome, where chariot racing was the most watched entertainment—especially since, unlike relatively rare gladiator games, by the second century A.D. chariot races were held on dozens of days every year, and the vast Circus Maximus could accommodate far more spectators than the Colosseum. Our word "circus" derives from the identical Latin word, meaning a circle or racecourse; the Circus Maximus in Rome was a truly immense stadium that could hold up to 250,000 fans.

The Romans used an oval track for their racing as we do today, but with a crucial difference; whereas we engineer race-tracks to minimize the danger of crashing, the Romans seem to have built theirs to encourage collisions, which were seen as part of the entertainment. This was because, after being spaced apart in the starting gates, the charioteers all had to steer for a single point if they wished to make the most economical turns. Also, unlike the wide, relatively gentle curves of an automobile racetrack, charioteers had constantly to make sharp, and highly dangerous, 180-degree turns. Chariots tended to pile up and crash while attempting such maneuvers, a calamity that the race fans referred to as being "shipwrecked." Today, the beginning and ending of car races are often signaled by the waving of flags. This custom has antecedents in antiquity: at the Circus, the starting signal was when the presiding official dropped a cloth known as a *mappa*.

Figure 3.5 *Relief showing a chariot race in the Circus Maximus. Note the unfortunate charioteer at the bottom, who has fallen out of his vehicle and is now being trampled beneath the hooves of one of his competitor's horses.*

Superstars: Champion and celebrity athletes

Victors at the Olympic Games were not awarded money or intrinsically valuable prizes; a simple wreath of olive leaves was the mark of victory. While today we reward the top three athletes in each event with gold, silver, and bronze medals, the ancient Greeks were only interested in the very best, and accordingly only recognized the winner. Right after each event ended, a crowning ceremony took place, the predecessor of our current medal ceremony. Various

Greek authors describe Persian incredulity that the Greeks would compete at Olympia for honor rather than for material gain. However, rewards came to Olympic victors after the games, upon their return home. Just as a winning sports team in New York City will inevitably be treated to a massive ticker-tape parade, a triumphant ancient athlete could expect to be greeted in his home city with a huge victory parade attended by adoring fans. While today successful athletes will profit from commercial endorsements, notable ancient athletes were showered with gifts of money and valuable objects, and were frequently granted free meals for the rest of their life at state expense.

Today, ancient Greek athletes are often exalted as exemplars of amateurism in sports, in contrast with the corruption of modern professional athletics. However, this supposed "purity" is a distortion of the reality. The ancient Greeks lacked a concept of amateur athletics and had no word for such a thing; the modern Olympics popularized the notion, which was Victorian rather than ancient. Any Greek male could compete at the Games (although wealthy competitors had an advantage in that their many months of training and travel to the festival were at an athlete's own expense). Thus, someone who, to our mind, would be considered an amateur athlete could win at the ancient Olympics; the first recorded Olympic victor, Coroebus of Elis, was said to have been a cook, and other professions attributed to Olympic victors included ploughman, cowherd, and fish-hauler.

But over time it was natural that training became more formalized, and more money and patronage were devoted to promising athletes because cities wanted their citizens to rack up victors' crowns. Especially during the Hellenistic era, money was pumped into sports, and athletes could earn a lot by devoting themselves to their sport full-time; sports developed into entertainment for spectators. Especially in Hellenistic and Roman times, the training of boys from all social classes en masse at a public gymnasium meant that promising athletes might be picked from the lower classes and given a chance to compete; they could hope to be subsidized by the state if they were able to win a victory crown.

Just as professional athletes train year-round today, the top rank of ancient Greeks similarly devoted all their time to preparation and competition. Although the Olympic Games occurred only every four years, there were various other athletic games which took place in the interim. Because games of one sort or another continued in an ongoing cycle, athletes often trained and competed continuously, as today.

Three other famous "crown games," also subject to a truce, existed in addition to the ones at Olympia: those at the religious sanctuaries of Delphi, Nemea, and Isthmia. They were staggered so that one of the "big four" competitions occurred every year. This is similar to the way in which modern tennis and golf tournaments are scheduled so that the best athletes can compete in all of them. The fact that the four ancient festivals were known collectively as "the periodos" (circuit) suggests how ancient athletes "made the rounds" at competitions. The Pythian Games at Delphi, dedicated to the god Apollo, awarded crowns of laurel, Apollo's sacred tree; the Isthmian Games originally awarded crowns of pine; and the Nemean Games awarded crowns of wild celery. The latter custom is explained by the legend that the Nemean Games began as funeral games in honor of a baby who was killed by a snake after having been laid to rest by his nurse in a patch of wild celery. More minor games also followed the custom of awarding vegetal crowns: white poplar at Rhodes, myrtle at Thebes and Argos, and barley at Eleusis.

Some games did offer material prizes, such as shields, silver cups (still a popular trophy today), fine olive oil, painted amphorae, and money. Plutarch claims that the law-giver Solon set maximum sums that could be awarded to athletes by the state: 500 drachmae for an Olympic victor (a very large sum in the ancient world) and 100 for an Isthmian one, which was still probably equivalent to at least a year's earnings for a working man.

Just as today, the most successful athletes became international celebrities and were honored in a variety of ways. Statues of Olympic victors lined the path into the stadium at Olympia, and lists of past victors were recorded on the walls of the gymnasium there. Cities erected statues and monuments to their greatest athletes, and poems were written in their honor. The poet Pindar wrote 45 victory odes in honor of victors from 16 states. However, unlike the showboating athletes of today who sometimes celebrate with elaborate victory dances, Pindar's ideal athletic victor was reserved and showed humility when being crowned. Scenes in art routinely depict victorious athletes with their eyes downcast. On the flip side, losers suffered shame and disgrace, sneaking home by back streets and subjected to taunting. While some athletes became every bit as egotistical and vain as some modern sports superstars, and gained a reputation for arrogance and shameful antics off the field, at least while actually competing they were forced to behave. At some events, men carrying whips stood by, ready to beat competitors who misbehaved or grew too unruly. Anyone familiar with the on-field tantrums of some modern athletes might wish we still employed such figures.

Superstitions about winning are not unique to lucky-charm-carrying and routine-obsessed modern athletes. Ancient athletes often consulted oracles and astrologers, and even hired magicians and wizards to help them achieve victory. Plutarch mentions an athlete who thought that his success was dependent upon using a certain oil flask or strigil (scraper), and would fall to pieces if it were lost. Magic charms have been found which were intended to bring victory to particular athletes. At times, the pressure became too much to bear; one *pankratiast* is said to have run away the day before his Olympic contest.

The tendency of sons to follow their fathers into sports that is sometimes observable today (the auto racing dynasties of the Earnhardts, Pettys, and Andrettis come to mind) also occurred in the ancient world. Hipposthenes of Sparta won the Olympic wrestling competition six times, while his son won five times in the same event. The island of Rhodes was home to a particularly famous dynasty of athletes; over three generations, the family of the Diagorids produced six Olympic victors, with nine crowns among them, and many victories at the other Sacred Games as well. The Olgaethidae of Corinth won 60 victories at Isthmia and Nemea before the family members Thessalus and his son Xenophon won Olympic crowns; in fulfillment of a vow to Aphrodite, Xenophon gave 100 slave girls to serve at one of her temples in exchange for her help in winning.

Some athletes were afforded the status of "hero" when they died, which brought a semi-divine aura; worshiped in their own cults, they were considered to be endowed with magical powers, and their statues were sometimes credited with the ability to heal worshipers. Indeed, even when still alive, their superhuman feats could inspire intimations of divinity, as in the case of Theagenes of Thasos, said to have won over 1,300 victories in his 22-year career; it was rumored that a god had fathered him (his "human" father was a priest, thus bringing his mother within the god's reach). The famous wrestler Milo of Croton even dressed up as the demigod Herakles (Roman Hercules), wearing his Olympic crowns in addition to the usual lion-skin and club, in order to whip up his men to fight a battle.

Inevitably, there was some backlash against the posh treatment of award-winning athletes, as when the writer Xenophanes complains about the feting of Olympic victors: "Even if he should become a most glorious symbol for his fellow citizens and win *prohedria* [seats of honor] at the games and his meals at public expense, and some especially valuable gifts from the state ... he still would not be so valuable as I am ... the city-state is not a bit more law-abiding for having a good boxer or a pentathlete or a wrestler or a fast runner ... There is little joy for a state when an athlete wins at Olympia, for he does not fill the state's coffers." In Xenophanes' words, we can hear echoes of modern critics who castigate the excessive adulation of athletes and their unquestioned status as positive role models.

The adoring mob: Fans and spectators

While modern sports fans are often regarded as having an unhealthy obsession with their favorite team or athlete, they are no more dedicated than were the fans in the ancient world. Many of the customs of ancient fans would still be familiar to us. This was especially true of that most popular of spectator sports in ancient Rome, chariot-racing. Roman racing pitted chariots drawn from different teams, called factions, against one another. The factions were identified by the colors their charioteers wore. The earliest were the Reds and Whites, followed by the Greens and Blues; a later attempt to add Gold and Purple ultimately failed. Fans of a particular faction wore its color in order to show their support when cheering on its riders. Just like contemporary football and soccer fans, on race day aficionados of the chariot-racing factions would dress up in their team's colors, march down to the stadium, and sit together in the stands. They would frequently engage in complex verbal chants urging on the chariots of their faction and denigrating those of rival ones. Such mass chants and songs are a familiar feature of modern sporting events, again particularly of soccer and football.

An unfortunate aspect of modern fan behavior is violence among fans. Particularly in South America and Europe there have been a number of notorious riots at soccer matches. Such unruliness is not unique to the modern world, however, since rioting among spectators at ancient entertainments was common. At Pompeii in A.D. 59 a riot broke out between the local Pompeians and the partisans of a neighboring rival town, which resulted in a number of deaths and pitched battles in the stadium and surrounding streets. As punishment, Pompeii was forbidden from hosting gladiator games for 10 years.

Figure 3.6 *Wall painting showing a riot in the Amphitheater at Pompeii. This violent disturbance, which broke out between fans from Pompeii and partisans of a nearby town, resulted in gladiator games being banned from Pompeii for 10 years.*

Even worse was the riot that erupted between the fans of the Blues and the Greens in Constantinople in A.D. 532. This riot, known as the Nika Riot because *nika*, meaning "victory," was a common chant of the fans, lasted almost a week, burnt down much of the city, and was only quelled when the army was called in. By the time it was all over, the death toll was said to have reached 30,000.

Also just as today, ancient sports could produce intense emotions among fans. In his *History of Rome*, Ammianus Marcellinus describes the fanaticism of crowds at the Circus thus: "To the people, the Circus Maximus is temple, home, community center, and the fulfillment of all their hopes. All over the city you can see them arguing fiercely about the races … They declare that their country will be ruined if at the next meeting their own particular champion does not come first out of the starting-gate and keep his horses in line as he brings them round the post. Before dawn on a race day they all rush headlong for a place in the terraces at such a speed that they could almost beat the chariots themselves" (28.4.28). Dio Chrysostom's description of fans attending athletic contests in Alexandria strikes a similar note: "When they enter the stadium, it is as if they come under the influence of drugs … When you go to the stadium, who would describe the yelling and uproar, the frenzy, the sudden changes of expression and color on your faces, and the terrible blasphemies you utter?" (32.74).

Zealous fans sometimes showed their support through the use of magic. They would buy or fashion curse tablets calling upon gods and demons to bring injury and loss to a certain charioteer or his team and then bury or conceal these in the stables where the horses were kept. One such curse tablet reads: "Help me in the Circus on 8 November. Bind every limb, every sinew, the shoulders, the ankles and the elbows of Olympus, Olympianus, Scortius and Juvencus, the charioteers of the Red. Torment their minds, their intelligence and their senses so that they may not know what they are doing, and knock out their eyes so that they may not see where they are going—neither they nor the horses they are going to drive" (quoted in Harris, 1972, pp. 235–6).

Female groupies pursued ancient athletes as well. At the Olympics, Lais, a famous courtesan, saw the sprinter Eubatas and, smitten, aggressively tried to seduce him; he resisted, and his wife had a statue of him put up in honor of his faithfulness rather than his athletic accomplishments. It is a cliché nowadays to say that fans live and die with the on-field fortunes of their favorite team or athlete, but in the ancient world this was not just a metaphor. At the funeral of a renowned charioteer of the Reds, a grief-stricken fan was so distraught that he threw himself on the pyre and burnt to death with his idol.

A roll of the dice: Games and gambling

Another popular leisure activity among the people of antiquity was board games. The tomb of one avid gamer excavated in Perugia actually contained 816 glass game pieces and 16 bone ones. The Greeks played a game on a white- and black-squared board that was similar to checkers, while the Roman game *Duodecim Scripta* ("Twelve Lines"), played using three dice and black and white pieces on a game board bearing 24 squares, was somewhat akin to backgammon. The Roman board game *Latrunculi* ("Robbers") was kind of like chess, in that the goal was to capture your opponent's game pieces, and one side was white while the other was black. A game piece was called a *calculus* (which also meant a pebble used as a counter in making mathematical calculations) and they had different identities, such as *latro* (robber) or *miles* (soldier, echoed in our word "military"). One aim was to raid your foe's sheep-pens (*mandra*) while safeguarding your own. The *tabula lusoria*, or "gaming board," could be either basic or, if you were wealthy, very fancy and expensive; in one of the earliest existing novels, *The Satyricon*, Petronius has his filthy-rich character Trimalchio own a gaming board made of exotic terebinth wood with crystal playing pieces, and Martial describes a two-sided gaming board that could be used to play both *Duodecim Scripta* and *Latrunculi* (*Epigrams* 14.17). *Latrunculi* was considered an intellectual game of strategy, just as chess is today.

Playing games of luck and skill inevitably led to widespread gambling in the ancient world. In the *Iliad*, Homer's Greek heroes were already wagering on the chariot races at Patroklos' funeral games. Perhaps the simplest form of gambling was the Roman game *micatio*, somewhat reminiscent of "Rock, Paper, Scissors," in which the two players would simultaneously stick out varying numbers of fingers of their right hand while calling out the total number of raised fingers, until one of them picked the right number; the Romans had a saying that an honest man was someone you could play *micatio* with in the dark. However, the most popular games of chance were dice and knuckle-bones, which were enjoyed by both children and adults. Dice (Greek *kuboi*, echoed in our word "cube," and Latin *tesserae*) had the numbers one through six etched on their sides like the dice we still use today. Among the Greeks, every different combination of numbers thrown evidently had its own

Figure 3.7 *A game-board that was carved into the steps of a public building in the city of Philippi. This game was probably similar to modern backgammon, involving moving counters around the indicated positions.*

name; the best throw, consisting of three sixes (the Aphrodite throw, named after the goddess of love), became a symbol of good luck. As in so much else, the Romans emulated the Greeks' love of dicing. Rolls had different values; the worst, known as "dog" (*canis*) throws by both the Greeks and the Romans, were evidently all ones. Knuckle-bones (Greek *astragaloi* and Latin *tali*), which came from the lower legs of four-legged animals, were used in two ways. In a game of skill, often played by children and women, the bones were thrown upwards and caught on the back of the hand. As a game of chance, knuckle-bones functioned like four-sided dice. Each side was associated with a number: the plain side with one, the convex side with three, the concave side with four, and the twisted side with six. You threw the knuckle-bones, either with a cup or your hands, onto a gaming-table (*abacus*). The Romans' luckiest roll, the Venus throw, named after the Roman goddess of love, resulted in one of each different side landing face up.

Gambling was extremely popular in Rome among everyone, from the poor playing in the alleys or in taverns up to the emperor himself—despite the fact that various laws were aimed at controlling it. The first emperor, Augustus, enjoyed dicing, and once wrote in a letter that he had "played all day long and kept the gaming board warm," with whoever threw a "dog" adding money to the pot, while whoever threw a Venus would collect it all (Suetonius, *Augustus* 71). His grandson, the Emperor Claudius, loved playing dice so much that he wrote a book on the subject and had a special, stable board fitted to his carriage so that he could play without his game being disturbed even when travelling (Suetonius, *Claudius* 34). Even Julius Caesar's famous statement as he was crossing the Rubicon River, *ilea acta est*, "The die is cast," came from dice-throwing; Caesar thus described his big political gamble with a metaphor everyone would have been able to appreciate.

While Claudius had a portable gaming-board that he could carry with him, the average person either had to go seek one out or else make his own. *Tabulae lusoriae* could be found in taverns—then as now, one of the most popular venues for gambling—and etched into the stone and marble surfaces of public areas all over town. Indeed, game boards and gaming-tables have been discovered not only in the Roman Forum and the Colosseum, but even in the House of the Vestal Virgins. If the opportunity and desire for a game struck, all the Roman gamer needed was a way to draw or cut the board onto the pavement or steps where he was sitting. If, when touring ancient sites, you keep an eye peeled for such game-boards, you will appreciate how popular board games and games of chance were in the ancient world, as they still are nowadays.

Betting on winning gladiators and horses was popular too, although there was apparently no organized, formal structure for betting as there is today. The bets were seemingly for smaller amounts than for dicing, which was the more likely way to lose your toga. None the less, fans talked obsessively about favored gladiators and charioteers, the pedigrees of the horses, and their past performances. As the historian Tacitus put it, "The distinctive and characteristic vices of our city, which it seems are already acquired in the womb, are the mania for actors, gladiator games, and chariot racing … How few are those whose everyday conversations concern any other topic" (*A Dialogue on Oratory* 29). When the writer Lucian described the many conversations that could be overheard in the streets about racing, statues of the drivers, and the horses' names, he labeled this phenomenon *hippomania* (horse-craze) (*Nigrinus* 29). Roman children even placed bets—on cockfighting, which was evidently seen as appropriate entertainment for kids. The avid fans who devour the many sports-related TV and radio shows and publications today and cite detailed statistics to one another would no doubt have empathized with the intensity of their interest.

A soothing soak: Baths and bathing

The next time you go to a spa to be massaged, plucked, waxed, or otherwise pampered; the next time you find yourself patronizing the steam room and the juice bar or socializing at a gym; or the next time you walk on a bathroom floor equipped with radiant heat, be aware that you are following in the (heated) footsteps of the ancients and are sweating in their shadow. The fancy multipurpose gym and spa facilities that are increasingly popular and prevalent today reflect an ancient model: the Roman bath complex. Soaking in a tub full of steaming water has become a symbol for renewing both body and spirit, but in addition to being aware of these benefits, the Romans put their own spin on bathing by using it as an opportunity for creating and strengthening social ties. Rather than providing "personal time" alone, having a bath made you feel part of society and of a social network. At the baths, you could find all sorts of goods and services and ways to please both mind and body.

While the Romans are famous for their obsession with bathing and their massive public baths, the roots of this tradition are evident in ancient Greece, whose culture Rome so often borrowed from and imitated. Homeric heroes in the *Iliad* and *Odyssey* savored hot baths after battles and long trips, and, as guests, experienced baths as part of their hosts' hospitality, as when the Phaeacian queen orders that a bath be prepared for Odysseus: "Arete bade her handmaids to set a great cauldron on the fire with all speed. And they set on the blazing fire the cauldron for filling the bath, and poured in water, and took billets of wood and kindled them beneath it. Then the fire played about the belly of the cauldron, and the water grew warm ... his heart was glad when he saw the warm bath ... when the handmaids had bathed him and anointed him with oil, and had cast about him a fair cloak and a tunic, he came forth from the bath, and went to join the men at their wine" (*Odyssey* Bk. 8, lines 433-457).

The Greeks claim to have the earliest known bathtub in Europe: a built-in terracotta model from Mycenaean times, painted inside with spiral designs, at the so-called Palace of Nestor in Pylos. Its small size suggests that the bather would have sat upright in it and been sluiced with water. Perhaps the fact that, in the *Odyssey*, Telemachus enjoys a bath as a guest at Nestor's palace contributed to the choice of name for these particular ruins. Small terracotta tubs were later used by the wealthy; in early times, a hot bath was a luxury unaffordable by the poor.

Some traditionally-minded Greeks saw the desire for hot baths as a corrupting, decadent trend dangerous to morality, and therefore bathed "Laconian style," using only cold water ("Laconian," deriving from Laconia, the location of Sparta, associated these hardy bathers with the tough, no-nonsense Spartans). The early Greek gymnasium included a place for bathing in its plan; the *loutron*, or cold water washing room, provided basins and sometimes showers. From the sixth century B.C. onward, Greek vase paintings depict many scenes of people washing themselves: women showering under boar- and lion-headed spouts, athletes rinsing off in a covered structure that resembles a communal shower shaped like a temple façade, and men drenching themselves (and one another) with water from basins using ladles and amphoras. The *loutron* can be identified in the remains of many gymnasia by its drainage system, rows of raised basins, and the animal-headed spouts (lion, panther, boar) used to supply running water—though not a means of heating it.

However, the prejudice against hot baths was ultimately doomed by both pleasure and practicality; athletes rubbed themselves with olive oil and dust before working out, which obviously rinsed off more easily with hot water than with cold. Moralists could not stop the renovation of gymnasia to supply hot water nor, in addition, the spread of actual public baths. One contributor to the trend was ideas about education. A primary focus on conditioning the body began to be complemented by a greater emphasis on developing the mind through philosophy, music, and the liberal arts. Reflecting this shift towards more intellectual pursuits, gymnasia began to incorporate libraries and spaces devoted to lectures. People could now go to gymnasia to exercise the mind as well as the body. Hot baths were no longer so threatening to an ethos less dependent on physical toughness ... although there were always naysayers who thought hot water would render men effeminate.

For the Romans, bathing was about a lot more than just getting clean. For their bath complexes, they built upon the model pioneered by the Greeks of a multi-purpose structure (the gymnasium) that could supply many activities and services at once—and which could act as a social hotspot. Unlike the more conservative Greeks, Romans for the most part felt that bathing should be a pleasurable—even luxurious—experience. Bathing was seen as being civilized rather than decadent or effeminate. However, as always, some traditionalists did object to a custom they viewed as compromising one's toughness. The Stoic writer Seneca is pleased to note that the Roman hero Scipio Africanus had only a tiny, dark bath in his villa that his own contemporaries would find horrifyingly primitive, and he extols his dirtier but more virtuous ancestors: "It didn't matter to Scipio whether he bathed in murky water, because he came to the baths to wash off sweat, not oily perfumes ... And he didn't bathe every day. Writers who have passed on to us the ancient customs of Rome say that our ancestors washed only their arms and legs every day, since these parts of the body were covered with dirt from farm work. The rest of the body was washed only once a week. Of course, someone will at this point say, 'Sure, but they were very smelly men.' And what do you think they smelled of? Of the army, of farm work, and of manliness!" (Seneca the Younger, *Letters* 86; quoted in Jo-Ann Shelton, ed., *As the Romans Did: A Sourcebook in Roman Social History*, 2nd edition, New York: Oxford University Press, p. 311). Seneca, who lived under the early Empire, was fighting a losing battle, however; public baths were required to make a city Roman, and visiting them was an integral part of Roman life.

While the very wealthy might have some manner of private bathing facilities in their homes and country villas, that did not prevent them from going to the public baths. The tenements in which the vast majority of people lived completely lacked provisions for bathing, but any Roman, regardless of class, could go to the public baths, which were either free or charged only a nominal fee. Like today, you would first leave your belongings in an early version of a locker room (though in ancient Rome, it was safest to leave a slave to watch over them to prevent theft). Your possessions and clothes were placed either

Figure 3.8 *Changing-room in a bath complex. The niches in the shelf on the wall were where patrons could leave their clothing before proceeding to the baths naked.*

in niches in the wall, which are still visible in the ruins of many Roman baths, or in wooden cabinets. You had to bring your own towels, oils, perfumes, work-out and bathing clothing, and a device called a *strigil*—a curved metal implement used to scrape oil, sweat, and dirt off your skin. Soap did not exist; olive oil was used in its place. The usual strategy was to exercise first, then bathe, and afterwards go home for dinner. Ball games were an especially popular way to work up a mild sweat before jumping into the waters.

The baths of the Romans actually offered more variety than any but the most elaborate modern bathing establishments. For the Romans, bathing was an important ritual, and baths became focal points of social interaction. By the third century A.D., Rome had hundreds of baths, some small, private, neighborhood ones and others gigantic public facilities. Admission to the great public baths was either free or required only a nominal fee, so that everyone could take advantage of them. These giant complexes built by the emperors contained far more than various pools of water, but were really social centers where a Roman might hang out all day long, and thus were often equipped

Figure 3.9 *Ruins of the Baths of Caracalla. Some sense of the colossal scale of this complex can still be obtained by the size of its ruins.*

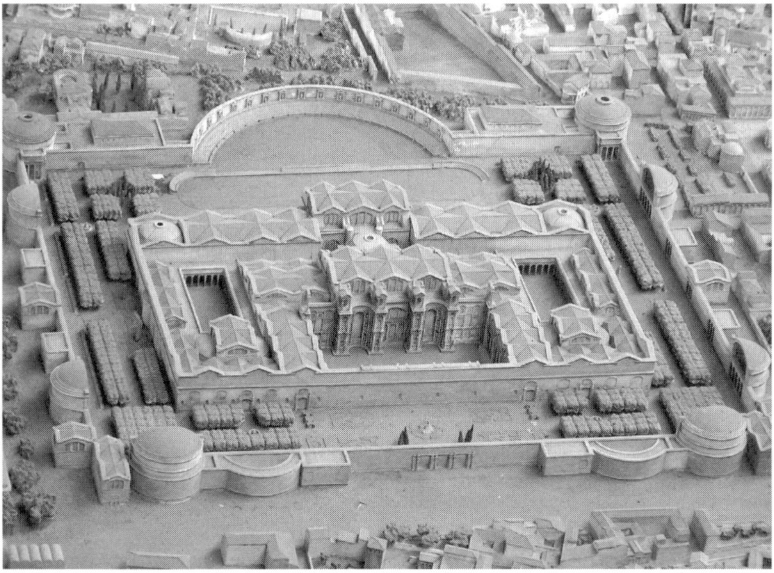

Figure 3.10 *Model of the Baths of Diocletian at Rome. Such complexes contained not only many pools of water of varying temperatures, but also athletic fields, gymnasia, libraries, food courts, and gardens.*

with athletic fields, gardens, lecture halls, art exhibits, libraries, food-courts, and spa-like amenities. The ground floor alone of the Baths of Caracalla occupied some 100,000 square meters, and this facility could accommodate 10,000 patrons at one time.

For an ancient, the process of bathing followed a pattern that typically took one through a circuit of rooms with varying water temperatures—from warm (the *tepidarium*), to hot (the *caldarium*), to cold (the *frigidarium*)—though you were free to alter this order to suit yourself. There were a variety of what we would call saunas. Ancient bathers could choose to relax in a "sweating chamber," that was either moist and hot (the *sudatorium*) or dry and hot (the *laconicum*), which was considered therapeutic. After bathing, you would rub yourself (or be rubbed by attendants) with oil or scented lotions. You might also elect to treat yourself to a massage—skilled masseuses could be found in any major bath complex. Also on hand and ready to provide services for a fee were cosmetic practitioners. One common worker of this type, known as the *alipilus*, specialized in removing unwanted body hair by plucking it out with tweezers. Too much hair-plucking could lead to suspicions of effeminacy, however; the poet Juvenal claimed that "a hairy body and coarsely furred arms indicate a manly man" (*Satire* 2 lines 11–12).

Beneath the floors of Roman baths was a heating system called the *hypocaust*, literally meaning "a furnace that heats from below." This consisted of a double-floor arrangement with the two floors separated by stacks of bricks. Hot air from the same furnaces that heated the water for the baths was forced into this zone between the floors, which resembled a crawlspace. The hot air rose and heated the floor above. Thus, even though Roman bath complexes typically had floors made of fine imported marbles, rather than being cold these would have been cozily heated by the underlying hypocaust system. Just strolling about such an environment would have been a sensual pleasure. In rooms of the bath in which it was desired that the temperature be even hotter, such as the *caldarium*, hollow terracotta tubes through which hot air could be sent were embedded in the walls, invisibly raising the temperature of the entire room.

The fact that baths were meant to refresh and soothe the body does not mean that they were a quiet, tranquil haven in the manner of today's spas. Because of the many types of activity that went on there, baths were a busy,

Figure 3.11 *Cutaway model of a Roman bath. The hypocaust system, consisting of double floors separated by stacks of bricks between which hot air was circulated, can be seen.*

noisy place. Perhaps Seneca's hostility can be partly explained by the fact that he lived in an apartment above a public bath, so that his studies were constantly disturbed by various noises emanating from the bathers below. His description of the sounds that he has to endure also offers a lively portrait of a typical day's activities at a public bath: "I live directly above a bath. Imagine, if you can, the array of noises which are so loud that I wish I was not able to hear. I can hear the bodybuilders hefting lead weights—when one is performing a hearty workout, or at least pretending to, I hear every grunt, and when he puffs out his exhaled breath, I hear every wheeze and gasp. Or perhaps I have to endure the sounds of a lazier fellow who is content with a quick rub-down, and I hear the slap of the masseuse's open or flat palms upon his shoulder. Next, along comes a ballplayer proclaiming his point total. That's all I need. Mix in the odd loudmouth, the petty thief, the dreadful sound of the man who likes to hear his own untalented voice singing in the bath, or the eager swimmer who causes a commotion plunging into the pool with a mighty splash … the chatty hair-plucker, who is never silent, except when he is making his victim shriek instead as he rips the hairs from his armpit. Then, too, there is the sweets-vendor hawking his varied wares, the sausage-seller, the confectioner, and all the sundry sellers of food, each one advertising his wares in a distinctive voice" (*Epistle* 56.1–2). The annoying characters described by Seneca are all too familiar to anyone who frequents a modern gym or a public swimming pool, and he captures some of the trying aspects of these for the most part pleasant venues.

As might be expected with any site that focuses so much on the body and that has so much muscular, bare flesh on display, ancient baths were also regarded as potential settings for sexual behavior. As some people today join a fitness club or hang out around pools as a way to pick up attractive mates, the ancient bath/gymnasium complex was rife with sexual tension. As ancient baths were usually segregated by gender, much of the preening and ogling that went on was among men. Seneca describes men who cruised the baths seeking to pick up attractive young lovers whom they would take back to their homes. In several poems, Martial portrays men gazing lustfully at one another in the baths, and even directly accuses one such unwelcome voyeur, "You, Philomusus, are constantly eyeing me up while I bathe" (*Epigrams* 11.63).

Going abroad: Travel and tourism

Exploring museums stuffed with famous artworks; bargaining with street vendors to buy cheap souvenirs imprinted with images of local tourist attractions; know-it-all guidebooks that describe detailed walking tours designed to hit all the key sights in famous cities; aggressive (and often unscrupulous) locals offering to be your guide; taking a trip to an exotic spa to relax or restore health; visiting locations associated with the lives of well-known celebrities; haggling with greedy hotel managers to rent overpriced rooms near famous sights; and uncomfortable travel on overcrowded forms of transportation. All of these are standard experiences of those who participate in the modern global tourist industry. Today, tourism is one of the top industries in the world, and masses of tourists routinely embark on lengthy and expensive vacations for the purpose of seeking fun and relaxation in picturesque spots and dutifully visiting famous cultural landmarks. All of the experiences described above will be familiar to the modern traveler, but every one of these was just as routine for the ancient Mediterranean tourist of 2,000 years ago. Reflecting on the timeless urge to go to distant places to see famous things, one Roman wrote: "We trudge along endless roads and traverse the waters in order to see what we ignore when it is right under our eyes. Nature seems to have disposed us to avidly seek what is far away but remain unmoved by what is close, or perhaps any desire that is too easily fulfilled loses its appeal. For whatever reason, there are numerous things in and around our own city [Rome] that we have never visited, but if the same things were in Greece or Egypt or Asia, we would have learned and read everything there was to know about them and eagerly viewed them" (Pliny the Younger, *Letters* 8.20.1–2).

While many of the experiences of the ancient and modern tourist are similar, technology has ensured that some of the means of transportation are quite different. Today's jet aircraft can sweep a person from one side of the globe to another in a matter of hours, but for ancient travelers, all journeys had to be made on foot, by riding animals, or aboard slow ships subject to the vagaries of wind and weather. Not only was travel slow, but it was dangerous, due to bandits, pirates, and other hazards. This perhaps accounts for the existence of a considerable body of superstitions concerning travel. Thus, if you dreamed of donkeys, it foretold a trip that would be safe but lengthy. To dream of owls or quails was ominous, since it supposedly meant that you might encounter bandits, and a dream of wild boars forecast storms.

Because sea travel was a great deal faster than land travel and could accommodate more baggage, nearly all but the shortest trips would include a sea voyage. Unlike today, where massive cruise ships convey tourists to desirable spots, the ancient world had no such dedicated passenger vessels, so tourists had to book their passage on a merchant ship. On the other hand, the ancient Mediterranean swarmed with such cargo freighters busily circulating between the major ports, so it was fairly easy to make use of these trade networks to get around. For example, the Apostle Paul, whom one could consider a sort of religiously motivated tourist, was able to travel all around the Mediterranean and do his preaching by hitching rides on Roman grain freighters.

Figure 3.12 *Mosaic of a Roman merchant ship. Such freighters also served as transportation for tourists who wished to visit foreign lands.*

Passengers had to bring on board everything they would need over the course of the journey, including their own bedding and sufficient food and drink for themselves and whatever entourage of servants might be accompanying them. Wealthier people might be able to book small cabins, but the typical traveler simply slept on deck. As today, a major practical concern of travelers was having enough money for the journey and obtaining appropriate currency when in foreign lands. The usual solution today is to carry a bank card with which you can draw local currency from an ATM. Ancient travelers had to make do without this handy banking technology, but nevertheless often found clever ways to avoid simply having to carry lots of cash. One solution was to get a kind of letter of introduction to a relative or patron of your family in another city who would advance you some money while you were in town. Merchants often had these sorts of reciprocal agreements with their counterparts around the Mediterranean.

Another issue was converting your money into local currencies. In the same way that an American tourist today can often get away with paying for things in foreign countries with U.S. dollars, especially in areas that specifically cater to tourists, there were certain currencies in the ancient world that were accepted far beyond the borders of the countries that produced them.

For example, the standard coins produced by the city of Athens were made of particularly reliable silver and were stamped with an easily recognized image of a big-eyed owl, the symbol of the goddess Athena. Such coins, referred to colloquially as "owls," were accepted as valid currency across the eastern Mediterranean, so a tourist journeying around at the times of Athens' hegemony could simply lay in a supply of Athenian "owls" and undertake his travels with reasonable confidence that they would be accepted wherever he went. Other such widely usable currency included a type of gold coin made in Persia. Later, when the Romans had conquered the Mediterranean, one could travel from Britain to Syria using a single currency. In this way, one might consider Roman money as a forerunner of modern attempts at broadly accepted currencies such as the euro.

Tourists, however, always tend to have greater amounts of cash on them than locals, and so inevitably attract the attention of pickpockets and robbers. In precisely the same manner that many tourists today wear a pouch beneath their clothing containing their passports and their money, ancient tourists were advised to carry their cash in a pouch hung around their neck under their clothing and, furthermore, not to wear flashy or ostentatious jewelry that would attract the attention of prospective thieves.

Before setting out on a journey, the savvy modern tourist will consult one of the multitude of guidebooks that provide supposedly up-to-date and knowledgeable advice on everything from where to stay to what to see and how best to get there. These same sorts of guidebooks existed in the ancient world. One category of these, called *itineraria*, focused on giving information about roadways, travel conditions along them, and where one might seek food and lodging. During the Roman period, such *itineraria* became quite detailed, listing exact distances between towns along the well-built Roman road system and identifying where one could find inns for food and lodging. Much like the road guides published today by Michelin and the AAA, some of these even employed symbols to rate the quality of inns and to indicate what amenities were available at each one. In addition, some guidebooks provided commentary on the actual condition of each stretch of road, with notations such as "mostly uphill but with a multitude of places to provide rest and refreshments," "can be covered in one day's journey by a good walker," "the road mostly goes through stretches of olive trees and forests," and, perhaps the most welcome comment of all, "is completely free of bandits."

The most famous of all ancient travel guidebooks was written in the second century A.D. by a Greek named Pausanias. He authored what was perhaps the first comprehensive tourist's guidebook to an entire country, the true forerunner of such books as the Baedeker, Frommers, and Lonely Planet series that are relied upon by modern tourists. His *Description of Greece* offers an in-depth account of the buildings, monuments, works of art, local traditions, history, myths, and products of every place that he covers. His work is divided into ten sections, each on a different region of Greece. The very first section, on Attica, includes a lengthy discussion of the famous city of Athens and its monuments. Just like in many modern guidebooks, his write-up on Athens presents a number of suggested walks through parts of the city, for which he gives detailed itineraries of exactly what a tourist following his directions will see. It is still possible to walk some of these routes today and to view at least the ruins of many of the buildings he describes. Pausanias' tone is informal and chatty; he is like an ideal tour guide who has a deep knowledge of the sites and wants to show them off, but is always concerned with keeping things interesting as well as informative.

When we turn to the motivations of ancient tourists and what sorts of sight they chose to visit, we find the same types of destinations patronized by modern tourists. They journeyed to five basic categories of places—locations that: 1) were famous for one reason or another; 2) offered rich cultural attractions; 3) claimed to improve one's health or cure diseases; 4) allowed one to attend a famous event or spectacle; and 5) promised fun in an exotic setting. Just as today, in practice, itineraries were often chosen to hit sights that combined several of these goals.

Some of the obvious tourist hot-spots of the ancient world included: all the major cities, such as Athens, Rome, and Alexandria; religious sanctuaries, such as those at Olympia, Delphi, and Delos; natural wonders, such as the active volcano of Mount Etna in Sicily; lands perceived as exotic and mysterious, such as Egypt; and the sites of famous mythological and historical events, such as the city of Troy and the battlefield of Marathon. Added to these were manmade wonders such as the Pyramids, the Colossus of Rhodes, and particularly large or impressive temples and statues. It was some time in the third century B.C. that the traditional list of the Seven Wonders of the Ancient World was compiled, and no doubt there were ancient tourists who boasted of checking off as many on this list as they could.

In the same way that there have been a number of contemporary fads for places that were mentioned in or served as the setting for best-selling books and popular movies, certain sites attracted ancient tourists because of their appearance in literature. One example was the Vale of Tempe in Greece, a pleasant but otherwise unremarkable wooded area that happened to become the subject of a number of famous poets.

Today, in cities such as Los Angeles, New York, and London, you can take specialized tours that will drive you past the houses of celebrities both living and dead (and the latter's graves too). Such sites were an ancient preoccupation as well. In Athens, tourists flocked to see the supposed house of Socrates; in Sparta, the house of Menelaos; in Pylos, that of Nestor; and in Thebes, that of the poet Pindar. An entire tourist industry focused around just the life of Alexander the Great. In Macedon, you could visit the school where he was taught by Aristotle; at the battlefield of Chaeronea in Greece, you could sit by an oak tree under which his tent had allegedly been pitched; near Tyre in Phoenicia, you could meditate at the stream beside which he napped and had a dream foretelling his conquest of the city; in Babylon, you could see a house he stayed at; and, best of all, at Alexandria in Egypt, you could pay homage to the great conqueror at his tomb and view his gold-encased corpse. Alexander's body suffered an undignified mishap when the Roman emperor Augustus, while visiting the tomb as a tourist, accidentally knocked the nose off Alexander's mummified body.

While Alexander was a historical figure, a mythological one whose relics were especially popular with tourists was Helen of Troy. On the island of Rhodes, a temple displayed a pair of bracelets that she allegedly wore. In southern Italy, it was possible to view one of her sandals. A version of her myth claimed that she was hatched from an egg and, rather remarkably, this egg could be visited in a temple at Sparta. At Delphi, visitors could see a necklace that supposedly once hung around her beautiful neck as well as the stool she habitually sat on. Thebes, however, claimed to possess the very same stool, and thus tourists had to choose which they believed was the authentic one. Finally, the most provocative relic was at Rhodes, where visitors could examine the cup she drank from, which had the additional titillating allure that it supposedly preserved the shape of one of her breasts.

The form that such myth-related objects took ran an impressive gamut. As is perhaps to be expected, there were numerous weapons and pieces of armor supposedly used by various heroes, but in addition one could see the tools employed to build the Trojan Horse, the steering bar from Menelaos' warship, the hair of the Egyptian goddess Isis, and the flute of Marsyas. Tourists also had a taste for what one might call curiosities or bizarre objects. More than one temple displayed the bones of giants—these are thought to have been mammoth bones, which are found in Greece. Other such temple collections included the jawbone of a whale, stuffed chimpanzees brought from Africa, the mummified body of a woman covered in hair, the skull of an elephant, mirrors that distorted the images reflected in them, a 100 lb. crystal, and what (from the description) seem to have been coconuts.

There were no true museums in the ancient world, but temples often served much the same function, as they were stuffed with famous artworks, war trophies, and curiosities such as the ones described above. Perhaps the first attempt at a kind of museum that was dedicated to the preservation of historical objects was a set of rooms in the palace of King Nebuchadnezzar II of Assyria in the sixth century B.C. There, he displayed inscriptions, statues, weapons, and objects from both his own and conquered peoples. The rooms were open to the public so they could come and marvel at the assemblage, and the name he gave to this institution was "The Wonder Cabinet of Mankind."

For tourists whose tastes ran to the high end of culture, there was no shortage of collections of famous sculptures and paintings that one was supposed to see. At the top of the list were several statues included among the Seven Wonders of the World, such as the statue of Zeus at Olympia, which had been made by the renowned sculptor Phidias. The Roman statesman Cicero once recorded a list of particularly famous artworks that drew throngs of tourists. This list is reminiscent of the sort of "greatest hits" art tours of Europe, which promise those who sign up for them that they will be able to boast of having seen Da Vinci's "Mona Lisa," Michelangelo's "David,"

Botticelli's "Venus," Van Gogh's "Sunflowers," Vermeer's "Girl with a Pearl Earring," Monet's "Water Lilies," and the Sistine Chapel. Cicero's list included a painting of Venus rising out of the ocean by Apelles, a statue of Europa being abducted by Zeus in the form of a bull by Pythagoras of Rhegium, a picture of an Athenian trireme by Protogenes, and a bronze cow sculpted by Myron. This cow statue seems to have attracted particular adulation. On display on the Acropolis at Athens, it was said to be a marvel of realism. Admirers claimed that not merely ordinary people but even cattle-herders as well as bulls could be fooled into thinking it was real.

Another thing that drew tourists abroad in large numbers was special events. In the same way that hordes of people will descend upon a city or country today when it hosts something like soccer's World Cup or football's Super Bowl, ancient national and international athletic contests attracted swarms of spectators. The greatest of all these athletic tourist magnets is the same today as it was over 2,000 years ago: the Olympic Games. Like today, the ancient Olympics were held on a four-year cycle and drew great numbers of aficianados who would travel considerable distances to observe them. Also, just as today, among these fans was always a sprinkling of celebrities, although in the ancient world there was occasional trouble when such VIPs included the more mentally unbalanced of the Roman emperors, whose inflated concepts of their own prowess led them to want to compete in the Games. In addition to the Olympics, there were three other great international competitions held on a rotating basis so that every year one of these major competitions was being held. There were also hundreds of local events so that a professional athlete could be constantly on tour, going from one to another in the same way that modern golf or tennis pros make the circuit of annual tournaments. Avid fans of certain sports or particular athletes could similarly be constantly on the move from one important event to another.

While we tend to associate tourism with pleasure-seeking or idleness, a substantial number of tourists, both in antiquity and today, undertake their journeys with a more serious motivation. This group consists of those who travel for the sake of their health, many of them seeking a cure for some disease or ailment with which they are afflicted. Today this phenomenon, sometimes known as "medical tourism," ranges from those who spend a week at a luxurious Mexican spa for some relaxation as well as inexpensive minor cosmetic surgery, to desperate victims of serious diseases who seek a miraculous cure at a religious site.

In the ancient world, the most popular medical destinations were sanctuaries devoted to the god of healing, Asklepios. Two of the most famous of these were located at Epidauros, which early on developed a reputation for divine healing, and on the island of Cos, which was the home of the great physician Hippocrates and his associated medical school. At a sanctuary such as Epidauros, the tourist/patient typically followed a fairly standard routine. He or she would take a purifying bath and then spend the night within the temple or sanctuary, engaged in prayers to the god. To accommodate the hordes of visitors, some sanctuaries had large dormitories, while at others visitors would sleep in the temple itself. It was believed that in your dreams you would be visited by the god, who would sometimes effect a miraculous cure. Perhaps more commonly, the temple attendants would prescribe for you some sort of drug, ointment, or regimen of special diet, exercise, and rituals.

There are numerous surviving testimonials from ancient authors claiming to have received a cure or at least to have had their sufferings alleviated by such a procedure. In gratitude, many of them made dedications at the temple. A common form that such offerings took was a clay or marble representation of the afflicted body part. Thus, a common sight in modern museums is a case filled with life-sized marble hands, feet, eyes, ears, lungs, intestines, wombs, and nearly every other organ or body part—all of which are ancient temple artifacts donated by healed visitors. If this sounds odd, it should not. Consider the approximately 5 million people per year who journey to Lourdes in France seeking a cure for a comparable range of ailments. These modern pilgrims leave behind similar offerings. Lourdes has vast collections of crutches abandoned by those whose foot and leg ailments were evidently cured. An exact parallel to the ancient world's offerings of clay body parts still exists in many countries, such as Mexico, although there the dedicated objects, known as Milagros, are traditionally miniature images of body parts fashioned from tin.

Figure 3.13 *Dedicatory ears. This dedicatory plaque was left at a healing sanctuary by someone suffering from a hearing disorder.*

Another type of health-inspired journey is the cruise, in which the restful shipboard life is meant to effect a cure through either the climate or simply relaxation. One of the more popular cruise itineraries in the ancient world was to take a trip up or down the Nile River, where leisurely shipboard days could be interspersed with visits to famous antiquities that were already old 2,000 years ago. The dry climate of Egypt was also thought to be particularly beneficial for those with respiratory problems, so doctors might advise such patients to undertake such a trip. When a slave who was a particular favorite of the wealthy Roman aristocrat Pliny the Younger contracted tuberculosis, the indulgent master sent the slave on a luxury cruise up the Nile in an attempt to restore his health. As late as the early twentieth century, doctors were still dispatching patients with respiratory ailments on trips to Egypt.

Those seeking aid at temples usually had fairly serious maladies, but another form of health-related travel that drew lots of tourists was simply to visit the sites of hot mineral springs. Bathing in such naturally heated and mineral-rich waters was regarded as both relaxing and healthful. This age-old practice, which grew particularly widespread during the Victorian era, continues today. Many of the sites of Roman mineral water spas are still actively in use for the same purpose by new generations of health-seekers. The springs of Wiesbaden were originally the Roman resort of Aquae Mattiacae; Vichy (home of Vichy water) was Aquae Calidae; and the aptly-named city of Bath in England was Aquae Sulis. Archaeological excavations at these sites have revealed another enduring custom: ancient visitors to fountains and springs also tossed in a coin for good luck, as evidenced by enormous hoards of ancient coins that have been discovered at the bottoms of these hot springs.

One location that was especially richly endowed with numerous hot springs was the area around the Bay of Naples in Italy, and this brings us to another category of tourist: those who enjoy visiting particularly beautiful spots, often including beaches, for no other purpose than to lie around and enjoy themselves. For the ancient Romans, the Bay of Naples was just such an attractive vacation destination. Particularly in the summer, Romans would escape the heat of the city by flocking to the beach, where the cool breezes off the water were far more pleasant than the fetid stench of the tightly-packed city. The entire region around the Bay of Naples was dotted with the villas of the rich, and numerous seaside resort towns catered to vacationers of all social and economic classes. Today, many young people on spring break like to converge on resorts such as Cancun in Mexico or the beaches of Florida. In Europe, the migration is to beaches along the Spanish coast and trendy places such as Ibiza, St. Tropez, and Portofino, which fulfill the same purpose for various economic classes. Just like their modern counterparts, certain ancient resort towns developed reputations for being sites of immoral behavior and drunkenness. One example on the Bay of Naples was Baiae, which featured both hot springs and beaches. Today's spring-breakers are infamous for scenes of debauchery such as wet t-shirt contests and binge drinking, but consider ancient descriptions of life on the Bay of Naples, which refer to "nude bathing parties" and "drunks staggering about the shore-line and raucous boating parties." One disapproving Roman elder characterized it as a place where "young women are shared by all, old men act like they're youths, and youths act like adolescent girls."

If all of this makes certain aspects of ancient tourism sound very familiar, there are a number of other travel-related experiences that appear to be equally timeless. One of these is the annoyance of disembarking at your destination only to be greeted by a noisy and pushy swarm of locals all clamoring for you to hire their services as your guide. In Greece, these pests were known as *periegetai*, or "leaders around," and were notorious for the aggressive way in which they solicited the business of tourists and their non-stop stream of chatter, much of which was of dubious accuracy. One ancient writer describes a typical encounter thus: "Immediately upon arriving at the colonnades of the Sanctuary of Dionysos, two or three people rushed up to me, offering to describe everything about the site for only a small fee." Locals were well aware of the potential income represented by tourists, and so often staged performances or offered experiences that would earn them some extra coins. For example, in Egypt there were several sites featuring sacred crocodiles considered to be reincarnations of the god Suchus. At one temple, the priest could be induced to summon their trained crocodiles and open their mouths for inspection—for a small fee, of course. At another, one could buy offerings to be made to the crocodile god consisting of a cake, meat, and sweetened wine, and then watch as the priest fed these to the hungry beasts.

A vacation to an exotic and distant spot is not complete for many tourists unless they return home laden with souvenirs to hand out to family and friends. The same was true of ancient tourists, and any popular tourist attraction would have been surrounded by stalls of vendors hawking appropriate tchotchkes. For famous statues and buildings, such souvenirs often took the form of miniature replicas. Thus, in the same way that many an American visitor to Paris returns home with a miniature Eiffel Tower in her suitcase or a European comes back with a little Statue of Liberty, ancient tourists bought miniature versions of things such as Myron's cow and the Pyramids. Today, you can photograph famous sights and bring back your own images of them. In the ancient world, of course, this was not possible. What you could do, however, was purchase a vast array of cheap household objects bearing a representation of the desired monument. One of the most common forms these took was the ubiquitous little clay lamps that burned olive oil and functioned as the main source of lighting in the ancient world. These could be mass-produced and stamped with images of things such as the Lighthouse of Alexandria. Another popular item was small glass bottles featuring pictures of important local sights conveniently labeled. Wealthier tourists could even purchase lifesize copies of famous artworks made out of bronze or marble that could be shipped home and put on display in their houses to illustrate both the range of their travels and their fine taste.

Finally, just as the highlight of many a tourist's trip abroad is shopping for goods that are supposedly local bargains, such as rugs in Turkey, there were similar local products that ancient vacationers tried to acquire at bargain prices. Predictably, in the eastern Mediterranean these included various textile products and exotic spices. Others were specific to a single location; for example, the bees of Mount Hymettus in Greece were supposed to produce the finest honey, so a visitor to the region might bring back a jar as a gift for a good friend. Some souvenirs, also like today, were of a religious nature. Thus, a traveler to Egypt who worshiped one of that land's deities might take home with him a bottle containing the sacred waters of the Nile. When ancient tourists returned home laden with souvenirs, they frequently had to pass through the equivalent of customs, at which they had to declare their purchases and pay tariffs on them.

One worry of travelers is the prospect of getting into trouble while in a foreign country. Today, if you encounter some sort of serious difficulty, the solution is to seek assistance from your consulate. Once again, such a procedure is nothing new. In the ancient Greek world, if you found yourself in some sort of predicament while abroad, you would turn to the local *proxenos* for aid. A *proxenos* was a citizen of your own country who was a permanent resident in another country and who had been designated a kind of ambassador to that country. Such men were often wealthy merchants whose business interests led them to live abroad, and while they technically received no salary for serving as *proxenos*, they were expected to render whatever assistance was possible to fellow citizens who happened to pass through the city in which they lived. Often this took the form of no more than providing lodging or food, but if there was more serious trouble, with his wealth and local contacts the *proxenos* could often resolve the issue.

Finally, tourists then as now have the unfortunate tendency either to try to bring home a bit of a famous object or to leave their mark upon it. Many famous sites and objects were damaged by eager tourists laying inquisitive hands on them or attempting to break off pieces to take with them as souvenirs. The example noted above of Augustus knocking off the nose of Alexander's corpse was plainly an accident, but nevertheless constituted a (literal) defacement of a treasured relic. Other ancient tourists did things such as make off with bits of rock from sites such as the pyramids in Egypt or, with curious fingers, unravel ancient garments that had belonged to famous people or possessed special qualities. Probably the most timeless way to announce that you had visited a site or seen a particular object was to inscribe your name upon it, and ancient travelers did not hesitate to do this. The most common graffito on famous monuments left by tourists both ancient and contemporary is some variant on the classic statement "So-and-so was here." On the walls of the tombs of the pharaohs located in the Valley of the Kings in Egypt, there are more than 2,000 graffiti left by tourists of the classical era. Another favorite Egyptian site for such messages was a colossal statue of Memnon that supposedly possessed the power of speech. Ancient tourists covered the reachable parts of the legs and feet of this statue with hundreds of inscriptions recording their presence. It was not merely uncouth youths or disrespectful hooligans who left such graffiti. Among the messages inscribed on Memnon's legs is one from Sabina, wife of the Roman emperor Hadrian.

4

Power to the people: Systems of government

We are indebted to the ancient Greeks and Romans for two systems of government that have deeply influenced politics throughout history and which continue to do so today: Greek democracy and the Roman Republic. Both of these systems of government experimented to varying degrees with what was, at the time, the revolutionary idea of sharing power broadly among the citizens of a country, rather than concentrating it in the hands of one person or just a few. For states that have favored a narrow distribution of power, the later phase of Roman history, in which Rome had an empire and an emperor, offered an alternative but equally compelling model for many ambitious, power-hungry rulers. Not only the structures, but also the vocabulary and symbolism derived from these forms of ancient government, continue to permeate our world today, and it is impossible to fully understand our modern forms of government without knowing about their classical inspirations.

Man, the political animal: Politics and the ancient city

Before we examine specific types of government, let us briefly consider where the idea of politics comes from. As for so much else, we can thank the ancient Greeks. The *polis* (usually translated as "city-state"), which first arose in the eighth century B.C., became *the* distinctively Greek form of social and political organization for at least the next 700 years. A *polis* was a geographic region consisting of a city and the area around it. Both the inhabitants of the urban center and those living in the surrounding countryside were *politai* (members of the *polis*), recognized as a single people and ruled over by the same central government. For instance, even if you lived 30 miles outside the city of Athens, as long as you were a resident of the overall territory called Attica, you still counted as an Athenian. *Polis* is the source of the words "politics" and "political," as well as adjectives such as "metropolitan" and "cosmopolitan."

In his work *Politics*, the philosopher Aristotle starts off by tracing the basic units in which people have grouped themselves, beginning with the household, then the village, and finally the *polis*, which he says "exists for the good life" (*Politics* 1.1.8), and is a sort of culmination of the ways in which human beings have cohabited. "Man is by nature a political animal" (*Politics* 1.1.9), he writes, defined by the need to gather with others and establish an orderly coexistence: "A man that is by nature and not merely by fortune cityless is either low in the scale of humanity or above it … a man who is incapable of entering into a partnership, or who is so self-sufficing that he has no need to do so, is no part of a state, so that he must be either a lower animal or a god" (*Politics* 1.1.9–12). It is unnatural for a person to remain in isolation; he or she is meant to be a "political" being—in other words, part of a *polis*.

At the same time that the *polis* was flourishing, another form of political and social organization dominated throughout vast swathes of Greece. The *ethnos*, meaning "tribe," "nation," or "people," although not politically unified and lacking a central government, none the less possessed a strong identity as a single people inhabiting a particular area who shared the same culture and worshiped the same gods. An *ethnos* might consist of a bunch of small towns or little villages who came together to fight a common enemy or deal with a major problem. This is the source of our word "ethnic." Not surprisingly, the Greeks living in city-states tended to consider themselves more sophisticated than their somewhat "backward" rural cousins—an attitude that seems to be as old as cities themselves.

The great experiment: Athens and the birth of democracy

It is often said that one of the Greeks' greatest contributions to the modern world was the notion of democracy. Let's jump straight to the topic of democracy and see how this earth-changing idea came to be. To do so, we need to go back to ancient Athens in the year 514 B.C. At that time, Athens was not a democracy, and for several generations had been ruled by a family of king-like strongmen known as the Peisistratids. The current generation of Peisistratids consisted of two brothers, and our story begins when the younger brother, named Hipparchos, became attracted to a beautiful young man of Athens named Harmodios. Now, this might not have been a problem except that, unfortunately, Harmodios already had a boyfriend, a man named Aristogeiton. When Hipparchos' amorous advances were rejected, he became angry, and in revenge refused to allow Harmodios' sister to carry a basket in the big state parade that was about to be held. This may all sound kind of silly, but carrying the basket in the parade was regarded as an honor, making this act a major insult to the family.

The young lovers Harmodios and Aristogeiton were so offended that they determined to assassinate Hipparchos and his older brother Hippias at the parade. They weren't very good assassins, however, and only succeeded in killing the younger brother, Hipparchos, while Hippias escaped. Both Harmodios and Aristogeiton were promptly killed by Hippias' bodyguards, and the incident seemed closed.

Why bother telling you all this? Actually, for a very good reason. The incident served as a rallying point for those opposed to these tyrannical rulers, and, a few years later, resulted in a revolution in which Hippias was expelled from Athens. And it was after the expulsion that the Athenians were then inspired to establish a political system which, for the first time that we know of, was based on the people wielding primary power in the state—or, in other words, the first attempt at a democracy. So, if you want to know the true origins of democracy, it all began with an incident of male-on-male sexual harassment.

Figure 4.1 *Statue of Harmodios. The sexual harassment of this young man eventually sparked a revolution at Athens that ultimately ended with the establishment of the first democracy.*

So it was that in 508 B.C., shortly after getting rid of the Peisistratid brothers, the Athenians were in the position of knowing that they wanted to make a major change in how their government was set up, but they were not sure how to go about it. They had been in a similar situation several hundred years earlier, and that time they had taken the bold step of picking a wise man named Solon, instructing him to design a new government, and then promising to obey whatever he devised. It had worked out pretty well, so they decided to repeat their Solon strategy of turning over all power to one man and charging him with fixing the state and coming up with a new, better government. Solon himself was long gone, but the wise man whom they turned to this time around, named Cleisthenes, set up what would be the first real democracy.

He realized, however, that the biggest obstacle to a democracy would be that the Athenians had become fragmented into different factions based on geography. These were the hill people, the coast people, and the city people. Each of these regions had different economic interests, and Cleisthenes knew that people from the same locale would band together and support policies that would only be good for their own little area rather than for the entire state. Cleisthenes cleverly solved this problem by dividing all Athenians up into 10 tribes. Each tribe was in turn composed of a mixture of citizens drawn from the three geographic territories. This set-up insured that no longer could the members of the geographic regions separate themselves, but rather that people would have to work together within their tribes with people from the other areas.

He then established a group called the Council of 500, which became the main legislative body of the state (the equivalent of the Congress in the United States) and which was responsible for making most of the major political decisions. There were, in addition, some elected officials, but the Council of 500 was the focal point of power, and was endowed with the ability to ratify legislation. Now comes the part that really made it a democracy—how the 500 members of the Council were selected. Every year, each of the 10 tribes sent 50 people to serve on the council. Those 50 representatives for each tribe were chosen by random lottery. All members of the tribe would put their names in a big pot, 50 would be drawn, and, if you were selected, then you would serve on the Council of 500 and would make the decisions that would govern the state for that year.

Unlike our modern representative democracies, in which we elect politicians to represent us, this system made Athens a true democracy, since it meant that every citizen had an equal chance of serving in the government. This was a truly radical system, and I sometimes wonder if the United States wouldn't have a better government today if we simply randomly chose 535 citizens and sent them to Washington each year to form the Congress. The way the odds worked out in ancient Athens, chances were that each person would serve on the Council of 500 twice in his lifetime. Athenian democracy underwent some further permutations, and one of the most important additions was a law that granted every citizen the right to get up and speak in the assembly of citizens—literally giving everyone a potential voice in politics.

Of course, the word democracy itself is derived from a Greek one composed of two parts: *demos* meaning "the people" and *kratos* denoting "power." Thus,

Figure 4.2 *The Acropolis of Athens. This large, rocky outcrop, adorned with spectacular temples and buildings, was the center of Athens, the state that pioneered democratic forms of government.*

a democracy is a form of government in which power is given to the people. While much praise is heaped upon the Athenians for their democratic form of government, it should be remembered that it was really only a democracy for those people who qualified for citizen status. And there were a great many groups that were excluded from citizenship in ancient Athens. Women did not count as citizens, children did not count as citizens, slaves did not count as citizens (and there were a lot of slaves in Athens), and finally, foreigners living in Athens permanently (of whom there were also a large number) did not count as citizens. All together, probably less than one in five of the human beings actually living in Athens counted as citizens and thus enjoyed the full fruits of their democratic system. Many other Greek states also came to embrace some form of democracy.

Democracy part I: The good

Today, many politicians and think-tank intellectuals like to claim that a democratic form of government produces a whole set of positive societal effects ranging from scientific creativity to economic prosperity. Western democracies also have a tendency to tout the link between their form of government and such abstract values as toleration, individual rights, and freedom of expression. Such rhetoric was particularly vigorous during the Cold War, when democracy was defined in contrast to communism, but if one looks at nearly any presidential speech of the last half-century, one will find constant assertions that democracy leads to a host of positive consequences in those societies that adopt it. While these assertions fit well within contemporary political discourse, they too are as old as democracy itself. In fact, the great-grandfather of all pro-democracy speeches was one given by the Greek statesman, Pericles, in 431 B.C. If you are familiar with this speech, the next time you hear a presidential address you will almost inevitably recognize various statements from it that are echoed (if not outright copied) in the modern oration. In this sense, Pericles' words are probably among the most plagiarized in all of history. Let's examine some of Pericles' specific claims that still have a familiar ring today.

This speech was supposedly given just after the outbreak of the Peloponnesian War, at a funeral held at Athens to honor the soldiers killed during the previous year's fighting. In the version recorded by the historian Thucydides (*The Peloponnesian War* 2.34–46), rather than enumerating the achievements of the individual men who had died, Pericles states that he will instead praise them by describing the city that produced them, including "the form of government under which our greatness grew, and the national characteristics from which it arose." The resulting "Funeral Oration" of Pericles was thus intended as a reminder to the people of Athens of the ideals of Athenian democracy.

He begins by noting that the Athenians chose not to copy other states' forms of government, and asserts that instead "we are called a democracy," which he succinctly defines as having "its administration … in the hands of the many and not of the few." Pericles proceeds to emphasize the role that equality plays in this system, and especially the crucial notion that all citizens are equal under the law regardless of wealth, status, or family: "The laws provide equal justice to all." Athens at this time, by the way, was famous for laws that afforded its slaves more legal protections against mistreatment and abuse than in most other states. Another key component of the legal system was that for most offenses, citizens were tried by a jury of their peers selected by lot from the citizen body. These juries were typically very large, ranging from 501 to 1,501 jurors. Their large size was thought to act as insurance against bribery and also meant that the verdict was likely to represent the opinion of the citizens as a whole and not just a few individuals. Other elements of the legal system stressing equality were that it was relatively easy for any citizen to bring a lawsuit and that, during the trial itself, the accuser and the accused were responsible for making their own speeches before the jury.

According to Pericles, the effects of this emphasis on equality were that, at Athens, rewards were based on merit, citizens were free to rise as high as their abilities would take them, and neither poverty nor obscure family origins prevented them from serving the state. This is identical to the modern emphasis on the "self-made" businessperson, as exemplified, for instance, in Horatio Alger's stories. Pericles further asserts that ordinary citizens, although they are not professional politicians and may be primarily occupied with their own business and affairs, are fully competent to serve as judges and to decide political matters.

Another of the basic principles of democratic Athens emphasized by Pericles is the idea of personal freedoms. He identifies several forms that these freedoms take, including the right of each citizen to do as he pleases within the limits of the law, or, as he puts it: "In public life we emphasize freedom, and in our private interactions we are not suspicious of one another, nor do we get angry with our neighbor if he does what he likes." According to Pericles, the Athenians were particularly brave in warfare because they were free men fighting to defend a state in which they each had a share. Another sort of freedom he notes is what we might today call freedom of speech. Since the most important decisions were reached as a result of debate and voting in the assembly, the concept of unfettered public discussion was central to the system functioning properly. Pericles states, "Rather than viewing debate as an impediment to action, we value the wisdom that it grants in order to prepare ourselves before we take action." Finally, even the private rights of non-citizens were respected: "Our city is thrown open to the world, and we never expel a foreigner or prevent him from seeing or learning anything." This statement also implies a degree of tolerance for those who are different, and indeed a large number of foreigners, mostly *metics* (citizens of other Greek states), made their permanent homes at Athens. The Athenians, while proud of their own heritage and identity, were certainly not above copying ideas from others, and the multicultural nature of their city made it easy to be exposed to and acquire new concepts and knowledge from all around the ancient Mediterranean world.

The openness of Athenian life certainly spurred economic activity and growth. Although the notion of a capitalistic economy did not yet exist, Pericles was aware of the vigorous economy that was one of Athens' strengths and that flourished under its unique form of democratic government. Pericles observed, "Because of the greatness of our city, the fruits of the whole earth flow in upon us, so that we enjoy the goods of other countries as freely as our own."

To Pericles, the benefits of democracy extended far beyond political and legal rights, and fostered a set of values and characteristics that distinguished Athens in other areas as well. Chief among these was that an open, democratic state would encourage cultural creativity and innovation among its citizens. He boasted that "We provide plenty of means for the mind to refresh itself" and "We are lovers of the beautiful, yet simple in our tastes, and we cultivate the mind without loss of manliness." Certainly Athens' achievements in the fields of art, architecture, philosophy, and literature during the fifth century B.C. seem to confirm Pericles' opinion. Towards the end of the speech, Pericles proclaims that Athens produces citizens who are "self-reliant, equal to any circumstance, and versatile." Furthermore, he declares that Athens is constantly at the forefront of achievement and innovation, and that it sets the standard to which other states aspire. This is reminiscent of much recent political rhetoric about "exporting" democracy to other countries and the supposed effects that this will have. Pericles' "Funeral Oration" is a dazzling summary of the positive characteristics of democracy, and if many of the statements quoted above sound familiar, that is because politicians in democratic states have been repeating Pericles' words and claims for the last 2,300 years.

Pericles (and his modern imitators) may be forgiven for overstating their case a bit because, even when the flights of fancy rhetoric are stripped away, the assertions that they are making about the benefits of democracy have a fundamental truth to them. Democratic forms of government can, and have, often produced many of the positive values and effects that its proponents assert. This is not to say, however, that democracy as a form of government does not have potential flaws as well.

Democracy part II: The bad

Today, just as there are many who unhesitatingly praise democracy, there are many who see places where it can go wrong or be corrupted by unscrupulous or self-interested groups or individuals. Interestingly, just as they were already fully aware of the good aspects of democracy, the ancient Greeks were also attuned to many of the very same pitfalls or weaknesses of this system that we continue to struggle with today. A number of these potential faults of democracy are revealed in a dramatic story involving a famous race between two ships, with the fate of an entire city hanging on the outcome.

In the summer of 427 B.C., a trireme (a type of warship) set sail from the port of Athens in frantic haste. Triremes, featuring long, narrow hulls tightly packed with hundreds of rowers, were designed to emphasize one quality above all others—speed—and it was speed that was desperately needed on that day. The ship flashed out of the harbor and set its course towards the east and, as the first set of rowers grew exhausted, they flung themselves down on the deck to sleep while their places were instantly taken by another set of men who kept up the relentless pace. So urgent was their desire for speed that the men did not even pause in their rowing for the few moments that it would take to eat, but instead gulped down barley cakes soaked in wine and olive oil at their stations. The reason for their haste was that they were engaged in a race with another trireme, but their rival enjoyed a head start of almost 24 hours. The finish line was the city of Mytilene, located on an island some 300 km (186 miles) away, and the stakes were neither money nor honor, but instead quite literally the lives of every citizen of Mytilene.

At this time, Athens ruled over a confederation of dozens of subject city-states, known as the Athenian Empire, of which Mytilene was one. The Mytilenians had revolted against their overlords, but the rebellion had quickly been put down by the Athenian military. The assembly of all Athenian citizens had met, and, in a vindictive frenzy, voted to punish the rebellion by putting to death the entire adult male population of Mytilene, innocent and guilty alike, and selling every single woman and child into slavery. Accordingly, a ship was at once dispatched to bring word of this terrible decree.

The very next day, however, the citizens of Athens began to reflect on the cruelty of their judgment and to reconsider its wisdom. Another assembly was hurriedly convened, and, after several emotional speeches, the people voted to cancel the earlier cruel sentence and instead to impose the more appropriate punishment of executing only the actual leaders of the rebellion. Another ship was then sent with the new order, and the race was on to see if the second ship could overtake the first before it reached Mytilene and enforced the mass death sentence.

This dramatic incident reveals some of both the strengths and the weaknesses of the democratic system of government. On the one hand, the initial vote for the excessively severe punishment demonstrates how, in the heat of the moment at an assembly, the people could be easily swayed by transitory emotions such as anger, or by the words of inflammatory orators, to take actions that were impulsive and cruel. On the other hand, the fact that they were willing to revisit and change their decision shows the flexibility of the system, which allowed for mistakes to be corrected. However, even this flexibility could be viewed as a liability, since it reveals one of the recurrent problems of democracies: the inability to stick to a policy, since what the group decides one day can be overturned on another. Such fickleness can make long-term planning and diplomacy extremely difficult. These are all problems that democracies still struggle with today. As for the end of the story, the ship bearing the decree of death for all did arrive first at Mytilene, and the sentence of doom had just been read out, when the second ship rowed into the harbor, just in the nick of time to prevent it from being carried out.

The Mytilene incident illustrates a few of the potential enduring flaws of democracy, but the ancient Greeks were aware of many more. The most obvious critique leveled against many democracies, then as now, is that frequently the rights of a citizen are only extended to a limited privileged group, at times comprising only a minority of the total population. In the

United States, consider the long, ugly struggle for African-Americans first to escape slavery, and then to gain equal rights. While the United States has existed as a supposed democracy that emphasizes the idea that "all men are created equal" for over 200 years, African-Americans have only truly been included in those ideals for a few decades. Similarly, for the majority of the time that the U.S. has existed, women were not allowed to vote or to participate in the political process as equals. Considering our own record, we should not be too quick to condemn Athens of 2,400 years ago for excluding women and slaves from full citizenship. Keeping this in mind, let's evaluate some of the other negative aspects of democracy through two main approaches related to ancient Athens: first, we will look at criticisms leveled at this system by Greek intellectuals themselves, and then we will examine some of the actions taken by Athens during the period when it was a democracy in order to see whether or not they consistently lived up to the lofty ideals expressed in Pericles' "Funeral Oration."

Very early in the history of democracy, Greek philosophers had already voiced a number of reservations that they had about this system and identified some of its potential flaws. One of the most fundamental of these was a concern that such a government afforded too much freedom to its citizens, who would either abuse this liberty or exploit it for selfish purposes rather than for the good of all. In *The Republic*, Plato notes that, in a democracy, "there is liberty and freedom of speech in plenty, and every individual is free to do as he likes" (557b). While such a degree of freedom might sound like praise to a modern audience, Plato meant this as a criticism. He goes on to describe what he sees as the consequences of such freedom: "There is no compulsion to exercise authority if you are capable of it, or to submit to authority if you don't want to; you needn't fight if there is a war, or you can wage a private war in peacetime if you don't like peace" (557e). Plato likens liberty to an addictive intoxicant: the more freedoms that the populace gains, the more they will crave, until all self-discipline disappears and, as individuals unrestrainedly cater to their baser natures, morality decays.

Plato thought that societal distinctions would eventually break down and be erased so that the young would disrespect their elders and children would even rebel against their parents. For Plato, the freedom permissible in a democracy would inevitably be abused as individuals selfishly pursued their own advantages to the detriment of society as a whole. Many of the ancient Greek philosophers had a fairly pessimistic view of human nature, believing that a central reason for the popularity of democracy was that it allowed people to indulge their desires, since "Most people prefer to live undisciplined lives, for they find that more enjoyable than restraint" (Aristotle, *Politics* 6.2.19–20). From their viewpoint, a true democracy would inevitably devolve into "an anarchic form of society" (Plato, *The Republic* 558c).

A second general area of criticism leveled by philosophers concerns the heavy reliance on random chance in the democratic system of Athens. Many government posts were filled by lottery, and some philosophers argued that, even in everyday life, there is no task for which one would prefer a randomly chosen person rather than someone with relevant training, skills, or experience. In one dialogue attributed to Socrates, he argues that "It is absurd to select the leaders of the city by random chance when no one would dream of selecting a pilot (to steer a ship), a carpenter, or a musician by lot" (Xenophon, *Memorabilia* 1.2.9). The Athenians were not averse to consulting experts, as is pointed out in another supposed speech of Socrates reported by Plato: "When we gather in the assembly to decide a matter dealing with constructing a building, we have builders advise us, and when it is a case of constructing ships, we send for shipwrights" (Plato, *Protagoras* 319b).

Yet when it came to running the state, the Athenians were willing to entrust this task to randomly selected people regardless of their intelligence or wisdom. Plato despairingly concludes that a democracy "treats all men as equal, whether in reality they are equal or not" (*The Republic* 558c). This perhaps overstates the situation, since the magistrates who were chosen by lot had to prove a basic competency, could be removed from office by the assembly, and were not truly "running the state"; but nevertheless the Athenians were willing to involve average citizens in administration to a surprising degree.

Many Greek intellectuals simply did not share Pericles' confidence that the typical citizen was competent to exercise supreme authority, and viewed the entire system as a means by which the poor exploited the wealthy. One famous critique attributed to an "Old Oligarch" bluntly defines democracy as "a kind of political regime in which the inferior sort of people govern at the expense of their betters" (Pseudo-Xenophon, "On the Government of Athens" 1.1). This view is echoed by many philosophers, including Plato, who stated that "Democracies begin when the poor gain victory, kill or exile their opponents, and share power and civil rights equally with the rest" (*The Republic* 557b).

The philosopher Aristotle stressed the role of wealth even more, asserting that a true democracy is not simply when power is placed in the hands of the majority, but that liberty and poverty must also be considered. For him, a democracy only "exists whenever those who are free, poor, and in the majority are in control of government." (*Politics* 1290b). He asserted that the goal of a democracy is to benefit the poor at the expense of both the wealthy and the good of the state as a whole (*Politics* 1279b). It is such skepticism about the abilities and motivations of the common man that led Plato ultimately to conclude that supreme power should only be placed in the hands of a small group of individuals rigorously trained in rational thinking, his "philosopher-kings."

In addition to the philosophical objections raised by ancient Greek intellectuals, history allows a second way of evaluating Athenian democracy, which is to consider the actions of the state during this period in order to see if the decisions made by the people were wise ones. A related test is to scrutinize this record with the goal of determining whether or not Athens adhered in practice to the idealistic principles expressed in Pericles' "Funeral Oration." Such an examination raises legitimate questions on both counts, because the record of democratic Athens is by no means a spotless one, and there is room to debate whether the achievements of democratic Athens outweighed its blunders.

One place to begin is to consider the period between the Persian invasion of 480 B.C. and the beginning of the Peloponnesian War in 431 B.C. This was the era when Athens was clearly the most powerful state in Greece and therefore had a lot of latitude in choosing how it would behave towards its neighbors. What Athens did during this stretch was to act as an imperialist power, dominating other states by military force, enslaving or killing those who opposed them, compelling other cities to pay tribute to Athens, and establishing Athenian colonies and garrisons in subjected territories. Another somewhat unsavory aspect of Athens' control over its empire was the Athenians' predilection for compelling supposed allies not merely to sign treaties, but to actually make all of their citizens swear "loyalty oaths" to Athens. A number of these survive, and in addition to the expected phrases promising not to revolt against Athens, not to give aid to rebels, and to pay the required tribute, they contain lines in which the citizens of other states must swear "to obey the *demos* (the people) of Athens" or even promise "to love the *demos* of Athens."

We have already seen one example of Athenian aggression in the events leading up to the race of the triremes to the island of Mytilene. This was not an isolated case. Another famous demonstration of the potential cruelty of the Athenian *demos* that happened around the same time was known as the Melian incident. The Athenians threatened the peaceful island of Melos, declaring that they must submit to the Athenian empire. When the Melians refused, saying that they valued their freedom, they were crushed by the Athenians.

Occurrences such as this certainly suggest that Athens did not always adhere to the value system implied in the "Funeral Oration," or at least that these principles were not employed evenly. In its treatment of its empire, the Athenians repeatedly displayed an unpleasant egotism, a sense that they were better than other states, and a belief that this superiority justified their taking actions that were arbitrary and morally questionable. There was clearly a double standard in regard to the ideals of freedom of choice and equality that lay at the heart of the political structure of Athenian government, but that were denied to citizens of other states such as Melos. These same negative tendencies are sometimes pointed out by modern critics in the actions of contemporary democracies. The United States, for example, has at times been accused of bullying other states, having a superior attitude, and engaging in questionable wars, all the while professing moral rectitude. For the purposes of this discussion, whether or not such charges are accurate is not the point. What is clear is that there is a pattern of democracies, admittedly sometimes with the best of intentions, being occasionally prone to such behaviors.

Democracy part III: And the ugly

Finally, the Greeks identified what is perhaps one of the greatest perennial problems in a democracy—that the people are liable to be conned by unscrupulous leaders who play upon their emotions or self-interest so that they make rash and foolish decisions. While the principle of free speech has its positive aspects, it also opens the door for those who are skilled at manipulating words to gain excessive influence. Not surprisingly, oratory, or the art of public speaking, reached a high level of sophistication in ancient Athens, and those who were good at it by talent or through training could use this ability to gain power.

The Greeks called such men demagogues and, while the original Greek word *demagogos* literally meant simply a "leader of the people," from the beginning it clearly carried the connotation of one who manipulates the populace for his own gain. Such figures were frequently targets of ridicule in comic plays. For example, Aristophanes' play *The Knights* offers a portrait of their characteristics—"a demagogue needs neither education nor honesty, he only has to be crude and a scoundrel" (190–2)—as well as of their methods: "Why, nothing could be easier … mangle, mince, and mash, jumble the facts all up together. Win over the demos with a healthy serving of greasy flattery. You have all the qualities a demagogue requires—a loud voice, low breeding, the vulgar vocabulary of the marketplace. You have absolutely everything that is needed for a successful political career" (214–19). Elsewhere in the same play, a character promises that he will win public debates because "I will yell louder than anyone else, I can shout down anybody" (285). Such statements seem reminiscent of modern politics, where the voices that get heard and tend to make the news are not the calm, reasoned ones, but rather those making the most inflammatory or sensational claims.

In addition to the dangers posed by demagogues, democracies are also susceptible to impulsiveness and allowing the emotions of the moment to lead them into questionable decisions. For example, during wartime, the Athenian assembly once voted to illegally execute some admirals who had fled the scene of a battle, allowing some of their men to drown. The men may well have deserved some sort of punishment, but in the heat of the moment they were denied a proper trial and in essence were executed by what was basically a lynching. Incidents such as this lent credence to another charge leveled against democracy—that it amounted to mob rule in which the people sank to the lowest common denominator of the group and were prone to arbitrary and rash actions.

In addition to the kinds of potential structural flaw already described, it is clear that the ancient Athenian democracy was not immune from political corruption and greedy or unscrupulous people who were able to cheat the system. Bribery, for example, was a serious problem, and politicians frequently exchanged allegations of having accepted bribes in return for advocating various policies. One of the most explosive of such accusations was to claim that a man was accepting money from a foreign state whose interests might be contrary to the good of Athens, which does seem to have happened regularly. Again, this is reminiscent of modern debates over the role that money-rich special interest groups and lobbyists should play in politics and in crafting laws.

From Watergate to more recent attempts to manipulate elections, dishonest politicians and their adherents have been all too prevalent. In addition to literary sources that give us accounts of ancient political corruption, there is also archaeological evidence for a unique sort of election-manipulation in ancient Athens. This evidence concerns a special type of election known as an ostracism. This was actually a kind of anti-election. Once a year, Athenians could vote, not for someone they liked, but instead for the person whom they hated the most. If more than 6,000 votes in total were cast, the person who got the most votes would be banished from Athens for 10 years. If he returned before the 10 years were up, he would be killed, but at the end of that time, he could come back and resume full rights as a citizen. The name derives from the fact that, to cast their votes, the Athenians used broken bits of pottery onto which they scratched the name of the person they wanted to be ostracized. Such a piece of broken pottery was called an *ostrakon*.

We know quite a bit about whom the Athenians disliked, since pottery is more or less indestructible, and after an ostracism they simply took all the *ostraka* and dumped them in a hole in the ground, enabling archaeologists to dig them up later. An interesting thing was noticed when these *ostraka* were analyzed. Often, a number of *ostraka* from the same ostracism were written in the same handwriting. What might we conclude from this evidence? Well, a

Figure 4.3 *Ostrakon from the Athenian agora. This object represents the vote of a citizen who wished to have the Athenian statesman, Kimon, the son of Miltiades, expelled from Athens for 10 years.*

positive-minded interpretation might be that not everyone could write, and so perhaps literate people were helping out their illiterate fellow citizens. A more cynical reading is that someone was attempting to stuff the ballot box with a bunch of false votes. Unfortunately, since the *ostraka* in the same handwriting usually all name the same individual, this second interpretation seems to be the correct one. Thus, even at the dawn of democracy, there was already political corruption.

In the end, it is truly remarkable that the Greeks were able to identify, so clearly and so quickly, the full range of both positive and negative tendencies inherent in the new form of government that they had developed.

Government by representation: The Roman Republic

While we in the United States like to think of ourselves as a democracy, we are not truly a pure direct democracy like ancient Athens, where ordinary citizens personally voted on important laws and policies, and where they were chosen randomly to fill key government positions. Instead, we are a representative democracy, in which we elect a set of politicians who, in turn, vote for us regarding important pieces of legislation. This sort of governmental structure, and in particular the version practiced by the United States, is directly based on that of another ancient Mediterranean society: the Roman Republic. Like the Roman Republic, the United States' form of government features elected representatives, is shaped around a series of elected offices, includes a senate, and employs a system of checks and balances among three branches. Later, we will look at the relationship of the Founding Fathers to classical antiquity and see exactly where they got their ideas from, but first let's examine the basic structural elements of the Roman Republic that continue to be imitated in one form or another today.

For the first couple hundreds of years of its existence, Rome was a monarchy. Often, these kings were not even native Romans, but rather were imposed by Rome's more powerful neighbors, the Etruscans. In 509 B.C. there was a rebellion, and Rome expelled the kings and established the Roman Republic. According to legend, what finally drove the Romans to revolt was a case of sexual assault: the king's brother raped a respectable Roman matron, Lucretia, who committed suicide as a result. This incident sparked an uprising against the king and his family by the outraged Romans. Thus, in an interesting parallel, it was acts of sexual harassment that prompted the birth of the two extremely influential types of government—the Athenian democracy and the Roman Republic—which have endured from the classical world into the modern one.

It took several centuries for the fledgling Republican government to gradually develop into its final form, but ultimately the main feature of the political system of the Roman Republic was a series of elected magistracies. Each of these offices had a number of things in common: they were filled through the process of all Roman citizens directly casting votes for each office; each had a minimum age requirement; each office was held for only one year; each office was collegial (meaning that more than one person was elected to the same title or position); and the more important the office, the fewer the number of people who held that office each year. The very topmost post in the government, roughly equivalent to President, was the consul, but, in keeping with the principle of collegiality, the Romans elected not one, but two, consuls each year. This ladder of elected officials can be thought of as the equivalent of the executive branch of government.

After a Roman had held any of these offices at least once, he automatically became a member of the Roman senate. Membership in the senate was for life, and senators would often go on to hold higher elected offices in the government once they reached the necessary minimum age. The senate served as a site for debate about government policy, it crafted proposals for legislation, and it served as an advisory body. Since it tended to include the wealthiest, most prominent men in the state, it had enormous prestige and exercised great informal influence in addition to its formal powers.

Finally, there were the Roman citizens themselves. They were always a tiny minority of the total populace. It is estimated that there were around 1 million citizens in the late Republic, and during the early Empire, when there were perhaps 50 million people living in the entire Roman Empire, there were only about 6 million citizens. As in Athens, to even be considered for citizenship, you had to be a free adult male, and then you either had to be the son of a citizen or else to have been granted citizenship. A big change came in A.D. 212, when the Emperor Caracalla declared that all free (male) inhabitants of the Empire were citizens. One of the main privileges of citizenship was being able to vote, and citizens voted both to elect government officials and to pass proposed legislation. When Roman citizens actually cast votes, depending on what sort of election it was (whether to elect various officials or to pass legislation), the citizens were divided up into groups, called assemblies, based on characteristics such as geographic origin or net worth.

This all sounds nice and democratic, but even though each citizen cast one vote, the assembly system had the practical effect of weighting some people's votes more than others. For example, in one assembly called the Tribal Assembly, all citizens were assigned to one of 35 tribes based on their place of geographic origin. In the actual election, each tribe collectively had one vote. Therefore, there was a total of 35 votes in the election. To determine how a tribe would cast its vote, the members of each tribe voted among themselves, and whatever the majority of the members decided, that was how the tribe's vote was cast. Thus, the system was similar to the electoral college system used in presidential elections in the U.S., whereby all the electoral votes of a particular state are given to just one presidential candidate. The Roman process at first glance seems democratic, but the system really favored the rich. Elections were held at Rome, and you had to be physically present to cast a vote. There were no absentee ballots, and everyone voted in one place. Therefore, if you wanted to vote, you had to travel to Rome, which required time and money, something only the rich had. Thus, unless you were a poor person who happened to live in or near Rome, you probably never actually got to vote.

If you find standing in long lines waiting to vote inconvenient, consider the Roman procedure: on the big day itself, everyone would show up at a huge field just outside the city limits called the Campus Martius. On this field were constructed long enclosures made of wood and ropes similar to cattle pens, or to the roped-off areas used to hold crowds waiting for rides at amusement parks such as Disney World. The apt Roman slang term for this was "the sheep pen." One of these enclosures, which has been reconstructed by archaeologists, measures about 300 feet wide and 1,000 feet long, contains 35 separate aisles for the 35 tribes, and is estimated to have been able to accommodate about 75,000 voters at one time.

The candidates would appear dressed in special unusually white togas produced by bleaching them and smearing them with lime. This stiff, spotless toga was called the *toga candida*. *Candida* in Latin means "shining white," and it is from this origin that we get our word "candidate"—even though modern politicians no longer wear togas while campaigning. Each voter was handed a small wax tablet like the ones used in schools. If it was an election for a candidate, they scratched the initials of their choice onto the tablet and then dropped it into an urn. If they were voting for a law, if they wanted to vote to pass the legislation, they scratched a V. This stood for *uti rogas*, meaning "As you have asked." If they wanted to vote against the proposal, they put an A for *antiquo*, meaning "Keep things as they have always been." Roman juries used a similar voting system: at a trial, if they wanted to acquit the defendant, they put an L for *libero*, meaning "I free him." If they thought he was guilty, they put a D for *damno*, meaning what it sounds like.

With the whole process of filing around through the pens, waiting to vote, and then counting the ballots, elections often lasted the entire day—another reason why the working poor were not able to vote much. After you had cast your vote, you were not allowed to leave the rope enclosure until everyone had voted to make sure that no one voted twice. Several hundred officials patrolled the area and handled the tablets in an effort to prevent cheating. Despite this, cheating and dishonesty were rampant, and in one celebrated instance several thousand tablets with the letters written in the same handwriting were found in the urns.

Politicians who wished to be elected relied on many strategies to win over the voters. One of the best accounts of this comes from a letter describing some of the tactics used by aspiring Roman candidates. Its advice is as relevant today as when it was written. Among the ploys that it suggests are to marshal and organize support among your circle of friends, relatives, and clients, to befriend and toady to influential people, to travel around to various towns campaigning and meeting voters personally, to arrange to be surrounded by a crowd of admirers whenever you appear in public, and to ingratiate yourself with those more powerful than you. Other recommended actions were to try to remember the names of as many people as possible (one type of slave commonly owned by politicians was a *nomenclator*, whose sole duty was to memorize the names of people so that the candidate could greet them by name), and to make lavish promises to the voters about what you would do for them. The letter cynically notes that you don't need to worry about actually being able to fulfill any of these promises once in office—only about getting elected. Finally, it urges politicians to always try to appear honest and moral (although, once again, it doesn't matter whether you really are this way; the only thing that counts is the image that you project to the voters).

Today, campaigning politicians deluge voters with television ads, stick signs with their names on everyone's lawn, and give their supporters bumper stickers to put on their cars. In ancient Rome, political advertising was no less visible: politicians and their advocates covered the walls with political graffiti and slogans. Over 1,500 instances of graffiti concerning political campaigns have been preserved on the walls of Pompeii, and these offer a glimpse into the workings of Roman politics at the local level. Candidates or their backers hired professional graffiti painters to cover the walls with slogans praising a candidate's virtues or urging citizens to vote for him: "If honest living is thought to be any recommendation, then Lucretius Fronto is worthy of being elected" (*CIL* 4.6626). One sign promises that, if put in office, one candidate will safeguard the treasury (*CIL* 3702), while another, written by a practical-minded person, exhorts: "Elect Gaius Julius Polybius to the office of *aedile*. He provides good bread" (*CIL* 4.429). These are reminiscent of the generic sort of laudatory TV ads that proliferate around election time. In the same way that modern politicians will target certain groups that they think likely to support them, such ads can be found in Pompeii as well: "Innkeepers, make Sallustius Capito *aedile*" (*CIL* 4.336). One effective strategy is the personal endorsement; thus, some graffiti offer recommendations of candidates by individuals or groups, such as "Magonius supports Cuspius Pansa for *aedile*" (*CIL* 4.579) and "The neighbors of Marcus Lucretius Fronto urge you to elect him to the office of *aedile*" (*CIL* 4.6625).

Today, one of the most heated issues relating to the political process is the perceived excessive influence of special interest groups, but, once again, this is nothing new. The most common type of Roman electoral graffiti expressed the endorsement of candidates by ancient special interest groups. Frequently, these were associations composed of people who shared the same profession: "The chicken vendors request that you elect Epidius and Suettius as *duovirs*" (*CIL* 4.6426), and "All the mule drivers request that you elect Gaius Julius Polybius to the office of *duovir*" (*CIL* 4.113). Among groups expressing various political opinions were the fruit-vendors, grape-pickers, fishermen, farmers, goldsmiths, carpenters, cloth-dyers, fullers, perfume-makers, millers, bakers, barbers, and porters. There is also an endorsement of a candidate by the members of a religious cult: "As a group, the worshipers of Isis demand the election of Gnaeus Helvius Sabinus as *aedile*" (*CIL* 4.787).

Pompeii's electoral graffiti even supply a glimpse of the dirty tactics that some politicians might employ. Victory in many recent elections has been attributed to the use of negative ads that attack one's opponents, and it seems that one strategy in ancient Rome was to slander your opponent by putting up graffiti that appeared to offer endorsements of him by undesirable groups. The opponents of a man named Vatia appear to have been particularly fond of this tactic, and painted a number of such notices, including: "The petty thieves ask you to elect Vatia as *aedile*," "The late sleepers ask you to elect Vatia as *aedile*," and "All the heavy drinkers ask you to elect Marcus Cerrinius Vatia *aedile*" (*CIL* 4.581, 576, 575).

Finally, one method of swaying voters has always been effective, if dishonest; you can simply bribe people to vote for you. Roman politicians did not hesitate to hand out cash to prospective voters, or to use slightly more indirect bribes, such as holding massive public feasts and giving out lavish gifts.

We have already seen how a number of words relating to politics, such as "candidate" and "senate," come from Latin, but there are many more, and often the origins of these words reveal something interesting about their meaning. For example, "inaugurate" comes from the Latin *inaugurare*, "to install in office"; but the original literal meaning of *inaugurare* was "to foretell the future from the flight of birds." This was because the Romans thought that, before placing any officials in office, it was necessary to make sure that the portents and omens from the gods were favorable, and one of the main ways in which the Romans divined the will of the gods was by observing the flight and feeding patterns of birds. Today, "plebiscite" is a fancy word for a bill voted on by the people, but it is derived from the Latin *plebs*, an often somewhat pejorative term for the common people. Even the word "republic," proudly used by both the Romans and ourselves as a label for our countries and their forms of government, is a compound of two Latin words: *res*, meaning "thing," and *publica*, meaning "public." Thus, the much honored and venerated term, "The Republic," has a rather more humble-sounding literal meaning of simply "the public thing."

Looking backwards to go forwards: The Founding Fathers and Classical Antiquity

The Founding Fathers of the United States were utterly steeped in classical culture by virtue of the classically-focused education that they had received. Therefore, they constantly looked to the ancient Greeks and Romans for their role models, and they were obsessed with the idea that they were following directly in their heroes' footsteps as they set about establishing their modern version of an ancient republic. As noted by the historian Carl Richard, it is little wonder that they labeled their legislative building "the Capitol," that they formed a "senate," that they co-opted the Roman eagle as their national symbol, and that they slathered Latin phrases all over their national emblems and currency (Richard, 1994: p. 50). To give just a few examples of the Founders' deep engagement with the classical world: Thomas Jefferson never went anywhere without his Greek grammar book; John Adams turned to reading Cicero as a refuge whenever he needed calming down; George Washington saw himself as a modern incarnation of Cato and, when his troops became disheartened at Valley Forge, decided that the best way to raise their spirits was to stage a play about his idol; Alexander Hamilton wrote essays under the pseudonyms Phocion, Publius, Tully, Metellus, Horatius, Camillus, and Pericles; John Witherspoon named his house "Tusculum" after the location of Cicero's villa; James Warren chose to deliver a speech commemorating the Boston Massacre while wearing a toga; and when Jefferson's wife died, the epitaph he chose for her tombstone was two lines from Homer's *Iliad*.

The source of the Founders' preoccupation with antiquity can be found in the educational system of the time. Eighteenth-century education focused almost entirely on ancient history and languages. For those who received it, elementary education consisted primarily of learning to read and write Greek and Latin and reading, memorizing, and studying classical authors such as Homer, Virgil, Cicero, Plutarch, Xenophon, Demosthenes, Livy, and Tacitus. A typical schoolday featured a strict regime of grammar drills and translation exercises from 8:00 to 11:00 in the morning and then again from 1:00 in the afternoon until dusk. Students were expected not only to be able to translate Greek and Latin passages into English, but also English to Greek and Latin, and even Greek into Latin. If a boy did not naturally take to such intensive language study, he was encouraged by liberal use of the rod.

The moralizing stories of Plutarch, Livy, and Herodotus provided a rich array of heroes and villains from which the boys took role models to emulate and negative examples to shun. It was generally believed that a classical course of education instilled not just knowledge about the past but, more importantly, a set of positive moral virtues. As John Adams explained to his son John Quincy Adams: "In company with Sallust, Cicero, Tacitus, and Livy, you will learn Wisdom and Virtue ... You will remember that all the End of study is to make you a good Man and a useful Citizen" (cited in Richard, 1994: p. 37). For those who moved on to higher education, the main admission requirement for colleges was the ability to read and write Greek and Latin. Once at a university, little about the course of study changed from one's earlier years of education, and most institutions required at least four more years of Latin and two more of Greek for all students.

The bestselling biography of George Washington by Parson Weems, first published in 1800, nicely encapsulates the range of classical references with which educated readers of the time were expected to be familiar. Weems characterizes Washington as being "pious as Numa, just as Aristides, temperate as Epictetus, and patriotic as Regulus ... impartial as Severus, in victory, modest as Scipio, prudent as Fabius, rapid as Marcellus, undaunted as Hannibal, as Cincinnatus disinterested, to liberty firm as Cato, and respectful of the law as Socrates."

Despite the compulsory nature of the educational system's classical curriculum, a surprising number of the Founding Fathers seem to have come away from it with a deep and sincere love for classical civilization, which functioned as a common cultural touchstone for the educated classes. Thomas Jefferson recalled how at William and Mary he immersed himself in the world of the ancients, studying 15 hours a day, and he was by no means unique in his devotion. Another measure of the depth of the influence exerted by this classical educational regimen can be traced in the notebooks of hand-copied quotations that it was customary for educated gentlemen of the day to keep. Filled with lines that they found inspiring or relevant to their own lives, such items, known as "commonplace books," are a good measure of the key intellectual influences on many figures of the time. As one might expect, their commonplace books were heavily weighted towards classical authors. Fully 40 percent of Jefferson's book consisted of quotations from classical authors—more even than from the Bible. Such quotations frequently found their way into the speeches, essays, and letters that they wrote. To use Jefferson as an example again, he sprinkled quotations in ancient Greek throughout his letters so copiously that John Adams, despite his own love of the classics, was driven to complain about it.

Admittedly, even among the Founders, Jefferson's passion for antiquity was notable, and it also exercised a wide-reaching influence. It was Jefferson's infatuation with Roman architecture that helps to account for the dominant Neoclassical style of many government buildings. As an active architect, he designed a number of prominent structures that directly imitated Roman models. The library at the University of Virginia is a near-exact copy of the Pantheon at Rome, and he based some of his other buildings on the Temple of Nerva Trajan and the Theater of Marcellus. His home, Monticello, has not only the style, but also many of the exact features, of a Roman villa. One particular inspiration seems to have been Pliny the Younger, who famously described the amenities of his villa in one of his letters. Among the elements that Jefferson copied from Pliny were porticos, underground passageways, the garden layout, brick-lined fish ponds, and even a type of birdhouse with a weather vane that could be rotated from inside the house. Structures planned by Jefferson but never completed included a Greek temple, statues of urns and nymphs, and, most amazing of all, a Roman-style triumphal column that would have been even larger than Trajan's famous 100-foot-high triumphal column. As if all this were not enough, Jefferson named his horses Tarquin, Diomede, Castor, Celer, and Arcturus.

In a very real sense, the intellectual world in which these men lived was one in which the figures and situations of the classical past were still vibrantly alive and fully as important, if not even more so, than contemporary events. Jefferson once commented that he preferred to read ancient authors rather than current newspapers because the occurrences of 2,000 years ago held greater interest for him. Nevertheless, the Founders were quick to apply the apparent lessons of the past to their own times. They interpreted much of ancient history as a story of heroic resistance against tyranny, and this framework had an urgent contemporary resonance in light of their ongoing struggle against what they perceived as the tyranny of the British monarchy. Their own attempt to establish a republic based on principles of liberty enabled them to live out their fantasies of emulating their childhood role models, and again and again they turned to ancient examples for inspiration. For them, the ancient past was directly relevant to the unfolding present. Concerning reading ancient authors, John Adams stated, "When I read them I seem to be only reading the

History of my own Times and my own Life," and "I seem to read the history of all ages and nations in every page, and especially the history of our country for forty years past. Change the names and every anecdote will be applicable to us" (cited in Richard, 1994: pp. 87 and 84).

In fashioning their new version of a representative democracy, the Founders looked to ancient authors for guidance regarding the key structures that would make it up. Several of the most important ideas they took from the Roman model were to divide power among different branches of government and to arrange those branches so that they created a system of checks and balances among them. A crucial passage inspiring their decisions was a famous section of the Greek writer Polybius' *History of Rome*, in which he analyzed the structure of the Roman constitution and determined that much of Rome's success stemmed from the way it distributed power. According to Polybius, the strength of the Roman Republic was based on the fact that "The Roman government has three branches, each of them possessing sovereign powers … and each of these several parts can, when they choose, oppose or support each other. The result of this power of the several divisions for mutual help or harm is a union that can survive any challenge, and a constitution that cannot be improved upon. For when any one of the three branches becomes overweening, and shows a tendency to be contentious and encroach upon the others, the mutual interdependency of all the three, and the possibility of the pretensions of any one being checked and thwarted by the others, must plainly quell this tendency. Thus, the proper equilibrium is maintained." (*History of Rome* 6.18). The influence of this well-known passage on the Founders and the structure of American government is obvious.

Another key concept that the Founders took from the Roman Republic was the ideal of the citizen/farmer/soldier. The first component of this identity is the farmer, and the Romans idealized farming as the most noble of all professions. They believed that many of the positive virtues of their citizenry were derived from values that naturally came from cultivating the soil. Farmers lived close to nature, and, through their own labor, produced the most basic necessity for life—food. They were self-sufficient and did not have to rely on others for survival. Farmers were regarded as being tough, frugal, practical, hard-working, and honest. In this ideology, farmers were content with their simple but virtuous lives and did not crave luxuries or celebrity. In contrast, the Romans thought that any sort of profession for which you were paid a wage or salary was inherently demeaning because you were selling yourself for the gratification of others and thus were reduced to a status similar to that of a slave. Any job that involved buying or selling goods or charging interest by definition involved deceit, and therefore was morally degrading. All other professions were parasitic to varying degrees, since their practitioners subsisted upon the food produced by farmers. As a result, only farming was considered a pure profession; thus, throughout Roman history, all politicians, if asked what their job was, would inevitably claim that they were just simple farmers, even if they rarely (or never) actually set foot on their farms.

The second element in the farmer/citizen/soldier formula, the citizen, was another identity that was extremely important to the Romans. They were very conscious of the fact that their Republic was a form of government that depended on their active involvement through voting and service in government offices. Being a citizen also carried with it important rights; indeed, one of the most powerful statements that one could make in the Roman world was *Civis Romanus sum*, meaning "I am a Roman citizen," since such a declaration immediately conferred significant legal rights and social status.

Finally, one of the duties of the citizen, at least during the earlier stages of Roman history, was to fight for his country in the army. Before Rome's army became professionalized, campaigning was often seasonal, so it was possible for men to farm most of the year while also serving in the military for brief periods. Many of the same positive stereotypes associated with farming, such as toughness, practicality, physical stamina, and strength, were obviously valuable in a military context as well, so good farmers were logically enough thought to make good soldiers.

The ideal of the citizen/soldier/farmer was a legendary figure named Cincinnatus. He was a retired general who lived on a tiny farm, tilling the soil, in the fifth century B.C. At this time, Rome had only recently overthrown its monarchy and become a republic. The experience of living under kings had left the Romans with a deep-seated hatred of any one man having absolute power, and under the new political system they went to great lengths to spread political authority among a variety of individuals and institutions. However, the Romans were a very practical people, so, despite their hatred of kings, they realized that in moments of extreme danger when the state itself was threatened with complete destruction it was sometimes necessary to put a single person with absolute power in charge in order to enable swift and decisive action. When such a person was appointed, he was called a dictator, and his appointment was strictly limited to no longer than six months.

In the Roman historian Livy's account of Cincinnatus, an enemy force had invaded Roman territory and succeeded in trapping the Roman army. The capture of the army would result in the destruction of the Roman state, so in this time of emergency the senate determined that a dictator was needed. They selected the retired general Cincinnatus, and a delegation of the senate was sent to inform him. They found the old warrior hard at work digging in a ditch on his modest three-acre farm. Cincinnatus put on his toga, accepted the appointment to the dictatorship, and quickly organized the Roman defenses. Through a series of brilliant maneuvers he completely defeated the enemy and rescued the surrounded Roman army. Although Cincinnatus had been granted the dictatorship for a period of six months, he immediately resigned from the post after holding it for only 16 days, and returned to his tiny farm (*History of Rome* 3.26–9).

This story illustrates the standard Roman themes of service to your country and placing the good of the state above your own. But the key moment in this story comes at the very end, and illustrates a different concept. After winning his victory and saving the state, Cincinnatus was beloved by everyone and at the height of his popularity. Not only was he the object of universal adulation; he was also still dictator, and thus possessed absolute power over the Roman state and everything and everyone in it. One might naturally assume that this would be the sort of position most people would aspire to and would want to savor as long as possible—loved by all and wielding total power. Cincinnatus, however, chose to defy this expectation, and instead of enjoying the power and fame that he had, after all, deservedly won through his own talent and efforts, he voluntarily resigned from the dictatorship and returned to laboring on his modest little farm.

Why would he give up fame, power, and fortune in exchange for obscurity, poverty, and hard work? The main answer, of course, is that he exemplifies the Roman Republican attitude of being uncomfortable with one person having too much political authority, even if that one man is oneself. The Romans were correct to try to curb the ambitions of prominent politicians since, in the end, the Republic did indeed collapse when they gained too much influence and power. Both for the Romans and for later civilizations, Cincinnatus became the paradigm for a type of altruistic behavior that was perhaps more ideal than reality—that talented individuals should use their gifts for the benefit and glory of the state, but not seek reward or fame for themselves.

Thus, the perfect Roman was a man like Cincinnatus: in times of peace, a hard-working, self-sufficient farmer; in times of war, a tough and hardened soldier; and at all times, an honest and engaged citizen. How much or how often reality differed from this ideal is less significant than the fact that the ideal existed, and that men like Cincinnatus were constantly being cited as role models to be emulated. Whether or not the majority of Romans really were simple farmer/citizen/soldiers, it is how they envisioned themselves and the standard to which they aspired. The Founders were equally obsessed with the story of Cincinnatus and the ideal of the citizen/farmer/soldier. They saw the largely agrarian fledgling United States as a reborn version of the old Roman Republic populated by simple but virtuous small family farmers. The idea, famously incorporated into the Constitution, of a "well-regulated militia" of citizens stems from the desire to imitate the supposed citizen armies of ancient Rome. In fact, this is something of a misunderstanding of history, since Rome's army could only be considered a citizen militia in its early phases. In the period when it actually conquered the Mediterranean, the Roman army was an entirely professional force of soldiers for whom war was their full-time job.

At the end of the Revolutionary War, the United States actually found itself a true Cincinnatus. At that point, George Washington found himself in a situation quite similar to that of Cincinnatus. Having unexpectedly won the war against the British, he was in charge of the military and extremely popular. He could have seized power and perhaps even made himself king of the new country, and there were many who both urged and expected him to do so. Instead, like Cincinnatus, he resigned from his position as commander-in-chief and returned to his Mount Vernon farm. For this selfless action, he became universally known as "the American Cincinnatus." Numerous poems and essays hailed his emulation of his antique model, and Lord Byron even referred to Washington in his "Ode to Napoleon" as "the Cincinnatus of the West."

A not inconsiderable part of Washington's fame at the time derived not so much from his military leadership as from his voluntary surrender of power. This was seen as a far rarer quality than being a good general. Washington himself seemed to enjoy this identification with Cincinnatus, and cultivated their similarities. After resigning from the army and withdrawing from public life completely, in letters dating to 1784 he calls Mount Vernon his "villa" and refers to himself as "a private citizen of America, on the banks of the Patowmac ... under my Vine and my own Fig-tree, free from the bustle of a camp and the intrigues of a court" (cited in Richard, 1994 p. 72).

One final way in which the cautionary tale of Cincinnatus influenced the Founders was to make them firm advocates of term limits for Presidents. In this, they again copied the magistrates and dictators of ancient Rome, whose exercise of absolute power was restricted by short terms in office.

The Founders occasionally looked beyond democratic Athens and Republican Rome for ancient models. With rather more idealism than accuracy, Samuel Adams once expressed the hope that Boston would become a Christian Sparta—characterized by "frugality, selflessness, valor, and patriotism" (cited in Richard, 1994 p. 73). Molded by their educations and inspired with the belief that they were both reliving and improving upon history, the Founding Fathers of the United States collectively were one of the most striking and prominent examples of a group constantly influenced and guided by classical models.

The Empire strikes back: Another Roman model of government

Although this chapter has focused on the democratic legacy of the ancient world, the classical world has also provided the inspiration for several other important types of government. Of these, probably the most significant is the way in which the Roman Empire, a vast political entity that was acquired by violent military conquest and ruled over by totalitarian emperors, has exerted a constant fascination upon later imperialistic empires and ambitious leaders. The Roman Empire would serve as the model for a long chain of would-be emulators, from Charlemagne to Hitler.

The word "emperor" itself is derived from the Latin term *imperium*, which was the power wielded by Roman magistrates to enforce the laws of the state. It could also refer to the geographical territory within which that *imperium* could be applied. From this root arose the English words "emperor" and "empire." Many of the terms used for later rulers are directly derived from titles given to Roman magistrates or emperors. For example, one name or title adopted by almost all Roman emperors was Caesar. In Russia, a form of this term became the name for the ruler of that country, the Tsar (or Czar). In imperial Germany, it became the Kaiser. In other languages as diverse as Swedish, Polish, and Turkish, variants of Caesar are also used to denote rulers.

The immediate, obvious heir to Rome was the Byzantine Empire, the former Eastern Roman Empire, which regarded itself simply as the true Roman Empire. But many other post-classical states with dreams of conquering their neighbors and expanding their territory also looked to ancient Rome as a model and precursor. Imperial Russia not only named its leaders after Caesar, but explicitly identified itself as the "Third Rome," after the original Roman empire and the Byzantine empire. During much of the Middle Ages, the barbarian nations that dominated Europe often co-opted Roman titles and names in an attempt to enhance their glory by presenting themselves as successors to or revivals of the Roman Empire. The high point of the career of Charlemagne, the most successful early medieval ruler, was when the Pope crowned him on Christmas Day, A.D. 800, and bestowed upon him the title of "Charles Augustus, Emperor of the Romans." The fact that the most impressive title that a Christian Pope could think of to give a barbarian king was "Augustus, Emperor of the Romans" says much for the power that the memory of Rome still exerted. Similarly, throughout the Middle Ages and beyond, one of the most coveted titles that European rulers could aspire to be designated was "Holy Roman Emperor," another conflation of Roman, Christian, and barbarian cultures. This was such an honored appellation that there was a continuous succession of Holy Roman Emperors from the tenth century all the way up until 1806, when the last one was deposed by Napoleon.

Napoleon himself was obsessed with the model of Rome and the Roman Empire, and imitated it in a number of ways. When he initially seized power, the title that he took was "First Consul," a reference to the consuls, the highest magistrates in the Roman Republican government. Later, when he had dropped the pretense of Republicanism, he then styled himself Emperor Napoleon. Another famous borrowing by Napoleon from ancient Rome was his adoption of the legionary standards of the Roman army, which consisted of a golden eagle atop a pole, as the standards of his new French army, and Napoleon's eagles became one of the most visible and well-known emblems of his forces. Around the same time, the legionary eagles of Rome were also being imitated by another self-perceived revival of Rome, the fledgling United States, which made the bird its national symbol.

Figure 4.4 *Roman sculptural relief of an eagle clutching a thunderbolt. The eagle was used on Roman legionary standards, a practice imitated by later armies, including those of Napoleon and Hitler.*

The British Empire of the Victorian era also looked back to ancient Rome as a model, although in their case the Victorians tended to focus on the idealistic perception that, just as the Roman empire brought peace, law, Christianity, technology, and "civilization" to a multi-ethnic empire of "barbarians," so too Britain was bringing the supposed benefits of its "superior" culture to its own vast, multi-ethnic colonial empire. The aristocratic elites who supervised the running of the British Empire were the products of a school system that was almost entirely devoted to studying the classics of Greece and Rome, and they were keenly aware of the similarities between themselves and their ancient predecessors. Many were the Victorian soldiers or bureaucrats dispatched to regions such as the Near East whose concept of the peoples and geography of the area had been entirely shaped by what they had read in Homer, Herodotus, and Xenophon.

Figure 4.5 *Roman sculptural relief showing fasces. The fasces, a bundle of sticks wrapped around an ax, was an ancient Roman symbol of the authority of the state and its magistrates, and is the origin of the word "fascism."*

In the twentieth century, the Roman Empire proved irresistible as a model to fascist leaders and movements. Even the very term "fascism" is directly derived from ancient Rome. It was the custom for Roman magistrates always to be accompanied in public by attendants known as *lictors*. These attendants each carried a bundle of rods wrapped around an ax, which symbolized the magistrate's right and power to enforce the laws of the state by punishing those who broke them; he did this by ordering his *lictors* to beat offenders with the rods and cut off their heads with the ax. In Latin, the name for this bundle of rods wrapped around an ax was a *fasces*, and it is from this root, with its connotations of absolute power, that the English term "fascism" was coined.

Figure 4.6 *Mussolini's "Square Colosseum." This office building is part of the EUR complex erected by the fascist dictator just south of Rome, which was intended to serve as an administrative and cultural center for his new Roman Empire.*

Mussolini declared that his fascist Italian state was a direct revival of the Roman Empire, and that he himself was the heir to the Emperors. Accordingly, he announced that his state was the "Third" or "New" "Roman Empire," and he equipped his legions with by-now-familiar eagle standards. To stir up interest in ancient Rome and further strengthen the supposed links between ancient and contemporary Italy, Mussolini initiated a number of excavations of ancient Roman sites, although due to his eagerness to uncover spectacular ruins, the methods employed by his workers often destroyed more than they revealed. He also erected grandiose new sets of buildings that were intended as modern versions of ancient *fora* and temples, such as the structures at EUR, a government complex he built just south of Rome, which includes the infamous "Square Colosseum," a masterpiece (or nightmare, depending on one's taste) of 1930s fascist architecture.

Another example of his attempts to link his activities with ancient Rome is the adornments of the Foro Italico (originally known as the Foro Mussolini), a sports complex near the banks of the Tiber river. Decorating the concrete plazas that connect its various stadia and venues are black and white mosaics done in a style closely imitating that of mosaics found at Roman sites such as the Baths of Caracalla and Rome's port of Ostia. Instead of depictions of ancient athletes, however, these mosaics show modern Italian athletes engaged in contemporary sports such as basketball. Even more startling, some of these mosaics portray Italian soldiers wielding machine guns and packed into three-quarter-ton trucks as they invade Ethiopia, in celebration of Mussolini's conquest of that country. Others show blackshirts giving the fascist salute while aircraft fly overhead. The contrast between ancient style and modern subject matter is quite jarring.

Figure 4.7 *Mosaic from Mussolini's Foro Italico at Rome. These mosaics, executed in imitation Roman style, adorn the athletic complex erected along the Tiber river, but depict Italian soldiers performing the fascist salute and hailing Mussolini as "Duce" or "Leader."*

The other notable fascist regime of the 1930s was, of course, Nazi Germany. Hitler had dreams of creating a vast new empire and, like Mussolini, looked back to the Roman Empire for inspiration. Thus, it should not be surprising that Hitler also decided to place golden eagles on the standards of the military units in his army, and, just like the United States, chose the eagle as a governmental symbol. Through an ahistorical bit of wishful thinking, the Nazis even

Figure 4.8 *Mosaic from Mussolini's Foro Italico at Rome. This panel, again exactly imitating the style of ancient Roman mosaic work, shows Italian soldiers in machine-gun-equipped trucks invading Ethiopia as the first stage of carving out a new Roman empire.*

convinced themselves that they had some sort of "racial" connection with the ancient Greeks. As will be discussed in the next chapter, Hitler looked to ancient Rome for architectural inspiration, and either built or planned to build a number of monuments that either imitated Roman arches and temples or employed the classical style of architecture. Like America's Founding Fathers, Hitler believed that studying ancient Rome was a useful guide to the present; he even wrote in *Mein Kampf* that "Roman history ... is and remains the best instructor, not only for today, but for all times."

At first glance it might seem odd, or even contradictory, that people as enlightened as many of the Founding Fathers and as depraved as Adolf Hitler would both find inspiration in the political forms and symbols of classical antiquity. What this really demonstrates, however, is the complexity and the originality of the systems of government that the Greeks and Romans developed, and the influence that their political models have exerted over subsequent history.

5

Understanding and shaping the material world: Architecture and science

The two most influential buildings in the world

In terms of providing inspiration for later structures, it could be argued that the two most influential buildings in all of history are both Roman ones. Probably everyone reading this book has set foot in multiple modern structures that are direct imitations of these two Roman buildings. One of them is the original model for most large sports arenas found all over the world today, including every major football, soccer, and baseball stadium. The other is the basis for a staggering number of monumental public edifices, including countless city halls, libraries, state Capitols, courthouses, museums, cathedrals, public libraries, university buildings, and such disparate structures as the Jefferson Memorial in Washington, D.C., the Reading Room of the British Museum in London, St. Peter's Basilica in Rome, and the Grand Auditorium of Tsinghua University in Beijing. Can you guess yet what these two famous Roman buildings are? The answer is the Flavian Amphitheater (more popularly known as the Colosseum) and the Pantheon. As an introduction to the general architectural influence of the classical world upon the modern one, let us begin by focusing on just these two structures, and consider how their distinctive forms have inspired later generations.

While the Greeks built many theaters and stadiums that functioned as spaces where plays, athletic competitions, and other spectacles could be held, none of these featured spectator seating that fully encircled the performance area. A fully enclosed oval structure in which spectator seating completely surrounded a central performance space would not be realized until the Romans developed the amphitheater. In some sense, the Roman amphitheater was like two Greek theaters joined back to back, and indeed there is some evidence that the Romans may have built an experimental wooden structure consisting of two theaters that could be rotated and joined together. The earliest amphitheaters were temporary wooden structures; the oldest known stone amphitheater is the one located in the city of Pompeii on the Bay of Naples. The first permanent stone amphitheater at Rome was not built until 30 B.C., when one was constructed in the Campus Martius by a man named Statilius Taurus.

Of course, the largest and most famous amphitheater and the one that has inspired generations of later imitators is the one known today as the Colosseum. This is actually a later nickname that was applied to the building; its proper name is the Flavian Amphitheater because it was erected by the Flavian family of emperors in the late first century A.D. It is a marvel of clever engineering, which admirably serves the purpose of providing a structure that could be quickly and efficiently filled with a very large number of people and then offer them an excellent view of the entertainment.

To support the great weight of the Flavian Amphitheater, a vast area was excavated and concrete foundations were poured that reached an impressive 12 meters deep. The footprint of the building overall consists of a huge oval, 188 meters on the long axis and 156 meters wide. The dimensions of the arena, the space in which the entertainments were held, is 86 meters by 54 meters. In its final form, the exterior rose through four distinct levels. The bottom level was a continuous ring of 80 arches of the simple Tuscan order. On top of this was another colonnade of 80 arches of the Ionic order, and above this was yet a third level consisting of 80 more arches of the Corinthian order. The fourth level was a solid wall divided into shallow bays by Corinthian pilasters and topped by a large, ornate cornice. Every other bay had a square window, and mounted above the highest layer were 240 wooden posts or masts used to support a retractable cloth awning that could shade the spectators from sun or rain. The total height of the four levels of the exterior wall was 48.5 meters.

Figure 5.1 *The Flavian Amphitheater (The Colosseum). With its iconic arched façade, the Colosseum is one of the most recognizable buildings in the world.*

Figure 5.2 *Model of the Flavian Amphitheater. In this reconstruction, the similarity between this building and its many later imitators in the form of sports stadiums all around the world is instantly apparent.*

The whole edifice consisted of a concrete and brick core with a facing of tufa and Travertine stone. It has been estimated that over 100,000 tons of fine Travertine stone were used in the facing of the amphitheater. This covering was attached to the structure with iron clamps which themselves weighed around a total of 300 tons. Corresponding to the outer layers, there were four tiers of seats inside and a standing-room-only gallery at the highest level. Altogether, the Flavian Amphitheater could probably have accommodated about 55,000 spectators—about the same number as most of today's major stadiums.

Upon entering one of the 78 ground level entrances, each of which was marked by a Roman numeral, spectators made their way to their seats through an extraordinarily complex network of ramps, stairs, and corridors. Those destined for the upper levels used different corridors than those whose seating was in the lower sections. Some scholars have argued that this system of passages and stairs could have allowed the entire building to be filled and emptied very quickly. For anyone who has waited in endless lines to get into or out of a modern sports stadium that has only a few passages for entry and exit, such a prospect sounds delightful. Roman spectators appear to have been given tokens much like modern stadium tickets, which listed the numbers of their seat's gate, level, section, and row. The seating was arranged as a microcosm of Roman society, with the spectators seated according to their status. The emperor or the presiding magistrate, along with his coterie, was seated in a special box, and prime seats at the lowest level were reserved for other important figures, including the Vestal Virgins and senators. An analogy could be made to today's expensive VIP seating and luxury boxes. The seats immediately above were similarly set aside for those holding equestrian rank. Poorer citizens filled the upper tiers or stood in the gallery at the highest level. If they were admitted at all, women and slaves seem to have been relegated to the gallery.

Beneath the floor of the arena were two subterranean levels that contained cages for wild animals as well as rooms for gladiators and equipment. This underground maze also included an elaborate system of trapdoors and elevators which could be used to raise scenery up into the arena or, perhaps most spectacularly, to disgorge combatants or wild animals, which would seem to spring forth unexpectedly from the ground itself. The exact number and operation of these trapdoors and elevators are a matter of some scholarly debate, but there seem to have been at least 32 of them, and possibly many more. The much smaller amphitheater at Capua, for example, featured no fewer than 62 trapdoors and elevators of varying sizes. Just think of the excitement it would add to a modern baseball game if, at random moments, a hungry lion were to burst up from the field!

One of the unpleasant trials of attending an event in the Mediterranean can be the hot sun, but the Flavian Amphitheater even made provisions for this irritant. The 240 wooden masts on the top level were used to support a retractable cloth covering called the *velarium*. This could be deployed or pulled back as needed to provide shade for the spectators in various sections. Precisely how this enormous retractable roof was rigged is another hot topic of scholarly contention, but apparently a contingent of sailors was stationed in the city to operate the ropes and pulleys. This feature seems to have been included even on earlier versions of amphitheaters, since there is a reference to its abuse by the sadistic emperor Caligula, who delighted in locking the exits and pulling back the *velarium* on an especially hot day, causing audience members to faint from the heat. In recent decades, retractable roofs have become a much-vaunted feature of some high-tech football and baseball stadiums, but modern architects have nothing on the ancient Romans, who anticipated such an amenity 2,000 years earlier.

Today, probably every major city in the world has at least one sports or entertainment venue that recalls the design of the Flavian Amphitheater. As a testimony to the skill of the Romans who designed it, the Flavian Amphitheater still stands today, albeit in ruins, and continues to provide a model and inspiration for new generations of architects.

Let us now turn to the second hugely influential Roman building, the Pantheon. It is the best-preserved Roman structure and also one of the most remarkable. The term "pantheon" means "a temple to all the gods," and its design was nearly unique among Roman temples. Most Roman temples followed their Greek and Etruscan forebears in being rectangular and having columns across at least the front, and often around all sides. The building that you see today in Rome is actually not the original version of the Pantheon, which was built in 27 B.C. by a Roman general named Agrippa together with a number of other structures he erected in the Campus Martius. Agrippa's

Figure 5.3 *Front view of the Pantheon. From this angle, with its columned façade and triangular pediment, the building resembles a standard temple, but the just-visible top of the dome reveals its true innovative nature.*

Pantheon seems to have been a fairly conventional rectangular temple, the foundations of which have been discovered several meters beneath the current building. This first Pantheon was damaged and restored several times, but then was entirely rebuilt on a new and much grander scale by the emperor Hadrian at the beginning of the second century A.D. The Hadrianic version of the building, which was revolutionary in design, is the one still standing today.

When viewed from the front, Hadrian's Pantheon at first looks entirely conventional in appearance. There is a podium (or platform) with steps leading up to a porch with several rows of columns. Above this is a typical triangular pediment. Hadrian even kept the original inscription so that, although this building has almost nothing to do with Agrippa's, the inscription emblazoned in giant letters just below the pediment still reads "M. AGRIPPA LF COS TERTIUM FECIT." ("Marcus Agrippa, the son of Lucius, consul 3 times, built it.") The only odd feature apparent from the front is that the pediment is unusually high in proportion to its width.

After entering through a set of massive bronze doors, one would expect to find oneself inside the usual cramped and dark rectangular temple interior. Instead, visitors to the Pantheon step into an enormous circular space some 43 meters wide. Even more astonishing, overhead, there is a colossal dome of equal height. The dome itself is a perfect half-circle, so that a sphere of the same diameter would exactly fit within the structure. The only source of light is a circular opening in the top of the dome 9 meters in diameter called the *oculus* (Latin for "eye"), which creates a dramatic circular shaft of light that moves around the interior over the course of the day. When looking upwards at the dome, you can see that it is divided horizontally into five rows of square indentations called coffers. These are scaled down in size as they go higher so that each level contains 28 of them, and they provide a pleasing grid-like frame that draws the eye upwards toward the *oculus*. The interior of the Pantheon is a truly stunning space. To suddenly find yourself within its vast circular expanse with the mighty dome soaring overhead is awe-inspiring, yet touches such as its graceful proportions and the clouds and sky visible through the *oculus* render the overall effect uplifting rather than ponderous.

Figure 5.4 *Model of the Pantheon. The size of the hidden drum supporting the immense concrete dome of the Pantheon is revealed in this side view.*

Figure 5.5 *Interior view of the Pantheon's dome. This view highlights the coffered ceiling panels and the opening of the oculus at the apex of the dome. The circle of light from the oculus moves around the interior over the course of a day.*

Even today, the Pantheon still possesses the largest unreinforced concrete dome in the world. Its dome is wider than those of the Capitol Building in Washington, D.C., the Hagia Sophia in Istanbul, and St. Peter's Basilica in the Vatican. The engineering of this marvel is particularly impressive. One secret is that the architects employed a wide range of materials so that the lower levels are constructed of thick, dense substances best able to bear the weight of the dome, while the materials grow increasingly lighter at progressively higher levels of the structure. The lowest sections are composed of solid stone (travertine and tufa), but this gives way to tufa and brick, and then just brick, at the middle levels, while the dome itself is of concrete with a light volcanic stone called pumice mixed in. The concrete of the dome itself steadily narrows in thickness from about 6 meters at the top of the drum that supports it to only 1.5 meters at the *oculus*. Thus, it is made out of lighter materials in the places where having less weight is advantageous, and heavier ones where they are needed to support the structure's weight. The Pantheon also employs other tricks, such as brick relieving arches originally hidden behind marble facing that directed the mighty weight of the dome onto massive piers connected to the foundations. The whole thing was so well made that, despite having to support such a huge expanse of roof without any internal struts, it stands intact today, some 2,000 years later. One reason for the Pantheon's survival was its reconsecration as a Christian church in A.D. 608, and for a while it even sported two rather unsightly bell-towers that were known by the derisive nickname "the ass's ears," and that were not removed until the late 1800s.

The Pantheon is arguably one of the most influential buildings of all time. Its basic formula of a rectangular columned façade surmounted by a triangular pediment fronting a huge dome and a circular internal space has become a stock design for innumerable buildings, especially those associated with large institutions such as the government, banks, and universities. Nearly every state Capitol building in the United States, including famous ones such as the Texas State Capitol in Austin, the Wisconsin State Capitol in Madison, and the California State Capitol in Sacramento, directly imitates the Pantheon. The basic architectural design of a temple façade backed by a dome can also be seen in the United States Capitol Building in Washington, D.C. and in innumerable churches, foremost among these being St. Peter's Basilica in Rome. Thousands of courthouses, libraries, and museums (such as the National Gallery in Washington, D.C. and the Reading Room of the British Museum) have copied this architectural model. While all of these buildings emulate the Pantheon's basic design, more exact models that almost exactly replicate the Pantheon also abound, including the Jefferson Memorial, the Grand Auditorium of Tsinghua University in Beijing, the Rotunda at the University of Virginia, and the Pantheon in Paris.

Given the admiration for the Roman Republic felt by the Founding Fathers of the United States, it is perhaps not surprising to find so many American government buildings that copy the Pantheon, but political leaders of all stripes have been drawn to its form. One of Adolf Hitler's unfulfilled plans was to construct the Volkshalle, an outrageously gigantic version of the Pantheon, in Berlin, which would boast a dome a fantastic 250 meters in diameter, or about six times that of its Roman inspiration. Just the *oculus* of this monstrosity would have been wider than the original Pantheon's entire dome.

Mapping where we live: City planning

While the Flavian Amphitheater and the Pantheon have exerted a particularly strong and direct influence over later buildings, classical antiquity provided the models for many other modern structures as well as for the ways in which these structures interact with one another and are arranged in relationship to one another. In fact, the whole concept of city planning originated with the Greeks and Romans.

The Greek word for city-state, *polis*, still lives in our language today as a root in words such as "politics" and "metropolis," and their developments in the field of city planning continue to influence us. One obvious pattern of city growth is organic, which can lead to a confusing accretion of winding streets and narrow alleys. Somewhat ironically, the great metropolises of ancient Rome and Athens were both examples of cities that developed organically, and as a result, both suffered from congestion in the streets. Another strategy, however, is to plan a city in a methodical fashion, following certain conventions. The era of Greek colonization, during which mother cities sent out bands of settlers to found colonies overseas, offered many opportunities to build cities from scratch. The "grid-iron" or "chessboard" plan, in which straight streets cross one another at right angles, probably arose on the west coast of Asia Minor in a Greek region known as Ionia. Hippodamos, a native of the Ionian city of Miletos during the fifth century B.C., was for a long time traditionally credited as the inventor of city planning; although this is now disputed, the ancient Greek grid pattern for cities is often still referred to as the "Hippodamian" plan. A shadowy figure, of whom little is definitely known, he is described as a long-haired dandy by Aristotle (*Politics* 2.5.1).

Whoever the originator of the principles of Greek urban planning actually was, the characteristics of this approach can be seen in various Greek colonies and cities. After its rebuilding in the fifth century B.C., Miletos itself was a model of order, with broad streets intersecting at right angles. Major streets were connected to the gates in the city walls. Greek cities were almost always built around a central open area known as the *agora*. This multi-purpose space could function as a marketplace, a site for political assemblies and speeches, a place for voting, a location where law cases could be heard, an arena for contests and spectacles, and simply a setting where citizens could congregate and exchange ideas, goods, and conversation. The *agora* was absolutely central to the Greek concept of a city and participation by its citizens in the city's life. The Roman *forum* would later serve many of the same purposes, and was just as characteristic of Roman city layouts.

For the Greeks to consider a place a real city, it had to have a certain minimum set of buildings. Some of these stereotypical structures included gymnasia, theaters, an *agora*, fountains fed by wells or aqueducts, temples, stadiums, *stoas*, and government buildings (such as a *bouleterion* or council chamber). This attitude is clear in the dismissive remarks of the Greek author Pausanius, who said of a town of mountain rustics, "... if you can even call it a city when it has no state buildings, no training ground, no theater, and no market-square, when it has no running water" (*Description of Greece* 10.4.1).

The Romans followed the Greeks in their approach to town planning but added their own distinctive structures, such as amphitheaters, baths, and circuses for chariot racing, to the list of features that any self-respecting city required. They also adopted the Hippodamian grid plan, at least for newly founded cities. Thus, although the streets of Rome itself remained a nightmarish tangle of alleyways, the colonies established by Rome became models of organization and orderly arrangement. The Romans were very good at surveying, and employed teams of professional surveyors who divided up the countryside into precisely measured rectangular plots. This process, called *centuriation*, was the basis for the careful records of land ownership maintained by the Romans.

A Roman twist on the Hippodamian plan derived from the Roman military, where it was the habit of legions on the march to construct an elaborate camp, known as a *castrum*, at the end of each day's journey. While varying in size according to the number of troops present, these camps had a rigidly standardized form based around a grid pattern of paths or streets. The layout of the *castra* was copied for more permanent military camps and outposts, and, as these in turn often became the kernels around which towns sprang up, the arrangement of the camps ended up constituting a kind of city planning. Many Roman colonies were founded by (or to house) veterans from the legions, and these towns also tended to be laid out on the military camp model. There is something of a debate concerning whether Roman army camps imitated Roman towns or whether Roman towns imitated Roman army camps, but the end result was a considerable degree of standardization among many towns founded by the Romans, whether they had begun as military camps or not.

The main characteristics of this design were that its streets followed the familiar grid pattern, with the main north–south road known as the *cardo* and the major east–west thoroughfare labeled the *decumanus*. The *cardo* and the *decumanus* usually met in the center of the town at the open area of the *forum*. In military camps, this corresponded to a sort of parade ground where the commander's tent was located and the legionary standards were placed. Many towns in England began as Roman *castra*, and this heritage can often be identified not only by the street layout but also by a city's name. The suffixes -caster and –chester, which are so commonly found at the end of the names of English towns, are anglicized versions of *castrum*, so that such names indicate that these cities began as Roman camps. All across Europe, many modern cities, from Barcelona in Spain (the Roman Colonia Barcino) to Cologne in Germany (the Roman Colonia Agrippinensium), similarly had their origins as Roman military settlements, and the layouts of their streets also testify to the long-lasting influence of the classical world.

One pleasant feature that the Romans often incorporated into their urban planning, and which is an admired aspect of many modern cities, is large public parks, or what we would now term "green spaces." Today, there are a great number of famous urban parks, such as Central Park in New York City, Hyde Park in London, the Tiergarten in Berlin, Retiro Park in Madrid, Stanley Park in Vancouver, and Golden Gate Park in San Francisco, that greatly add to the appeal of living in those cities. These sorts of large urban green space have their roots in antiquity, where parks every bit as splendid, or even more so, graced several famous ancient cities. There was a long-standing tradition in Roman society of wealthy individuals opening up their gardens to the public, and large sections of ancient Rome were taken up by very pleasant parks equipped with shady marble colonnades, ponds, fountains, groves of trees, and decorative landscaping. The urban populace was free to wander through these parks and make use of their amenities. The idea of public pleasure gardens, known as *horti* (a root in our word "horticulture," literally meaning "garden cultivation"), seems to have been derived from earlier Greek Hellenistic cities, which often included such zones. The most famous of these was Alexandria in Egypt, which, incidentally, was also one of the best examples of a planned city using the Hippodamian grid, and was renowned for its unusually broad streets. It is estimated that over one-fourth of Alexandria was given over to luxurious parks and gardens. In Rome, some of the most famous *horti* were those around the Theater of Pompey and those of Julius Caesar, Sallust, and Lucullus. For city dwellers, many of whom were crammed into tiny apartments, the availability of such verdant urban spaces for their use and relaxation would have been a major factor in making urban life more pleasant—or even bearable in the first place.

The bones of a city: Infrastructure

Another aspect of urban planning which the Greeks and Romans excelled at and which provided a model for later eras was what we would today call infrastructure. While often hidden or underappreciated, constructs such as roads, sewers, drains, water supply mechanisms, bridges, and highways are the vital underlying bones of any city, which enable it to function and which make life there possible for its inhabitants.

First of all, there are the roads that allow movement through the city and link it to other places. The Romans were particularly adept at road-building, and there is indeed considerable truth in the old adage that "All roads lead to Rome" in the ancient world. The Roman road system constituted the best-built and most extensive road network up until very recently. Not only did the Romans build a lot of roads, but they made them solid, with carefully laid paving, and they made them to last. Our very word for "street" derives from the Latin *sternere*, which means "to pave."

The first major Roman road was the Via Appia, begun in 213 B.C. by the man whose name became affixed to it, Appius Claudius. It connected Rome with Brundisium (modern Brindisi) at the heel of Italy, which was a departure point for ships sailing to the east. By the end of the second century

Figure 5.6 *Roman road in Pompeii. The Romans constructed thousands of miles of well-constructed roadways, many of which remained in service for centuries.*

B.C., additional roads, such as the Via Flaminia and the Via Aurelia, ran up and down the length of Italy, joining the cities of the peninsula with a web of well-built roads. As the Roman empire expanded outside of Italy, the Romans doggedly extended their network of durable roadways into the provinces. Legions stationed around the Mediterranean spent much of their time constructing roads, and a typical Roman soldier spent far more time digging than fighting.

The main Roman roads were marvels of practical engineering: first, a deep and solid foundation was excavated; then, gravel or sand provided a base; and finally, the roads were often covered with carefully fitted paving stones. Major roads were usually at least 15 feet wide and were built with a crown, so that rainwater quickly flowed to the sides and into drainage ditches. The Romans also prided themselves on making their roads straight and level no matter what the terrain was, so that even if there were a mountain in the way, they would drill a tunnel through it, or if there were a valley or river, they would erect a bridge over it. As a measure of the quality of their construction, at least 350 Roman bridges are still standing today, many of them bearing modern traffic. Just as today's roads are punctuated with mile markers, the Romans placed stones at one mile intervals along their roads which were not only inscribed with a declaration of the distance traveled (usually measured in miles from Rome) but also often proudly listed the name of the magistrate or emperor who had had the road built and frequently even the military unit which had actually constructed it. The total length of the Roman road network, consisting of both large and small roads, has been estimated at around 50,000 miles, and by Rome's high point, one could travel every step of the way from Spain to Jerusalem on well-crafted Roman paving.

These roads served many purposes. They helped the Romans maintain control over their empire by enabling troops to be rushed to trouble spots. They encouraged and facilitated long-distance trade, and bolstered the economy. They sped up communication among the different regions of the empire, a function that was aided by an imperial messenger service. Finally, they served as a powerful symbol that a territory was indisputably Roman. Like an animal marking its territory, the presence of Roman roads sent the unmistakable signal that an area belonged to Rome.

In addition, the Romans were skilled bridge-builders. The road network around the Mediterranean was carried over ravines and gullies by solidly-built bridges, and the city of Rome itself had nearly a dozen bridges connecting the right and left banks of the Tiber river. The Romans were excellent practical engineers, and many of their bridges remained in active use long after the Roman period. The Roman word for bridge was *pons*, and the oldest and most famous bridge in Rome was the *Pons sublicius*. Originally, there were a number of important religious ceremonies associated with this bridge and with the Tiber, and the chief priest of Rome was called the *Pontifex Maximus*, or literally "the greatest bridge-maker." Later, the Christians appropriated this term for the spiritual leader of their church, and the official title of the head of the Catholic Church is today still Pontifex Maximus. The more familiar term "Pope" is derived from the Latin phrase, though few remember that the title of Pope was originally linked to Roman bridges.

One of the most fundamental requirements for any town or city is an adequate supply of water. Providing for this basic human need must always be one of the principal concerns of urban planners, and water has to be managed in two ways. First, water must be brought to the city in sufficient quantity and of sufficient purity to be drunk by the populace. In addition to water for drinking, a city consumes substantial amounts of water for several other basic functions, including cooking and cleaning. Second, and equally important, arrangements must be made for removing unwanted water, either because there is too much of it and there is a risk of flooding, or because the water has been contaminated by human use and poses a health hazard. This second provision involves disposing of the now soiled water which had been brought to the city by human action as well as unwanted water due to natural weather processes such as rain, snow, and floods. By any standards, ancient or modern, Rome was extraordinarily well supplied with the means both to bring water to the city and to take it away.

Nowhere is the Romans' ability to manage water more impressively demonstrated than at their capital city. By the early fourth century A.D., the city of Rome was being supplied by 19 aqueducts which collectively were capable of bringing over a million cubic meters of fresh water to the city every day. This bounty was distributed to the populace through a complex network of pipes and tanks that delivered water to nearly 1,500 public fountains and pools and almost 900 public and private baths. This system was overseen by a high-ranking state official who supervised a large staff of specialists including engineers, and was maintained by 700 well-trained slaves organized into several divisions.

Natural springs together with the Tiber River provided adequate water for Rome for several hundred years, but as the city grew it became obvious that additional fresh water would have to be brought in by aqueducts. Accordingly, in 312 B.C., a man named Appius Claudius Caecus undertook the construction of the first aqueduct bringing in water from outside the city's borders. This first aqueduct, named the Aqua Appia after its builder, took its water from springs approximately 14 miles outside of Rome. It had a capacity of approximately 75,000 cubic meters of water per day, and contrary to the modern stereotype of Roman aqueducts as a series of tall stone arches, this first aqueduct was mostly located underground. Later aqueducts included some sections carried on impressive above-ground arches, but even in the fully developed system, the overall percentage of aqueducts that ran along such arches was less than 10%.

Figure 5.7 *Roman aqueduct. This dramatic section of aqueduct carried atop arched colonnades is located just outside of Rome, and is a familiar sight to passengers aboard trains traveling south to the Bay of Naples.*

Over the next several centuries, more aqueducts were added, some of them bringing water from as far as 91 km away. To distribute the water, thousands of basins and fountains were built. Under the emperor Augustus alone, more than 700 basins, 500 public fountains, and 130 distribution reservoirs were either erected or renovated. Not only were these structures functional, but they were beautiful as well. Augustus' additions were adorned with 300 bronze or marble statues and 400 marble pillars (Pliny, *Natural History* 36.121).

One of the interesting characteristics of the Roman water supply system that differentiates it from modern ones is that it was a continual flow system, meaning that the water kept passing through the fountains and basins constantly, whether people were actually using them or not. Overall, there were very few valves to turn the flow of water on and off. The entire water system operated by gravity. There was minimal to no use of pumps, so that the elevation of the water was of vital importance, and the entire course of the aqueduct had to be carefully graded so that the water flowed fast enough to prevent stagnant pools or backflow, but not so fast that it became difficult to deal with. The average gradient in the Roman aqueduct system seems to have been about a 3-meter drop in elevation per kilometer of distance. The velocity of the water in the pipes would have been around 1 to 1.5 meters per second, although in some spots it might have flowed as quickly as 4 meters per second. At these typical rates, it might have taken about a day for water to travel from the furthest source to the city. Channels through which the water flowed were made from a variety of materials, including stone lined with hydraulic cement and pipes of clay or lead.

Only a tiny fraction of Romans had running water in their dwellings, but fountains or basins were located at nearly every street intersection. These probably served as focal points of neighborhood social interaction, where people gathered to draw water and exchange gossip, somewhat analogous today to the office water cooler. Naturally, if you lived many stories up in a building, the daily routine of hauling water to your dwelling could have been quite arduous. Wealthy Romans would likely have had slaves to carry jars of water to their homes. One profession in ancient Rome was the *aquarius*, the neighborhood water delivery-man who would bring water to your door for a fee. The satirical poet Juvenal mentions the *aquarius* as a stereotypical figure with whom sexually frustrated women would find relief (*Satire* 6.332). You might recognize *Aquarius* ("the water-carrier") as a term applied to one of the signs of the zodiac, portrayed as a man pouring water out of a jar.

In today's high-tech, electronics-based society, the necessary infrastructure, in addition to water, includes such things as electricity, cable, telephone service, and internet access. One of the greatest challenges for the companies that supply such services is people illegally tapping into the networks and getting the services without paying for them. While this might seem a uniquely modern problem, it has an ancient analogue. One of the greatest challenges faced by those charged with maintaining the Roman aqueduct system was the problem of private individuals illegally tapping into a conduit. People would bore holes into the aqueduct and then attach their own pipes to bring water to their dwellings or businesses. This was such a problem that the government had to have officers constantly patrolling all the exposed sections of aqueduct, and they were continually removing such illegal taps and fixing the holes they made. One of the administrators in charge of Rome's water supply in the early second century A.D., a man named Frontinus, identified illegal tapping as a serious problem that could divert up to half the capacity of an aqueduct. He indignantly reported that his men had found "fields, shops, apartments, and even brothels illegally hooked up to the system with private water taps" (*Aqueducts of Rome* 2.76).

The Romans built aqueducts not only for the capital city but all over the empire as well, and some of these provincial aqueducts feature some of the most impressive architecture. The Pont Du Gard in southern France is an astonishing engineering achievement consisting of a multi-level arcade 50 meters in height built to carry an aqueduct across a gorge. The town of Segovia in Spain has a lengthy section of well-preserved and imposing aqueduct, and the city of Vienne in Gaul was served by no less than 11 aqueducts, although these were considerably smaller in size than Rome's. Although the Roman examples are more famous, the Greeks also built aqueducts and similarly took great care to provide their cities with an adequate supply of fresh water.

Overall, the Roman water supply system was a truly impressive achievement and one that the ancients themselves marveled at. Frontinus himself boasted: "How could you compare such an array of indispensable structures carrying so much water with the idle pyramids or the useless although famous works of the Greeks?" (*Aqueducts of Rome* 1.16). Another proud Roman, Pliny the Elder, similarly argued: "If we take into careful account the plentiful supply of water to public buildings, baths, pools, canals, homes, gardens, and villas near the city; if we contemplate the distances traveled by the water before it arrives, the raising of arches, the tunneling through mountains, and the construction of level courses across deep valleys, we will have to concede that nothing more remarkable has ever existed in all the world" (*Natural History* 36.24.123).

In modern cities, the drainage system and the sewage system are separate networks, but in ancient Rome, as in most cities until quite recently, the two were combined. The earliest Roman drainage system was clearly built in order to deal with the problem of excessive water rather than as a way to get rid of sewage. The site of Rome, with its many springs, proximity to the Tiber, and low-lying valleys situated between hills, meant that these valleys had an excess of water and, at least during parts of the year, seem to have taken on the character of swamps or marshes. A number of literary sources emphasize the swampy nature of early Rome, and the situation was so bad that there was apparently a regular ferry that operated among the main hills during the wet season. These marshy areas included some of the most important sites in Rome, so the development of the city depended upon rendering these areas drier and more habitable on a year-round basis. The earliest public work known at Rome was intended to accomplish exactly this purpose.

Rome's first drain would develop into its most famous: the Cloaca Maxima, literally "the great sewer." The earliest version, constructed by the kings, drained the Forum and emptied into the Tiber. It seems to have originally been an open ditch, and as late as the third century B.C. there was still a danger of pedestrians in the Forum falling into it (Plautus, *Curculio* 476). The kings had to employ compulsory labor to construct this drain, and according to legend, the work was so arduous that some laborers committed suicide rather than continue to work on it.

Eventually, later reconstructions of the Cloaca Maxima transformed it into a completely underground conduit, and numerous other drainage sewers were added to serve other sections of the city. In their fully developed form, these sewers were impressive engineering achievements made of concrete or even high quality stone. The capacity of the sewers was also impressive. Portions of the Cloaca Maxima are more than 4 meters tall and 3 meters wide, leading Pliny the Elder to claim that one could drive a fully loaded wagon of hay through Rome's sewers (*Natural History* 36.108).

This system played an essential role in keeping the low-lying areas of the city dry, and would also have helped to expedite the drying-out process in the aftermath of a flood. A secondary function was to carry away waste, particularly the estimated 100,000 pounds of excrement produced daily by Rome's inhabitants. The majority of sewage that found its way into the system did not come directly from latrines; only a tiny handful of houses had toilets linked directly to the sewers, and there were very few public latrines. Most waste was dumped in the streets, and from there, might find its way into the sewers.

Ancient authors expressed great awe at Rome's sewers, even counting them as one of the greatest wonders of the city, and their admiration is summed up in one author's rhetorical question: "What other city can compare with Rome in her heights, when her depths are so incomparable?" (Cassiodorus, *Variae Epistolae* 3.30.1–2).

Another area in which Rome excelled was the supply system established to bring food to the city. By the first century B.C., the population of Rome was approaching one million, and no other city, at least in the Western hemisphere, would reach a comparable size until the nineteenth century. Thus Rome was uniquely similar to modern metropolises in having to import massive amounts of food to feed its inhabitants. Like today, the most efficient way to transport large quantities of bulk goods, such as grain, was by water, so Rome developed the first great waterborne shipping system. Practically all the excess food from the entire southern half of the Roman empire, including Italy, Sicily, Spain, North Africa, and Egypt, was collected, put on boats, and sent to Rome to feed its gigantic, hungry populace.

For a long time, however, the city lacked a really good harbor. The available existing harbor of Ostia lacked a safe anchorage for ships. In A.D. 42, the emperor Claudius finally tackled this problem by excavating a new artificial harbor some 1,000 yards wide out of the Italian coastline. This immense basin was connected to Ostia and the Tiber river by a series of canals. Although Claudius' harbor, known as Portus ("Port"), was equipped with large breakwaters, it still seems to have been a dangerous anchorage, since in A.D. 62 a storm sank over 200 ships. Rome at last got a first-rate harbor when the emperor Trajan rebuilt Portus and added an inner harbor where ships could be completely safe. This inner harbor was a giant hexagon 700 yards wide and lined with well-made quays and mooring points. The modern airport that serves Rome was partially built over Portus and, if you look carefully, you can still see the outline of Trajan's hexagon as your plane comes in for a landing today. Hundreds of Roman freighters busily plied the Mediterranean, bringing an estimated 600,000 tons of vital grain, olive oil, and wine to Rome every year. The size and sophistication of Rome's harbors and docks were unrivalled before the most recent few centuries, but would not look out of place in a modern port.

The Romans were able to build such impressive harbors, quays, docks, breakwaters, and so on because they developed a special kind of concrete that could be poured directly into wooden molds underwater, and it would harden there despite being immersed. This hydraulic cement, which employed a volcanic sand called pozzolana as one of its ingredients, was a key component in Roman engineering. Waterproof, the cement was also used in aqueducts and sewers. Exhaustive technical analysis of its composition has revealed that Roman cement was as effective as, and in some cases, even more so than, its modern equivalents.

Putting it together: Building methods and design elements

The Romans made widespread use of concrete in other structures as well, and indeed some architectural historians speak of Roman architecture as heralding "the concrete revolution." Although forms of concrete had existed before the Romans, they made use of this versatile material in a far more extensive and creative way than anyone before them, and really, more so than anyone else afterwards up until the twentieth century. Although the stereotypical image of a Roman building is one of shining marble—and it is true that almost all monumental Roman structures gave an outward appearance of being made of marble or other fine decorative stones—this marble was almost always just a thin layer applied over a structural core composed of humble bricks and concrete. Roman bricks and concrete were cheap, durable, and flexible materials to work with, and they are the secret behind how the Romans could quickly build such enormous, long-lasting structures. Because concrete can be poured in almost any shape, it allowed Roman architects far greater versatility in terms of design than their Greek forebears. Together with the Romans' extensive use of the vault, concrete allowed Roman buildings to span huge interior spaces without needing a forest of internal columns to hold up the roof. Concrete also allowed rooms and buildings to break free of the rectilinear constraints earlier imposed on them, and architects to experiment with curved walls and round shapes.

Roman architects were good at making sturdy, functional buildings, and their philosophy is best summarized by one of their number, Vitruvius, who lived in the first century B.C. and wrote an influential book called "On Architecture." In it, Vitruvius states that buildings "should exhibit the principles of soundness, utility, and attractiveness. The principle of soundness will be observed if the foundations have been laid firmly, and if, whatever the building materials may be, they are selected with care but not excessive frugality. The principle of utility will be observed if the design allows faultless, unimpeded use through the disposition of the spaces and the allocation of each type of space is properly oriented, appropriate, and comfortable. That of attractiveness will be upheld when the appearance of the work is pleasing and elegant, and the proportions of its elements have properly developed principles of symmetry." (*On Architecture* 1.3.2). Even today, these three core principles are featured on the emblem of the Society of Architectural Historians (*Utilitas Firmitas Venustas*), and Vitruvius' statement offers a good sense of how the Romans ideally approached building design. Roman architects are known to have drawn plans for their structures much like modern blueprints and to have constructed three-dimensional models out of wood, stone, and clay.

When we think of buildings from the classical era, probably the single thing that is most associated with them is rows of columns. This cliché is fundamentally accurate, since the Greeks and the Romans made extensive use of columns as both structural and decorative features in their buildings, but it is just one aspect of the classical style of architecture. Over subsequent centuries, many later architects seeking to imbue their work with the reflected glory of ancient empires have emulated the look of classical buildings, particularly for monumental edifices such as government buildings, banks, churches, and museums. While the classical style has enjoyed moments of greater or lesser popularity, its influence is so pervasive that it is hardly possible to walk down almost any block of any major city around the world today without seeing at least one structure boasting classical-style columns or other classical architectural details on its façade.

Given their ubiquity today, let's look in a little more detail at the main styles of architecture that originated in the classical world in order to understand how they have exerted such a powerful and constant influence on all subsequent architecture. The Greeks created three basic styles that are sometimes referred to as the orders of architecture: the Doric, Ionic, and Corinthian orders. To them can be added another pair developed by the Romans, based on the earlier Greek models: the Tuscan order and the Composite order.

When the classical orders of architecture are discussed, they are often thought of in terms of their type of column, and indeed the easiest way to distinguish one order from another is to look at this feature. However, the orders are really about more than just columns. They imply a whole set of proportions which the entire building is supposed to reflect. One might think of the orders as a combination of ornamental style and modules of dimensions that can be combined and arranged in different ways like building blocks, but because they all share certain ratios of proportions, the overall structure will have a coherence and balance in its dimensions.

The Doric order seems to have developed on the Greek mainland in the late seventh century B.C.; the Ionic order arose about the same time or slightly later in eastern Greece; and the Corinthian was a relatively late Greek development, although it was much used by subsequent Hellenistic and Roman architects. The Doric order, often thought of as the most basic one, has columns and proportions that are relatively squat when compared to the others. It also has the simplest decoration. In the Doric order, the capitals (or tops of the columns) consist of a simple, unadorned concave swelling, known as the *echinus* (meaning "sea urchin," because it was thought to resemble one), leading to a plain, square block known as the *abacus*. Ionic columns have longer and thinner proportions than Doric ones, and their capitals feature a volute, which resembles an upside-down scroll curling around at each side of the column. Finally, Corinthian columns have even more attenuated proportions, and their capitals are the most complex, with a set of intricately sculpted, curling leaves of the acanthus plant. Typically, in all three styles, the shaft of the column is fluted, meaning that there are shallow, vertical grooves extending from top to bottom. The Romans added the Tuscan order, which is a kind of simplified Doric order with unfluted columns. A fifth style, which is sometimes attributed to the Romans, is the Composite order, which, as the name implies, incorporates elements from several of the others to create a highly ornate order.

In addition to the major orders, architecture today makes use of many details and smaller elements devised by the ancients, especially the Greeks. A few examples which might be familiar from their appearance on buildings today are dentils, which are a row of squarish, toothlike projections; fasciae, which consist of three progressively projecting horizontal bands; friezes, which are horizontal bands of decoration; the top element in the entablature, the cornice, which forms the eaves along a building's sides; and pediments, which are the triangular spaces on the front or back of a structure formed by the two sides of a sloping roofline.

Theaters for entertainment, arches for boasting

We began this section with perhaps the two most famous Roman buildings, each of which has spawned innumerable imitators. While there are many sorts of ancient structure that have influenced the modern world, we will end this discussion by focusing on two more specific building types that have inspired many copies. One of these is a very practical type of Greek building, the theater, and the other is an entirely decorative sort of Roman structure, the triumphal arch.

Since the Greeks are credited with developing theater as an art form, they also had to devise appropriate structures in which to hold plays. The main requirements were a space that could seat or otherwise accommodate thousands of spectators in such a way that they could both see and hear the actors clearly. The result was the distinctive D-shaped Greek theater, which became the model for all subsequent performance spaces. The standard Greek theater consisted of an open area called the orchestra, which was where the actors performed, and then a large half-circle around it where the audience sat. Originally, most Greek theaters were constructed against hillsides, where the natural slope of the hill could be used as the seating area, with the orchestra at the base. The Theater of Dionysus in Athens, which rests against the slope of the Acropolis and which was the site where many of the most famous Greek plays were first performed, is an example of this.

Early on, spectators probably just sat on the hillside itself, but wooden benches eventually provided more formal seating, and finally, stone theaters were constructed with concentric rows of marble benches. The Theater of Dionysus probably seated around 20,000 spectators, but the largest later theaters may have been able to accommodate nearly twice that number of

Figure 5.8 *Theater. These structures, some of which could seat up to 40,000 spectators, were the venues for the famous tragic and comic performances of Greek and Roman playwrights.*

people. One of the most impressive aspects of Greek theaters is that they were carefully designed to maximize the acoustic properties of the structure. This was a necessity in an era without any artificial means of voice amplification, and these buildings were so well constructed to meet this requirement that, at many of them, it is possible to hear a person whispering in the orchestra from the back row—a fact that Greek guides delight in demonstrating to tourists today.

The Romans copied the basic structural elements of the Greek theater, and most of the surviving ruins of theaters today are Roman-era structures. A variant on the theater was the odeon, which had the same shape but was roofed over, and was used for musical performances as well as other types of entertainment. Almost any auditorium, concert hall, or opera house that you might attend today owes its basic form to the Greek theater, which makes it one of the more significant and commonly encountered architectural legacies of the classical world.

Our final type of ancient structure is one that is much rarer in the modern world than theaters, but nevertheless has produced some notable imitators. This is the triumphal arch, first constructed by the Romans. The triumphal arch probably had its origins in the celebratory parades known as triumphs that were awarded to victorious Roman generals, for which decorations were temporarily placed on the city gates through which generals and their men marched. The parade would continue through the streets of the city, and over time, honorific arches commemorating generals and their conquests began to be erected along this route. These took the form of free-standing arches with one to three openings that were typically covered with carvings of Romans slaughtering barbarians and carrying booty back to Rome. On top of an arch there would be a statue of the victorious general riding in a four-horse chariot known as a *quadriga*. These monuments proliferated until there were over 50 in Rome, at least another 50 throughout Italy, and yet more scattered across the Roman empire.

Figure 5.9 *The Arch of Constantine. Located near the Colosseum, this arch was decorated with panels taken from earlier triumphal arches.*

Of the 50 arches in the city of Rome, only three survive intact today: the arches of Titus, Constantine, and Septimius Severus. The Arch of Titus is a good example of a relatively modest triumphal arch. It is a single-opening arch 15 meters high and 13.5 meters wide. Built in A.D. 81 just after the death of the emperor Titus and located along the Sacred Way between the Forum and the Colosseum, it commemorates Titus' military victories in Judea. It is decorated with several famous panels of Roman soldiers carrying away loot from the Great Temple of the Jews in Jerusalem, including one remarkable scene in which a group of soldiers can clearly be seen struggling to haul away the temple's gigantic *menorah*, the traditional seven-branched Jewish candle-holder.

Figure 5.10 *Detail of decoration on the Arch of Titus. This panel shows victorious Roman soldiers carrying loot taken from the Great Temple in Jerusalem, including the sacred seven-branched candlestick holder, the menorah.*

Particularly since the revival of interest in classical architecture beginning with the Renaissance, later rulers and governments have seized upon the triumphal arch as a way to honor themselves or their heroes, and this has resulted in a spate of imitations. These can be found around the world, from the Narva Triumphal Gate in St. Petersburg, Russia, to the Brandenburg Gate in Berlin, to the Victory Gate in Laos erected to celebrate independence from France, to the Arch of Victory in Australia commemorating World War One.

The most famous of such gates by far, however, is the Arc de Triomphe on the Champs-Elysées in Paris. Begun by Napoleon to celebrate his victory at the battle of Austerlitz, at 50 meters tall and 45 meters wide it is larger than any Roman arch ever was. As impressive and well-known as this victory arch is, however, it is not actually the largest in the world. That honor belongs to the Arch of Triumph erected in Pyongyang, North Korea, by Kim Il-Sung. This mammoth 60-meter-high, 40-meter-wide structure, inaugurated in 1982, is inscribed with the lyrics of a song honoring the North Korean leader.

I've got a question: The first scientist-philosophers

In Western Europe up until about the last 350 years, science had not advanced a great deal from where classical thinkers had left it. The writings of Euclid and Archimedes remained the final word on geometry, Aristotle and Pliny were the acknowledged authorities on what we might now call the natural sciences, the texts of Hippocrates and Galen were regarded as the best reference works on medicine and treating illness, and Ptolemy's theories on astronomy were still prevalent. Despite antiquity's long domination over scientific thinking, the classical world did not really have a term equivalent to our modern word "science." The closest that existed were probably the Greek concepts of *philosophia*, or "love of wisdom," and *episteme*, or "general knowledge." Nevertheless, the Greeks and Romans provided the foundations upon which modern disciplines such as physics, biology, chemistry, zoology, botany, and astronomy would be based and from which these fields would develop.

In addition to this core body of knowledge, the ancient Greeks also, and perhaps even more importantly, bequeathed to the modern world the beginnings of the scientific method—the crucial idea that, in order to learn about the natural world, one should pose hypotheses, conduct experiments, and observe results. The very word *hypothesis* is an ancient Greek one meaning "proposal," "suggestion," "supposition," or "subject proposed for discussion," which Plato employs in one of his philosophical dialogues after first attributing its use to mathematicians of the time. Before one can investigate the world, one has to pose questions, and the Greeks were very good at doing this.

In the writings of another ancient Greek, we have an account of one of the very first recorded experiments. As told by the historian Herodotus, "King Psammetichus of Egypt desired to know if his country was the oldest of all nations, but he could not settle the matter by inquiry alone, so he tried a test. He took two newborn babies of common parents and gave them to a shepherd to raise among his flocks. The shepherd was instructed to make sure that no one ever spoke a single word around the children. They were to be raised in a secluded hut. The shepherd tended to all their needs and brought them goats to provide milk. Psammetichus arranged all this because he wanted to find out what word the children would speak first without any outside influences, when they were old enough to start talking. And things worked out according to his plan. The shepherd followed the king's orders for two years, and then one day when he opened the door and went into the hut, the children both ran up to him with outstretched arms and distinctly said *becos*. The king then made a general inquiry to find out what nation used the word *becos*, and discovered that it was the Phrygian word for bread. From this, he concluded that the Phrygians were actually the oldest culture in the world, and the Egyptians could no longer make the claim themselves. I learned that these were the real facts of the matter from the Egyptian priests of Hephaestus at Memphis" (*The Persian Wars* 2.2).

In this story, the king is clearly applying a precursor of the scientific method—he poses a question that he wants to answer, he creates an experiment to explore the question, and he observes the results. Naturally, the entire experiment is fundamentally and terribly flawed because it is based on the erroneous assumption that language is innate rather than learned. This flaw is less important, however, than the fact that it is a true attempt to conduct an unbiased scientific experiment in order to discover information as opposed to simply looking to superstition or tradition for answers. As such, it exemplifies the spirit and interests of the ancient Greeks, who were drawn to stories of such experiments and who first began to systematically seek rational answers to questions about the world around them.

Consider what attitudes towards natural phenomena were like before the Greeks began to ask these sorts of questions. Confronted with a world full of puzzling natural phenomena such as wind, rain, and lightning, many ancient cultures came up with folk-tales and mythologies to explain why the world functioned as it did. One strategy is animism, in which spirits inhabit everything around us. The ancient Greeks, for instance, told stories about nature spirits (nymphs) such as dryads and hamadryads (tree nymphs), oreads (mountain nymphs), and nereids (sea nymphs). Another strategy is to assign inexplicable phenomena to gods possessing special, superhuman powers. Thus, Zeus, king of the gods, wields thunderbolts; his brother Poseidon controls the sea and causes earthquakes by striking the ground with his trident; and the seasons change because Demeter, the goddess of agriculture, neglects her job while she mourns in winter for her kidnapped daughter Persephone, and joyously revitalizes the earth when they are reunited in the spring. Eventually, however, in the late seventh century B.C. in ancient Greece, some radical thinkers emerged who rejected these sorts of tale, and instead sought logical explanations for the things they observed—science rather than stories. It was out of this new impulse to question the world around them and to seek logical explanations for natural phenomena that the foundations of science as we know it today were laid.

We call this very first wave of Greek scientists—or, as they were known at the time, philosophers—the Ionian Rationalists. Also sometimes called the Pre-Socratic philosophers, meaning the Greek philosophers who came before Socrates, they got started around 600 B.C. The term Ionian Rationalists, however, is a more descriptive label, and one that tells us much more about who they were. Let us begin with the second word, "Rationalist," and consider what it means in relation to these men. They were among the first to look at the world around them and attempt to come up with logical explanations for why things happened. Rather than simply accepting mythological causes for natural phenomena such as rain, wind, the seasons, and so on, which typically attributed all these things to the actions of the gods, this group of thinkers tried to interpret these phenomena in a way that we would today call scientific. This was a truly radical way of thinking about the natural world, and to those who strictly adhered to religious beliefs of the time it would have been regarded as sacrilegious.

The inquiries of these men led them in a number of different intellectual directions. Those who concentrated on explaining the natural world became particularly interested in measurement, standards of weights and measures, mathematics, and geometry, since the very first step towards understanding the world around you is being able to describe it with accuracy and precision. Those whose focus was on more abstract concerns, such as speculating about the fundamental nature or organization of the universe, developed logic, reason, and critical thinking.

Skepticism, meaning that you do not accept anything that you are told without some sort of proof, was a major component of the Rationalists' approach, and led to an emphasis on personal observation to verify facts. A logical next step was to conduct experiments in order to test a hypothesis, and we see many Rationalists carrying out such experiments in a variety of fields. These were all ground-breaking ideas. Up to this point, most people had simply accepted what they had been told, and had been trained to see the world as a fundamentally mysterious place ruled by inexplicable forces. The Greek Rationalists challenged and changed all this, and the science-based and technologically advanced world that we live in today and take for granted is the direct end result of the process begun by these thinkers so long ago.

The first word in the phrase, "Ionian," is significant as well. The movement embodying these characteristics began and thrived in a region called Ionia, which was an area on the coast of Asia Minor. Today, this coastline and the islands just offshore are mostly owned by Turkey, but in antiquity they were part of the Greek cultural world.

The Ionians were located in an interesting place geographically, since they were right on the border between the Greek world and the older inland civilizations of the Near East and Mesopotamia. They were at the crossroads of the major trade routes that joined East and West. Ionia was a border zone where all kinds of disparate philosophies, religions, and cultures came together. It was a place where Egyptians, Persians, Jews, Medes, Phoenicians, and Greeks all intermingled in the streets. Not only was Ionia characterized by a volatile intellectual climate, but its political life was similarly unsettled. The region was contested territory claimed by both the Greeks and Persia. In addition to the threat of external invasion, Ionia was troubled internally by factionalism, civil war, and class strife.

The first of the Ionian Rationalists is usually considered to be a man named Thales of Miletus. He was a merchant who, in pursuing his business, had travelled to Egypt, where he was probably exposed to Egyptian and Chaldean ideas about and knowledge of mathematics and astronomy. One of Thales' most famous achievements was using his understanding of mathematics and astronomy to predict a total eclipse of the sun in 585 B.C.

Thales' biggest contribution was simply to question the traditional explanations for how the natural world functioned. He posed two questions which would obsess all subsequent Ionian Rationalists and continue to challenge thinkers up through the present: "What is the world made of?," and "What is the basic unit of which all things are composed?" Thales called it "the antecedent of all things" or "the first element" and reasoned that, since all things appeared to be nourished by water and needed it to survive and grow, water must be the first element. Today we might call this primordial unit the atom, a concept so fundamental that we refer to our time as the Atomic Age—the period after the detonation of the first nuclear bomb in 1945. The international symbol for the atom, with several electron orbits drawn around a central nucleus, has become an icon of modernity. But even though the minute workings of the protons, neutrons, and electrons could not be observed until the twentieth century, the roots of atomic theory extend back to these basic questions of Thales.

Later, in the fifth century B.C., Leukippos and his student Demokritos invented and refined the theory that everything in the universe is composed of an infinite amount of unchanging, indivisible, eternal particles too tiny to be seen by the human eye. They also came up with the idea of void—nothingness, or the empty space through which bodies move. This infinite number of invisible particles circulate through the void, occasionally colliding, getting tangled together, and forming larger compounds. Demokritos was the first to label such a particle *atoma* (an uncuttable or indivisible thing), the source of our word "atom." All things and all causation could be ascribed to the movements of these atoms.

Thales also speculated about the nature of the universe. He theorized that the earth was a flat body that floated on top of water like a raft. Thales was plainly moving away from traditional pagan concepts of the gods. He believed that god or the divine was in everything, that people possessed souls that were linked to all other souls, and that all beings were thus related to one another.

One of his key characteristics of the soul, and by extension of all living things, is that they are capable of movement. Since he observed that magnets can move, he therefore speculated, perhaps playfully, that they too must have souls. Even after he became a philosopher, he did not lose his instincts as a merchant, and according to legend he used his knowledge of astronomy to predict the ripening of the olive crop, which enabled him to corner the market and make a financial killing.

One of Thales' students, Anaximander, expanded on his teacher's theories. He is the first individual known to have made a map of the world, which in itself reveals his interest in geometry and measurement. He was also the leader of a colony and enjoyed wearing fancy and impressive clothing. He claimed that the first element was not water or any other substance, but was instead something called "the indefinite." His take on the structure of the universe was that the earth had originally been covered in water that dried up under the heat of the sun, exposing the land. He speculated that mankind was therefore descended from fish-like creatures, making Anaximander a kind of forerunner to evolutionary theory.

Another important Ionian Rationalist was Xenophanes. By profession he was a poet, and the main direction of his theories was to challenge conventional notions of the Greek gods. He ridiculed the idea that the gods looked just like people, and said that this concept of the gods was egotistical and anthropocentric. To illustrate this point, he wrote that "If cattle or horses had hands so as to paint and produce works of art as men do, they would paint their gods and give them bodies in form like their own—cattle like cattle, and horses like horses." His vision of religion was explicitly monotheistic, positing that there was one omnipotent divine being who was "not like mortals in either body or mind. He is all sight and all mind and all hearing, and he remains in one place, not moving. It is not seemly that he should be now here, and now there. He moves all things without effort by his thought."

Xenophanes believed that the world had experienced alternating phases between when it was dry and when it was covered in water. He based this on the observation that fossils of fish could be found in the mountains, and correctly deduced that these imprints must have been left at a time when that region was under water.

One of the most colorful and important figures of the next wave of Ionian Rationalists was Pythagoras. He liked to call himself a lover of wisdom, or a *philosophos*, from which our term philosopher derives. He, too, is alleged to have traveled widely, visiting Egypt and sites in the Near East, where he may have picked up elements of Eastern thinking. Pythagoras' ideas fall into the two categories of mathematics and mysticism, although he himself did not see these as being different.

He came up with many of the cornerstones of geometry, including the Pythagorean Theorem. He thought that the first element was "number." He called the number one the Monad and said that it was male and that number two, the Dyad, was female. This is reminiscent of the modern concept of binary number systems used in computers, and we might therefore even regard Pythagoras as the "grandfather" of computers. He also made important advances in astronomy regarding the movements of the planets. In Pythagoras' view, the universe was put together along mathematically precise lines. In addition, he believed that mathematics and music were interrelated, which led to his famous idea that the movement of astronomical bodies along perfect, harmonious paths created beautiful sounds—"the music of the spheres."

Pythagoras was none the less also very superstitious. He said that you should never poke a fire with a knife because you might injure it, and that you should always spit on your nail clippings to prevent them from being magically used against you. He was a believer in reincarnation, and the transmigration of souls, even into animals. He claimed that he could remember his past four lives, including one in which he had lived at the time of the Trojan War. One story about him is that he once saw a neighbor beating a dog and asked him to stop, saying that he recognized the dog as the reincarnation of a friend. He advocated vegetarianism so that you could avoid unintentionally eating deceased friends and relatives. Pythagoras was a flamboyant figure who habitually dressed in eccentric outfits such as a golden hat, long white robes, and trousers.

The rationalists emphatically believed that the human mind possessed the power both to comprehend and to make sense of this world, and that the solutions to human problems and questions could be reached through rational thought and logical analysis, a belief that continues to motivate scientific inquiry today.

Practical and not-so-practical science: Engineers and inventors

Later Greek thinkers continued the work of the Ionian Rationalists. One of them, Aristotle, in his youth had been a student of the famous philosopher Plato at his Academy. Aristotle, however, went on to develop interests very different from those of his teacher. Where Plato had focused his inquiries on aspects of the mind and pure thought and believed that the physical world was an illusion, Aristotle devoted enormous effort towards a close study of the world around him.

Aristotle was interested in virtually everything, and wrote influential treatises about a dazzling array of topics, including politics, ethics, physics, biology, literature, music, rhetoric, zoology, theater, logic, and metaphysics. His study of the natural world led to his groundbreaking efforts to catalog and classify fish and animals. He believed in systematically collecting data and then drawing conclusions from them. The modern Linnaean system of biological classification owes much to the earlier example of Aristotle.

The Hellenistic Era, which followed the death of Aristotle's pupil, Alexander the Great, was a period that witnessed important new inventions and discoveries in the fields of science, medicine, engineering, and mathematics. The mathematician Euclid, known as the "Father of Geometry," lived and worked in Hellenistic Alexandria. His most important contribution was a book called *The Elements*, which laid out all the basic principles of geometry. He came up with many of the geometric proofs and theorems still used today, as well as being a pioneer in axioms involving shapes and angles. *The Elements* is probably the most successful school textbook ever written. All the way from antiquity up until the last century, Euclid's book was used to teach basic geometry to students.

One of the most brilliant scientists and inventors of the era was Archimedes. A citizen of the Greek colony of Syracuse on the island of Sicily, he was an inveterate tinkerer who crafted numerous ingenious machines, including pumps, pulleys, and a variety of military devices. He was also talented in the field of mathematics, establishing the value of *pi* and finding methods for calculating the area and volume of complex shapes. He delighted in building contraptions that could move water from one level to another, such as Archimedes' screw, which remains the basis for many pumps. Similarly, he had a flair for using levers, pulleys, and block and tackle systems in order to magnify force and move or lift heavy objects. One of his most famous sayings was "Give me a lever and a place to stand and I can move the world."

The most well-known anecdote about Archimedes concerns the local ruler's request that he solve a complex problem involving the purity of a golden crown. Archimedes was stumped by this conundrum and decided to take a break and visit the local bath for a relaxing soak. As he stepped into the bath, he noticed that his body displaced an equal volume of water, leading to his sudden realization of a way in which he could use this observation to solve the problem of the crown. Elated, he leapt up and ran home through the streets, naked and dripping, shouting "Eureka!, Eureka!," meaning "I have found it." As memorable as it is, this story may actually be a later invention, but it certainly captures an accurate sense of the great scientist's obsessive devotion to his intellectual pursuits.

Unfortunately, this very same dedication would result in Archimedes' death. Syracuse was attacked by the Romans, and although Archimedes was able to prolong the city's defense by crafting a number of ingenious war machines, the Romans eventually broke in and began looting it. The Roman general had given his men specific orders not to harm Archimedes, because the Romans hoped to gain his services for themselves. When soldiers burst into his laboratory, however, he was so intent on a complex mathematical diagram that he ignored their questions as to his identity, and so he was killed. He was buried in a tomb decorated with a sphere and a cylinder, symbolizing one of his mathematical insights.

A few other notable Greeks and their inventions or insights include: Straton of Lampsakos, who anticipated one of the basic laws of physics by demonstrating that falling bodies accelerate; Meton, a master of precise astronomical calculations, who was only 30 minutes and 10 seconds off in calculating the time it took the earth to revolve around the sun; Aristarchos of Samos, who used geometry to calculate the distances to the sun and the moon and proposed (correctly) a heliocentric model of the solar system;

Eratosthenes of Cyrene, who was especially interested in geography and not only made some of the earliest accurate maps, but also calculated the earth's circumference with only a tiny degree of error; and Diokles, whose pioneering work in optics became the basis for all telescopes.

Some inventions of scientists working during the Hellenistic era include cogged gears, pulleys, the screw, glass-blowing, hollow bronze-casting, surveying instruments, an odometer, the water clock, and a musical instrument known as the water organ. Greek inventors devised several different ways to accurately measure time, such as water clocks, which were based on the amount of time it took for a given volume of water to drip or run out of a container and which were often employed in courts to limit the length of time speakers had to make their cases, and sundials, which made use of the sun's daily movements to measure time. There were even portable sundials that could be considered the ancient equivalent of wristwatches. Often, however, rather than being applied to practical concerns, the ingenuity of these scientists was instead devoted to trickery.

For example, Hero of Alexandria, who was nicknamed "the Mechanic," constructed an automated puppet theater, complete with doors that appeared to open on their own, statues that seemed to come to life and move their arms, and never-emptying bowls that poured out wine from invisible reservoirs. Many Hellenistic inventions would today be considered the kinds of thing used by magicians or illusionists. A particularly elaborate example of this was a gold statue of the goddess Nike (Victory) that was crafted so that it appeared to emerge from the Temple of Athena Nikephoros in the city of Pergamum and then place a crown upon the head of King Mithridates Eupator. The Greek word *mechane*, from which the word "mechanic" is derived, originally meant "a trick." Perhaps Hero "the Mechanic's" most potentially revolutionary invention was a prototype of a steam engine. If this had been widely applied for practical purposes, the Industrial Revolution might have occurred thousands of years earlier, with incalculable results on history; but like most of his other machines, it was only employed to perform the equivalent of parlor tricks.

A source of funding and patronage for many inventors was the rulers of the Hellenistic kingdoms. These autocrats were fond of staging lavish public spectacles, and practiced what we would now refer to as conspicuous consumption. For example, Ptolemy II of Egypt organized a parade in Alexandria that puts modern counterparts such as the Rose Bowl parade and the Macy's Thanksgiving Day parade to shame. Ptolemy's procession included not just his army, equipped with chariots and war elephants, but immense floats carrying larger-than-life-sized mechanical statues of gods and heroes that moved their limbs, more floats with giant paintings of historical and mythological scenes, actors dressed as satyrs, 120 boys carrying saffron on golden platters, and a special float bearing a colossal wineskin stitched together from leopard pelts that had a 30,000 gallon capacity and spewed free wine into the spectators' eager mouths. There was also a menagerie of exotic animals in the parade, consisting of giraffes, antelopes, parrots, elephants, a gnu, camels, peacocks, a rhinoceros, a white bear, ostriches pulling carts, 2,000 gold-painted oxen, and 2,400 dogs. To top it all off, there was a 180-foot-long, gold-plated phallus with a giant ribbon and bow tied around it.

The city of Alexandria was a center of learning which boasted the famous Library of Alexandria. This great collection of knowledge had as its goal to acquire a copy of every book in existence. It is estimated to have contained half a million scrolls. All ships that docked at Alexandria were searched by customs officials, and if they found a book that was not yet owned by the library, it was confiscated until a copy could be made.

Attached to the library was an institution called the Museum, or literally "the house of the Muses." This functioned as both a place to collect interesting objects and a kind of center for advanced research that attracted scholars from all over to come to Alexandria to study and work. There they would do research, collect data, perform experiments, and then write treatises on their findings. The subject matter of these essays ranges from a review of known poisons and their antidotes, to texts on agriculture and bee-keeping. Research reached a high level of sophistication, and soon began to attract the timeless criticism often directed at scholars that their work focused on hopelessly obscure topics that had no practical applications. So that you can judge for yourself, here are the titles of some actual texts written during this period: "A collection of the rare words used by Democritus," "On words suspected of not being used by earlier writers," and one that must have been a particularly riveting read, "On changes of names of fishes."

The Ptolemaic rulers of Egypt funded the library and took great pride in it. Being intensely competitive, the other Hellenistic kings soon established their own competing libraries, and a kind of war of books developed to see who could own the most. None of the other libraries, however, really got close to matching the Great Library of Alexandria. Mirroring their patrons' animosity, rival scholars also engaged in bitter academic feuds over erudite topics in a manner that would be familiar at any large research university today.

The Hellenistic era was not only an era of academic disputes, but a time of nearly constant real warfare among the various kingdoms that formed out of the break-up of Alexander the Great's empire. As is often the case during wartime, the desire for more powerful weapons spurred technological innovation. Military engineers devised larger, more efficient catapults and cranes to be employed on the battlefield and in sieges, and portable pontoon bridges that allowed armies to ford rivers. The great inventor Archimedes spent much of his time designing military equipment, including catapults of assorted sizes and a machine supposedly resembling a giant claw that snatched up Roman ships and overturned them. Even before this time, the historian Thucydides mentioned an early flame-thrower, consisting of a cauldron linked by a pipe to a pair of bellows, reportedly used to burn down the wooden fortifications of Delium and Lecythus in 424 B.C.

A healthy body and a healthy mind: Medicine

The next time you read a study that advises you to eat well, hear someone say "Everything in moderation," try to figure out what your dream of the night before was trying to tell you, or have a long, relaxing soak in the tub when you are feeling low, rest assured that the ancients were there before you in their quest for health and long life.

The modern symbol of medicine and doctors is two snakes entwined around a rod. Given the fairly sinister reputation of snakes (especially in the Christian tradition), one might well be puzzled as to why this image should be associated with the medical profession, whose goal is to help rather than to harm. The answer lies in the ancient world, where this symbol would have been instantly identifiable as the *caduceus*, carried by the messenger god Hermes (Mercury for the Romans) as he led the souls of the dead to the underworld region of his uncle Hades. However, the *caduceus* also had the power to bring the dead back to life, even though this was rarely made use of.

Although the *caduceus* is primarily known as Hermes' attribute, another Greek god was commonly portrayed holding a staff entwined with snakes: Asklepios, the god of healing, medicine, doctors, and patients. Alternately portrayed as either the son of the god Apollo (himself often seen as possessing the abilities both to heal and to inflict disease) or as a mortal hero promoted to divinity after his death, Asklepios was so skilled at his art that he could reportedly revive dead people; perhaps this is why the *caduceus*, with its less-known resuscitative power, began to appear in depictions of Asklepios. Ironically, Asklepios' triumph over death led the king of the gods, Zeus, to kill him with a thunderbolt, for fear that he would upset the balance between life and death.

Figure 5.11 *Statue of Aesculepius (Asklepios). The god of healing is identifiable by his staff entwined with a serpent, which has become the symbol of the medical profession.*

The sacred nature of the snake in Greek religion might also have contributed to its identification with Asklepios. In order to establish a new shrine to the god of healing, a sacred snake from the mother temple had to be transported there. Similarly, when the Greek god first appeared at Rome and put a stop to a terrible plague, it was said that he swam up the Tiber in the form of a giant serpent and hid among the reeds of Tiber island, where the Romans built a temple to him in gratitude. (Tiber island preserves this ancient connotation with healing, as it eventually became the site of a Christian hospital still in operation today).

Among Asklepios' children were: the Greek goddess of health, Hygieia (often portrayed with a snake in one hand and a cup in the other, or sometimes with the snake drinking from the cup), the source of our word "hygiene"; the Roman goddess of health, Panacea, the source of our word for a cure-all; and two sons, Machaon and Podalirius, who were skilled physicians appearing in Homer's *Iliad*. At his shrines, ill supplicants of the god were treated with baths, exercise, and diet regimens (all still familiar therapies today), as well as with a procedure called incubation: the patient would go to sleep in the shrine, hoping that the gods would send a dream revealing how to treat the illness, or might even effect a miraculous cure. Dream interpreters at the shrine were often employed as consultants. While incubation might at first sound odd to us, we should consider the role that dreams continue to play in the modern world. The ancient practice of interpreting dreams might be seen as foreshadowing the theories and therapies of Freud, himself an avid lover of the classical world and another great believer in the significance (and interpretability) of our dreams. Dream interpretation also suggests the link between mind and body, between psychological and physical health. The importance of the idea of treating the entire person in the ancient world is represented by the fact that sanctuaries to Asklepios resembled sanatoria, equipped with theaters, gymnasia, and baths, so that there was stimulation and attention given to both the mind and the body.

While the Hippocratic Oath, usually attributed to the famous Greek doctor Hippocrates (c. 430 B.C.) or his followers, is still invoked today as a touchstone for doctors, some of its dicta are more familiar to us than others. While most of us have probably heard the phrase "help rather than harm," we should perhaps consult a translation of the original to see what else it advises:

> I swear by Apollo the healer, by Aesculapius, by Health and all the powers of healing, and call to witness all the gods and goddesses that I may keep this Oath and Promise to the best of my ability and judgment.
>
> I will pay the same respect to my master in the Science as to my parents and share my life with him and pay all my debts to him. I will regard his sons as my brothers and teach them the Science, if they desire to learn it, without fee or contract. I will hand on precepts, lectures and all other learning to my sons, to those of my master and to those pupils duly apprenticed and sworn, and to none other.
>
> I will use my power to help the sick to the best of my ability and judgment; I will abstain from harming or wronging any man by it.
>
> I will not give a fatal draught to anyone if I am asked, nor will I suggest any such thing. Neither will I give a woman means to procure an abortion.
>
> I will be chaste and religious in my life and in my practice.
>
> I will not cut, even for the stone [i.e., kidney stones], but I will leave such procedures to the practitioners of that craft.
>
> Whenever I go into a house, I will go to help the sick and never with the intention of doing harm or injury. I will not abuse my position to indulge in sexual contacts with the bodies of women or of men, whether they be freemen or slaves.
>
> Whatever I see or hear, professionally or privately, which ought not to be divulged, I will keep secret and tell no one.
>
> If, therefore, I observe this Oath and do not violate it, may I prosper both in my life and in my profession, earning good repute among all men for all time. If I transgress and forswear this Oath, may my lot be otherwise.
>
> *(Translation by J. Chadwick and W. N. Mann, in "Hippocratic Writings," New York: Penguin, 1950, p. 67)*

While invocations of the gods and familial bonds with one's teachers are no longer required, many of its guidelines remain in force: doctor–patient confidentiality, a ban on sexual harassment, the charge to help rather than harm, and staking one's professional reputation on one's obedience to the rules. Certain ethical issues currently being debated, such as abortion and euthanasia, are addressed and settled in a way that is now being revisited and questioned.

The oddest clause, to modern sensibilities, is probably the stricture against performing surgery ("cutting" the patient). However, for most of history until relatively recent times, the professions of physician and surgeon were kept separate, with surgeons looked down upon as closer to butchers than to doctors: hence the job of "barber-surgeon," whose practitioners cut both hair and bodies. However, one can see in this clause a recognition of fields of specialization still in effect today—"Leave the cutting to those who know how to cut" might now be rendered as "Send the patient to the relevant specialists if his illness is beyond your knowledge." Similarly, the call for chastity and religiousness in one's profession would now probably be expressed as a more general call for moral behavior and seriousness of purpose. But even without these transpositions into more modern sentiments and language, the original Hippocratic Oath obviously still exercises a strong influence on the medical profession.

Hippocrates and his followers left behind a whole corpus of medical writings that offer some still relevant advice. They stress moderation as an important prescription for and indicator of health, as in the following aphorisms: "Neither a surfeit of food nor of fasting is good, nor anything else which exceeds the measure of nature" (*Aphorisms* 2.4); "All excesses are inimical to nature" (*Aphorisms* 2.51); "Sleep and wakefulness, exceeding the average, mean disease" (*Aphorisms* 7.72). They offer suggestions for proper diet and exercise to combat various diseases and conditions, and while some of these might sound fanciful or arbitrary, they none the less indicate an awareness of the importance of diet and exercise to good health. They also recognize how mental attitude affects physical wellbeing: "In every illness, a healthy frame of mind and an eager application to victuals is good. The reverse is bad" (*Aphorisms* 2.33). Bed rest is seen as a valuable remedy: "Rest, as soon as there is pain, is a great restorative in all disturbances of the body" (*Aphorisms* 2.48).

While the Hippocratic corpus emphasizes diet, exercise, and rest as general aids to good health, there is an awareness that specific conditions require specific remedies: "Remedies are beneficial only through correct applications, but they are harmful when applied wrongly" (*The Science of Medicine* 5). Throughout, different diet and exercise regimens are prescribed according to type of ailment. In fact, Hippocrates and his followers compiled what might comprise the earliest medical case studies. Each begins with a brief reference to the patient being discussed: for example, "the unmarried daughter of Euryanax," "a man who dwelt in the park of Delearces," and "Cleanactides, who lived on the hill above the temple of Heracles." The initial symptoms are listed, and then a day-by-day description of the progress of the illness. Although many of these seem to end with "death" as the specified outcome, there were some successes. It was thought that these case studies could be used to aid in the diagnosis of future patients: "They [physicians] compare the present symptoms of the patient with similar cases they have seen in the past, so that they can say how cures were effected then" (*The Science of Medicine* 7). Hippocrates expresses annoyance at those who criticize and question the science of medicine because not all patients recover. Modern doctors might sympathize with Hippocrates' annoyance at patients who don't follow their doctor's directions: "As if doctors can prescribe the wrong remedies but patients can never disobey their orders! It is far more likely that the sick are unable to carry out the instructions than that the doctors prescribe the wrong remedies" (*The Science of Medicine* 7). However, Hippocrates also stresses that physicians should take responsibility for faulty practices: "Although the art of healing is the most noble of all the arts, yet, because of the ignorance both of its professors and of their rash critics, it has at this time fallen into the least repute of them all. The chief cause for this seems to me to be that it is the only science for which states have laid down no penalties for malpractice." (*The Canon*)

In the ancient world, Greek was the language of medicine; the Roman writer Pliny the Elder states that "medical writers, unless they write in Greek, are not accepted as authorities even by the ignorant or by those who do not know Greek. Indeed, people tend to trust advice about their own health less if they understand the language in which it is spoken" (*Natural History* 29.8.17). Ironically, while Roman doctors needed to speak Greek (rather than their native Latin) to impress with their medical learning, today's doctors use Latin in the same way. Somewhat paradoxically, while the Romans viewed Greek doctors as the best ones available, they also distrusted Greek medicine, as suggested by this quotation from the poet Martial: "Until recently, Diaulus was a doctor; now he is an undertaker. He is still doing, as an undertaker, what he used to do as a doctor" (*Epigrams* 1.47). Perhaps this skepticism sprang partly from the fact that, unlike today, there were no medical licenses and no formal process of certification; anyone could set himself up as a doctor, as Pliny the Elder complains: "Medicine is the only profession … where any man off the street gains our immediate trust if he professes to be a doctor … for doctors, and only doctors, there is no penalty for killing a man" (*Natural History* 29.8.17–18).

While Greek practitioners of medicine tried to develop it into a science, the Romans were initially skeptical of it, and many continued to prefer traditional magical and religion-based cures, a topic that will come up again in the next chapter. In his multi-volume *Natural History*, Pliny the Elder alternates logical-sounding medical advice with superstitions and bizarre folk remedies. Thus, he addresses issues of diet, exercise, and therapeutic treatments that might seem familiar to us today: "To fast from all food and drink, sometimes only from wine or meat, sometimes from baths, when health demands such abstinence, is held to be one of the most sovereign remedies. Among others are physical exercises, voice exercises, anointing, and massage if carried out with skilled care … Especially beneficial however are walking, carriage rides of various kinds, horse riding, which is very good for the stomach and hips, a sea voyage for consumption, change of locality for chronic diseases, and self-treatment by sleep, lying down, and occasional emetics" (*Natural History* 28.14.53–4). He offers other reasonable advice as well, such as "Mother's milk is for everyone the most beneficial" (*Natural History* 28.33.123), and "Sunshine too, best of remedies, we can administer to ourselves … [and] it is [healthful] to drink cold water before a meal and at intervals during it …" (*Natural History* 28.14.55). Until recently, medical practice agreed with Livy that stomach ulcers could be soothed by drinking milk (*Natural History* 28.54.196). One Roman aristocrat, heeding Pliny's dictum that "By far the greatest aid to health is moderation in food," embarked upon a regimen foreshadowing current diets that carefully control portions, and employed a sort of proto-personal trainer: "L. Lucullus gave charge over himself to a slave to enforce control, and he, an old man who had celebrated a triumph, suffered the very deep disgrace of having his hand kept away from the viands even when feasting in the Capitol, with the added shame of obeying his own slave more readily than himself" (*Natural History* 28.14.56).

Yet Pliny also records more unusual medical remedies. Some involve animals directly: "Sneezing and hiccups are relieved by touching with the lips, it is said, the nostrils of a mule" (*Natural History* 28.15.57); "I find that a heavy cold clears up when the sufferer kisses a mule's muzzle" (*Natural History* 30.11.31); "By the touch of the [elephant's] trunk headache is relieved, more successfully if the animal also sneezes" (*Natural History* 28.24.88). Some utilize parts of animals and animal products: "Rubbing with ants' eggs prevents hair in the armpits of children" (*Natural History* 30.13.41); asthma can be treated by ingesting "21 millipedes, soaked in Attic honey and sucked through a reed" (*Natural History* 30.16.47); swan's fat is praised as the best means of clearing the complexion and smoothing wrinkles (*Natural History* 30.10.30); and scrofula is helped by eating the middle part of a snake with the ends cut off, "with much greater benefit if the snakes have been killed between two wheel ruts." (*Natural History* 30.12.37). Various types of dung and animal fat or grease (especially bear's grease) are frequently recommended for their healing properties. Sympathetic magic is probably at work in some of these suggestions, for instance placing a wolf's-tooth amulet on a baby to soothe teething pain (*Natural History* 28.78.257) and wearing an amulet containing crabs' eyes to cure ophthalmia (*Natural History* 32.24.74).

Despite the bizarreness of these remedies, some of them would undoubtedly have worked, such as the cure for lethargy advising one to "apply to the nostrils a vinegar-soaked callus from the leg of an ass" (*Natural History* 28.67.230) and rubbing oneself with mouse dung as an anti-aphrodisiac for men (*Natural History* 28.80.262). Although Pliny at times refers to some of these more fanciful cures as "lies" or expresses skepticism as to their efficacy, his inclusion of them suggests that people might have followed such advice, or at least did not automatically think it absurd. Perhaps if we consider some of the cures currently being practiced, such as injecting one's skin with botulism, ingesting sharks' cartilage and royal jelly, and drinking one's own urine, the folk remedies mentioned by Pliny might seem more familiar than we initially thought.

Ancient assessments of the female body probably bear some of the responsibility for assumptions about women's inferiority that persisted for thousands of years. Aristotle famously referred to the female of the species as "a deformed male" (*Generation of Animals* 2.3.25–30; 737a25–30), who developed imperfectly due to her moister, colder composition; the hotter male was stronger, more equipped to defend himself, and altogether more perfect. Woman's lack of heat was responsible for all her inadequacies, according to Aristotle, even her intellectual and moral ones; he characterizes women as "more impulsive," "more easily moved to tears," "more void of shame," "more false of speech," "more deceptive," "more apt to scold and to strike," "more difficult to rouse to action," and less courageous than men (*History of Animals* 608a32–b19). While he also describes women as "more compassionate," "more attentive to the nurture of the young," and "of more retentive memory," these traits obviously do not outweigh all of the negative ones he attributed to them.

The Hippocratic corpus, while offering some sound advice, also supplied reasons for women's supposedly greater tendency towards irrationality and madness. Because her flesh is softer and more porous than a man's, it absorbs moisture more readily and even blood; if this blood is not discharged by menstruation every month, it builds up, causing illnesses and even madness. It was thought that virgins tried to hang themselves and jump down wells because this blood pooled around their hearts; menstruation and sexual intercourse would offer relief.

Similarly, the uterus was a source of trouble. Our word "hysteria" derives from the Greek word for womb because it was thought that typical hysterical symptoms, such as the loss of one's voice or consciousness, or the inability to breathe, were caused by the womb moving around. If it became too dry and light (most often from lack of sexual intercourse), it could migrate and "wander" around the body, wreaking havoc with a woman's health. If it refused to return to its proper position, doctors used various treatments to lure it back, for instance by burning sweet- or noxious-smelling substances either under a woman's nose or under her vagina in order to attract or drive the uterus in the appropriate direction. Like a creature in its own right, the uterus was capable of motion, prone to mischievous behavior, and even sensitive to odors. By implication, women weren't in control of their own bodies, which no doubt reinforced the idea of their mental instability and emotional changeability.

Sadly, women were sometimes denied credit for one crucial ability that they possessed and men lacked: having babies and thus allowing humanity to continue. In Aeschylus' play *The Eumenides*, the god Apollo defends Orestes against the charge of matricide (which he readily admits to) by arguing that: "The woman you call the mother of the child is not the parent, just nurse to the seed, the new-sown seed that grows and swells inside her. The man is the source of life—the one who mounts. She, like a stranger for a stranger, keeps the shoot alive unless god hurts the roots" (*The Eumenides* lines 666–71).

Ancient medicine was an odd mixture of some very misguided ideas, a smattering of sound principles, and lots of attempts at magical, or sometimes what we might optimistically call homeopathic, cures. Just as with science, some of the most important legacies of the ancient world to the modern lie in the realm of methodology. The Hippocratic writings created an ethical code for the practice of medicine which is still relevant today, and the casebooks of other early physicians such as Galen paved the way for modern medical textbooks that emphasize the observation of symptoms in order to classify diseases, recommend treatments, and predict outcomes.

6

Understanding and shaping the spiritual world: Superstition and religion

Better safe than sorry: Superstitions

Despite our proud belief that we in the "modern" world are now in an era of scientific progress and rationality, many of us still avoid black cats, knock on wood, refuse to walk under ladders, read our daily horoscope, play our lucky numbers in the lottery, and feel a slight sense of uneasiness on Friday the 13th—sometimes acknowledging our credulity with a laugh, and saying it is better to be safe than sorry. In the ancient world, observing superstitions was one way to impose order on a confusing world full of randomness, and people espoused a wealth of them—some of which will probably strike us as very familiar.

We already encounter a list of superstitions in the eighth-century B.C. text "Works and Days," written by the farmer Hesiod, who mixes pragmatic advice about the seasonal rhythms of agriculture with admonitions not to leave the ladle resting on a mixing-bowl of wine because this will bring bad luck (744) and not to face the sun when urinating (727). However, some of these make a kind of sense from the perspective of health and hygiene, such as not to urinate in springs, and this cleanliness assumes moral overtones reminiscent of our notion that "cleanliness is next to godliness": you should make sure you've washed your hands before pouring a libation to the gods or else they will ignore your prayers (724), and you should pray and wash your hands free of wickedness before crossing a river or else the gods will punish you later on (737).

The Roman writer Pliny asks a series of questions about customs intended to bring good luck, some of which we still observe today. "Why on the first day of the year do we wish one another cheerfully a happy and prosperous New Year?"; "Why do we say 'Good health!' to those who sneeze?"; "Why on mentioning the dead do we protest that their memory is not being attacked by us?" (a Roman version of "God rest his soul" or "May he rest in peace") (*Natural History* 28.5). He mentions instances of magic formulae recited to ease illnesses like sciatica and gout, and that, after being in a serious carriage accident, Julius Caesar used to always repeat a prayer for a safe trip three times over before departing—"a thing that we know most people do today," Pliny adds (28.4.21). He tells us that prayers are written on walls to prevent fires, and that if a fire gets mentioned at dinner, you should pour some water under the table to keep one from occurring (28.5.24), since talking about something might cause it to happen. He cites a superstition that is still prevalent today: "According to an accepted belief, absent people can divine by the ringing in their ears that they are the object of talk" (28.5.24). Other current variations are that burning or itching ears signify the same thing.

The Greeks and Romans believed in lucky and unlucky numbers and days. Hesiod tells us that the first, fourth, and seventh days of the month are holy; that the eighth and ninth are "good for the works of man"; that the twelfth is best for sheep-shearing and harvesting and for a woman to set up her loom for weaving (*Works and Days* 770); but that one should not begin sowing on the thirteenth day (780), and the fifth day is just altogether bad (802). (Tellingly, he refers to the unlucky days as "stepmother" days.) Pliny says that the odd numbers are more powerful than the even ones, and that a sudden silence will occur only when there is an even number of diners at the table—a situation that also presages danger to their reputations (*Natural History* 28.5.27).

Why is a black cat crossing one's path considered bad luck? The common identification of cats, especially black ones, as the familiars of witches, from the Middle Ages onwards, is probably the more immediate cause, but why is the color black so often associated with evil or the Devil (for example, the "Black Mass" allegedly celebrated during the witches' Sabbath)? In ancient times, black animals were traditionally sacrificed to the dead and to gods of the Underworld, while white animals were sacrificed to "bright" celestial divinities. As the color of night and darkness, black was the obvious choice for symbolizing a region thought to be deep underground. With the arrival of Christianity, the pagan Underworld (where transgressors suffered cruel punishments) somewhat naturally became identified with Hell, and its king, Hades or Pluto, with the Devil.

In English folklore, huge black saucer-eyed demon dogs (still echoed in Conan Doyle's Hound of the Baskervilles) appear on rural roads and woodland paths, frequently heralding death. Black birds, such as ravens and crows, are often traditionally seen as portents of ill luck or death (although this probably also arises from their prevalence on battlefields, where they are notorious for plucking the eyes out of corpses and scavenging carrion). The common superstitions that a crow flying over or landing on a house means death for one of its inhabitants and that a crow cawing three times signifies imminent death have precedents in antiquity: Hesiod says that it is bad luck if a cawing crow lands on your house (*Works and Days* 746); Pliny refers to the crow as "ill-omened" (*Natural History* 10.14); Phaedrus connects the raven with prophecy and the crow with "unfavorable omens" (*Fables* 3.18); and Aesop in his *Fables* states that seeing a single crow is bad luck, although two crows bring good luck. Aesop's distinction was still being made in nineteenth- and early twentieth-century Britain, with sayings like "One crow sorrow,/Two crows joy." One ignored omens at one's peril. It was said that, soon after leaving his house one day, the Roman politician Tiberius Gracchus stubbed his toe and had a tile dropped at his feet by three cawing crows flying overhead (Valerius Maximus, *Works* 1.5.2). Instead of sensibly turning around, he ignored this bad portent, and was soon after beaten to death by his political enemies.

The calf-sized demon-dogs of Britain and the "hell-hounds" that appear in modern popular culture are almost certainly connected to the famous three-headed dog Cerberus, who guarded the entrance to the Underworld in Greek myth. The fact that in modern folklore ghostly dogs tend to materialize at crossroads (where deals with the devil are often transacted) can also be traced back to Greek myth. Hekate, known as the goddess of the crossroads, magic, witchcraft, and the moon, had dogs as her special animal, and she was often depicted with Cerberus; like him, she had three heads, all facing in different directions, befitting a deity known to linger where roads intersect. The ancients invoked her name when practicing witchcraft and putting curses on people; one incantation to incite love intones, "The dogs howl in the city … The goddess is at the crossroads" (Theocritus, *Idyll* 2). Perhaps one of the most famous modern incarnations of this imagery is found in Blues songs, in which the crossroads, deals with the devil, and hell-hounds all make frequent appearances. The great Mississippi bluesman, Robert Johnson, who has been labeled the "most influential blues musician of all time," had much to do with this, recording the songs "Cross Road Blues" and "Hell Hound on My Trail," which have done much to keep this imagery alive in popular culture. Today, some Wiccans have embraced Hekate as a woman's goddess (her three faces representing the maiden, the matron, and the crone) and widened her domain to include the liberation and empowerment of women.

Like us, the ancients believed in the importance of a good start. If a Greek or Roman messed up during a religious ritual such as a sacrifice, he had to start over from the beginning and repeat it until he got it perfect. Similarly, our phrase "to get off on the right foot" might well echo Roman superstitions about embarking on a new enterprise. When a Roman left his home, crossed a threshold, or went into or out of a city or country, if he started out by stumbling or went over any boundary left foot first, this was a very unlucky omen. The Roman playwright Terence nicely sums up the sorts of negative sign one might identify—bird calls, black dogs, unlucky days, unnatural things raining down from the heavens—by listing a reluctant bridegroom's excuses for putting off his marriage: "He could say, 'I've had so many warnings … a strange black dog came into my house, a snake fell from the tiles through the skylight, a hen crowed, a soothsayer spoke against it and a diviner forbade it. Fancy starting on anything new before the shortest day!'" (*Phormio* 705–10).

However, now as then, there were also many skeptics who felt that everything could be explained rationally. For instance, the Epicurean philosopher Lucretius devoted his work *De Rerum Natura* ("On the Nature of Things") to dispelling superstition and fear of the gods by explaining the laws of nature.

However, he went beyond a rejection of superstition to critique religion as well. He pictured humankind as "groveling upon the ground, crushed beneath the weight of religion" and terrified by "fables of the gods" (1.62-68) and the threat of punishment after death. In Lucretius' model of the universe, an infinite number of atoms tumbling through infinite space collide and combine, thus creating things. Therefore, just because the universe exists doesn't mean that there have to be gods who created it, and if there are no gods, then people need not live in constant fear and trembling.

While Lucretius' scientific outlook made him uncomfortable with religion, the Sceptic school of philosophy (the source of our words "skeptic" and "skeptical") went even further, arguing that knowledge is unattainable and rejecting the idea that anything whatsoever could be known for certain. But there were also many who expressed awareness of a dividing line between appropriate religious observances and inordinate superstition. For instance, when the statesman Pericles was bed-ridden with the plague, he reportedly let the women of his household put an amulet around his neck, but seemed quite sheepish about having gone along with this bit of "folly"; and in Plato's *Republic*, there is a negative portrayal of "soothsayers" who claim that they can use spells and incantations to bend the gods to their will. The Roman word *superstitio*, originally positive in meaning, ultimately came to have negative connotations, suggesting a loss of one's dignity through excessive credulity.

Unnatural powers: Magic and witchcraft

The word "magic" derives from the Greek word *magos*, which the Greeks originally used to refer to Persian wise men, whom they thought of as especially skilled practitioners of astronomy, astrology, and magic in general. (Nowadays, the most commonly encountered usages of the word are probably in the Bible: the wise men, or Magi, from the east, who bring offerings to the newborn Christ child in Matthew's Gospel, and Simon Magus—Simon the Sorceror—who converts to Christianity but is reprimanded by Peter for trying to buy the power of receiving the Holy Ghost in *Acts* 8:9–24, which, given his background, he was probably interpreting as a potent form of magic.) The

Greeks particularly associated magic with Egypt and Eastern cultures, and attributed to mages the ability to interpret dreams, practice divination, and summon the dead. The Roman writer Pliny attributes the invention of magic to the Persian prophet Zoroaster (or Zarathustra), the founder of the religion of Zoroastrianism (*Natural History* 30.3). Pliny writes that magicians claim to practice divination using "water, balls, air, stars, lamps, bowls, and axes" and "to hold conversations with ghosts and the dead below" (30.14), but he is skeptical of their powers, and says these have been disproven as false (though the fact that he devotes so many pages to recording their alleged abilities suggests the degree of their fame).

Witches and sorcerers were feared figures in antiquity. Two famous witches of Greek myth, Circe and Medea, set the pattern of ruthlessness and powerful women sexually enslaving men. Medea (a barbarian from the Caucasus, east of Greece) kills lots of people, including her own brother, and tricks others into death (Pelias she dismembers into a boiling cauldron after saying he will regain his youth—one of the earliest instances of a witch's cauldron—and the princess who replaces her in her husband Jason's affections she gives a poisoned robe that burns her to death). According to Homer's *Odyssey*, Circe (sometimes referred to as Medea's aunt) turns the men who visit her island into animals, thus metaphorically revealing their bestial natures. When Odysseus lands there, his men ingest her potions and turn into swine; forewarned, he alone avoids this fate by protecting himself with a magic herb, but she manages to keep him trapped on her island as her lover for quite a while.

This ancient connection between magic and sex was very strong. Witchcraft was a way to control the world—and the people—around you by gaining power over them, including sexual power. It was widely believed that witches worked erotic magic by "drawing down the moon," which they invoked in their love spells and from which they collected the "moon-juice" that it deposited on plants, which they incorporated in their love potions. The Greek region of Thessaly was particularly notorious for its powerful witches and their proficiency in drawing down the moon; one writer even says that every Thessalian girl could draw down the moon. The influence of the moon over human beings is reflected as well in the notion that a full moon can drive people crazy—the word "lunacy" derives from *luna*, Latin for moon— or

Figure 6.1 *Pages of a book of magic. Two of 11 metal leaves comprising a book of magic spells written in Greek.*

turn them into werewolves. Our use of "moonstruck" to mean either mentally unbalanced or unable to think clearly due to being in love reflects the moon's ancient association with magic. Thessalian witches figure prominently in Apuleius' novel *Metamorphoses*; one works love spells to attract men and rubs on a lotion that turns her into an owl (a symbol of wisdom). When the unfortunate protagonist Lucius tries to emulate her, he instead turns into an ass (revealing his true nature, for he starts out both sex-obsessed and rather stupid), and has to spend the rest of the novel striving to learn self-control and become human again.

Love potions (*philtra*), charms, and spells were widely employed in antiquity as a way to incite passion in the object of one's unrequited desire. Love magic could be performed on hairs, nail clippings, or clothing from the beloved to irresistibly draw him or her; in Apuleius' *Metamorphoses*, an unfortunate mix-up results in an inflated wineskin made of goat hide becoming animated and floating to a witch's door because the hairs she obtained came from it rather than the man she desired (in fact, the idea that you could work magic on people using their nail and hair clippings endured even into the nineteenth century).

Spells and charms were often aided with the use (and abuse) of what we would call voodoo dolls. Magic rituals were performed in which miniature figures representing the person to be harmed were stuck through with nails and needles, and ones made of wax were melted. For love spells, male and female figures symbolizing the two lovers were often used in conjunction. One spell lists the various parts of the doll that should be pierced, and with how many pins: "Take thirteen bronze needles and insert them into the brain while saying, 'I pierce your brain [insert her name]'; insert two into her ears, two more into her eyes, one into her mouth, two below her rib cage, one into her hands ... and two into the soles of her feet, while on each occasion saying once, 'I pierce the [insert name of part] of [insert her name], so that she may think of no one except me [insert your name] alone'" (cited in Ogden, 2002 p. 248).

Later in the same spell you are told to draw some magic symbols and inscribe a heart shape around them, which sounds kind of like the custom of carving two sweethearts' names in a heart into a tree—though in a much more disturbing way. The idea was that treating the doll in this way would immobilize it and place it in your thrall; these were called "binding" spells or curses because they would bind or restrain the victim. As well as controlling a love object, they could be used to harm or defeat rivals, or to seek justice. The popularity of such binding curses is suggested by the fact that about 1,600 of them survive. They were often inscribed on lead curse tablets and put in places thought to communicate with the Underworld, like graves, wells, and springs. These spells often run through every single part of the body, cursing each one individually. One particularly thorough example reads: "Spirits of the underworld, I dedicate and hand into your power, Ticene of Carisius. Let everything she attempts turn out badly. Spirits of the underworld, I dedicate to you her limbs, her face, her body, her head, her hair, her shade, her brain, her forehead, her eyebrows, her mouth, her nose, her chin, her cheeks, her lips, her speech, her breath, her neck, her liver, her shoulders, her heart, her lungs, her intestines, her stomach, her arms, her fingers, her hands, her navel, her entrails, her thighs, her knees, her calves, her heels, her soles, her toes. Spirits of the underworld, if I witness her wasting away, I promise that I will joyfully present to you a sacrifice every year" (*CIL* 10.8249). The victim of one such binding spell describes its effect thus: "[He] said that at that moment his body felt drawn tight as if by purse strings, with his limbs being crushed together" (Porphyry, *Life of Plotinus* 10).

Why do we refer to an unlucky person as being "jinxed" and avoid bragging about our good fortune because we don't want to "jinx" it? This, too, possibly stems from magical practices in the ancient world, with a brief detour into bird taxonomy. The genus jynx is a group of Old World woodpeckers, one of which, the wryneck, is thus called because of its ability to turn its head through almost 180 degrees. When it feels threatened, it reacts by hissing and twisting its head around in a snake-like manner. In his "History of Animals," Aristotle describes this display, mentioning that, like a snake, it keeps its body perfectly still when its head swivels, and that it has a very long tongue that it sticks out and pulls in, again like a snake (504a).

Perhaps it was this uncanny-looking behavior that attracted the notice of ancient witches. It was said that if a man wore a wryneck's right eye under a lapis lazuli stone, he would attract desire, gain the approbation of his fellows, and win law-suits, while the left eye would do the same for a woman. The bird was also called upon for assistance in love spells: "Wryneck, draw this man to my house," a witch repeats as a refrain in one lengthy spell (Theocritus, *Idyll* 2). Apparently, *iynx* or *iunx* also referred to a magical device consisting of a little wheel strung on threads that you pulled to make it spin around rapidly; you can still see children playing with such a toy nowadays. The god of love, Eros (Cupid to the Romans), was sometimes shown with one, because of its use in love spells. The whirling motion was thought to induce love. The two *iunxes* could be employed together; the fifth-century B.C. Greek poet Pindar says that Aphrodite, the goddess of love, "yoked fast the variegated wryneck [*iunx*] … to a four-spoked wheel and brought the bird of madness to men for the first time" (*Pythian* 4.211–50), and gave this weird contraption to the hero Jason to help him seduce the witch Medea. (In an alternative myth, it is said that a nymph named Iynx or Iunx invented the device, which she used to charm Zeus into falling in love; in revenge, Zeus' angry wife Hera transformed her into the iunx bird.) Today, a "jinx" is a much milder sort of curse, echoed in "jink" (to make a quick, evasive turn—recalling the wryneck's twisty head) and "high-jinks" (playful, boisterous behavior and frolicking—perhaps suggested by the *iunx's* rapid spinning motion).

Necromancy, the art of communicating with the dead and re-vivifying corpses (derived from the Greek words *nekros*, dead body, and *manteia*, divination) was another form of magic described by the Greeks and Romans. In the epic poem *Pharsalia*, the first-century A.D. Roman poet Lucan describes how the powerful witch Erichtho transfuses the corpse of a recently dead soldier with boiling blood, "moon-juice," rabid dogs' froth, snakes' eyes, lynx guts, and various other noxious substances in an attempt to bring him back to life, and how she goes around collecting all the different parts of dead bodies to employ in her spells and potions (6.667; 6.507). The Romantic poet Percy Bysshe Shelley was a fan of Lucan's work, and it is possible that he familiarized his wife, Mary Shelley—the author of a famous episode of reanimation involving the collection and sewing together of body parts in her novel *Frankenstein*—with this scene.

Greek incantations and curses often incorporated magical "nonsense" words, the most famous of which we still hear today: abracadabra. We first hear this word mentioned in a poem on medicine, *Liber medicinalis*, written by Quintus Serenus Sammonicus (died A.D. 212), a tutor to the future emperor Caracalla and his brother Geta. In it, he gives remedies for various illnesses, including semi-tertian fever, for which he advises the following: the word abracadabra should be written repeatedly in column form with the final letter removed each time, in the shape of an inverted triangle. The patient wore this magic formula folded up in an amulet, which would allegedly break the fever's power over him (*Liber medicinalis* 51.932–9). The origins of the word are obscure, although it has been suggested by some that it comes from the Aramaic language and means roughly "Create as I say." During the Middle Ages, this magical word expanded its supposed potency until it was deemed capable of inducing all sorts of magic—not just treating a specific type of fever. That is why today abracadabra has become a sort of all-purpose magical chant. No doubt the reason why this particular magic word caught on is due to its mellifluous sound.

One of the most famous pop-culture instances of a magical incantation going awry occurs in the Disney film "Fantasia," when Mickey Mouse, the apprentice to a sorcerer, animates a broom to fetch water and it refuses to stop, causing a huge flood. While the more immediate inspiration was "Die Zauberlehrling," a poem written by Goethe in 1797, which "Fantasia" adheres to precisely, the German poem stems from an ancient source: a second-century A.D. text by the Greek writer Lucian (*Philopseudes* 33–6). In Lucian's text, one man tells another about an Egyptian magician he befriended and travelled with. Every time they arrive at an inn, the magician takes a broom, a pestle, or the bar from the door, drapes it in a cloak, says some incantations, and then it walks around and does chores like fetching water and cooking for them; everyone else sees it as a human being. He calls it "the perfect servant." Wanting to perform magic himself, he eavesdrops on his friend and overhears the magic words, but when he uses them to animate a pestle and sends it to fetch amphoras of water, disaster ensues, since it ignores his orders to stop and floods the house. Desperate, he chops it in two with an axe, but this only results in each half getting up and continuing to fetch water. Only the return of the magician puts an end to the out-of-control pestle.

Keep away from me: The evil eye

Belief in the "evil eye" and methods of averting it, which are still common in Mediterranean countries today, where eye-shaped amulets are a popular tourist item, were prevalent in the ancient world. It was thought that certain individuals, just by looking at you, could cause you to fall ill, wither away, and die. The idea that eyes are the windows to the soul has ancient roots, but eyes could communicate negative emotions as well as positive ones like love, as in "love at first sight"; Plutarch says that "when people consumed by envy rest their eyes on persons … these eyes, being situated adjacent to the soul, draw evil from it and attack the persons as if with poisoned missiles … people think that anti-evil eye amulets help against envy, because they draw off the gaze by their bizarreness, so that it rests less on those that are affected by it" (*Moralia* 680c–683b). Such a glance, often a sidelong one (*obliquo oculo*), could blight the fertility of both crops and humans. Witches and sorcerers, the most skilled practitioners of the evil eye, were considered to be frequently motivated by envy.

Throughout ancient Greece, apotropaic (evil-averting, from the Greek word *apotrope*, "turning away") eyes were painted on the prows of ships to prevent shipwreck, on shields for protection in battle, and on drinking cups. The Gorgon (a female monster depicted with crazy eyes, sharp teeth, and a large, protruding tongue, the most famous of whom was Medusa) frequently appeared on the pediments of archaic Greek temples and their heads on warriors' shields, as a way to scare off evil—perhaps echoed in our gesture of sticking out the tongue as a sign of rejection. The gargoyles and grotesque figures carved on medieval cathedrals served a similar function.

Figure 6.2 *Roman good luck charm. This apotropaic charm is in the shape of an erect phallus hung with bells. Similar amulets were commonly placed about the house or worn around the neck.*

The phallus (a distracting sight indeed) was another popular apotropaic image, often worn as an amulet, especially by young Roman children, who were considered particularly vulnerable to the evil eye. The ancients thought that spitting and making certain gestures could also dissipate the evil eye's power, customs still practiced today. Many superstitions in rural areas of England involve spitting (often three times) as a way to ward off bad luck or evil. Ovid describes one such Roman gesture used to repel ghosts: "... then gestures with his fingers wrapped around his thumb, lest ghosts should come near him . . ." (*Fasti* 5.2.433–6). Pliny asks, "Why do we meet the evil eye with a special attitude of prayer?" (*Natural History* 28.5.22), and advises that if a baby is looked at, the nurse should spit three times to protect it (28.7.39).

It's all in the stars: Astrology

Another magical practice we owe to the ancient world is the casting of horoscopes. Today, millions of people check their daily horoscopes in order to gain insight into upcoming events, to determine their lucky numbers for the day, or just for entertainment. In the ancient world, the East (specifically Mesopotamia, and the Chaldean culture) was known as the birthplace of astrology and the home of its most skilled practitioners, but the art also spread to Greece and Rome, where it became very popular. Originally, astronomy and astrology were virtually synonymous and equally respectable. Babylonian astronomers were the first to divide the heavens into 12 sectors and designate each month with a zodiacal sign, but this knowledge had spread to the Greek world by the fourth century B.C., where it became strongly rooted in Egypt, and from there expanded to Italy in the second century B.C.

The earliest astrology focused on kings and the fate of their kingdoms, but eventually developed into a way for any individual to seek self-knowledge and foretell his or her destiny. Horoscopes were being cast for the average person in Egypt under the reign of the Greek dynasty of the Ptolemies. Then, as now, the location of the planets in the zodiac at the time of one's birth was thought to influence one's character and determine one's future. Even the great scientist Aristotle accepted that the stars could exert influence over earthly life, and in his work *Tetrabiblos*, the famous geographer Ptolemy tried to demonstrate scientifically that the stars were able to do this. Indeed, the basic beliefs of astrology—the control exerted by the stars and planets over our lives and their role in predicting fate—became common knowledge accepted by the majority of people and cultures in the ancient world. This assumption was not strongly shaken until the ascendance of Christianity; in the fourth century A.D., St. Augustine rejected astrologers as frauds and denied that our fates could be read in the stars.

The word "zodiac" has its origins in the Greek term *zodiakos kuklos*, "circle of animals" (*zodion* meant "little animal"), since the majority of the astrological signs were envisioned as animals. The first known representation of the 12-sign zodiac that we are familiar with today appears on the ceiling of a chapel dedicated to the god Osiris within a temple to the goddess Hathor at Dendera, Egypt, dating to around 50 B.C. Aries, Taurus, Capricorn, and Scorpio are readily identifiable, although some of the signs are given an Egyptian twist; Aquarius, the water-bearer, is depicted as Hapy, god of the Nile flood, pouring water out of two jars, for instance. The necklaces people wear today to show off their sign of the zodiac are nothing new; the Romans liked to wear amulets and charms inscribed with astrological signs as well.

Rulers often kept astrologers in their permanent employ in order to consult them about important decisions and the most auspicious time for taking action. The Roman emperors were great patrons of astrology; for instance, the second emperor Tiberius had a long-lasting relationship with his astrologer Thrasyllus, who supplied him with predictions for over 40 years. Tiberius was said to be extremely superstitious, and many were disturbed by the powerful influence wielded over the ruler of the world by a fortune-teller. Before we scoff too much at Tiberius, consider that President Ronald Reagan's schedule was supposedly sometimes determined by the predictions of his wife, Nancy. While some people were alarmed to find that Nancy Reagan consulted astrologers and used horoscopes to advise her husband, she was merely doing what many leaders had done before—trying to hold on to and exercise power by reading the stars.

Tiberius also owned a pet snake that accompanied him on all of his journeys. One day, Tiberius opened up the snake's box to discover to his horror that his beloved snake had died and was being eaten by ants. Interpreting this as a negative omen, he immediately canceled the trip that he had just embarked upon. Other emperors were also highly superstitious. Even Augustus, the model of a good, rational emperor, had a number of superstitions. For example, if he accidentally put a shoe on the wrong foot when getting out of bed in the morning, he took it as a bad omen for the day; and he carried a small piece of sealskin with him at all times, believing that this would protect him from lightning.

Ancient people used other methods to attempt to predict the future as well. One of the more creative of such endeavors sounds almost exactly like an ancient equivalent to the Ouija board, which is still sold in toy stores today as a game (available now in a glow-in-the-dark version), stripped of its original supernatural menace. The ancient variant consisted of a tripod of laurel branches with a ring suspended by a string from the apex. This contraption was placed over a metal dish inscribed with the letters of the alphabet and, after posing a question, the ring was tapped, causing it to swing back and forth and supposedly spell out the answer in the same manner that the planchette of a Ouija board spells out answers to questions that have been asked of it. The creators of this ancient fortune-telling device came to an unfortunate end, however, when it was reported to the emperor that they had used it to inquire as to the identity of the next emperor. The current emperor interpreted this as treason and had them executed.

The supernatural: Ghosts, werewolves, and vampires

Ghost stories told late at night around the campfire have long been used to induce an exciting thrill of fear in listeners. Today, the popularity of ghost stories endures, though more often translated onto the big screen as horror movies and the little screen as television shows about ghost-hunters. Almost anywhere they travel, tourists can visit famous haunted sites or take tours of, for instance, "Haunted London." Currently there are several popular ongoing TV series about people who seek out supposedly haunted places and try to document or make contact with the spirits who dwell there. When did our fascination with ghosts and our idea of being haunted by them begin?

Those of us who have been to a large zoo have likely seen a genuine Roman "ghost." In this case, the explanation is natural rather than supernatural, and is the animal known as a lemur. Due to its nocturnal life-style, its eerie vocalizations, its huge reflective eyes, and the difficulty of spotting it in its forest habitat, the lemur derives its name from the Latin word *lemures*. These were spirits who returned to haunt their former household during the festival of the Lemuria, on May 9th, 11th, and 13th. This was a more hostile visitation than the one that occurred during the benign Parentalia (discussed in Chapter 2), when ancestors and relatives were honored.

An alternate name for one of these Roman ghosts was *larva*, which nowadays refers to a newly hatched, often formless-looking insect. How did this happen? During the Middle Ages, "larva" also came to mean a frightening mask (which is an interesting development, given that the Romans made and displayed masks of their dead family members that were called *imagines*—singular form, *imago*). In the eighteenth century, "larva" underwent a transformation from superstition to science when the Swedish botanist Linnaeus (popularly known as the father of modern taxonomy) adopted it to mean an immature insect that "masked" its adult form. Linnaeus also came up with the term "imago" for the last phase in an insect's development before it becomes an adult—the same word the Romans used for their masks of the dead. Finally, Linnaeus was the one who, in 1758, gave the lemur its name because it reminded him of a ghost. Linnaeus' seeming obsession with Roman ghosts has therefore informed biology and our perception of the animal kingdom.

The idea that a proper burial is necessary or else a spirit, unable to reach the afterlife, will remain in this world as a ghost, haunting people, originates in antiquity. It was believed that if a body was not buried with a coin to pay the ferryman, Charon, its spirit would remain stranded on the earthly side of the Styx River, unable to cross to the Underworld. Today, it is commonly thought that ghosts are the spirits of those who have suffered an injustice, died or were killed in some horrible way, or have some sort of unresolved issue that keeps them bound to this world and unable to rest in peace. In ancient Greece, *psychagogoi* ("soul-drawers") were those able to call forth the dead. The first known record of this occurs in Homer's *Odyssey*, when Odysseus summons the shade of the seer Teirisias by sacrificing an animal and pouring its blood into a lake that communicates with the Underworld. A throng of spirits hurries forth to crouch by the lake and lap up the blood, which holds the memory of life. *Psychagogoi* could attract a soul by sacrificing an animal and using its blood as a draw, as in the *Odyssey*, or they could locate the body by leading a black sheep until it sat down on the spot and then sacrifice it there, accompanied by complex spells. After doing this, "they mark off and walk around the place and they listen to the ghosts as they speak and ask the reasons for their anger." This form of exorcism was somewhat like talk therapy to help a spirit work through its anger issues so that it could find rest.

Why do we think of ghosts as rattling chains? Those who have read Charles Dickens' "A Christmas Carol" might assume that this image comes from Marley's ghost, who appears to Scrooge encircled with and dragging heavy chains burdened with reminders of his earthly profession. However, the roots lie much deeper. In the first century A.D., Pliny the Younger recorded the influential story of a ghost in a haunted mansion that established a number of supernatural archetypes that would last for many centuries to come (*Epistles* Bk. 7, letter 27). Chief among these are a chain-rattling ghost and a creepy old house that is haunted. In the story, the sound of rattling chains presages the appearance of a hideous ghost with chains wrapped around his wrists and ankles, who terrorizes the inhabitants of the house until they either perish from sleeplessness and fear or desert it.

A philosopher named Athenodorus comes to Athens and finds this large, spacious house on the market for a suspiciously cheap price. When he discovers why, rather than being deterred, he buys the house and decides to engage in some ghost-hunting. When night falls, he sits down with writing tablets and a pen to occupy his mind so that he won't start imagining things. At last, he hears the sound of clanking chains approaching ever nearer, but he just keeps concentrating on his writing until he realizes that the ghost is right next to him, beckoning with a finger. In an amazing display of sang-froid, the philosopher gestures to the ghost to wait a minute while he finishes what he is working on, but the ghost impatiently rattles the chains over his head until he follows. The ghost, moving slowly as though weighed down by his chains, leads him to the courtyard and vanishes. Athenodorus marks the spot, and the next day has it dug up, discovering a pile of bones intermingled with chains. After these are given a proper burial, the ghost is apparently satisfied, for he never appears again.

We can thus observe an interesting evolution in those seeking to exorcize ghosts. In the ancient world, it is the rational, level-headed philosopher who fulfills this role. From the Middle Ages on, it is the priest, with the support of God and religion, who can lay ghosts to rest. Today, ghost-hunting aspires to be a scientific pursuit, as experts in the paranormal (humorously exemplified by the techno-babble-spouting heroes of the *Ghostbusters* films) lug around equipment that detects sudden drops in temperature or picks up the movements of shadowy figures.

Strictly speaking, vampires do not appear in classical literature, though creatures with vampire-like tendencies do. One third-century A.D. text tells the story of a handsome young philosopher named Menippus, whose one weakness is sex. He falls in love with what seems to be a beautiful, gentle, wealthy woman, and they embark on an affair. When he is on the verge of marrying her, one of his associates forces her into telling the truth. All of her fine possessions vanish, and she reveals that she is an *empousa*—a female ghost that craves sex and human flesh. She had been "fattening up" Menippus with pleasure in preparation for eating his body; she admits to particularly enjoying beautiful young men because their blood is pure (Philostratus, *Life of Apollonius* 4.25). Tales of dead young women deceiving men into sleeping with them were relatively common; by dying young, they had missed out on the pleasures of life, which they sought to experience even though dead. Greek folklore was also rife with accounts of female ghosts eating their male lovers; another type of ghostly female was called a *lamia*.

Werewolves also show up in Greek and Roman texts. The historian Herodotus mentions that he has heard of a people called the Neuri who turn into wolves for a few days each year and then become human again, although he expresses skepticism (*The Persian Wars* 4.105). A story recorded by the Greek writer Pausanias (*Description of Greece* 6.6.7–11) describes the ghost of a rapist who comes back to kill off members of the community that stoned him for his crime. The villagers are instructed by the Pythia (the local prophetess) to give the ghost a virgin bride every year, which appeases it. But one year, a man falls in love with the victim, fights the ghost, and drives it away. A painting of the ghost depicts him wearing a wolfskin, with the caption "Lycas/Alibas" ("Wolfy" or "Corpse").

In his novel *The Satyricon*, Petronius describes a man's transformation into a werewolf; he takes off his clothes, pees around them in a circle, becomes a wolf, starts howling, and runs off into the woods. His horrified companion later discovers that a savage wolf ravaged the flocks that same night, draining their blood, and was stabbed through the neck. When he returns home, his friend is there with a doctor tending to his wounded neck, and it becomes clear that the man was a werewolf or shape-shifter (61–2). Pliny scoffingly relates the story that a certain Arcadian family draws lots to decide which member will have to become a werewolf for a period of nine years. The unlucky man removes his clothes, goes off into the forest, joins a pack of fellow werewolves, and, if he abstains from eating human flesh during that time, can become a man again and return home—though his human form will have aged nine years.

However, the phenomenon of lycanthropy (or wolf-man disease; Greek *lykos*: wolf and *anthropos*: man) is also discussed scientifically in a second-century A.D. medical treatise, in which the author calls it a form of melancholia, lists the symptoms (dry tongue, sunken eyes, weight loss, turning into a wolf in the month of February and hanging out by graveyards until dawn), and supplies a cure (bleed the patient, bathe him, give him wholesome food and a certain medicine, and give him sleep-inducing drinks and opium when the "disease" starts to take effect). It is interesting to note that lycanthropy manifests itself in February—the month when the Lupercalia ("wolf festival") took place at Rome, beginning at the cave (the Lupercal) where the she-wolf suckled Romulus and Remus. (The Lupercalia is described in more detail in Chapter 2.)

A world full of gods: Greek and Roman religious beliefs

While we tend to divide religion and superstition into separate categories, in antiquity they both existed on the same continuum of spiritual beliefs that tried to explain the world so that it made sense and so that we could devise ways to deal with it. The difference was that, when beliefs were taken too far and resulted in excessive or immoderate behavior, this was bad, whereas piety and the proper, decorous observation of religious rituals was a good thing.

Although the pagan religions of the classical world are (for the most part) no longer practiced today, their influence can still be discerned—even in the practices and beliefs of that most anti-pagan religion, Christianity. But before we consider specific interactions between pagan beliefs and Christianity, let us look at some of the more general notions bequeathed to us by Greek and Roman religion.

Like us, the pagan Greeks and Romans said prayers, conducted religious ceremonies, celebrated religious festivals, and worshiped higher powers. But unlike many of today's major religions, such as Christianity and Islam, which are monotheistic, they were polytheistic, meaning that they believed in many gods. Probably the most commonly known ones today are the 12 Olympians, thus named because they lived on top of Mount Olympus in northern Greece, who all belonged to the same (not always happy) family. (The number sometimes appears as 14, when Hades, god of the Underworld, and Dionysos, the god of wine, are added.) Although the Olympian gods originated in Greece, the names that the Romans gave them have more thoroughly infused the English language. "Cereal" comes from Ceres (Demeter), the goddess of agriculture and especially grain crops; "martial" from Mars (Ares), the god of war; "volcano" from Vulcan (Hephaestus), the god of fire and forges. Several of them were grandchildren of the Earth, the goddess Gaea; they had to fight and defeat the intervening generation, the Titans, to gain control. From the Titans, who were literally mighty giants, we derive our words "titan," someone gigantic in size or power (often in a figurative sense) or known for towering achievements, and "titanic."

However, the Olympians were not the only gods. In pagan belief systems, there are many gods and demi-gods who exert power over the natural world. In addition to the famous pantheon of gods dwelling on Mount Olympus, the ancient Greeks envisioned a world full of nature spirits inhabiting every mountain, river, and tree. This belief that there are spirits present not just in humans but in all things, called animism (from the Latin word *anima*, "soul"), is common in many early religions. Nymphs, the minor female divinities who dwelt in and had power over a particular place, object, or natural phenomenon, were divided into many categories: nereids were sea-nymphs; oreads were mountain-nymphs; naiads governed lakes, springs, and brooks; dryads and hamadryads lived in trees. Rivers were ruled over by male river gods; male woodland spirits (sporting goats' legs, tails, animal ears, and horns) called satyrs (fauns by the Romans) took part in the revels of the wine-god Dionysos and spent much of their time chasing nymphs (from which we get the terms satyr to denote a lascivious man and satyriasis to refer to uncontrollable, excessive sexual desire in men). The shepherd-god Pan (similarly endowed with goats' legs, horns, and lustiness) invented the Pan pipes after a failed conquest; the nymph Syrinx was transformed into reeds to escape his embraces, so Pan settled for fashioning a musical instrument from her and learning to play it beautifully. The word "panic" also comes from Pan, whose shout could induce irrational terror in an enemy army, causing them all to flee. These demi-gods suggest a connection between human sexuality and the fecundity of nature.

It has been posited that, early on, Roman religion bordered on animism, in that spirits were thought to infuse everything. Sacred woods, springs, and caves, inhabited by spirits called *numina* (the source of our word "numinous," meaning "filled with a sense of divine presence") dotted the natural landscape. These spirits at first did not even assume human form, and were worshiped at open-air altars at the places where they dwelt. The people who held sway over Italy before the Romans rose to power, the Etruscans (who were themselves influenced by the Greeks who had colonized Italy), are often credited with having bequeathed to the Romans both anthropomorphic gods who could be represented as statues and the idea of building permanent temples where they could be worshiped rather than just open-air altars. *Numina* came to inhabit things (such as crops), actions (like traveling), and abstract concepts (virtue and loyalty, for example) as well as places. Some developed concrete identities, appearances, and personalities, and turned into gods. However, invisible spirits retained an important role in Roman religion. The *genius* (literally "the begetter") was the guardian spirit of a person or place; its derivation from the Latin *gignere*, "to produce," is reflected in our use of "genius" to mean the power to create things and those who possess that power. Each individual had his or her own *genius*, a bit like our concept of a guardian angel. A man's *genius* was what allowed him to sire children. The Roman family had its own special *genius* that the entire family worshiped to ensure its continuing existence. The *genius loci* (Latin for "spirit of the place") was a form of address you employed when you were not sure about the name of the deity to whom you were sacrificing—a polite way to say "Hey, you" without offending the deity.

While most people no longer believe that every plant and body of water harbors a spirit, perhaps we can observe the echoes of this notion in the works of the American Transcendentalists such as Emerson and Thoreau, and even in modern attitudes towards nature. Instead of many spirits, Emerson saw one spirit infusing nature, which reflects the unity of all things as ordered by God. The immanence of God that he saw in nature may be analogous to nature's infusion with spirits in the pagan worldview; both speak of the power and majesty of the natural world, and explain why it affects us so deeply. The environmental movement, which urges us to be kind to "Mother Earth," personifies our world in a way that harkens back to the Greek goddess Gaea (or Ge), Mother Earth, who first gave birth (both by herself through parthenogenesis and with her husband Uranus, the Sky) to life. The Gaia Theory, postulated in the 1960s by the British scientist James Lovelock, which suggests that the earth might be considered as a single living organism, derives its name from the ancient goddess, as do the disciplines of geography and geology.

Hero worship, still a common phrase today, originated in ancient Greece, albeit with a different meaning. Whereas hero worship nowadays typically denotes reverence for a respected figure, often a child admiring someone older, originally hero worship was literally the worship of heroes: religious devotions directed towards a group of demi-gods, or heroes, situated between humans and gods. These were often literally half-divine: the children from unions between gods and humans, like Herakles (Roman Hercules), a son of Zeus, and Theseus, a son of Poseidon. (In particular, the male gods' frequent lusting after mortal women meant that there was no shortage of demi-gods, although female gods went after men as well.) The graves of heroes were sites of cult activities such as sacrifices, and worshippers left gifts there to honor the dead hero and procure his help or protection.

Like the nature spirits mentioned above, the hero was restricted to a specific place, the area where his grave was located, and thus often played an important role in establishing group identity for a nearby city; if more than one city claimed a particular hero (and hero's grave, or *heroon*) as its own, this was therefore an impossible situation, and the dispute had to be settled. However, a hero's bones could sometimes be moved, if sanctioned by an oracle's pronouncement, in order to protect a new place; for instance, the general Cimon found what was allegedly the hero Theseus' grave on the island of Skyros and had his large corpse brought to Athens and interred in a temple, the Theseion. (Heroes' corpses and bones, like their reputations and powers, were typically huge; the hero Orestes' coffin was said to be 7 cubits long.)

As protector of a city or tribe, a dead hero might appear at a battle to help fight the enemy, either huge and superhuman in appearance or invisible but exerting his powers none the less. He could also supply healing, good harvests, and omens if shown the proper respect by worshippers. If neglected, however, heroes could harm rather than help. Due to their terrifying nature, snakes were seen as manifestations of heroes; Theophrastus says that the superstitious man will build a *heroon* where he spots one (*Characters* 16.4). If you visit the Athenian agora, you can still see the base of the famous ancient "Monument of the Eponymous Heroes," which originally bore bronze statues of the heroes who gave their names to the ten Athenian tribes established by Cleisthenes around 508 B.C. These were chosen from a preliminary list of about 100 heroes submitted by the Athenians to the Delphic Oracle, who picked the top ten. Over the centuries, a few new heroes were added (and then removed) according to the political situation. This monument came to function as a sort of civic bulletin board, where official announcements, proposed laws, the schedule for court hearings, and news about the tribes were all posted along the base.

Thus, the Greeks and Romans worshiped all sorts of gods, demi-gods, nature spirits, superhuman heroes, and even personified concepts (such as the Greek Nike, or victory, a winged goddess whose name was appropriated for a popular brand of sneakers, and the Roman Fortuna, the goddess of luck, often depicted with a spinning wheel signifying how fortune is constantly changing—perhaps best known today as a popular game-show). The Greek thinker often credited as the first philosopher, Thales of Miletus, famously stated that: "All things are full of gods." How did a world in which divinities dwelt everywhere and new gods were constantly being discovered and adopted turn into today's world, where the two biggest religions, Christianity and Islam, are monotheistic?

You can have only one God: The rise of Christianity

Christianity arose in the Roman world, and its initial suppression and persecution played a crucial role in the formation of Christian identity. Tales of martyrs who died, usually in horribly gruesome ways, rather than renounce their faith circulated widely, and were eventually gathered in extensive lists called martyrologies. Stories of how joyously and fearlessly Christians embraced death probably piqued the interest of pagans and inspired conversions, since they lacked a concept equivalent to heaven. The ancient Greeks and Romans did not have a well-defined, consistent vision of an afterlife. Some believed death was the end; others believed in a shadowy underworld ruled over by Hades in which some suffered punishments for their behavior in life while the majority drifted around as shades. The Elysian Fields, described by Homer as an idyllic paradise with perfect weather, were at least initially reserved for heroes and those who were related to the gods, so most people had little hope of admittance there. Christianity offered the promise of Heaven for all believers, a new and appealing idea.

The sense of equality of all believers before God was welcomed by the many disempowered groups in Roman society, which was highly stratified, with rigid class and status distinctions. If you were poor or a woman, you had little value; if you were a slave, you had been reduced to a piece of property. But in Christianity, you had value in the eyes of God, and could gain distinction for your religious devotion. In its early days, women were even allowed to serve as deaconesses, and poverty was extolled as a virtue rather than looked down upon.

Christianity's insistence on monotheism inevitably led to conflicts with the Roman authorities, who were perfectly willing to accept the Christian God as yet another in their ever-expanding pantheon, but could not understand why He had to be the only god. Also, the empowerment of those who had long endured discrimination posed a threat to the status quo and social stability. Persecution forced many Christians to worship in secret. If you walk through the first-century A.D. Christian catacombs that lie beneath the city of Rome, you will see a fish outline consisting of 2 curved lines etched here and there. Why did the fish become an important Christian symbol? The Greek word for fish, *ichthys*, can be read as an acronym for the phrase "Iesous Christos,

Figure 6.3 *Christian tombstone. This very early Christian tombstone found near the Vatican features an image of fish, and the inscription says "fish of the living," referring to those born again through the ritual of baptism.*

Theou Yios, Soter," or "Jesus Christ, son of God, Savior." It is said that the early Christians used this symbol to mark their tombs and meeting places and as a way to differentiate fellow believers from potential informers in a hostile environment. For those in the know, the fish meant Christianity; for the uninitiated, it was just a simple drawing of a fish. It is interesting to note that another significant, common early Christian symbol was the dove, the bird of peace—which also happened to be the bird of the goddess of love, Aphrodite/Venus. Was this a conscious appropriation of a pagan symbol of erotic love to instead signify Christian love?

So how did Christianity change from a persecuted minority religion with little influence, into the most powerful religion in the world, which shaped all aspects of life during the Middle Ages? While people tend to envision the Roman emperors persecuting Christians, they also *became* Christians, and made Christianity the official religion of the Roman empire. When Constantine converted after dreaming that Christ showed him the Chi Rho symbol (the first two letters of Christ rendered in Greek) and said "In this sign, conquer" (his troops, with the Chi Rho painted on their shields, indeed routed the enemy), this was the first step in a major transition. In A.D. 313, Constantine issued the Edict of Milan, which proclaimed freedom for all—including Christians—to worship whatever god they pleased, and also decreed that the property confiscated from Christians during earlier persecutions should be returned to them.

Figure 6.4 *The Emperor Constantine. This head of the first emperor to convert to Christianity was once part of a colossal statue of which only the head and feet survive intact.*

Later, Christianity's adoption as the official state religion of Rome would help even more to spread it throughout the vast Roman empire. Perhaps a less-known fact is that, in addition to promoting Christianity, the later Roman emperors also began to vigorously persecute paganism, and engaged in such persecutions for several centuries until it was finally wiped out. Roman emperors passed edicts banning animal sacrifice, divination, and augury, shutting down oracles, and forbidding the use of pagan temples for religious ceremonies.

Finally, in A.D. 380, Theodosius I decreed Catholic (Nicene) Christianity the official state religion and, from A.D. 389 to 392, he issued stringent anti-pagan decrees aimed at sweeping away any remnants of paganism: he outlawed blood sacrifices; he closed Roman temples; he dissolved the Vestal Virgins; he had pagan feasts declared workdays; and, in A.D. 393, he even put an end to the Olympic Games because they were associated with the worship of pagan deities. In A.D. 435, Theodosius II declared that all pagan temples should either be destroyed or converted into Christian churches. Justinian, who reigned between A.D. 527 and 565, persecuted pagans in ways both minor and major. He banned pagans from civil service jobs, denied government stipends to pagan teachers (and had them exiled and their property confiscated if they refused baptism), and closed down pagan centers of learning such as Aristotle's Lyceum, the Skeptic Academy, the Stoic Porch, and the Epicurean Garden. He also decreed death for those who secretly sacrificed to the gods, and for baptized Christians who reverted to pagan practices. In the end, the tables had been turned, and paganism became the minority religion forced to practice in secret. Thus, the Roman emperors may have been good at persecutions, but these were aimed at pagans as well as Christians. One might speculate as to what would have happened if the Roman emperors had stuck with paganism instead of converting to Christianity.

It could even be argued that the momentous split of Christianity into Catholicism and Protestantism was affected by attitudes towards antiquity. Did the Reformation grow at least partly out of latent fears of paganism? At the time of the Reformation, religious icons and art were venerated in Christian churches throughout the world, but some saw a hint of pagan idolatry (the worship of images or objects rather than God) in this practice. For example, the Christian saints, somewhat like the pagan gods, were represented with specific iconographic symbols (often references to how they had been martyred) and functioned as the special patrons of various professions, cities, and problems. When these saints became popular later in the Middle Ages, and people prayed before the statue of a saint asking for divine intercession and help with their troubles and left offerings there, it almost amounted to a revival of the old polytheistic tradition of many gods, each of whom was associated with a specific region, profession, or problem. The Reformation revived a suspicion of idolatry, resulting in an outbreak of iconoclasm—the destruction of any religious images that might be considered idolatrous. Statues of saints, paintings, and stained glass windows were smashed, as earthly distractions from true religious feeling.

Pope Leo X, who sat on the papal throne when Martin Luther began comparing the Papacy to the Antichrist, had received a humanistic education and loved art, the Greek and Roman classics, and the works of the Renaissance humanists who were reviving classical culture. Martin Luther was upset by this revival of antiquity, and doubly annoyed that the Pope was a patron of the arts who helped to finance it. His pronounced distaste for the ancients is suggested by an anecdote in which his fellow reformer Ulrich Zwingli, who has been arguing with him heatedly about theological doctrine, looks forward to a time when they will both be at peace in heaven, with all their questions answered, fraternizing with Socrates, Plato, and Aristotle. Luther, deeply shocked, protests that they are unbaptized pagans burning in hell. When Zwingli defends them as virtuous men led by their consciences, Luther angrily accuses him of not being a Christian.

The artist Lucas Cranach the Elder, a friend of Luther's, produced a series of woodcuts contrasting Christ's humility with the prideful pope's attachment to earthly pleasures; like a corrupt Roman emperor, he delights in power (wearing a crown, having his feet kissed by the nobility, sitting on a throne, being carried in a litter) and its trappings (he is surrounded by ornate architecture, eating and drinking to excess). The title of Luther's tract "The Pagan Servitude of the Church" (1520) uses "pagan" as a dirty word, reflecting his belief that pagan accretions and practices had to be stripped away from the Church to restore its original purity. Had Martin Luther been educated in Italy and learned to love ancient art and literature, he might not have developed into such a vocal critic of the Church and the Pope and such a zealous reformer. Perhaps the Reformation did not take hold as strongly in Italy, which remained a Catholic country, because of its deep-rooted attachment to the longstanding "pagan"-tinged traditions that troubled Luther.

How to worship: Prayer, sacrifice, priests, and divination

Next, let us consider how the pagans worshiped their gods, and the major similarities to or differences from the religious ceremonies we practice today.

There were two main ways in which the Greeks and Romans communicated with their gods: prayer and sacrifice. Their prayers had some similarities with modern monotheistic practices: they talked to a god directly; they acknowledged his or her power; they made requests; they followed certain verbal formulas (as do Christians by always ending with "Amen"). The gesture they made when praying—extending the arms and lifting them skywards—was absorbed into Christianity. If you walk through a Christian catacomb, you will likely see wall paintings of Christians with their arms outstretched and raised, palms turned outwards, signifying that they are praying. Known as "orans" figures, these frequently appear in early Christian art. This same gesture (the orant posture) is still made today by the priest officiating at a Roman Catholic mass when he is praying on behalf of the entire congregation. In more recent decades, this attitude of prayer has become increasingly popular in Charismatic churches, where members of the congregation adopt the pose as well. Thus, even when engaged in Christian prayers, we might unconsciously be assuming a pose of very great antiquity, used for centuries before the birth of Christianity.

Figure 6.5 *Plaque with Christian images. This carving illustrates two important early Christian symbols, the Chi-Rho icon made famous by Constantine's vision, and a dove bearing an olive branch, flanking a praying woman in the orant posture.*

However, unlike Christian prayers, ancient pagan ones in some ways resembled a business transaction. The prayer always contained a reminder of what the worshiper had done for the god in the past, whether through offerings, sacrifices, or temple-building. This pointed reminder of past services would hopefully persuade the god to give the worshiper something in return by fulfilling his request. Also, whereas the Christian god is considered omniscient and can hear all of our prayers, even the most powerful pagan gods were incapable of this. If they were busy or distracted or just in the wrong place, they might not hear your prayer. Therefore, like letters, ancient prayers were often "addressed" to a list of places considered especially sacred to the god, where he might well be hanging out. This would make it more likely that your prayer would be heard. In a similar vein, the answer to Plutarch's question "Why are boys made to go out of the house when they want to swear an oath?" is so that the oath-taker can't hide from the god of the sky, who will witness his promise and hold him to it.

While nowadays we like to speak of making sacrifices (and remind others of the sacrifices we have made for them), these tend to be figurative ones rather than the very literal ones practiced in the ancient world, which generally involved the killing of animals. The Latin word *sacrificium*, an offering to the gods, derived from combining *sacrum*, meaning "sacred," and *facere*, meaning "to do or make." When you offered a sacrifice, you were literally making it sacred or holy by giving it to the gods, whose property it became. There were both blood sacrifices (animals) and bloodless ones (typically grain or wine). In blood sacrifices, it was important that the animal went to its death willingly; any sign of struggle was a bad omen, and any mistakes in the ceremony meant that it had to be done over again from the beginning. The Greek hecatomb was the sacrifice of 100 cattle, but small-scale sacrifice was more usual. A popular Roman sacrifice was the *suovetaurilia*, in which a pig, a sheep, and a bull were killed. Certain gods liked to receive certain animals; the sacrifice of choice for Asklepios, the Greek god of medicine, was a rooster, for example. Celestial or sky gods favored white animals, while chthonic (underworld) gods required black ones.

However, even though the sacrifice technically became a god's property, that did not prevent worshipers from eating the meat. Typically, some

Figure 6.6 *Relief showing a sacrificial procession. The bull in this image is about to be sacrificed. The man with the round mallet over his shoulder will strike it on the head and then the man in front will cut its throat with his triangular knife.*

portions would be consigned to the flames on the altar as burnt offerings (Homer often refers to "thighs wrapped in fat"), and the gods would enjoy the savory smell rising up to Mount Olympus, but they themselves ate ambrosia and drank nectar rather than human food. Rather than letting all that meat go to waste, the Greeks had a feast, so that a sacrifice was kind of like a combination religious ritual and big barbecue.

Semitic peoples such as the Hebrews also engaged in animal sacrifice, like the ram that Abraham kills in place of Isaac, and they made burnt offerings as well. The metaphorical comparison of Christ's death with the sacrifice of a lamb has sometimes been interpreted as a rejection of pagan (and early Jewish) practices. Since animal sacrifice was so clearly pagan in nature, the early Christians rejected it. In contrast to the party atmosphere of the pagan sacrificial feast, the Last Supper is a somber occasion. However, by describing Christ's death as a sacrifice and by likening the Eucharist to the post-sacrificial feast (the wine as his blood, the bread as his body), the early Christians were expressing their beliefs in the sort of language and metaphors that everyone in the ancient world could understand—even the pagans—which might have helped with conversions, by making a new belief understandable through ideas and traditions that people already knew about. By willingly going to his death, Christ echoes the animals in pagan blood sacrifices, but he is truly conscious of his fate and aware of what it signifies, unlike the dazed or drugged animals being led by halters.

In Christianity, a symbolic sacrifice is made by worshipers observing Lent, the 40-day period leading up to Easter, the celebration of Christ's ultimate sacrifice of his life, which functioned as the very genesis of Christianity. In emulation of Jesus, who fasted in the desert for 40 days, worshipers abstain from meat or give up something they particularly enjoy to express their repentance and self-denial.

While Christ's self-sacrifice and resurrection were central to the formation of Christianity, the idea of a god who suffers, dies, and is resurrected had already existed for centuries in Egypt and the Middle East. Mystery religions, thus called because they were practiced in secret and were only open to initiates, had appeared in Greece by the sixth century B.C. Members underwent initiation rites that tended to involve cleansing and purification, and a more direct, personal sort of relationship between the individual and a god (without the need for a priest's intervention) was sought. Mystery religions devoted to the gods Isis and Mithras grew very popular in Rome during the early Empire. Because their rituals were often described in coded language, many of them still remain mysterious to us today. The emphasis typically found in these mystery religions on rituals of rebirth, cleansing rituals involving water, initiation rites, divine intervention, and life after death may have directly influenced many aspects of Christianity, including rituals such as baptism, and core concepts such as heaven.

Finally, the Greeks and Romans had priests who functioned as intermediaries between human beings and the gods and sought to interpret and communicate their will, as priests and theologians still do today. In ancient Greece, the *hiereus* (priest) and the *hiereia* (priestess) were known as such because they watched over the *hiera* (the "sacred things") kept in the sanctuary of a temple. (Our word "hierarchy" comes from the Greek *hierarkhia*, rule of a high priest, and the connotation of holiness is preserved in "hieroglyph," "sacred writing".) By tradition, priests usually served male gods and priestesses female ones. They conducted religious rituals, performed sacrifices, ran religious festivals, and presided over solemn ceremonies such as weddings, funerals, purification rites, and oath-taking. A temple might have only a single priest or priestess to look after it, but larger temples sometimes required a whole staff of specialists to run them, such as libation bearers, holy-water carriers, wine pourers, musicians, and key holders. The role of the *exegetai* ("interpreters of sacred law") is echoed in the practice of Biblical exegesis, the interpretation of the Bible, and the *diakonos* (the source of our word "deacon") was a servant in charge of temple chores.

In Rome, powerful priesthoods practiced rites meant to maintain a positive relationship between the gods and the state, rather like official government ambassadors to the divine. However, unlike priests today, Romans were priests only part-time, and had day jobs, so to speak (often in politics, since they were drawn from the Patrician class). Priests were members of the secular community, not separated from it as a distinct, especially holy caste. They were grouped in "colleges" and "brotherhoods," and there were many different types of priests with varying responsibilities and duties.

The Roman priests' emphasis was primarily on carefully following ritual procedures, since any mistake endangered the entire state by potentially bringing bad luck. If a priest severely screwed up a ceremony, he was expected to abdicate his office; Livy mentions one doing so after mishandling the entrails of a sacrificed animal (26.23.8). Certain priests wore a special hat called the *apex*, resembling a flat disk with a rod sticking out of the top, or were identified by special costumes. Some priests were also governed by strict taboos, particularly the main priest of Jupiter known as the *flamen Dialis*: he could never see armed soldiers in battle ranks; he could not wear a ring or any knots whatsoever on his body; he could neither touch nor name a female goat; he could neither see nor touch a dog or a dead body; his hair and nail trimmings had to be buried beneath a healthy tree; it was illegal for anyone else to sleep in his bed; and he could not remove his underwear except in a covered place, so that Jupiter would not see him naked—to name only a few of the regulations that governed his highly restricted existence.

The Romans thought that one could learn the gods' will by observing signs (*auspicia*); thus, we now call an occasion "auspicious" when we feel we can predict that success seems likely, and we say "under the auspices of" to indicate the endorsement or approval of some institution. (For the Romans, such endorsement could come only from the gods.) Omens could take various forms, though phenomena associated with the sky were especially popular: for instance, thunder, lightning, and bird flight were seen as carrying divine messages. Indeed, the word *auspicia* was derived from the combination of *avis* and *specio*, meaning literally "to look at birds." "Augury" probably derives from the same root as *auspicia*, and *augurs* read signs from birds, such as their flight patterns, feeding habits, and the sounds they made, in order to determine whether the gods approved or disapproved of a particular course of action; like a magic eight-ball, they provided only a "yes" or "no" answer.

Our word "inaugurate" comes from the Latin *inaugurare*, to seek omens from the flight of birds, because this was standard procedure before a Roman official could be consecrated and installed in office. Today, politicians are still sworn into office at an inauguration, though without the benefit of avian advice. Another popular form of divination was extispicy—"reading" the entrails of sacrificial animals in order to predict the future. The *haruspex* ("gut-gazer") was an expert at interpreting the gods' will by examining entrails such as the liver and the gallbladder, and seeing messages in their appearance. So-called bronze "training" livers have been found that are marked off into little sections, each of which bears notations in Etruscan. (The Etruscans, known as the inventors of extispicy, were considered especially skilled at it.) Regardless of the type of divination being practiced, extensive study and training were required, and only specialists were capable of it. The average person needed a priest to interpret omens for him; he could not do it himself.

Feriae, or festival days, were devoted to religious rites honoring the gods. People could visit temples to observe the prayers and sacrifices being conducted by the priests, though they could not take part in public, state-run rituals. Everyone, even slaves, was supposed to rest on these days. Varro referred to them as "days instituted for the sake of the gods" (*De Lingua Latina* 6.12), and Cicero wrote that on such days freedmen should avoid lawsuits and slaves labor (*Laws* 2.29). The agricultural work that could be done on these days was

Figure 6.7 *Drawing of a bronze liver. This bronze liver, marked into regions, was probably used as a training device to instruct novice priests how to interpret signs from the gods, which appeared on these organs that were inspected as a part of sacrifices.*

restricted, and in Rome, *flamines* (a type of priest) were not supposed to see any labor being done, so heralds walked in front of them calling for all work to cease so that the day's holiness would not be impaired.

This all sounds rather similar to the notion of observing the Sabbath by stopping all work in order to devote oneself to honoring God. However, not everyone bothered to go to the temples; there were Romans who took advantage of the day off as the opportunity for a holiday, and even pious Romans often had fun after they had done their worshiping. *Feriae* were originally known as "feast days" because the rich were supposed to provide a meal for the poor. One is reminded how, in the Catholic Church, saints' days are also called "feast days"; perhaps in the Middle Ages a holy day was also a time for rest from labor and a good meal.

Ancient worshipers engaged in religious processions, still practiced by churches today, especially in Mediterranean countries, where holy statues and relics are often borne aloft. There were various types of sacred procession in antiquity, some modest and others involving thousands of people.

Supplicationes were processions from temple to temple to worship the gods. The *lustratio*, a purification ceremony aimed at banishing hostile spirits from an object, group, or territory, was sometimes conducted as a procession around a piece of land, in which a luck-bringing object would be slowly carried along, with pauses for prayer and sacrifices. Such rituals were intended to eliminate inimical or dangerous spirits from the region, and the Catholic Church still performs analogous ceremonies. Portable shrines were sometimes carried, as can still be observed today. In the *pompa*, a ritual procession that took place during festivals and funerals, wagons called *tensae* pulled around statues and other emblems of the gods; this is the source of our word "pomp," a magnificent or dignified display, which is most commonly heard describing military funerals and in the march "Pomp and Circumstance" that is played during the processional at many high school and college graduation ceremonies.

A visit to church: Christianity borrows from paganism

Christian reactions to paganism were of two types: either defining Christianity as the complete opposite of paganism, or absorbing and assimilating certain aspects of paganism in order to make the new religion more understandable and palatable to pagans in the hope of converting them. Or, in a more ambitious strategy, the two approaches could be combined, using pagan ideas as a starting point but then putting a Christian spin on them and emphasizing the difference. Let us consider some comparisons (and contrasts) through the concrete example of a visit to a Catholic church.

Imagine you are attending a Catholic service in one of Europe's fine old cathedrals. You enter through large doors, often surrounded with carvings to inspire you for the service: scenes of the Last Judgment in the tympanum, the semi-circular area above the doors, and rows of saints clutching their attributes at each side. The very fact that you have gone *inside* a building to attend the service can be traced to ancient Greek and Roman religious practices. The Greeks and Romans generally performed their religious rituals and ceremonies outdoors, in front of or on the steps of their temples rather than inside them; it was a public event that all passers-by could witness—a part of official, state-sanctioned cultural life.

Figure 6.8 *Door of Notre Dame Cathedral in Paris. This entrance, surrounded by statues of saints and surmounted by a semi-circular tympanum, packs an enormous amount of Christian religious iconography into a small space.*

At its beginnings, Christianity was in contrast one of hundreds of mystery religions, so called because their teachings and rituals were performed in a private setting and kept secret from everyone other than the worshipers; what practitioners of mystery religions did was indeed a mystery to outsiders. Therefore, early Christians worshiped indoors rather than outdoors, in buildings derived from Roman architecture. This indoor worship defined them as being fundamentally different from pagans, which led to lots of suspicion and misunderstandings. Pagans were puzzled as to why Christians would want to worship inside where they could not be observed, which made them suspect that Christian rituals were unsavory or disturbing in some way. Thus, when pagans heard garbled rumors of Christian doctrine ("Love thy brother and love thy sister" sounded potentially like incest, and the Eucharist like human sacrifice and cannibalism), they tended to believe them, because who knew what they were up to, and what did they have to hide?

While Christians initially met in private homes in order to avoid detection, the eventual acceptance of Christianity created a need for official (and more impressive) places of worship. While today, the word "basilica" signifies a large, important church, such as St. Peter's Basilica in Rome where the Pope celebrates mass, a basilica was originally a secular structure; the Roman *basilica*, a rectangular public building used for meetings or as a courtroom, offered a practical model for early Christian churches. The Latin word *basilica*, by the way, derives from the Greek *Basilike Stoa*, or "Royal Hall," basically the government headquarters of fifth-century B.C. Athens, where the *Archon Basileus* ("King magistrate") and the *Areopagus* (the civil and criminal court) were situated. It was eventually realized that, by taking two basilicas and superimposing them at right angles to one another, a building shaped like a cross would be formed—an ideal shape for a Christian place of worship. The cruciform church plan became a standard one during the Middle Ages—but it began as two pagan government buildings stuck together.

In a Catholic cathedral, you might initially stop at the baptismal font (located near the entrance to remind you of your initiation into the Church through baptism) to dip your fingers in the holy water and cross yourself. The association of water with religious ritual was a common one in the ancient world. While Jewish precedents for ritual purification by water (by immersion in a ritual bath called a *mikvah*) are often cited, the Greeks and Romans also insisted upon cleansing themselves before religious ceremonies such as animal sacrifices by washing their hands or sprinkling themselves with water. Raised stone basins containing water for purification (somewhat resembling a baptismal font) called *peirrhanteria* were often located in Greek religious sanctuaries, and a special metal vessel (the *khernibeion*) was used to hold water for ritual cleansing. This might remind one of the aspergillum (derived from the Latin verb *aspergere*, "to sprinkle"), an implement used to sprinkle holy water on worshipers during Roman Catholic and Anglican ceremonies.

The modes of decoration you encounter after entering the cathedral also owe much to classical precedents. Although stained glass windows were a medieval innovation, many other details would have been familiar to the ancients. Christian artisans took the mosaics so beloved by the Greeks and Romans and transformed them to suit their own purposes. Rather than floors, they now covered walls and ceilings; mythological scenes gave way to depictions of Christian figures, stories, and doctrine; and rather than the tiny bits of marble and stone used by the Romans, pieces of sparkling glass that would catch the light and glimmer were preferred. Elaborate marble designs inlaid upon the floors would probably have reminded a Roman of the gorgeous interior of a public bath—and indeed, Roman baths were often converted into Christian churches. Columns, derived from classical precedents, often had their capitals altered to look less pagan; instead of the scrolls and acanthus leaves of the Ionic and Corinthian styles, these church columns might be topped with entwined plants, animals, human figures, and grotesques, sometimes illustrating biblical stories and sometimes primarily decorative in nature.

The focal point of services, the altar (Latin *ara*), stands at the front of the church. Its essential presence in Christian religious ceremonies also characterized ancient Greek and Roman practices (even though the ceremonies involved were obviously different). The typical Greek altar, constructed of whitewashed bricks or fitted stone blocks and often decorated on its sides with volutes, is not that far removed from early Christian examples, except for one major difference: the Greek altars depicted in vase paintings are typically splashed with blood in token of the many animal sacrifices conducted there. Also, the pagan altar stood outside the temple; in keeping with the public nature of religious ceremonies, sacrifices were made on the steps of the temple, not inside it. "Fragrant altars" was a stock phrase frequently employed by the ancients (e.g., Homer, *Iliad* 8.48; Hesiod, *Theogony* line 545; Ovid, *Metamorphoses* Bk. 4, line 1049) because of the practice of burning incense as an offering, the fragrance of which became identified with sacred ceremonies. Catholic ritual still creates a sacred atmosphere with clouds of incense, as censers and thuribles swung on chains dispense the instantly recognizable aroma.

The area around the church altar is called the sanctuary, which comes from the Latin *sanctuarium*, a consecrated place. (The Greek equivalent, the *hieron*, was an area sacred to the gods, which could be either with or without a building, or could consist of a natural feature such as a piece of land, a grove of trees, a spring, or a cave.) Today, we also use "sanctuary" to mean a place of refuge or immunity from prosecution, and the image of a fugitive hurrying into a church to escape arrest is still a part of our mental landscape. Indeed, under English law from the fourth to the seventeenth century, a person could not be arrested in a church or sacred place, until James I did away with this loophole.

But whereas we associate Christian churches with sanctuary or asylum (from the Greek *asylon*, "refuge"), ironically they were for a time denied this role. The idea of sanctuary in sacred places was one of great antiquity. Many Greek temples functioned as a place where supplicants could seek shelter, protection, divine aid, and justice; the Temple of Apollo at Delphi in particular was famous throughout the ancient world as a place for fugitives to find sanctuary. Physical contact with the altar, such as grasping it, was the most common way to invoke divine protection; in ancient Rome, a person who sat on or beside an altar could not be killed. In ancient Greece, criminals, slaves, and those fleeing harm also sought asylum by standing next to or touching the cult statue of a god. Two famous examples include the Trojan princess Cassandra trying to avoid being raped by the victorious Greeks by clutching the Palladion (the sacred statue of Athena) after the fall of Troy, and the Greek hero Orestes seeking sanctuary at the temple of Apollo after murdering his murderous mother, Clytemnestra.

However, Roman law initially denied Christian churches sanctuary status, and did not extend it to them until the end of the fourth century A.D., reflecting Christianity's rise in importance and influence. Thus, in A.D. 532, members of the Blue and Green chariot factions who had committed murder were able to seek asylum in a church sanctuary in order to avoid being executed by the Emperor Justinian—an event that helped spark the infamous Nika riots. Eventually, pagan sanctuaries and temples were being actively suppressed and either destroyed or converted into Christian churches, which became the place to seek sanctuary, with laws stretching the protected area ever further outwards; in A.D. 419, the zone of sanctuary was extended out to 50 paces from the church door, and in A.D. 431, it included the entire courtyard of the church. Churches in Anglo-Saxon England often had a frith ("peace") stool, a stone seat next to the altar reserved for those seeking sanctuary—a practice reminiscent of the pagan altar as a locus for asylum-seekers.

The wall and ceiling behind the church altar are likely dominated by a large image of Christ, who undoubtedly also appears in numerous scenes throughout the church. How he is depicted probably reveals pagan influences as well. Often he is shown as the Good Shepherd surrounded by sheep that symbolically represent either his Apostles or the entire Christian flock, or occasionally even with a sheep draped across his shoulders. The image of Christ as the Good Shepherd can be traced all the way back to Greek archaic statues of actual shepherds carrying their animals upon their shoulders. Sometimes he is portrayed as a teacher instructing his followers in Christian doctrine, as in the Sermon on the Mount. In these instances, the figure of the ascetic pagan philosopher, so prevalent in the ancient world, offered a ready model for both Christ as teacher and for saints and hermits who fled from society in order to pursue their religious studies without earthly distractions. For example, the misanthropic Greek philosopher Diogenes lived in a discarded amphora and threw away his one possession, a cup, as being too much of a luxury, and Socrates' use of analogies and the Socratic method of posing questions strongly resembled Christ's use of parables to make his listeners think about his message. During the earliest stages of Christianity, Christ was most often depicted following one of these two models, as the shepherd or the teacher.

How often have you seen Christ shown with a halo of light around his head? This too has its origins in pagan imagery. Converted pagans often tried to understand their new religion by associating Christ with the gods they were already familiar with, so they sometimes portrayed him as the sun god known as Helios or Apollo, who was conventionally depicted with a round halo of light around his head or with rays emanating from it. Excavations of a third-century A.D. Christian mausoleum beneath St. Peter's in Rome discovered a particularly fine example of this: a mosaic of Christ as Apollo/Helios, his head encircled by the sun's rays, driving the sun-chariot through the sky.

Another popular early image of Christ portrays animals clustering around him in a worshipful fashion, tamed by his presence. Early Christian representations of Jesus sometimes linked him with the legendary Greek musician Orpheus, whose singing and lyre-playing could calm wild beasts—an image appropriate as a reminder of how even animals recognized Christ's divinity, a

Figure 6.9 *Christian mosaic. This mosaic on the interior of a church dome depicts Christ and other religious figures with halos, an iconographic convention derived from pagan precedents.*

theme also repeatedly emphasized in medieval and Renaissance Nativity scenes, where all the barnyard creatures in the manger bow down to the baby Jesus.

Is Christ shown as a baby sitting on Mary's lap, being suckled? This image reaches back even further, to ancient Egypt and another mystery religion—the cult of Isis—which became popular in the Greco-Roman world. Statues commonly represent the goddess Isis breastfeeding the baby Horus who sits on her lap, and there is even a death and resurrection in her story, though it is her husband Osiris rather than her son who is sacrificed and revived.

Have you seen portraits of Christ in which he is seated on a throne, wearing purple robes, his head encircled by a golden halo, or is seated on a globe or holding an orb in his hand? When Christianity became the official religion of the Roman empire (and of the Roman emperors), Christ began to appear in the guise of a Roman emperor, who traditionally wore purple robes, and was often shown seated on a throne with a globe of the world either held in his hand or as his seat. As Christ Pantokrator (a Greek word variously translated as "the Almighty," "the All-powerful," and "the Sustainer of the World"), he is imagined as a mighty secular ruler decked in imperial regalia. The model for this image of Christ was also the Roman emperors, the most powerful earthly rulers that anyone of the time could imagine.

Thus, the artistic depiction of Christ reflected the changing status of Christianity. Early on, when it was still a persecuted minority sect, he tended to be a humble shepherd, teacher, or philosopher. When Christianity became the dominant religion of the state, he started to look more like a king or emperor ruling over heaven and earth, as he does in many glittering Byzantine mosaics. Of course, the most famous depiction of Christ is the Crucifix, which shows him dying to redeem humanity. But even this image is based on an aspect of Roman culture. Crucifixion was a form of Roman execution that was seen as especially humiliating and was reserved for those of low social status, typically slaves, pirates, and enemies of the state. Death by crucifixion was prolonged and particularly painful ("excruciating" derives from *ex*, "out of," and *cruciare*, "to crucify"); this public display of agony and of bodies left hanging on roadside crosses served as a highly visible warning to dissuade potential criminals. The suppression of Spartacus' slave rebellion, for instance, ended with the bodies of hundreds of crucified slaves lining the main road into Rome.

The halo, which is such an important symbol denoting the holiness of angels and saints as well as of Jesus, deserves further discussion. The Greek word *halos* meant the disk of the sun or the moon or the ring of light around it—a definition which took on a scientific dimension early in the sixteenth century, when it came to denote a circle appearing around the sun or moon caused by light refracted or reflected by ice particles in the atmosphere. The word "halo" wasn't actually applied to the circle of light around a holy person's head until the 1640s, but a disk of light did often occur in Greco-Roman art to denote divinity.

As might be expected, this disk initially most often encircled the heads of those celestial siblings, the sun god Apollo (or Helios) and the moon goddess Artemis (or Selene or Diana), and therefore had rays protruding from it in all directions; the most famous modern version of such a crown is on the Statue of Liberty (who was modeled on the Colossus of Rhodes, a giant statue of Apollo wearing the sun headdress). But a circle of light or a crown of rays came to represent an aura of divinity for other gods and goddesses, especially in Hellenistic times. The Romans used the disk on their gods (especially Sol Invictus, the "invincible sun") and ultimately also on their emperors, at first on coins and eventually in Byzantine church mosaics. The earliest Christian art occasionally identified Christ with Helios, the sun god, by placing the rayed diadem around his head, but for the most part the earliest images of Christ did not wear a halo.

Strangely enough (from our perspective), the halo was transferred from the Roman emperor to Christ rather than the other way around. As a symbol of the Roman emperor's semi-divine status, the golden disk/crown only became prevalent on depictions of Christ in majesty, assuming the Emperor's role. Yet, even after the Roman empire converted to Christianity, the emperor continued to be shown with a halo—for example, Emperor Justinian (a Christian!) in the mosaics of the church of San Vitale at Ravenna. Early haloes tended to resemble flat circular gold plates suspended behind the head. Sometimes, you may notice a cross drawn within Christ's halo, such that three spokes jut out at the top of his head and by his ears. These are often characterized as symbolic of the trinity, and no doubt they were—although they also look a lot like an abbreviated illustration of the sun-god's crown. Only with the discovery of perspective did haloes begin to float or hover above and slightly behind the head (first seen in paintings by Giotto), and the hollow halo that is only a thin gold ring suspended above the head (the kind seen on Halloween angel costumes) didn't really become popular until the Renaissance.

The huge significance of the number three in Christianity, due to the Holy Trinity, is obvious. But even before Christianity, three was a sacred number in the ancient world. Greek deities were often grouped in threes or in multiples of three: the Three Fates, the Three Graces, the Three Horae (goddesses of time and the seasons, often translated as "the Hours"), the Three Furies, the three judges in the Underworld, the nine Muses, the 12 Olympians. The three Olympian brothers Zeus, Poseidon, and Hades divided the world among them into three kingdoms—the heavens, the seas, and the underworld—and each had a tripartite attribute: Hades had the three-headed dog Cerberus, Poseidon had a trident (Latin for "three-tooth"), and Zeus had a thunderbolt that was often depicted in art as being triple-pronged (the Greek word for trident, *triaina*, derives from a proto-Greek word meaning "three-fold"). The Romans often worshiped gods in groups of three called triads. The most famous of these, the Capitoline Triad (thus called because the three deities shared a renowned temple on the Capitoline hill), originally consisted of Jupiter, Mars, and Quirinus, though it later shifted to the more well-known combination of Jupiter, Juno, and Minerva. The mystical allure of the number three was even felt by the mathematician Pythagoras, who called it "the number of harmony," which was equal to unity (the number one) plus diversity (the number two).

Figure 6.10 *The Capitoline Triad. This important triad of Roman gods can be identified by the birds at their feet: Minerva, the goddess of wisdom, has an owl; Jupiter, the king of the gods, an eagle; and his wife, Juno, a peacock.*

If a Catholic mass is underway in our hypothetical cathedral, you might hear it being recited in Latin, the traditional language of the Christian liturgy. Although Latin was originally the only language church services were conducted in, it has been falling into disuse in recent times, but there is currently a movement within the Catholic Church, led by groups such as the Latin Liturgy Association, to restore the use of the Latin liturgy. ("Liturgy," by the way, comes from the Greek *leitourgia*, public work done on the behalf of the people; a *leitourgos* was "one who performs a public service.") And while Latin became the international language for Church ritual during the Middle Ages, we are indebted to ancient Greek for allowing the spread of the New Testament. When the New Testament was first written down, it was in Koine Greek, the common language spoken throughout the eastern Roman empire. (The Greek language had originally spread east with the conquests of Alexander the Great.) This greatly increased the number of people who could understand the text—and be converted.

Finally, if the congregation is singing a hymn, they are imitating the ancient Greeks, who sang prayers to the gods set to music (*hymnoi*). Among the earliest examples of Greek literature are the *Homeric Hymns*, 33 hymns devoted to praising individual Greek gods. (Though the authors of these hymns are unknown, they were labeled "Homeric" because any very old piece of Greek literature used to be attributed to Homer.) Singing and music were a part of religious ceremonies from the very beginning. However, one important ritual role of music that we no longer require was to drown out the ill-omened noises made by animals being sacrificed; the Romans employed double pipes, the flute, and the lyre for this purpose. Today, organ music (the Greek *organon* means "instrument") is often associated with church services; but in the ancient world, the ancestor of our modern church organ—an instrument called the water organ (the *hydraulis*, invented by Ctesibius of Alexandria in the third century B.C.)—was often played at public entertainments such as circus games. Today, organ music is still associated with sporting events as well as religion, especially baseball and hockey games. Between the 1940s and the 1960s organ music was closely identified with baseball stadiums; hockey games continue to be punctuated by short organ tunes; and the brief but iconic "Baseball/Hockey Charge Stadium Organ Theme" remains instantly recognizable.

Gods or devils? The demonization of paganism

When Christianity displaced paganism, it naturally demonized it—often in a very literal way, as Greek and Roman gods were transformed into demons, certain pagan rites became equated with demonic possession, and pagan symbols came to signify evil.

One possible example is the serpent who tempts Eve to sin in the Garden of Eden, who is generally interpreted either as the Devil himself or his representative. In antiquity, snakes (often depicted with a little beard on the chin) were typically seen as sacred creatures. The *Agathos Daemon* (the "Good Spirit"), who had to be offered a libation before wine-drinking, was depicted as a serpent. The snake was a positive symbol of prophecy and healing, as is suggested by the snakes entwining the staff of Asklepios, the god of healing, which has been adopted as the emblem of doctors worldwide; the snake was thought to bring the god's cure to the patient. In fact, whenever a new temple to Asklepios was founded, it was necessary to transfer a sacred snake from his major sanctuary at Epidauros to the new site. The Romans believed that Asklepios, incarnated as a snake, traveled from Epidauros to Rome in 293 B.C. to cure an outbreak of the plague, and settled on Tiber Island, where they built him a temple in gratitude. (In its place, a Christian hospital established in 1584 now stands, continuing this island's reputation as a place of healing.) It was thought that heroes and the dead appeared in the form of snakes. The serpent's shedding of its skin was seen as a symbol of renewal and rebirth. Christianity thus caused a major reversal in the snake's reputation.

One Greek myth perhaps absorbed into Christianity is that of the first woman, Pandora, who unleashes all evils into the world from a jar (now often referred to as a box) that she has been specifically warned never to open, but her curiosity gets the better of her. Her name, "All-gifted," is ironic in that her "gifts" are all the bad things that plague the world. In a similar fashion, Eve, tempted by curiosity, eats from the tree of knowledge, leading to the Fall. In both stories, the first woman becomes the source of all evil due to uncontrollable curiosity. Interestingly, some writers add the detail that Pandora's brother-in-law, Prometheus, shaped humankind out of clay or mud, and the gods similarly molded Pandora and sent her to Prometheus' brother, Epimetheus, as a bride as punishment after Prometheus stole forbidden knowledge (fire) to benefit mortals. In some versions of the story, the goddess Athena breathes into the clay man to animate him, as God breathes life into the first man, Adam. This myth—with people being created out of dust, woman as the source of evil, and stolen knowledge leading to punishment—certainly resonates with the Christian story of creation.

Christianity also changed the pagan notion of possession by a god into a horrifying possession by demons, which must be violently exorcised. Oracles were thought to operate by a god entering and temporarily taking over the seer. "Enthusiasm" comes from the Greek *enthousiasmos*, inspiration, from *enthousiazein*, to be inspired, or to be possessed by a god; *entheos*, possessed by a god, literally meant "within is a god," a state in which the god speaks through a person, often using a strange voice to say unintelligible things that require interpretation, and even causing uncontrolled bodily movements. This state of being was also commonly referred to as "mania"—a frenzy or madness—and religious mania is today sometimes cited as one of the symptoms of bipolar disorder. The experience of the oracle sounds rather like *glossolalia*, or "speaking in tongues" (from Greek *glossa*, "tongue," and *laleo*, "to speak or make sounds"), currently still practiced in Pentecostal and Charismatic Christianity, where it is seen as being caused by the descent of the Holy Spirit into a human vessel. The "speaking in tongues" explicitly mentioned in the New Testament five times (and even more times implicitly) has been cited as the precedent for this phenomenon. Poetic inspiration was envisioned as working in a similar fashion, a belief that especially appealed to the Romantic poets, who had a great love of and familiarity with classical literature.

In the New Testament, there is a clear distinction drawn between "speaking in tongues" (a sign of grace which comes from the Christian God) and possession by demonic spirits or pagan gods, which must be exorcised and cast out. The word "demon" is derived from the Greek *daimones*, a class of supernatural beings situated between the gods and mortals. In fact, Homer sometimes even seemed to use the words *theoi* (gods) and *daimones* interchangeably, as if they were the same thing (*Iliad* 2.1.222). The term originally had a neutral sense, and in fact often a positive one, since *daimones* frequently functioned as guardians of human beings and exerted a benevolent influence. The great philosopher Socrates claimed to have a *daimonion* that spoke to and guided him by urging him away from ill-chosen plans of action.

A hint of negative overtones associated with *daimones* eventually appeared and seemed to grow stronger in the Hellenistic world, where a distinction was made between good demons (the *eudaimon* or *agathodaimon*) that resembled guardian angels and bad ones (the *kakodaimon*) that led people astray. Aristotle famously wrote in *The Nicomachean Ethics* that the highest good that could be achieved by humans was *eudaimonia*, frequently translated as "happiness" or "well-being"; but this could be interpreted more literally as "having a good *daimon* looking after you." Christianity completed the transformation of *daimon* from a neutral or even positive term to an ambiguous one that could be either good or bad to one suggesting only evil, and the *eudaimon*'s role was taken over by the guardian angel.

Christianity relegated demons, who used to dwell among humankind, to hell. Do hell and the king of demons, Satan, have any Greek or Roman precedents? While connections cannot be definitively made, there are some parallels. The ruler of the Underworld, Hades (also known as Dis or Pluto), was later identified with Satan, and "Hades" is sometimes used as a synonym for hell. But another pagan god offers an interesting model for the fallen angel Lucifer. Hephaistos (Vulcan to the Romans) was thrown down from Mount Olympus by his father Zeus because of his lameness and ugliness, and he fell for an entire day before crashing to the earth. The god of fire and blacksmiths, he practiced his craft in forges that were thought to be located under volcanoes. While he was ultimately readmitted to Olympus, he spent a lot of time in hot, fiery underground regions where he was surrounded by giant, monstrous-looking, one-eyed Cyclopes, who were his assistants. In *Paradise Lost*, Milton depicts the pagan gods as fallen angels, and one of them, whom he calls Mulciber, is obviously modeled upon Vulcan. Mulciber's day-long fall from heaven to earth and ultimately to hell after he is cast out by Jove (1.740–751) clearly parallels when Lucifer, cast out of heaven, is "Hurl'd headlong flaming … to bottomless perdition" by God (1.36–48).

Part of Hades' realm, a deep pit called Tartarus, functioned as a place of punishment for evildoers and those who offended the gods. Some of these punishments are so famous that they've become part of our vocabulary. Tantalus stood in a pool of water with a laden fruit tree bough hanging over his head, but when he tried to drink, the water receded, and when he tried to pluck the fruit, it pulled away from him; thus, for all eternity, he was in a state of being constantly tantalized—a word derived from his name. The phrase "a Sisyphean task" comes from the punishment of Sisyphus, condemned to push a huge rock up a hill only to have it roll down to the bottom again, resulting in a never-ending cycle of constant labor. Three judges in the Underworld decided who was confined to Tartarus and what their punishments would be. The Olympian gods also had a habit of throwing any major threats to them into Tartarus, so the Titans, the giants, and quite a few monsters ended up there—for instance, the giant monster Typhon (Greek for "whirlwind" and the source of the word typhoon), who fought an epic battle with Zeus before being consigned to the pit. This vision of Tartarus as a place of torture and punishment for earthly misdeeds in some ways resembles the Christian hell, often referred to as "the pit" or "the pits of hell."

Finally, when we look at the wall paintings in Etruscan tombs, we see grotesque demons of the Underworld that would not look out of place in medieval depictions of hell. Charun (the Etruscan version of the Greek ferryman of the dead, Charon), a blue demon with red hair, feathered wings, and a snake, holds either an ax or a hammer (the tools employed to dispatch sacrificial animals), with which he struck the victim on the head. Tuculcha has the beak of a vulture (appropriately, a scavenger who eats corpses), the ears of a horse or donkey, either snakes for hair or two snakes growing out of his head like horns, and snakes grasped in his hands. The female herald of death and escort of the dead, Vanth, has eyes all over her wings that render her all-seeing.

While there is a common perception that religion and attitudes towards spirituality are areas in which the modern world is most unlike the ancient, as we have seen, there is a surprising continuity between many of the religious rituals and images from the classical world and those of today. Although Christianity began at a time when the Mediterranean world was dominated by polytheistic beliefs, it ultimately became the official religion of Rome, and because of that status, spread along with Roman culture to every corner of the empire. In the process, it incorporated and adapted many of the rituals, beliefs, images, and customs of classical paganism.

When we turn to less formal attitudes towards the numinous and to the world beyond our rational understanding that can be grouped under the category of "superstitions," we find even greater direct similarities, parallels, and borrowings that unite ancient with modern. People of all eras have sought to find comfort, solace, justification, inspiration, and advantage in the spiritual realm, and the commonality of these impulses is one of the defining characteristics that make us human.

7

Words, ideas, and stories: Language, law, philosophy, and literature

The building blocks of language: The alphabet

How have the Greeks and Romans influenced the modern languages that allow us to communicate with one another? An obvious place to start is with the very letters that we use to form words. The word "alphabet" comes from the first two letters of the Greek alphabet, *alpha* and *beta*, compressed to stand for the whole thing, as we do when we say that children are learning their ABCs. How did such a crucial invention as the alphabet start, though? Here, the Greeks owe a debt to a yet earlier civilization. In ancient Mesopotamia trade flourished, and merchants marked the jars of goods that they exchanged to keep track of the contents. It is theorized that these stylized marks developed into pictographic writing—a system where pictures represent words. This works well for things that can be depicted visually; for example, you can draw a little cow, and over time, you might simplify matters by drawing just a cow head to mean "cow." But there are many words that can't readily be indicated with pictures, so the next step was to use written symbols to represent first syllables and then sounds, which could be combined to make words. The Mesopotamians devised letters that represented the sounds of consonants, but vowels were not written. In the Middle East today, modern languages such as

Arabic and Hebrew continue this pattern by either leaving out vowels entirely or only suggesting their presence with diacritical marks.

Sometime around the ninth century B.C., the Greeks "borrowed" the letters that had originated in Mesopotamia from one of the Middle Eastern peoples they traded with, the Phoenicians, and began using them to write Greek. Although they altered the letters somewhat, the similarities are still clearly evident. However, the Greeks decided that vowels would be useful too, so they added some of these. They also found other convenient applications for letters beyond simply recording language, such as standing for numbers (as the Romans also did with their system of Roman numerals) and writing down music. In fact, their system of notation for vocal music forms the underlying basis for the system still used nowadays.

If you go to Greece and Russia today, you might be struck by a certain similarity in the scripts visible on their street signs. However, in English and other European languages, the capital or upper-case letters are directly drawn from the letter shapes visible on the Romans' stone-carved Latin inscriptions, a likeness which you can observe when walking through museums and Roman ruins. Why the difference? Despite how different many of the letters may look, the Romans were indebted to the Greeks for their alphabet. Two variants of the early Greek alphabet developed, one known as the Western and the other as the Eastern. It is thought that the Western Greek alphabet (also known as the Euboean alphabet or the Cumaean alphabet) was taken to Italy by the Greek colonists who settled there. The dominant group in Italy at that time, the Etruscans, adapted it to their needs, and then passed it on to the Romans, who further altered it, until ultimately it became the Latin alphabet. In Greece itself, the Western Greek alphabet died out, and the Eastern Greek alphabet (also called the Attic-Ionic alphabet) took over. This Eastern Greek alphabet functioned as the basis for Russia's Cyrillic alphabet; although the Eastern Greek script has been somewhat altered, you can still detect its influence.

Incidentally, when examining those Roman monuments and Latin inscriptions, you may also notice that J, U, and W are missing. The Latin alphabet originally consisted of only 23 letters. Eventually, the V split into V (the consonant form) and U (the vowel form); I split into J (consonant form) and I (vowel form); and W was an entirely new letter, which explains why it appears most often in Germanic languages and comparatively little in Romance ones. Thus, if you ever see Julius Caesar written as Iulius Caesar, this is not a typo, but actually a closer rendition of the original Latin.

That explains our uppercase letters, but where do our lowercase letters, which are clearly absent from Latin inscriptions, come from? These were a later addition from Carolingian times, reflecting the strokes made by writing with a quill pen. The ancients didn't give us everything, after all.

Many Americans are probably most familiar with Greek letters from seeing them over the doorways of college fraternities and sororities, which are known as Greek letter organizations or as part of the Greek System. "Greek" is the adjective of choice because members identify themselves with the Greek letters (typically two or three) on their house. Why do they still use Greek letters when hardly any of their members know Greek? It began at the College of William and Mary in 1776, when Phi Beta Kappa was founded; now famous as an honor society, it started out as a social fraternity, and has the distinction of being both the first collegiate Greek letter fraternity and the oldest honor society for the liberal arts and sciences in the United States. Phi Beta Kappa stands for the organization's motto, *philosophia biou kybernetes*; now translated as "Love of learning is the guide of life," this was originally (and more literally) rendered as "Love of learning is the helmsman of life," since *kybernetes* means pilot, steersman, or helmsman. In another first, Phi Beta Kappa thus set the precedent for naming fraternities and sororities with the Greek letter initials of their secret mottoes (which are no longer secret, of course). Other examples include Delta Upsilon, with the motto *dikaia upotheke* ("Justice, Our Foundation") and Alpha Kappa Lambda, with the motto *alethia kai logos* ("The Truth and the Word").

Many Greek letters have acquired a life beyond mere membership in the alphabet. Alpha, beta, and gamma are frequently used to denote the first, second, and third items in a series—for instance, alpha test case and beta test case. As the very first letter, "alpha" naturally confers a sense of preeminence. The alpha male is the highest-ranking animal in a group and its leader—a term most often associated with a wolf pack, though it is sometimes used somewhat jocularly to refer to a confident, take-charge man. (When the alpha male dies, the beta male, who had occupied the second-ranked position, takes over from him.) In astronomy, alpha is the symbol assigned to the brightest star in a constellation.

Alpha and omega (*alpha kai omega*), as the first and last letters in the Greek alphabet, tend to be linked together. "Alpha to omega" used to be our version of "A to Z," as a way to suggest that something is thoroughly complete and exhaustive. (For Americans who wonder why the British refer to and pronounce the letter Z as zed, this is derived from the Greek letter zeta.) In the Book of Revelations, the phrase "I am the Alpha and the Omega" (1.8) expresses the eternal nature of God, and Christ says "I am Alpha and Omega, the beginning and the end, first and last" (Rev. 22.13). That is why, in early Christian art, you will sometimes see an Alpha painted to the left of Christ's head and an Omega to his right, sometimes within the circle of his halo, or else suspended from the left and right arms of the Crucifix, as a visual reminder of that famous biblical statement.

On a completely different note, if you ever wondered why the Charlton Heston movie "Omega Man" (1971) had that title, it was because he was potentially the last uninfected human after an apocalyptic plague. The omega reference also recalls the Apocalypse in the Book of Revelations, which is fitting, since the movie depicts what might be the end of humankind. Returning to the topic of animal behavior, the omega male is the very lowest in the social hierarchy, who is subordinate to everyone else and is the last one allowed to eat. You may have noticed that the word omega contains "mega," a Greek prefix that means large, great, or powerful, as in the Greek-derived megaphone ("big voice") and megalomania, a mental disorder characterized by delusions of grandeur. That is because omega literally means "the great (or long) O."

While alpha and omega get a lot of mileage out of their relative positions in the alphabet, some Greek letters have made an impression with their shape. The geographical feature of the delta, an area of silt that builds up at a river's mouth, is so-named because it resembles that letter's triangular shape, and the deltoid muscles in our shoulders get their name from being triangular as well. If you do any gardening, you may have encountered the gamma moth, a vegetable-munching insect with silver spots on its wings that resemble the letter gamma. Iota, the smallest Greek letter, naturally enough came to mean the most minuscule quantity, and entered Middle English by way of Latin as "jota" or "jote." Sometime in the early sixteenth century, "jote" morphed into "jot," so that when the King James Bible was published in 1611 it had Jesus declare: "Till heaven and earth pass, one jot or one tittle shall in no wise pass from the law, till all be fulfilled" (Mt. 5.18) rather than "Not one iota shall pass from the law," as the Greek version read. (Yodh, the smallest letter in the Hebrew alphabet, possessed a similar figurative meaning as the tiniest of things and was the equivalent of the Greek letter iota, so perhaps he would have said "Not one yodh.") Nowadays we say we're going to jot something down, as in make a brief note of it, a meaning first recorded in 1721 that probably also stems from iota's smallness.

Two Greek letters have staked out a highly significant role in Christianity. Rendered in Greek, Christ's name begins with the letters chi and rho which, combined, form a symbol for Christ that emerged at the very origins of Christianity, and has been widely used ever since. In Christian art, the chi-rho often appears as a reference to Christ, sometimes bracketed with the letters alpha and omega, as a shorthand rendering of Christ's statement "I am the Alpha and the Omega." The letter chi, X, also came to function as shorthand for Christ, as in the abbreviation Xmas, and X stands for the crucifix or cross as well, an association perhaps reinforced by its physical resemblance to one. Today in the USA, this identification of X with the cross appears even in that most mundane of objects, the traffic sign, where PED XING is a standard way of warning drivers of a pedestrian crossing.

Recently, the letter lambda has gotten a lot of exposure in the movie "300," where it appears on the shields of the Spartan warriors. In fact, this is a historically accurate detail, although in real life the lambda was painted onto a wooden shield rather than molded in relief on a metal shield, as in the movie. Why do they have as their symbol the Greek equivalent of our letter L? The region of Greece in which Sparta is located was called Lacedaemonia or Laconia in ancient times, and they were also referred to as Lacedaemonians—hence their choice of lambda to represent their identity.

Dead languages live again: The influence of Greek and Latin

Although no country today speaks Latin or ancient Greek, these "dead" languages are the ancestors of many current languages. All the Romance languages such as French, Spanish, and Italian are descended from, or, if you prefer, are watered down versions of, the Latin language spoken by the ancient Romans. Although English is technically considered a Germanic language, English-speakers also hear echoes of the classical past in their language. Over 60 percent of all English words have Greek or Latin roots, and this percentage rises even higher in certain disciplines; in the fields of science and technology, for instance, roughly 90 percent of the specialized vocabulary stems from Greek and Latin, and roots from these 2 languages continue to provide the majority of new scientific terms. Indeed, the word "technology" itself is a combination of the Greek words *techne* (art or artifice) and *logos* (word or discourse), while "science" comes from the Latin *scientia*, knowledge. To coin science-related words, bits of Greek are put together in new ways, and sometimes Greek and Latin elements are even combined to form hybrids that would have distressed the language-loving Greeks, who considered all non-Greek speakers barbarians—including the Romans who eventually conquered them.

The Greeks managed to transfer this attitude of their innate superiority to their conquerors, as the Roman upper classes began to speak and write in Greek to demonstrate how cultured they were, and sent their children to Athens to get the best possible education. Today, this same type of split is often reenacted, with English standing in for Greek. In fact, linguistic domination of the majority of the world by a single language is not a new phenomenon, since both the Greeks and the Romans managed this centuries before the current contender, English, had begun to evolve. Attic Greek, the version spoken at Athens, spread across the entire Mediterranean, from Spain to Afghanistan, functioning as the language of trade and administration. It was called "the common talk," *he koine dialektos*, from which we get our word "dialect," and it had to overcome more than 20 dialects of Greek in Greece itself, in addition to infiltrating numerous foreign kingdoms.

While Greek spread far and wide through colonization and, most spectacularly, the military conquests of Alexander the Great, what allowed its influence to outlast the rise of other empires and charm them into adopting it? The Greeks thought they were more civilized than everyone else, but why did so many people they looked down upon as "barbarians" seem to accept that this was true, and strive to learn Greek? There were other literate societies; in fact, there were a bunch of them in the Middle East, from where the Greeks had borrowed their alphabet. Why didn't these catch on instead?

The answer may lie in how the Greeks chose to use their language. Rather than restricting it to practical endeavors such as record-keeping, the Greeks wrote about their ideas and emotions, used it to theorize, philosophize, and speechify, recorded poetry and plays for posterity, and invented all sorts of new genres, such as history writing and travel guides. Their language acted as a vehicle for their culture, and "barbarians" took to it as eagerly as they did to wine (another Greek gift). Romans and Gauls alike had their children educated in Greek, and Parthian kings enjoyed attending Greek plays. During the Punic wars, the conquering Roman general Scipio quoted lines from Homer's *Iliad* about the sack of Troy as he watched Carthage burn to the ground. Clearly the Greeks knew how to use language so skillfully that many foreigners were moved and entertained by what they wrote. As the Roman poet Horace famously wrote (albeit in Latin), "Greece, the captive, made her savage victor captive, and brought the arts into rustic Latium" (the region around Rome) (*Letters* 2.1.156–7). With the rise of Christianity, Greek also got a boost from Christians wanting to be able to read the New Testament.

Latin eventually achieved the same feat that *koine* once had, expanding along with the Roman empire, and brought to all its provinces by its soldiers, merchants, and settlers, until it could be understood in most of the known world. This situation planted the seeds for what would develop into Europe's romance languages. However, the army grunts were not speaking Latin as it is taught in our classrooms—what we think of as Classical Latin. Instead, they were speaking "vulgar" Latin—a term used by the Romans themselves. *Vulgus* could mean the common people, the masses, or even a flock of animals—not the most flattering word. The adjective "vulgar" therefore meant "everyday" and "belonging to the common people," and Vulgar Latin was only spoken, never written; there was no agreed-upon spelling and standardization. Because Vulgar Latin was purely conversational, we know about it primarily through texts by ancient grammarians criticizing its many errors, and the dialogue spoken by the slaves and lower-class characters in the plays of Terence and Plautus. In contrast, the upper classes spoke and wrote the purer form of Latin that was inscribed on monuments and used to create literature, but this was not yet known as Classical Latin.

If you have ever heard the Bible referred to as the Vulgate and have wondered why, it is because, in A.D. 383, Jerome (later Saint Jerome) began a series of revisions and translations of existing texts of the Bible, in order to produce a standard version to be employed in the Latin churches. This was a momentous occurrence, since, for many centuries to come, Jerome's Bible was the only Bible in general use. It came to be called the *versio vulgata*, "the commonly used translation," and was ultimately adopted by the Catholic Church as the definitive, authorized version of the Latin Bible for over a millennium. All of the vernacular versions of the Bible produced throughout Western Europe were in a sense the descendants of the Vulgate.

When the western Roman empire began to fall apart around the fifth century A.D., Latin lost its ascendancy as the empire-wide spoken language of choice. As localized linguistic pockets grew more isolated from one another, types of Vulgar Latin diverged from one another at an increasingly accelerated rate. Throughout Europe, these developed into the various Romance languages, which now boast more than 800 million native speakers worldwide. Thus, the Romance languages, so often noted for their beauty, started out from a "vulgar" tongue spoken by the uneducated, illiterate masses and looked down upon by lovers of literature and language. When spoken Latin began to die out, that is when written Latin was designated "classicus"—"classy" Latin as opposed to the common sort being spoken by the lower classes.

The lowly beginnings of the Romance languages are connected to the definition more familiar to us today, when a romance is either a love affair or a novel about one. The adjective "Romance" was at first used to describe anything written in the Roman vernacular, the speech of commoners, as opposed to Classical Latin, which was reserved for high literature and serious subjects. In early medieval Europe, the most popular genre of stories was about love. These were written in the Roman vernacular so that they could be enjoyed by a wide audience, not just literary types, and because the frivolous subject matter would have been too undignified for Latin. Hence they became known as romances—a reminder of their "vulgar" Roman origins.

A few words about words: Some classical words and phrases

Anyone who has attended a course on how to take the SATs or expand one's vocabulary (from Latin *vocabulum*, "a term," from *vocare*, "to call") has encountered long lists of Greek and Latin root words to memorize as an aid to improving one's English. Common prefixes, suffixes, and stems from Greek and Latin that are frequently used to form new words include: tele- (far off), poly- (much or many), meta- (among, between, over or above, after), pseudo- (false), dis- (prefix indicating separation, negation, or reversal), ex- (prefix meaning out, from, or former), post- (behind, after), -scope (derived from the verb "to see"), -logy (from the verb "to speak," indicating a specific or specialized kind speaking), and -tion (a suffix derived from Latin that is used to make nouns out of verbs). But there are seemingly infinite numbers of them, as you will discover if you page through a dictionary and look at the word origins, or etymologies (from the Greek *etymos*, the true literal sense of a word, and *logos*, description; the Greeks even had a verb specifically meaning "to analyze a word and find its origin," *etymologeo*). The suffix tacked onto etymology, -logy (Greek *-logia*, from *legein*, to speak), is what we add to a root word to designate it as the science, doctrine, or theory of a thing; for instance, psychology, the study of *psyche* (Greek for the soul). You can see its connection to the Greek word for "word," *logos*, which in the Bible is *the* Word that God utters to create the world and which he incarnates in Christ.

The ancients gave us the words that we use to write about speech. The Greek word *glossa* (*glotta* in the Attic dialect), tongue, meant both the organ of speech and the language it was capable of forming, and the Latin word for tongue, *lingua*, shared this dual definition. While our words "language" and "linguistics" (the study of a language's structure and development) obviously come from *lingua*, *glossa* is also still firmly planted in our vocabulary, sometimes by way of Latin. If a book you're reading has a glossary in the back defining specialized words or terms to make your reading experience easier, you can thank the ancients, who came up with the idea. The Greek word *glossa* could also signify an obsolete or foreign word that requires explanation. Aristotle used *glotta* to refer to "strange" and "rare" words, such as one might encounter in a local dialect or as an archaic term in an old piece of literature.

The ancient Greeks, who were so obsessed with their language and their literary classics, not surprisingly began to compile all sorts of lists of obscure or archaic words. One reason was to help readers better understand old classics that might contain antiquated vocabulary by listing the old, unfamiliar words next to a word currently in use that meant the same thing; for instance, dozens of fragments of glossaries to Homer's epics survive, while hundreds more undoubtedly perished. The Romans imitated this practice by devising word lists for their own writers, such as Vergil and Cicero, and bilingual glossaries that listed Latin words and their Greek equivalents side by side catered to people trying to acquire basic Latin for everyday use as well as Latin speakers learning to read Greek texts.

But the Greeks also seem to have enjoyed collecting words purely for their weirdness. Such word collections were especially popular in the city of Alexandria during Hellenistic times, when scholars from all over the world gathered to study at the famed library there, and many seemingly vied to outdo one another in the arcaneness of their research. Later, the Romans adopted *glossa* to mean a collection of unfamiliar words, and the Latin *glosarium* became the term for an unusual, difficult, or foreign word that needed to be explained. In the Middle Ages, the *glossarium*, a collection of foreign, antiquated words, became a popular genre, and scholars delighted in adding "glosses" to texts—comments written in the margins or between the lines that would help readers understand a complicated or confusing point. Hence our word glossary, a list of definitions of vocabulary that might stump us by being too obscure, antiquated, foreign, or specialized.

The ancients also supplied us with the words we use to write about writing, and these give us a sense of the original close connection between writing and drawing. After all, remember how writing probably started out as drawing small pictures that grew increasingly simplified until they became the abbreviated symbols we call letters. The Greek verb *graphein* (to write, draw, or represent using lines) is the source of -graph, as in "autograph" (literally something one writes oneself) and "telegraph" (literally something written from far off). *Graphe*, a writing, drawing, or representation, gives us the words "graph," a diagram composed of lines, and "graphite," the type of carbon in pencils. The meaning of *graphikos*, literally "belonging to painting or drawing," is reflected in our word "graphic," which can mean "of the graphic arts" or "described in realistic and vivid detail," like a life-like painting. Latin also connects writing and drawing. The verb *scribo* means to draw, trace, represent by lines, or draw a likeness of, as well as to inscribe or write, put down in writing, make a record of, or compose. From this come our words "scribe" (Latin *scriptor*), "inscribe," "inscription" (Latin *scriptum*), "script," and "manuscript" (because *manus* means hand, literally "written by hand"). The Romans had a unique word, *scriptura*, to refer to the expression of ideas in writing, as opposed to orally. Perhaps the Bible became known as Scripture (or the Scriptures) in order to emphasize the fact that it was written down. This was a big deal, since paganism had no central written text, so the fact that the Bible was written distinguished Christianity from the pagan religions it was challenging.

As it so happens, the Bible gets its name from a plant. The ancient Greeks referred to the Egyptian papyrus plant as both *papyrus* (the source of our word paper) and *bublos* (or *biblos*). The pith from the stems of this plant, when mashed, flattened into a sheet, and dried, turned into a perfect material to write on. From a very early date (c. the eleventh century B.C.), rolls of papyrus were shipped from Egypt to the Phoenician coastal city of Gubla (Hebrew Gebal), now in present-day Lebanon, which was a center for the manufacture and trade in papyrus. In fact, the Greek name for Gubla was Byblos because it was their major source of papyrus. Because basically all books at that time were made of papyrus, the Greek term for book was also *biblos*, and, for a small book, *biblion*. *Biblos* sometimes carried the additional sense of sacred or magical writings. Given this background, it is perhaps not surprising that, by the second century A.D., the early Christians had started calling their sacred text *ta Biblia* ("the books")—or, perhaps more literally, "the little books," because it consisted of many chapters, and *biblos* could also mean the parts a larger book was divided into (Book 1, 2, etc.). By the time it had evolved to Old French, Bible had switched from the plural to the singular: *the* Book.

If you have ever wondered why a library is a biblioteca in Italy and Spain, a bibliothèque in France, and a Bibliothek in Germany, look no further than the Greek word *bibliotheke* (from *biblion*, book, and *-theke*, a form of the Greek verb *tithenai*, to place). As literally "a place to put books," the word's most common definition was bookcase, with library or collection of books as a secondary meaning. Perhaps this is because, in the ancient world, the library as a public institution was just being invented. Some individuals, mainly scholars, rulers, and those both literate and wealthy enough to afford (and appreciate) such an expensive item, collected books and such people might have a private library, but even these were rare. Library, by the way, comes to us from the Latin word for bookcase, *librarium*; the Latin for book was *liber*. (Interestingly, French bibliothèque can mean either a bookcase or a library, so maybe this is a holdover from Latin.) When you see bookshops in Italy and Spain displaying the sign "libreria," and in France, "libraire," you might assume that these are connected to the notion of a library, except that you will (unfairly?) be charged. In fact, the Latin word for bookshop was *libraria*, so they are simply following the Romans' lead.

One of the sneakier ways that Latin still gets used in speech and writing today, often by people who don't even realize that they are doing so, is through abbreviations that represent Latin phrases. Some of the more common of these include: i.e. = *id est* (that is to say); e.g. = *exempli gratia* (for example); et al. = *et alii* (masc.) or *et aliae* (fem.) (and others); etc. = *et cetera* (and other things; and the rest); ibid. = *ibidem* (in the same place in a book); *idem* = the same as above; *op. cit.* = *opere citato* (in the work quoted); Q.E.D. = *quod erat demonstrandum* (which was to be demonstrated); N.B. = *nota bene* (take note); A.D. = *Anno Domini* (in the year of our Lord); and *ad hoc* = for this (particular purpose).

Finally, even many of the most common names that we bestow upon our children and use to label ourselves are in reality Greek or Latin words or compounds of words. Just as with abbreviations, however, often the original meaning of these words has been forgotten, even by those who bear the names containing them.

A selection of some of the most common are: Amanda (Latin "worthy of love"); Andrew (from Greek *andreios*, manly); Angelo, Angela (from Greek *aggelos* = messenger, source of "angel," divine messenger, in the Bible); Barbara (from Greek *barbaros*, foreign); Basil (from Greek *basileos*, king); Bella = Latin for beautiful; Cassandra = the prophetess predicting disaster whom no one believes, in the *Iliad*; Daphne = Greek for laurel tree; Diana = Roman version of the virgin goddess of the hunt, Artemis; Eugene (from Greek *eugenes*, well-born); Felix = Latin for happy; George (from Greek *georgos*, farmer); Irene = Greek for peace; Lawrence and Laura (from Latin *laurus*, laurel tree); Martin (from Latin Martinus, a diminutive form of Martius, meaning "of Mars"); Melissa (an attested ancient Greek name; Greek for bee; *meli* = Greek for honey); Paul (from Latin *paulus*, little or small); Peter (from Greek *petros*, rock); Philip (from the ancient Greek name *Philippos*, "fond of horses," from *philos*, loving, and *hippos*, horses); Sylvia (Latin meaning "of the woods" or "sylvan"); Sophia (Greek for wisdom); Stella (Latin for star); Stephen (from Greek *stephanos*, anything circling the head, like a crown, garland, or wreath); Theodore and Dorothea (Greek for "gift from God," since *dorea* = gift and *theos* = god); Timothy (from Greek for "to honor God," from *timeo*, to honor, and *theos*, God); and Victor, Victoria, and Vincent (all derived from the Latin for conqueror).

The way that we think about the world around us and express our thoughts to one another is through the medium of words, and, as we have seen, the very letters, words, and languages that we use to communicate are deeply rooted in the classical world. Three of the most profound ways in which we use words are to craft the basic laws that underlie our civilization and make it possible, to speculate about the composition and the most profound secrets of the universe and human nature, and to tell stories to one another. These three applications of words and language are among the defining qualities that make us human, and once again, they are all areas in which the influence of the ancient world has left an enduring legacy. The remainder of this chapter will explore these.

And justice for all: The law

One day, a Roman decided that his slave was looking a bit scruffy, so he sent him to a barbershop to get a shave and haircut. The barbershop happened to be next door to a gymnasium, where some athletes were tossing a ball back and forth. One of the athletes threw the ball, a second failed to catch it, and the ball flew into the barbershop, striking the barber on the arm while he was shaving the slave and causing him to cut the slave's throat with his razor. The slavemaster, angry at the loss of his slave, decided to seek legal action to recover the cost of the slave. The question was, whom to sue? Should it be the first athlete, who threw the ball? The second athlete, who failed to catch it? The barber who actually killed the slave? Or even the city, for allowing a barbershop to operate near a potentially dangerous playing field? This is a law case (perhaps hypothetical) preserved in the very large body of Roman legal texts that have survived from antiquity. As evidenced by this example, the Romans developed an extraordinarily complex body of law that could deal with all sorts of cases, however improbable. The body of Roman legal statutes, cases, and associated legal commentary provided the basis for almost all the legal systems used around the world today, and, as such, constitutes one of the most important legacies of the ancient world to the modern one.

Law codes are absolutely vital in order to have civilization and cities. In small settlements or villages it is possible, and in fact common, for disputes among individuals to be handled by family elders. Such systems usually work because everyone knows everyone else, or is at least bound by extended kinship ties; but once urban centers begin to have bigger populations, you end up with large numbers of strangers living and interacting with one another. In such circumstances, conflicts inevitably arise, and you need a way to mediate these in a relatively impartial manner. Otherwise, you just have chaos and lots of people killing one another. This is the great contribution of law codes: they provide a clear set of rules to impersonally adjudicate such disputes and resolve them.

The earliest surviving law code is that of Hammurabi, developed in Mesopotamia around 2000 B.C. Considered by modern standards, Hammurabi's law code might appear somewhat harsh and unfair. The prescribed punishment for a great many offenses was death, and all human beings were most certainly not treated equally, with different rules and punishments for such groups as women, the poor, and slaves. Whatever its quirks, Hammurabi's code represented a huge step forward for civilization by even making it possible for large numbers of people to live together in cities. Other civilizations followed, and by the time of the Greeks, the precedent of law codes was well-established.

Each of the Greek city-states developed its own set of laws, which were often attributed to a semi-mythical "founding father" figure who established them. Thus, Sparta attributed its laws and governmental system to a man named Lycurgus. Athens was particularly rich in such figures, ascribing its systems to famous men, including Solon, renowned as the wisest man in the whole world. One of the earliest of Athens' lawgivers was a man named Draco, literally "the Snake" (and the source of our word "dragon"). He was a somewhat mysterious figure who supposedly set up the very first law code and courts for Athens. His laws, however, were legendary for being extremely strict, since nearly every offense, even minor ones, resulted in the death penalty. One contemporary noted that Draco's code was not written in ink but in blood. All but one of Draco's laws have been lost, however, so it's impossible to judge the accuracy of this assessment. A memory of the harshness of his code survives today in the English adjective "draconian," meaning unusually severe or cruel.

The later fully developed Greek legal systems typically relied heavily on juries composed of randomly chosen citizens to reach decisions in important cases, and this habit formed an important legacy to later legal thought and practice. The famous trial of the Greek philosopher Socrates, for example, was conducted before a jury composed of 501 Athenian citizens, a large enough percentage of the total citizen body that whatever decision they reached could confidently be regarded as reflecting the opinion of the majority of citizens. There are over 100 surviving speeches from either the defense or the prosecution in Athenian law cases, and these give us a good idea of the procedures and strategies used in these trials.

The earliest Roman legal code was a document known as the Twelve Tables, so named because it originally consisted of 12 actual bronze tablets set up in the Forum, each of which was inscribed with statutes pertaining to one aspect of the law, such as crimes, inheritance, property, and so on. Rome at this time was a fairly simple agricultural society, and the laws of the Twelve Tables were pretty basic. Over the centuries, however, Roman law grew into a far more complex and sophisticated system. Our knowledge of Roman law is mainly due to the actions of the emperor Justinian, who lived in the sixth century A.D. By this point, the western Roman empire and Rome itself had already fallen to barbarians, but the legacy of Rome had been preserved in the eastern half of the empire, ruled from its capital city of Constantinople. This eastern empire is often called the Byzantine empire, and Justinian was one of its greatest emperors. He ordered his ministers to collect together and compile a massive work consisting of the writings of Roman legal scholars. Published in A.D. 533 and known as the *Digest of Roman Law*, it runs to over 800,000 words. To this, Justinian also added several supplementary publications, such as the *Code of Roman Law* and the *Institutes*, and collectively these texts served as a summation and explanation of Roman legal thought covering a broad range of categories, from interpersonal crimes to inheritance law.

The real global impact of this work began to be felt around the eleventh century, when the Roman law code, as preserved by Justinian, became particularly influential at the great early law school established in Bologna, which thrived during the Middle Ages. The code of Roman law was then used as the basis for the legal systems that evolved in Europe. Subsequently, during the era of colonialism, this influence expanded throughout much of the rest of the world. Thus, countries as apparently dissimilar as Germany, Argentina, and Japan all use legal systems derived either directly or indirectly from Roman law. Although England deviated by developing English Common Law, much of its terminology and structure were nevertheless shaped by and derived from Roman Law as well. In the long run, the single most wide-ranging and significant effect of the Roman world on the modern one might well be in the realm of law, where Justinian's Code laid the basis for almost all modern legal systems. The only exceptions are a handful of countries, mostly in the Middle East and Africa, which use legal systems derived from Islamic Sharia law.

One other aspect of Roman law is worth noting. Like Athens, Rome had many high-profile trials involving famous individuals. Such trials were usually held before a jury in public spaces where large numbers of spectators could come and watch. Rome had no true class of professional lawyers, but ambitious aristocrats who were good at public speaking would often volunteer or be asked to deliver speeches for the prosecution or the defense at these trials. This was a way in which they could bring themselves into the public eye and enhance their reputations. This was especially true during the first century B.C., an era known as the Late Roman Republic. The many sensational cases of this time drew large crowds of random spectators and, because of their public nature, the speakers played as much to the audience as to the jury. In many respects, these trials were similar to the modern phenomenon of televised celebrity trials, such as the media circus surrounding the O. J. Simpson trial.

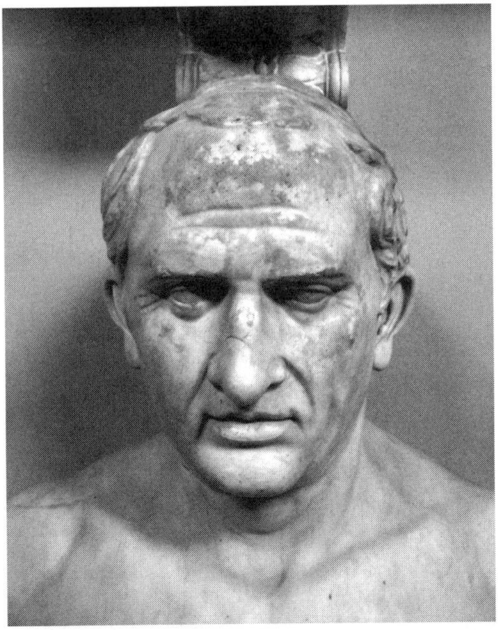

Figure 7.1 *Portrait bust of Cicero. One of the greatest public speakers of all time, Cicero made use of a sophisticated arsenal of oratorical tricks and strategies to win over audiences and juries.*

We know quite a bit about the kinds of tactic that ancient orators employed to win over juries and audiences, mostly due to the copious writings of one man who was the most famous public speaker at the time, as well as one of the greatest orators of all time, Marcus Tullius Cicero. Despite coming from an obscure family, Cicero made a successful political career for himself, eventually rising to the highest elected post in the government, on the basis of one skill. He had a talent with words. He possessed an extraordinary ability to get up in front of crowds and persuade them of what he wanted them to believe. Among his many writings are several handbooks describing in great detail how to be an effective orator, as well as copies of his speeches, works of philosophy, and even seven books collecting the letters he wrote to other people. More material survives from Cicero than from any other author in the ancient world and, because of him, the Late Republic is one of the best understood periods in ancient history. Cicero's first case was defending a man accused of killing his father, and, even though he was probably guilty, Cicero managed to get him acquitted.

Let's look in more detail at Cicero's ideas about oratory and how to be a persuasive public speaker. The key to Cicero's overall strategy is the belief that people are ruled by their feelings; therefore, if you can touch their emotions, you can make them believe what you want them to. He claims that the purpose of this sort of oratory is not to appeal to logic or science, but to engage the audience's feelings—if you can get an audience emotionally involved, you can get them to vote however you want. As he put it, "To sway the audience's emotions is victory; for among all things it is the single most important in winning verdicts" (*Orator* 69) and "Nothing else is more important than to sway the hearer's emotions" (*On Oratory* 2.178).

A second rhetorical trick is to make use of props and physical objects when speaking. He asserts that these can be very effective in provoking strong emotions. Cicero compares an orator to an actor and, like an actor, he has to prepare his stage and furnish it with the necessary props. For example, when prosecuting a murder case, some of the items that Cicero lists that can be used to elicit strong emotions in the crowd include "swords encrusted with blood, bits of bone taken from wounds, and the bloodstained clothing of the victims." If no good props were available, an orator might create one by commissioning a dramatic painting showing the crime being committed. All of these techniques are familiar to anyone who watches courtroom dramas on television, but remember that Cicero had all this worked out over 2,000 years ago. A final type of prop that Cicero made use of was living people. On one occasion, Cicero delivered a speech for a defendant while cradling the man's baby in his arms, with the result that "the Forum was filled with sobs and tears." Another time, he had a defendant's elderly parents stand behind him while he delivered his speech, thus implicitly saying to the jury and audience, "How could you leave these nice old folks without anyone to take care of them?"

The most famous example of using a specially prepared prop comes from a rival of Cicero's. For his speech after the assassination of Julius Caesar (the "Friends, Romans, Countrymen ..." speech in Shakespeare's "Julius Caesar"), Mark Antony had a larger-than-life naked wax figure of Caesar made, complete with every injury and stab wound inflicted by the assassins accurately and bloodily marked. He mounted this gruesome effigy upright on a revolving stand, and as he gave his speech and described the death of Caesar, he pointed out each injury on this model. In this instance, he was very effective in rousing the crowd's anger, since they spontaneously rioted and burned down the senate house.

Another modern-sounding piece of advice from Cicero was to employ rhyming phrases. The rationale for this is that people remember rhymes and like catchy slogans. This preference forms the basis for almost all modern advertising jingles. An example from one of Cicero's speeches is the line *audaciter territas, humiliter placas*, meaning "You blusteringly threaten, you cringingly beg." Such rhyming slogans are not unique to ancient Roman law courts. We have only to recall the most famous quote from the O. J. Simpson trial, when his lawyer Johnny Cochrane memorably declared, "If the gloves don't fit, you must acquit."

A large part of the effectiveness of Cicero's oratory derived from the way in which he gave his speeches—in other words, his delivery. He realized that how you give a speech is as important as what you say, and that a poor speech with great delivery is better than a brilliant speech with bad delivery. The greatest Greek orator, Demosthenes, expressed this idea when he was once asked, "What are the three most important aspects of oratory?" to which he replied, "Delivery, delivery, and delivery." Part of effective delivery was using compelling body language, to which Cicero and other Roman orators devoted much effort.

They even developed a kind of sign language, or system of gestures, that could be used to enhance the delivery of their speeches. Unlike today's sign language, however, their gestures did not mean the same thing as their words. Instead, they used gestures to add an emotional gloss to their words. The Romans believed that making certain gestures would cause people to feel certain emotions in response. Therefore, if you knew what gestures to make, you could manipulate an audience's feelings. Cicero explained this by saying that, just as certain musical tones and chords can make you feel sad, happy, tense, and so on, certain postures of the body or hand motions could make you feel certain emotions. He claimed that the body is like a lyre (a musical instrument) and that the orator must learn to "play" his own body (*On Oratory* 3.216).

Cicero was critical of fellow orators who did not use gestures in this way. He abused one such with the words, "You, Marcus Calidus, there was no trace of agitation in you, neither of mind nor of body. Did you smite your brow? Did you slap your thigh, or at least stamp your foot? No! In fact, so far from touching my feelings, I could scarce refrain from going to sleep then and there" (*Brutus* 278). Conversely, Cicero praised another orator's use of gesture by saying that: "Your wagging finger made me tremble with emotion" (*On Oratory* 2.188). Gesture and delivery were a huge part of oratory, and their importance is summed up in a quote by another famous Roman orator, Quintilian: "The hands may almost be said to speak. Do we not use them to demand, promise, summon, dismiss, threaten, supplicate, express aversion or fear, question or deny? Do we not use them to indicate joy, sorrow, hesitation, confession, penitence, and measure quantity, number, and time?" (*Insitutio Oratoria* 11.3.86–7).

There was a danger in this, however: gesticulating too much or in an undignified manner might make the orator look silly. One orator who was in the habit of violently flailing his arms around inspired many negative comments, including that it looked like he was trying to drive away flies (*Brutus* 216–17). Another man said it looked like he was trying to keep his balance in a wave-tossed boat. Perhaps most embarrassing was the case of an orator named Sextus Titius, who habitually swayed from side to side in an overly supple and languid way. This resulted in a popular dance of the time being named "The Titius" (*Brutus* 225).

Today, politicians hire expensive consultants who try to teach them how to employ effective gestures and body language when giving speeches, but they could probably save a lot of money by simply consulting the ancient, but still entirely relevant, advice of Cicero. We've discussed only a few of the oratorical strategies and tricks advocated by Cicero that have a modern feel to them. Others include: repetition, guilt by association, exaggeration, personal insults and mud-slinging, labeling, fear-mongering, us-versus-them strategies, and appeals to the gods or religion. While we might deplore many of these techniques, there is no doubt that they are effective, and we have only to look at the latest political campaign ads to see almost all of them being employed.

Thinking big thoughts: Philosophy

One of the greatest legacies of the ancient Greeks is their fundamental contribution to how we think rationally about the world around us and how it works, and how we explore human thought and human nature—or, in other words, the discipline of philosophy. The first and slightly earlier wave of Greek philosophers were the Ionian Rationalists, whom we examined in Chapter 5. They had concentrated their efforts on asking questions about the natural, physical world, but in the fifth century B.C. there appeared a second significant group of philosophers with a different emphasis, known as the Sophists. They were still all about asking questions, but they narrowed their focus from the natural world to the internal world of the human mind. Many Sophists accordingly had interests in human behavior, ethics, politics, history, and psychology. The philosophers associated with this movement include some of the greatest of all time, such as Plato and Socrates, whose ideas and methods continue to engage us today.

When they were not philosophizing, the Sophists earned a living by teaching what we would today call debate skills, for a fee. They taught the techniques of verbal argumentation to the young men of Athens and other Greek states. Particularly in cities like Athens, whose government encouraged citizens to speak at public assemblies, such oratorical skills could lead to political power. Their teachings, however, made the Sophists very unpopular with many people, especially those of a more traditionalist, conservative mind-set. Their critics viewed them as parasites and tricksters, who posed a threat because, at times, they appeared to advocate moral relativity. Their rhetorical techniques were sometimes seen as verbal trickery, and their complex theories as just argument for argument's sake.

Their reputation was not helped by the esoteric nature of many of their philosophical musings. A good example of this is a work by one of the most famous Sophists, a man named Gorgias. He wrote a book that demonstrated through lengthy and complex logical arguments that it was not possible to prove that anything really existed. This would have been problematic enough, but then he went on in a second section to show that nothing exists, but that if it did exist, we wouldn't really be able to understand or properly comprehend it. And finally, he added a third section arguing that nothing exists, but that if it did, we wouldn't be able to understand it, and if by some miracle we could understand it, then we wouldn't be able to communicate it. For the average person, worried about getting in the crops on time or putting food on the table, such abstract theorizing seemed neither comprehensible nor particularly helpful, and therefore the segment of the populace most drawn to the Sophists was young, idle, rich men who liked the idea of challenging their elders.

Fifth century B.C. Athens also boasted one of the greatest thinkers of all time—the philosopher Socrates. Although often lumped together with the Sophists by contemporaries, Socrates never accepted money, and may well have disputed the notion that he was a teacher. He himself wrote nothing, and is known to us only through the writings of others, chiefly his disciple, Plato. Socrates viewed himself as being on a divinely sanctioned quest for knowledge, and he is famous for developing a methodology of inquiry composed entirely of simply asking questions. This became known as the Socratic method. He would begin by posing a seemingly simple and innocent question to some person who was supposedly wise, and then keep asking further questions. Often, these additional questions would challenge the assumptions of his subject or point out flaws in his statements, so that the poor victim of Socrates' inquiries would eventually become trapped in a maze of contradictions and would be compelled to admit his ignorance. This was a form of instruction based not on giving answers, but rather on forcing people to reach their own conclusions and to rethink their convictions. The Socratic method is still regarded as one of the best and most effective means of teaching, and instructors in all areas, not just philosophy, continue to emulate the model established by Socrates.

Another favorite rhetorical technique of Socrates was to use analogies both to make arguments and to help others grasp difficult concepts, and this too has persisted as an important instructional technique. Unfortunately for Socrates, his methods made him unpopular with many in Athens, particularly those whom he publicly embarrassed by exposing their ignorance. This culminated in a trial in which he was partially scapegoated for the actions of some of those who had followed him. In a shameful episode, he was condemned to death by an Athenian jury, and, defying expectations that he would simply flee Athens, Socrates stayed and willingly drank the fatal cup of hemlock.

We know of Socrates' life mostly through the writings of his student, Plato, who became one of the most famous philosophers of all time in his own right and who developed a distinctive and influential view of existence. In a nutshell, he posited that the world that we can perceive with our senses is not actually reality. There is a second world that can only be reached through pure thought, and all things exist there in their perfect, ideal, true forms. All things that we sense in this world are just pale, imperfect shadows of those ideal forms.

Plato attempted to explain this theory with a famous analogy called the Parable of the Cave. He asks us to imagine people imprisoned from birth in a dark underground cave, fettered in such a way that they can't move and can only look straight ahead. A fire burns behind them, and objects modeled on real things are being carried back and forth in such a way that the prisoners can see only their shadows cast on the cave wall, as in a shadow puppet show. Thus, they are viewing merely shadows of imperfect copies of the real things that exist outside the cave, but mistake these for reality. This scenario reflects the plight of human beings bound by the evidence of their senses to the material world and unable to see beyond appearances to the true world of ideal forms. The commonly heard terms "Platonic forms" and "Platonic ideal," denoting something at the height of its perfection, refer to this metaphor.

The notion of "Platonic love," used nowadays to signify a non-sexual bond, originated with Plato's theory that loving another human being should function merely as an initial step on the path leading the soul upwards towards the world of forms and love of the divine; love of a particular individual's physical beauty should be transformed into a love of beauty as an abstract to love of the divinity that is the original source of all beauty.

If you have ever wondered why people speak of looking for their "other half," this might well stem from Plato's influential story of the sphere people in his dialogue *The Symposium*. To explain the impulse of attraction that draws people together to form couples, one of the symposium guests describes how, at one time, human beings were formed like perfect orbs, consisting of two people fused together. They could walk in either direction, but to run, they had to do cartwheels like a rolling ball. Angered by their pridefulness, Zeus punished them by slicing them in two in order to render them weaker. As a result, each half longed to find the other half it had once been joined with, and if the two halves finally met, they would eagerly embrace, trying to achieve their original oneness. Each of us is a half striving to become a whole again. Incidentally, Plato's story had the added benefit of explaining both heterosexuality and homosexuality, since the spheres could consist of either two males, two females, or a male and a female.

In general, Plato's ideas stress order and unity, such as his rather totalitarian portrait of an ideal state in *The Republic*. He represents a turn away from the experimentation and natural science of the Ionian Rationalists, and towards a form of philosophy focused purely on abstract thought. Plato's many dialogues really laid the foundations for all of Western philosophical thought, and all subsequent philosophers have had to work in his shadow.

Out of the break-up of Alexander the Great's empire emerged a confused time known as the Hellenistic era, which was characterized politically by constant warfare and frequent oppression. This period seemed to spark an intellectual response in the shape of several new schools of philosophy concerned with the question of how to live a moral or proper life during troubled times.

One of these new philosophical schools was Epicureanism, named after its founder, Epicurus. The Epicureans believed that the goal of existence was to achieve a state of tranquility in which one was free from pain and fear. This was accomplished by avoiding those things that caused pain and unpleasantness, and by seeking experiences that were pleasurable. Today the word Epicurean carries connotations of excess, particularly in regards to food, but a key aspect of ancient Epicureanism was moderation. The idea was that one should enjoy physical pleasures, but should studiously avoid overindulgence in them.

The Epicureans believed in withdrawing from society, not participating in politics, and living a quiet, intellectual life. This attitude is the very opposite of the earlier Greek emphasis on active civic involvement, but reflects the new political realities of the Hellenistic era. It was a philosophy of seclusion, especially popular with wealthy men who retreated into their country villas, where they socialized with a circle of close friends, didn't worry about the world's problems, and tried to make their lives as nice as possible.

An alternative school of philosophy, Stoicism, which was founded by a man named Zeno, had a very different response to the problems of the Hellenistic Age. The Stoics were rather more pessimistic in outlook and believed that the world was probably a bad place overall, but that one nevertheless had to endure whatever one encountered and to press on even in the face of adversity. They had a strong ethos of helping others, and thus, unlike the Epicureans, espoused an outward-looking philosophy that taught that it was one's duty to stay involved in society and to do the best one could, even when such actions were futile or doomed to failure.

The key concept for the Stoics was the idea of virtue. Virtue was the highest good; it was acquired through positive actions, and if one possessed it one could achieve contentment. If virtue was attained, then all else—including health, wealth, and status—was utterly irrelevant. This was a philosophy that mixed acceptance of misfortune with the effort to make things better.

Incidentally, the Stoics got their name from the fact that they originally met at a *stoa* in Athens—one of those multi-purpose colonnades that people used for all sorts of varied purposes. Additional meanings later accrued to the term "stoic" because of their philosophical beliefs.

The beliefs of the third major Hellenistic philosophical school can also be viewed as a response to negative aspects of the culture of the time, but their ideas were by far the most radical. These were the Cynics, who advocated living a life of unreserved, brutal honesty. This led them to reject all forms of authority, government, and even everyday social structures and conventions, which they held to be artificial constructs having no basis in nature. They maintained that people were basically animals, and that to pretend otherwise was pure hypocrisy. Accordingly, they also shunned all the material products of civilization, including personal possessions, and were usually encountered homeless and in a state of nakedness.

This extreme lifestyle led their critics to refer to them scathingly as "dogs." This nickname stuck and actually gave them the name by which they became known, since the term Cynic is derived from the Greek word *cuon*, meaning "dog" (which, by the way, is also the root of the English word "canine"). They were drop-outs from society, and their adherence to a life of absolute honesty often resulted in their being considered rude and obnoxious, since they told people exactly what they thought, and took pleasure in ridiculing the pretensions of society.

In keeping with their anti-authoritarian stance, they did not recognize any founder or leader even among themselves, but the most famous Cynic was a man named Diogenes. There are many stories about Diogenes that illustrate the Cynic mind-set. He supposedly went around naked and lived in a large abandoned pot, and the only object that he owned was a crude wooden bowl. One day, he witnessed a poor farm boy drinking from a stream out of his cupped hands—a sight which immediately filled Diogenes with self-disgust at his own indulgence for having the luxury of a bowl and which resulted in his immediately smashing it.

Diogenes ended up at Athens, where he had a run-in with the famous philosopher Plato. At a lecture, Plato offered a definition of man as an animal that walked on two legs and lacked feathers. Overhearing this, Diogenes grabbed a chicken, plucked it, and then mockingly presented it to Plato, declaring, "Here is Plato's man."

Another story featuring a well-known historical figure recounts that one day, as Diogenes was lying in the sun by the side of the road, Alexander the Great and his entourage rode by on their horses. Recognizing Diogenes and admiring him for his honesty, Alexander stopped and said that he desired to reward the philosopher and would give him anything that he asked for.

Figure 7.2 *Statue of Diogenes. This modern statue, erected in his hometown of Sinope, shows the Cynic philosopher with the urn that he supposedly lived in, a dog (from which the term Cynic was derived), and a lantern with which, at least according to legend, he searched for an honest man.*

Supposedly Diogenes merely glanced up sourly at the ruler of the world and snarled the reply that the only thing that he wanted from Alexander was for him to move along because he was blocking the sunlight.

All three of these Hellenistic schools of philosophy have given rise to modern English words—epicurean, stoic, and cynical—which still to some degree reflect their beliefs, but in an oversimplified, somewhat misleading manner. "Epicurean" today primarily suggests a fondness for luxury and sensuous pleasures, particularly food and drink, with the crucial elements of regulation and moderation left out; "stoic" now mainly connotes indifference to both pleasure and pain and the ability to completely repress emotion, omitting the Stoics' stress on virtue, helping others, and civic responsibility; and "cynical" means doubting the sincerity and goodness of people's motives and actions and believing that everyone is inspired only by selfishness, but fails to communicate the dedication to honesty and self-criticism that somewhat leavened the original Cynics' disagreeableness, since they were as harsh on themselves as they were on others.

Universal archetypes: Classical myths

Human beings are storytellers. This characteristic is universal to all societies and times. We innately seem to take pleasure in crafting narratives and then telling them to one another. Such tales can take innumerable forms and be conveyed through many different types of media, from poems to plays and movies to comic books, but these all reflect the basic act of storytelling. In these stories, the same themes, characters, and archetypes often recur, such as the quest, the coming-of-age story, the noble hero, and the cruel villain. The myths of ancient Greece and Rome were full of these, and the specific forms that they took have had a particularly profound influence on how later Western cultures have told their own stories.

The entertainment that we seek, whether in the form of movies, TV shows, or books, is frequently described as "escapist." Yet the things we like to read about and watch often mirror our deepest concerns and fears, but projected onto fictional characters or other people. The basic tensions that arise in people's relationships, both romantic and familial, are among the richest veins to be mined by writers and directors. Novels present sprawling family sagas full of conflict and intrigue; memoirs expose painful family dynamics; sitcoms poke fun at the ever-thorny interactions between in-laws; and talk shows and self-help books try to fix dysfunctional relationships, to give just a few examples. Many of the same stereotypes and themes recur over and over again: the straying husband, the jealous wife, sibling rivalry, the vengeful ex, the conflict between the older and younger generations. This same material never seems to get old no matter how often it is recycled in new shapes and forms. If we look back in time, we will find that many of the same problems and tensions that fascinate us today were memorably expressed by the Greeks and Romans in ways that remained influential throughout the Western tradition, and that continue to influence how we talk about them. Let us consider some of these ancient stock characters and stereotypes.

The original dysfunctional family was the offspring of Mother Earth, Gaia or Ge, who fought an epic battle between the older and the younger generations. Gaia's children, the Titans, were the first generation of gods to rule. One of them, Chronos, had usurped power from his own father, Uranus (the Universe), and castrated him. Not surprisingly, Chronos became so afraid of his own children doing the same thing to him that he swallowed every one of them until his wife managed to sneak their baby son Zeus away (Chronos swallowed a stone in his place). Chronos' prophecy became self-fulfilling, because Zeus inevitably grew up to be an angry god with revenge in his heart. He forced Chronos to vomit up his siblings, who joined him to fight the Titans in a great battle. When the Titans lost, he threw them into a deep pit and imprisoned them forever. This story captures intergenerational strife in a particularly graphic and literal way. The second generation, the Olympians, thus came to power, and established their own dysfunctional family on Mount Olympus. Sibling rivalry immediately cropped up, as the brothers Zeus, Poseidon, and Hades bickered over who should be in charge of the gods. Their solution was to divide things up so that Zeus ruled the heavens, Poseidon the seas, and Hades the Underworld—even though it is obvious that Zeus was the overall leader.

Marriage has always been a rich topic exploited for both comedy and tragedy, for us to laugh at while perhaps anxiously thinking about our own situations. The stereotypes of the henpecked husband and the nagging wife and of the philandering husband and the jealous wife can be traced back to the King and Queen of Mount Olympus, Zeus and Hera. They argue, yell, and carp at one another, then have make-up sex. Hera spies on Zeus and sends others to trail him, trying to catch him in his infidelities. Because he is a god, Zeus can indulge himself with mortal women the whole world over, and he has all sorts of tricks not available to the average guy. For instance, when pursuing the vast majority of his love affairs, he ends up transforming either himself, his lover, or both of them into an animal or some other form. Yet despite all his attempted deceptions, Hera always finds out in the end, gives him a good tongue lashing, and usually punishes the other woman (often by changing her into an animal or object).

As an example, when Zeus is dallying with the nymph Io, Hera spots them, so he turns Io into a lovely white heifer. Hera, not fooled, seizes the cow and places her under the guard of a giant named Argus Panoptes ("All-Seeing") because his body is covered with one hundred eyes (making him, quite literally, the first private eye called in by a wife to intervene in a case of adultery). Zeus sends in the god Hermes to tell him a boring, endless story, which gradually puts Argus to sleep, one eye at a time; then Hermes kills him and frees Io. Not done, Hera sends a gadfly to chase Io (an apt choice for hassling a cow), which stings her all the way to Egypt. Hera takes all of the eyes from Argus' corpse and puts them on the tail of her favorite bird, the peacock. Take away the fanciful elements and the metamorphoses, and you have a classic story of an unfaithful husband confronted by an angry wife who tries to get even with the other woman.

The jilted, vengeful wife or lover is a common stereotype, memorably portrayed in modern times by Glenn Close in the movie "Fatal Attraction" as killing and boiling a pet rabbit before escalating towards greater acts of violence. The original angry wife discarded for a younger woman and driven to acts of unspeakable violence was the powerful barbarian witch/princess Medea, who threw away everything for love—leaving her homeland, her family, and her high status to help her beloved, Jason, obtain her father's treasured Golden Fleece—and then found herself tossed aside by an ungrateful husband whom she had literally killed for repeatedly (even her own brother). When Jason put her aside and married a pretty, much younger princess, Medea went ballistic, sending a poisoned gown to the bride (who died a fiery death) and killing her own sons in order to hurt her husband.

There is a classical archetype for the happily married couple, however. Ovid tells the story of how Zeus and Hermes, in disguise, became discouraged by the selfishness of human beings, who turned them away when they sought hospitality. Only one elderly couple, Baucis and Philemon, offered to share their humble meal. In return for their kindness, their wish was granted that they should die at the same time, and, turned into trees, they spend eternity growing more and more intertwined with one another.

The evil mother-in-law doesn't get much worse than the goddess Aphrodite (called Venus by the Romans), who does not approve of her son Eros' (Cupid's) marriage to a mortal woman named Psyche (which means "soul" or "spirit"), and therefore forces her to perform a series of impossible fairytale tasks such as sorting a roomful of different grains into individual piles in one night. (Luckily, friendly ants converge on the room and help her out so she completes the chore in time.) Before this, Psyche had been forced to deal with a hostile stepmother and two jealous stepsisters, further piling on the evil stock characters out to get her. The story also has jealousy between the mother-in-law and daughter-in-law thrown in for good measure; Eros (the god of love) falls in love with Psyche in the first place because his mother is angry that people are worshiping the girl as more beautiful than the goddess of love herself, so Aphrodite sends her son to shoot Psyche with one of his arrows and make her fall in love with a disgusting monster. Eros instead pricks his own finger and falls deeply in love with Psyche, and "love" marries "soul." This of course makes his mother even angrier—her own son has taken the side of her rival! Because Eros has always been something of a mama's boy, his rebellion is even more shocking. The tale of Psyche and Eros is first recorded in Apuleius' second-century A.D. novel *The Metamorphoses*, where it functions as an allegory or fable about the nature and progress of love.

Parent–child relationships also have a longstanding classical heritage. The closeness of the mother–daughter bond is reflected in the story of Demeter, goddess of agriculture, and her daughter Persephone, which shows how traumatic marriage can be in ripping apart mother and daughter. Persephone's uncle, Hades, kidnaps her to be his queen in the Underworld, and Demeter is so distraught that, in the worst case of "empty nest" syndrome ever, she plunges the world into perpetual winter. Only when Persephone is allowed to split her time between her mother and her husband does summer return to earth—only to depart when Persephone returns underground, like a flower going dormant.

It has become trendy to stress the crucial role of mentoring in the development of both children and careers, so that someone older or more senior in rank offers advice and support to a young person in need of guidance or encouragement. This model was first memorably illustrated in Homer's *Odyssey*, where Odysseus' long absence leaves his young son Telemachus desperately in need of a father figure. Before departing, Odysseus appointed one of his loyal friends and advisors to look after his household and charged him with watching over his son as a guardian and teacher. Throughout the

Odyssey, this trusted older man frequently advises the youthful Telemachus, and urges him on in his quest for news about his father. His name? Mentor.

The classic codependent relationship is mirrored in that of Narcissus and Echo. Narcissus is incredibly handsome, but also so full of himself that he falls in love with his own reflection in the water. The nymph Echo falls in love with him in turn, but she has been doomed to only repeat the last few words that she overhears (an ironic curse from Hera, whom she had distracted from Zeus' love affairs by talking excessively). Pining for the self-centered Narcissus, she fades away until only her voice is left, and she literally becomes only an echo. Narcissus stares at the beautiful youth he can't ever touch until he starves to death and is transformed into the narcissus flower. This is the source of our word narcissism, meaning excessive egotism and self-centeredness. The field of psychology has adopted this term to indicate a personality type that is self-absorbed to an unhealthy degree.

In fact, the modern field of psychology has derived many of its terms and much of its vocabulary from the ancient world, specifically from Greek mythology. The great pioneer in the field, Sigmund Freud, grew up in nineteenth-century Germany in a society steeped in classical culture. German scholars were obsessed with establishing ways to study the ancient world, its languages, and its cultural remains. Heinrich Schliemann had found the ancient city of Troy, and archaeology was a "hot" topic; it also offered the useful metaphor for excavating further and further down through layers to reach a core buried long ago and very deeply, which was how Freud came to view his work uncovering the formative experiences of his patients. Freud looked to the myth of Oedipus to illustrate his theories of psychosexual development. In the myth, Oedipus is abandoned as a child, raised by adoptive parents, and, as an adult, unknowingly kills his biological father and then marries his biological mother. For a student exam, Freud had actually translated part of Sophocles' tragedy *Oedipus Rex*, and he had a bust of Sophocles and a statue of the Sphinx (the monster whose riddle Oedipus must solve) in his Vienna office, which was decorated with a profusion of ancient art objects and artifacts. Freud used Oedipus' story to characterize what he saw as a young boy's intense attachment to his mother and resulting jealousy of his father (he extrapolated from his own childhood experiences to deduce that this was a universal phenomenon). The Oedipus Complex has become famous, even to those with little knowledge of psychology.

Freud's office also contained an entire case full of statues of Eros, the winged god of desire, previously mentioned as the husband of Psyche. That is because the very term psychology drew its name from the Greek word *psyche*, meaning "soul," "spirit," and "butterfly," as well as being the name of Eros' wife, who was often depicted with butterfly wings. Freud's colleague, Carl Jung, adopted the Latin term for spirit or soul, *anima*, for use in his influential theory of the collective unconscious. Jung split the term into female and male versions, the *anima* and the *animus*, to refer to psychological traits belonging to the opposite sex that are buried in a person's unconscious. A man possesses an *anima*, a feminine inner personality, while a woman has an *animus*, a masculine inner personality. Because, during conscious existence, these hidden characteristics are usually repressed, they often emerge in dreams, which, like the Greek physician Hippocrates, Jung studied for clues about a person's mental state. Whether or not their theories are correct, Freud and Jung embedded fragments of the classical world in the newborn field of psychology.

People have always had a tendency to gaze back longingly towards an idealized past ("the good old days") that was a far better time than their own. The ancients came up with an influential myth to epitomize this idea. We still speak of a "Golden Age" of this or that to mean its heyday or high point, but in Greek myth there was an actual Golden Age, under the reign of the god Chronos (to the Romans, Saturn), when people didn't have to work because the earth willingly produced grain and fruits for them to use as they liked, their lives were extremely long, the only season was Spring, and evil, war, laws (they were unnecessary), misery, and old age did not exist. This time of innocence in some ways sounds rather like the Garden of Eden. Hesiod memorably describes the tale of humanity's decline in his *Works and Days* (lines 106–201). After this "golden race" of humans, the Olympian gods created a much inferior "silver race," and then, after growing angry at them, a yet further reduced "bronze race," followed by a brief improvement in the era of demi-gods and heroes (like those who fought at Troy), but finally hitting bottom with the age of the "iron race," during which Hesiod laments that he must live; he predicts that things will deteriorate until justice and shame are banished, all forms of evil thrive, and babies are born with gray hair. The gradual reduction of the metals' worth effectively sums up the decline in humanity's fortunes. People's lives grew shorter and shorter (they originally lived for several centuries) and they even diminished in size and strength, since it was believed that the heroes had been nine feet tall, based on giant bones that were dug up.

Another archetype linked to the myth of decline is that of the great flood that descends to sweep away an irredeemably corrupted human race; the Greeks (and the Mesopotamians) told stories of a flood sent by the gods that predated the Biblical story of Noah's flood by many centuries. When Zeus decides to destroy everyone with a flood, the Titan Prometheus warns his son Deucalion and tells him to build a boat. He and his wife Pyrrha drift around for nine days before their boat runs aground on Mount Parnassus (in the Bible, Noah lives to be 950 years old, reflecting the original extended lifespan of humankind, and his ark settles atop Mount Ararat). The myth ends with Deucalion and Pyrrha advised by the gods to throw the bones of their mother back over their shoulders; realizing that this means Mother Earth, they cast stones, and find that the ones thrown by Deucalion turn into men, and those thrown by Pyrrha become women, so that the world can begin anew.

And finally, Greek mythology supplied a wealth of tales that memorably illustrate the old adage, "Pride goeth before a fall." People who are too full of themselves and prone to excessive boasting get their comeuppance, usually by challenging one of the gods to a contest to demonstrate their own superior talent and then suffering punishment as a result. For instance, the woman Arachne was such a skilled weaver that she bragged that she was as good at it as the goddess Athena, who promptly appeared to call her bluff. For the contest, Athena wove a tapestry depicting stories of arrogant mortals who had been penalized by the gods for their presumption; Arachne responded by weaving scenes of the gods' ridiculous behavior and scandals. Enraged, Athena turned her into a spider—Arachne is the source of our word "arachnid"—but there is some irony in the fact that she nevertheless remained extremely talented at spinning. Another example is the satyr Marsyas, who challenges

Apollo to a music contest, and literally loses his skin when Apollo triumphs; as punishment, he is flayed alive.

Today, we refer to this human tendency towards self-aggrandizement as "hubris," meaning arrogance stemming from overweening pride—the fatal flaw of the heroes in Greek tragedies. In fact, the Greek idea of *hubris* had additional overtones; in the Athenian law-courts, it denoted swaggering around or behaving in an overbearing or abusive manner, and you could bring a law-suit against someone for *hubris*. Even if the gods didn't punish you, the lawyers still could.

From epic to slapstick: Poetry and theater

If you enjoy reading or writing poems, you owe much to the ancients, who not only composed a lot of influential poems that were widely imitated, but also gave us the vocabulary to talk about poetry, defined many very specific genres of it, and came up with theories of poetics that have shaped our responses to it.

If catapulted back in time, we might well think that the Greeks were poetry-mad. Even before the written word was used to record poetry, traveling bards roamed the countryside, reciting seemingly never-ending epics from memory as entertainment for appreciative audiences. The legendary blind bard Homer, the most famous one, became such an important figure in Greek culture that education largely came to consist of memorizing his works, the *Iliad* and the *Odyssey* (the preeminent works of epic poetry), and learning how to cite and interpret them. Nowadays Homer has become an adjective; we speak of the Homeric Age (around 1200 B.C., the period about which Homer wrote, although he actually lived four or five centuries later) and Homeric heroes, and many of us still read the *Iliad* and the *Odyssey* in school. Chances are that, even if you haven't read Homer's poems, you've none the less heard the phrases "Achilles' heel," "Trojan horse," "Beware Greeks bringing gifts," "the face that launched a thousand ships," "the wine-dark sea," and even "bite the dust" (a reference to how warriors fell face-first in death)—all of which derive either directly from his work or from myths and writings related to it. Perhaps you've referred to a complicated trip you made as an odyssey (although it was probably not as long or as convoluted as Odysseus' ten-year journey home from Troy). Given the original meaning of *epopoios* (epic poet), which literally, and somewhat dryly, translates as "a composer of hexameter verses (*epe*)," it is amusing to consider the grandiose connotations of our word "epic"; defined as grand, imposing, and impressive (as well as a type of long, narrative poem), this adjective has come to reflect the awe-inspiring nature of Homer's oeuvre.

The ancient Greeks even engaged in poetry as a sort of competitive sport. In the fifth and fourth centuries B.C., professional poetry reciters called rhapsodists (*rhapsodos* meant "song-stitcher," since poems were often sung) traveled to games and festivals throughout Greece to compete for prizes. Not surprisingly, Homer's epics were an especially popular subject. The recitation of epic poetry was called *rhapsodia*, the source of our word "rhapsody." Whereas we now most often use "rhapsodic" to describe praise that is extremely enthusiastic, "rhapsody" also denotes an instrumental composition of free, irregular form suggestive of improvisation (think of Gershwin's "Rhapsody in Blue" or Rachmaninoff's "Rhapsody on a Theme from Paganini") or any extravagantly fervid speech or writing. However, these additional meanings can be traced back to ancient Greek ideas about poetry as well.

Just as religious enthusiasm and oracles were believed to come from possession by a god, poetic inspiration was also thought to originate from the same cause. *Aut insanit homo aut versus facit*, the poet Horace wrote: "The fellow is either mad or is composing verses." To write poetry of genius (yet another type of indwelling spirit), you had to be possessed by the gods and gripped in a sort of divine madness. As you can tell by the word itself, "inspiration" was thought to be caused by a god literally breathing into you—the same way in which God brings Adam to life in the Bible. "Divine afflatus" was a term used by Cicero to describe poetic inspiration sent by the gods: "No man was ever great without a touch of divine afflatus," he wrote in *On the Nature of the Gods* (2.167). "Afflatus" in a literal sense meant "a breath or blast of wind," so that to be inspired was to be blown upon (or into) by a divine wind; somewhat deflating this model of poetic inspiration is the fact that "flatulence" is derived from the same linguistic root.

None the less, the Romantic poets latched onto the notions of divine breath and afflatus, and filled their poems and their theories about poetry writing with these ideas from antiquity. The Aeolian harp or wind harp (named after Aeolus, the god of the winds) became popular during the Romantic era, to the point where people had them in their homes as novelty items. This instrument made music passively, by the wind blowing across it and causing the strings to vibrate. The Aeolian harp was beloved by Romantic poets as a metaphor for the divine wind inspiring art. The harp image was particularly suited to refer to poetry writing because of how lyric poetry was originally sung by the ancient Greeks accompanied by music on a harp-like instrument called a lyre—the source of its name. The great Romantic poets Shelley and Coleridge both include Aeolian harps in their writings, and Coleridge even wrote a poem called "The Aeolian Harp." Keats' famous theory of negative capability—that the poet must remain constantly receptive to the world around him and its natural phenomena—expresses the same sense of openness and susceptibility to being "taken over" by forces outside oneself.

These Romantic poets were so enamored of ancient Greece that not only was their poetry greatly influenced by it in form and content, but they became involved in Greece's contemporary political situation. At the time, Greece was under the domination of the Ottoman Turks, and, dazzled by Greece's classical legacy of democracy and freedom, they became vocal supporters of Greece's struggle for independence. The great poet Lord Byron actually went to Greece to join the revolutionaries, but ended up dying there of a fever.

The ancient Greeks were especially good at coming up with all sorts of different genres of poetry, quite a few of which are still around today, although sometimes in different forms. Epic poetry and lyric poetry are perhaps the most famous, but there were many others. One of the most common contexts in which people sing today, even those who do not have much musical ability, is in church, where the singing of hymns forms an important component of worship. The English word hymn is directly derived from the Greek *hymnos*, meaning a song honoring a god or hero. Originally, of course, the god being praised would have been pagan rather than Christian, but modern Christian hymn-singing has its origins in these songs.

Figure 7.3 *Statue of Lord Byron at Athens. This statue portrays the Romantic poet expiring in the arms of a personification of Greece. In Greece today, Byron is regarded as a national hero for dying while participating in the nineteenth-century Greek independence movement.*

How often have you heard someone feeling the pressures of a modern, hectic, urban lifestyle expressing admiration or longing for the supposed simple life as it was practiced in the "good old days," living in the country or on a farm? Such sentiments are not new, and formed another genre of literature that goes all the way back to the Greeks. They called it *boukolika*, bucolic or pastoral poetry, and its most famous practitioner was Theocritus, in the third century B.C. His *Idylls* (from the Greek word for "little pictures"), describing things like the allegedly simple joys of rural life, were much imitated by the Romans (such as Vergil) and, later, by the English Renaissance poets. In contrast to epic poetry concerned with exceptional heroes, bucolic poetry had as its subject ordinary people in the countryside, like herdsmen (*boukoloi*) and the women they pursued romantically. Although *boukolika* literally means "cow-tending" poems, the rural setting depicted by Theocritus is beautiful, and the rustic lifestyle he portrays is one of peacefulness and contentment, punctuated with romantic episodes (another meaning of "idyll" no doubt inspired by Theocritus' poems). Pastoral poetry was another term for this genre because *pastor* is the Latin word for shepherd (which has also become our word for a clergyman who leads a church or congregation, just as a shepherd leads his flock). This type of poem was particularly popular in the urban, highly cosmopolitan centers of the Hellenistic and Roman worlds, where it was easy to disregard all the hard work and muck of rural life and imagine lounging around in an idealized lush green landscape far removed from the hectic big city.

The epigram form was another Greek innovation. Derived from *epigramma*, "inscription," epigrams were initially often epitaphs—inscriptions in stone memorializing the dead—and were frequently written in the first person to make it seem as if the dead person were speaking through his or her gravestone inscription. The American poet Edgar Lee Masters adopted this conceit for his much-read *Spoon River Anthology* (1915), in which each poem features a dead person reciting his or her own epitaph, so that, collectively, they formed a portrait of an entire small-town community. Starting in the fourth century B.C., "epigram" also began to denote short poems, with love and wine as common topics. In the first century A.D. under the Romans, the defining feature of ending an epigram with a twist or a witticism, the sense in which we use the word today, became prevalent. One famous poetry collection, the Palatine Anthology, included 3,700 epigrams, giving a sense of the high volume being written and the popularity they enjoyed. Even many people who are not ardent fans of poetry enjoy epigrams in the broader sense. Today these often take the form of clichés, "folk wisdom," or just "sayings." A few examples from a wide variety of sources are: "Little strokes, Fell great oaks" (Benjamin Franklin); "It's not the size of the dog in the fight that counts, it's the size of the fight in the dog" (Dwight D. Eisenhower); "Brevity is the soul of wit" (William Shakespeare); "All of us are in the gutter, but some of us are looking at the stars" (Oscar Wilde); and "It's not whether you get knocked down, it's whether you get up" (Vince Lombardi).

Some other poetic types pioneered by the Greeks that might not be as familiar today include the *paean*, originally a hymn sung to Apollo the Healer, which came to mean a song dedicated to any of the gods; the *enkomion* (Latin *encomium*), a type of hymn praising a person rather than a god, which was often sung by a group at the end of a dinner party; the *threnos*, a type of *enkomion* lamenting a dead person; and the *epithalamion* (meaning "at the bedroom"), a wedding song sung by a group outside the newlyweds' bedroom door on their wedding night (Spenser wrote a famous poem in this genre, by this name). The Greeks also came up with elegiac verse sometime in the late eighth century B.C.. Written in couplets and addressing a variety of topics (though today, an elegy tends to be a poem lamenting a dead person), elegies remained popular with the Romans and even throughout the Renaissance. A Roman poet particularly renowned for his elegiac verse about his unhappy love affair was the poet Catullus.

If you enjoy plays or going to the theatre, if you have sung in a chorus, or if you have ever referred to something as a "tragedy," you are indebted to the ancient Greeks, who invented much of the trappings and terminology connected with dramatic performances. Greek theater really got going in the fifth century B.C. at Athens, when most of its forms and conventions were developed. This was also the golden age of Greek tragedies, when the three most famous tragic playwrights lived and worked.

When you attend a play, chances are that you will be ushered into a semi-circular seating area surrounding a stage. In Chapter 5, we discussed how the Greeks created the first theaters and engineered them in such a way as to maximize the audience's enjoyment of the show, and our theater designs often imitate the Greek originals. *Theatron* means "viewing place," reflecting this focus on the audience's experience. There may be a space in front of the stage for an orchestra, which originally functioned as the area where the Greek chorus performed. The chorus (Greek *choros*), which we now think of as a group of singers, in ancient Greece was actually a group of singer-dancers, and *orchestra* in Greek literally means "dancing place." It is thought that Greek tragedy might have evolved from a type of performance called a *dithyramb*, in which a large group sang and danced in a big circle. Whereas we now imagine a play being all about acting, it used to be more about dancing.

The very earliest plays were simple affairs, with a single actor and the chorus exchanging lines. By tradition, a Greek named Thespis was considered the first person to add speech to the chorus' song and dance and to appear as a character distinct from himself; you might recognize his name as the origin of one of our words for actor, "thespian." The ancient Greek word for actor was actually *hypokrites*, meaning "interpreter" or "answerer," a term which we now apply to a person who is good at professing attitudes and standards that he does not really live up to—someone who, like an actor, is good at pretending.

The Greeks came up with two types of play—tragedy and comedy—which they performed at contests in honor of the god of wine, Dionysos. *Tragoidia* means "goat-song," though we are not sure if this is because it started out as a song performed at the sacrifice of a goat or because a goat was the prize at the earliest tragedy contests. Therefore, when you say that something is a tragedy, you are actually literally saying that it is a "goat-song," even though its current meaning of a distressing or terrible event stems from the catastrophe-filled plots and unhappy endings of Greek tragedies.

The three most famous Greek tragic playwrights, Aeschylus, Sophocles, and Euripides, all entered plays in the contest honoring Dionysos (the Dionysia) and were winners. Aeschylus was allegedly the innovator who upped the number of actors from one to two, while Sophocles added a third. The chorus offered commentary on the action of the play, as a sort of representative of the broader community and tradition. Despite the horrific plots, which often featured multiple bloody murders, nothing gory was ever depicted onstage; the audience had to use its imagination. Playwrights entered a set of three tragedies and one satyr play at the Dionysia. The satyr play was what it sounds like—one that featured goat-men behaving badly. Perhaps some comic relief was necessary to counteract the gloom of the preceding tragedies.

While Greek plays originally consisted just of the chorus and actors speaking their lines, scenery was eventually added. Sophocles was supposedly the one who introduced panels of painted scenery to the stage—the ancestor of today's often elaborate stage sets. The *skene* ("scene-building"), originally a kind of tent or hut where actors changed their costumes and in which painted scenery panels were stored, evolved into an elaborate two-story wooden structure decorated with columns and with multiple entrances and exits; this is the source of our word "scene." Over time, ancient stagecraft developed so that a wheeled platform was devised for rolling out set pieces, and a crane (*mechane*) was employed to lower actors onto the stage from above. These were frequently gods, who thus seemed to descend from the heavens, often to resolve a seemingly intractable situation. Referring to this practice, the Roman poet Horace coined the Latin phrase *deus ex machina* ("god from the machine") to mean something improbably introduced to solve a seemingly insoluble plot point, and he warned his fellow poets against doing this. Playwrights were in fact critiqued for excessive use of the *mechane*; over half of Euripides' surviving plays resort to it. To mock him, the comic playwright Aristophanes has a character named Euripides lowered onstage by a crane in one of his plays.

The origins of comedy are not entirely clear, but comic actors apparently often wore ridiculous-looking padded costumes with exaggerated bellies, buttocks, and penises, as well as grotesque masks. The actors in tragedies also wore masks, however. Whenever you see two masks, one laughing and one contorted with sorrow, used as symbols for drama and the theater, these reflect the ancient Greek tradition of actors always concealing their faces behind masks—even though stage actors stopped wearing masks many centuries ago.

During the Hellenistic era, the theater was one of the more popular forms of entertainment. The urban masses often flocked to the theatre, seeking not challenging intellectual fare, but light diversion. Instead of dealing with the atmosphere of political upheaval, chaos, and war that plagued the Greek world after the fragmentation of Alexander the Great's empire, these plays dealt with normal, everyday concerns and offered audiences escapism. In particular, audiences enjoyed a genre of plays called New Comedy, and if we were to see one of these plays today, we could easily imagine that we had turned on a TV and were watching a sitcom.

Just like the modern television sitcom, these plays dished out a steady stream of stock characters and stereotypes placed in broad comic situations and often presented against a stage backdrop sketchily set up to resemble two city apartments, with a few doors and a division indicated between them (rather like a studio set for a live sitcom). Whereas the comic plays of Classical Athens focused on the Greek city-state (the *polis*) and politics, the action of plays during the Hellenistic era was meant to occur over the course of a single day (rather like the episodic nature of a sitcom) and deal with the misadventures of a typical family in a domestic setting.

The most famous Greek New Comic playwright, Menander, wrote about interpersonal relationships and family dynamics. A sense of his subject matter can be gathered from a few of his titles: "The Double Deceiver," "The Girl from Samos," "Unfaithful," "The Woman-Hater," "The Man She Hated," and "The Grouchy Man" (which sounds eerily similar to the 1993 Jack Lemmon–Walter Matthau comedy, "Grumpy Old Men"). Characters bicker, scheme, try to deceive one another, and are themselves deceived. There are thwarted lovers, seductions, love affairs, misunderstandings, mistaken identities, illegitimate and long-lost children, weddings, and happy endings, as in many modern soap operas. Stock characters included the hooker with the heart of gold, the pimp, the gold-digger, the tyrannical old father, the cook, the lustful old man chasing younger women, the stingy old man, the braggart soldier (today's equivalent would perhaps be a not-so-bright athlete excessively proud of his muscles), and the slave who is cleverer than his master. A typical plot might involve a forbidden love affair between a youth and a girl deemed unsuitable by his dictatorial father because she is poorer, lower-class, a prostitute, or a slave. A wily slave aids the young man because he enjoys outsmarting his old, ill-tempered master—a reflection of the seemingly ageless human tendency to root for the underdog to come out on top in the end. It might transpire that the girl, abandoned at birth, is not who everyone thought she was, and is actually an okay match.

The Romans imported this type of comedy from the Greek world, employing many of the same stock characters and plots but adapting them to suit a Roman audience. The most famous Roman imitators of New Comedy, Plautus and Terence, borrowed freely from Menander, sometimes mashing together multiple plays. Plautus sought to amuse his audience by including lots of puns, jokes, double entendres, physical comedy and slapstick, and asides that addressed the audience directly. There were even song and dance routines, reminiscent of today's musical theater and light operettas. Plautus seems to have particularly delighted in turning social conventions upside down, poking fun at Rome's highly conservative, hierarchical, and patriarchal society. When the youth and his cunning slave ally managed to defy the father's authority and ultimately get their way without any repercussions or punishments, this was a daring twist. Greek New Comedy and its Latin imitators exerted a lasting impact, through the Renaissance and beyond, suggesting that people found the same sorts of things funny over a long time span. Shakespeare's early comedies were influenced by the works of Plautus; for instance, he based his "Comedy of Errors" on Plautus' "The Brothers Menaechmus," with bits from the sex farce "Amphitruo" added.

If you want to experience a modern take on a New Comedy play that is actually set in the ancient world, attend a staging (or even rent the movie version) of the popular Broadway hit, "A Funny Thing Happened on the Way to the Forum." The enduring popularity of these plays and their modern sitcom equivalents is strong testimony to the basic human impulse towards broad slapstick humor as a way to brighten our existence and, along the way, to poke fun at those who sometimes take things too seriously.

The joy of reading: Novels, biographies, and advice manuals

If the ancients had had bestseller lists, what sorts of books would have been on them? Of course, this is a flawed question, because literacy in the ancient world was limited, and so was access to books, which were costly and labor-intensive to produce. But what sorts of genres were popular? Many would not be out of place on today's bestseller lists: novels, romances, adventure stories, biographies of famous people, history, and how-to books. However, while we know that these various types of book existed, our knowledge of them is limited because few have survived in their entirety.

Homer's epic poem *The Odyssey* might be considered one of the earliest adventure stories, full of dangers and excitement. In his ten-year quest to return home after the Trojan War, the hero, Odysseus, assumes disguises and fake identities, fights and kills monsters, and uses his wits to escape death time after time. But the story ultimately turns into a tender romance extolling the values of marital love and fidelity. It has it all: one-eyed monsters, sexy witches, the summoning of ghosts, feats of strength, fighting, killing, lust, love, and revenge. Homer's other epic, *The Iliad*, was the first in-depth war story, transporting the audience onto the battlefield alongside its warriors. In the ancient world, everyone knew Homer's works; they formed the basis of a classical education, and they were imitated by writers for centuries to come. Homer's vivid tales even became shorthand for a universal human experience; today, when we encounter a series of difficulties when trying to accomplish something, we still say that we have been through an odyssey.

Greek novels arose during the Hellenistic period, as long narratives often focused around a romance, and novels became popular among the Romans as well, but today only five Greek examples and two Latin ones remain, along with fragments. A common plot involved two lovers who are separated, experience various improbable and perilous adventures, and are then reunited at the end to live happily ever after. Incidentally, "star-crossed" lovers refers to the astrological theory that our destinies are governed by the stars, which are the original cause of the lovers' tribulations. The "Romeo and Juliet" scenario thus has ancient roots, though even more important than familial animosity were class discrepancies—the strictures against the rich marrying the poor, the urban aristocrat marrying the country hick, and the free person marrying the slave. The modern archetype of a girl or boy falling for someone "from the wrong side of the tracks," much chronicled in pop music and teen movies, still resonates today, with racial prejudice added as another potential barrier to young couples.

Today's adventure or romance novels often feature a series of improbable plot twists, but such a structure was already a standard feature of ancient novels. The oldest surviving romance novel, dating perhaps to the mid-first century A.D., is Chariton's *Chaireas and Kallirhoë*. The eponymous lovers marry, but Chaireas, tricked into thinking his beautiful wife has been unfaithful, kicks her, and she collapses. A funeral is held for Kallirhoë and she is interred in a tomb, but when pirates come to rob it she wakes from a coma and seemingly rises from the dead. The pirates sell her as a slave, her master falls in love with her and marries her, but she fails to mention that she is already married to (and pregnant by) Chaireas. Meanwhile, Chaireas finds out that she is alive and goes searching for her, but is himself enslaved. By coincidence, the Great King of Persia, Artaxerxes, hears about their situation and must judge which husband is her true one but, awed by her beauty, considers taking her for himself. When a war breaks out, Chaireas becomes involved in the fighting, wins a victory against the Persians, and ultimately regains Kallirhoë. Reunited, they head for home; she tells her second "husband" to bring up the son he thought was his and send him along when he is grown up. The interesting twist is that this improbable-sounding story was based on real people who lived centuries before the author, although Chariton took a lot of liberties with the actual events (for instance, when the real-life model for the heroine was killed by soldiers, she stayed dead) and included characters who did not really live at the same time. But by setting his novel in a period earlier than his own and writing about "real" people (no matter how inaccurately), Chariton came up with an early version of the historical romance novel.

From this plot summary, you get a sense of some of the popular elements in ancient novels: a romance, adventures, misconceptions that must be dispelled, twists of fate, coincidences, and seemingly miraculous occurrences, especially the "fake death." Achilles Tatius' novel, *Leukippe and Kleitophon*, in which the eloping lovers suffer a shipwreck and are captured by bandits in the Nile Delta region of Egypt, also features two falsified deaths. Kleitophon thinks he sees Leukippe die not just once but twice, first sacrificed using theater props and fake blood, and later decapitated (but another woman was in her place). There are betrayals, a love potion, madness, kidnapping, other men falling in love with Leukippe, other women falling in love with (and marrying) Kleitophon, and an attempt at framing him for murder, though in the end, the long-suffering lovers are finally reunited and married.

Longus' novel *Daphnis and Chloë* employs another popular ancient plot device that still features commonly in books and movies: babies abandoned at birth with tokens that will later reveal their true identities when they grow up. Daphnis and Chloë are both raised by foster parents in a pastoral locale among herds of goats, sheep, and cows (a setting popularized in the aforementioned bucolic and pastoral poetry of the Hellenistic era). After many perilous adventures (kidnapping by pirates, falling into a wolf pit, being beaten up), the lovers are reunited with their biological parents, who recognize them by their birth tokens, and the novel ends with their marriage and their return to the idealized countryside. Today's soap operas and potboilers still exploit the motif of the mistaken (or deliberately concealed) identity as a way to miraculously solve seemingly intractable problems.

Probably the two best-known novels from the ancient world are Petronius' *Satyricon* and Apuleius' *Metamorphoses* (also known as *The Golden Ass*). The *Satyricon* (probably from the first century A.D.) combines satire with "lifestyles of the rich and famous" in its depiction of the vulgar nouveau riche freedman Trimalchio, who hosts outrageously luxurious feasts and lives amidst ridiculous wealth. Apuleius' second-century A.D. novel is entitled the *Metamorphoses* because of the protagonist Lucius' transformation into an ass, which he spends the rest of the story seeking to reverse. There are witches, magic, sex, violence, bandits kidnapping brides, bestiality, and a religious conversion experience. Lucius' episodic adventures have a picaresque quality, and Apuleius' characters tell numerous stories within the main story; for instance, the tale of Cupid and Psyche comprises about one-fifth of the narrative. But despite the remarkable things that happen, the people speak in a chatty, colloquial way that keeps the story seemingly grounded in everyday life.

Another genre that originated in antiquity was the fable populated by talking animals but illustrating morals that apply to humankind. Though not their inventor, Aesop, a slave who lived sometime in the sixth century B.C., was their most famous practitioner, well-known throughout the ancient world for centuries to come; the historian Herodotus even referred to him as "the Storyteller." Animal fables remained popular throughout the Middle Ages (the tales of Reynard the Fox, for example), and the conceit of talking animals mirroring human concerns continues today, especially in children's books and movies and satirical novels (such as Orwell's *Animal Farm*).

Another type of book that appears on contemporary bestseller lists is the biographies or autobiographies of famous people. It seems basic to human nature that we are fascinated by the lives of public figures such as politicians, athletes, and celebrities. All too often, such books have a rather voyeuristic emphasis, focusing on salacious or scandalous aspects of these people's lives. The racy biography was also a well-established ancient literary genre, especially biographies of rulers and military heroes. Perhaps the most famous examples were written by the Greek author Plutarch, who made an entire career out of composing dozens of biographies of famous people, known collectively as the *Parallel Lives*, and the Roman Suetonius, whose *Lives of the Caesars* included Julius Caesar and the first 11 Roman emperors. Plutarch took the more serious approach, deliberately discussing his subjects in pairs, one Greek and one Roman—hence the *Parallel Lives* title. Many of the pairs were followed by an explicit comparison of the two individuals. Plutarch's intention was, through examining the lives of famous men, to give examples of virtue and vice. He wrote about politicians (the Gracchi brothers and Cicero), generals (Pericles, Pompey, and Mark Antony), and even mythical or legendary figures (the Greek hero Theseus and Romulus, the founder of the city of Rome). His most famous pairing, however, is probably Alexander and Great and Julius Caesar, two charismatic leaders whose lives inspired many subsequent rulers, emperors, and aspirants to power.

Incidentally, the works of Plutarch are important to lovers of Elizabethan theater whether they have read them or not, since they functioned as the major source of information for William Shakespeare. The first English edition of Plutarch's *Lives*, translated by Thomas North, appeared in 1579, and Shakespeare paraphrased and directly quoted from North's translation of Plutarch in at least five of his plays, including "Julius Caesar" and "Antony and Cleopatra," which were particularly indebted to Plutarch. Scholars have pointed to Plutarch's *Lives* of Caesar, Brutus, Antony, Coriolanus, Alcibiades, and Theseus as providing material for Shakespeare.

Suetonius took a different approach. His sensationalistic biographies of the early Roman emperors often focused on sex, violence, and the depravity inspired by absolute power. He included juicy anecdotes (some perhaps questionable) and scandals, and adopted a chatty tone, describing the idiosyncrasies of the emperors and even the flaws in their looks. Rather than just talking about their public roles and actions, he focused a great deal on their personal lives, supplying minor details if they shed any light on an emperor's personality. His biographies would have made for better beach reading (if that had been done in antiquity). To give you a sense of Suetonius' inclinations, two of his works that no longer survive except in fragments were another set of biographies entitled "*Lives of Famous Prostitutes*" and a book that compiled obscene Greek insults.

Other types of book examined the natural world and animals (Pliny's multivolume *Natural History* and Aelian's *On Animals*), described foreign or exotic cultures (Herodotus practically invented ethnography in his *History of the*

Persian Wars, and Tacitus wrote about the German "barbarians" and the tribes in Britain), and collected the speeches of famous orators. History writing was pioneered by Herodotus and Thucydides (author of *The Peloponnesian War*), and the Romans gave us satire; the satirical works of Juvenal, with their dark humor, most closely resemble our modern idea of the genre.

A common sight on modern non-fiction bestseller lists is the how-to book, dispensing advice on all kinds of activity and aspects of life. The ancient world had how-to books as well, which were often written in the form of poetry, on varied topics: farming (Cato, Varro, Columella), dice-playing (the emperor Claudius), picking up women (Ovid's *Art of Love*), giving speeches (Quintilian), hunting (Grattius and Nemesianus), and fishing (Oppian). The third-century B.C. writer Nikander of Colophon left two such so-called didactic poems: the *Theriaca*, describing snakes and poisonous creatures and offering the most effective remedies for their bites, and the *Alexipharmaca*, which gives the antidotes for poisoning by an extensive array of plants, animals, and minerals. The ancients did not have the same sort of highly developed economy that we do today, so one popular genre of books—how to invest money and play the stock market—was unknown to them. However, they could be just as ruthless as any Wall Street trader in their advice on how to hold on to money. In his book on how to successfully run a country estate, Cato the Elder suggested that when a slave had gotten too old and feeble to work efficiently, you should just get rid of him.

Retelling old tales: Modern versions of ancient stories

In the modern world, we not only continue to read genres of books pioneered in antiquity—we also read books *about* antiquity. The mystery genre in particular abounds with detective novels set in the ancient world, such as Lindsey Davis' Marcus Didius Falco mysteries (20 so far), Steven Saylor's *Roma Sub Rosa* series (12 so far), and John Maddox Roberts' SPQR series. Historical novels by Steven Pressfield (on the Persian Wars, the Peloponnesian War, and Theseus and the Amazons), Colleen McCullough (the Masters of

Rome series set in the Late Roman Republic, seven novels so far), and Simon Scarrow (the Eagle series of Roman military fiction) have proven popular, as have novels set in the modern world but with classical themes; Donna Tartt's *The Secret History*, a psychological thriller in which Classics students alternate between quoting Greek classics to one another and taking part in drug-addled Dionysiac rites, made a splash when it came out in 1992. (*The Secret History* happens to also be the title of an attack on the Emperor Justinian and his wife Theodora by the fifth-century A.D. author Procopius, who filled it with court scandals and unsavory rumors about Theodora's past.)

We like to read about the ancient world in non-fiction as well as fiction. Biographies of figures from antiquity even occasionally make the bestseller list. However, in contrast to the biographies written in the ancient world, which usually focused on important men, today's popular biographies often feature powerful women from antiquity who, demonized or criticized in their own time, have now developed into proto-feminist heroines. Cleopatra in particular is a famous figure with so much symbolic weight that she seems almost legendary. Since 2000, six high-profile books on Cleopatra have been published, including an award-winning, critically acclaimed one that reached number three on the New York Times Bestseller List: *Cleopatra: A Life* (2010), by the Pulitzer Prize-winning biographer Stacy Schiff. In that very same year, a second biography, by Duane Roller, also came out. Other recent titles and sub-titles give a sense of the range of identities we see in her: *Cleopatra and Egypt* (2008), by Sally-Ann Ashton; *Cleopatra of Egypt: From History to Myth* (2001), edited by Susan Walker and Peter Higgs; *Cleopatra and Antony* (2010), by Diana Preston; and *Cleopatra: Histories, Dreams and Distortions* (1991) and *Cleopatra: Queen, Lover, Legend* (2006), both by Lucy Hughes-Hallett. Both her special status as a woman ruler in the ancient world and her reputation as a temptress who wins the love of two of the most powerful men of the time, Julius Caesar and Mark Antony, have made her irresistible to both writers and film-makers.

Helen of Troy has recently inspired a similar surge of interest, resulting in books such as Laurie Maguire's *Helen of Troy: From Homer to Hollywood* (2009) and Bettany Hughes' *Helen of Troy: The Story Behind the Most Beautiful Woman in the World* (2007). Bettany Hughes' earlier book about her, *Helen of*

Troy: Goddess, Princess, Whore (2005), caused a stir by allegedly seeking the "real" Helen and in the process upending the usual stereotypes of her found in Greek myth. In the place of the beautiful woman who is a passive prize traded between the men of royal families, Hughes somewhat improbably posits a powerful Bronze Age princess (and trained fighter) of Sparta described by one reviewer as "bald-headed, bare-breasted, and bloodthirsty." These women were also natural protagonists for historical fiction. The bestselling novelist Margaret George wrote about both of them, in *Helen of Troy* (2007) and *The Memoirs of Cleopatra* (1998).

Figure 7.4 *Mosaic portrait of the Empress Theodora from Ravenna. Wife of the Emperor Justinian, Theodora was a controversial figure, much reviled by her enemies, who seems to have been an unusually energetic and forceful woman who took an active role in politics.*

Theodora, wife of the Roman emperor Justinian, has also been reassessed. She started life as an actress, dancer, acrobatic circus performer, and (perhaps) prostitute, which led to much harsh invective against and defamation of her, epitomized in Procopius' *Secret History*, in which he refers to her as "Theodora from the Brothel." Recent books, such as Paolo Cesaretti's *Theodora: Empress of Byzantium* (2004) and J. A. S. Evans' *Empress Theodora: Partner of Justinian* (2003) instead stress her political influence, her role as Justinian's advisor and "partner in government," and her efforts to aid her fellow women by pushing legislation against rape, to regulate pimps and brothel-keepers, and to increase women's marriage and dowry rights, and by helping prostitutes and girls sold into sexual slavery. Stella Duffy's recent novel *Theodora: Actress, Empress, Whore* (2010) tries to take advantage of all the juicy, salacious background material while offering a sympathetic portrait of a complicated, powerful woman. (It also seems to suggest, yet again, that books about ancient women must always include a three-part sub-title with paradoxical overtones.)

Finally, popular novels aimed at the young adult audience often include classical and mythological elements. Despite the Christian themes of C. S. Lewis' Narnia books, Narnia is populated by many creatures and beings from Greek and Roman mythology: fauns, winged horses, centaurs, griffins, minotaurs, nymphs, dryads, naiads, maenads, Bacchus (the Roman god of wine), Silenus (his satyr-like companion), and Pomona (the Roman goddess of fruit trees). More recently, in Rick Riordan's *Percy Jackson & the Olympians* series of five fantasy novels, the Greek gods and monsters still exist in the modern world, and the protagonist has discovered that he is actually the son of the god Poseidon (a common enough occurrence in Greek myth).

In the magic-charged universe of J. K. Rowling's Harry Potter novels, the wizards-in-training recite spells in Latin and encounter a herd of centaurs, a chimera, a sphinx, a hippocampus, a hippogriff, a basilisk (a creature mentioned by Pliny the Elder, Lucan, and Aelian), a manticore, and a unicorn (both first mentioned in Ctesias' book about India, the fifth-century B.C. *Indica*). Dumbledore has a pet phoenix (first mentioned by Hesiod, described by Herodotus, and written about by Ovid, Pliny, and Tacitus) and Hagrid makes a pet of the big three-headed dog who guards the trap-door to the Philosopher's Stone, clearly modeled on Hades' watchdog Cerberus, whom he calls "Fluffy." (Fluffy can be lulled to sleep with music, just as in myth the musician Orpheus sings and plays his lyre to put Cerberus to sleep.) One of Rowling's centaurs (Firenze), who is unlike his wild woodland brethren, goes to teach at Hogwarts; he resembles the wise, mild-mannered centaur Cheiron, who was the teacher to young Greek heroes such as Achilles and Jason.

Figure 7.5 *A relief of a griffin. Mythological monsters such as this one have become staples in popular culture through novels, movies, and games.*

Humans have always been entertained by a good story. While all these genres of literature may seem just to recycle, imitate, and emulate the forms, characters, and plots of ancient tales, human creativity continually finds a way to make old stories and forms seem fresh again. Thus, they perpetually remain relevant and fascinating to new generations of readers.

Conclusion

You can't escape the past: Popular culture and antiquity

Down the hole: Rediscovering antiquity

At Rome, sometime in the late fifteenth century, a man accidentally fell into a hole in a hillside, and quite literally dropped into another world and time. He found himself in a vast network of underground corridors and hallways made of fine marble whose walls and ceilings were entirely covered with incredible paintings and molded sculptures depicting a fantastic assemblage of humans, animals, gods, and monsters. These were the remains of the spectacular palace known as the Golden House erected by the emperor Nero, which, over the centuries, had been built over and claimed by the earth. Soon, curious explorers were lowering themselves on ropes down into the ruins in order to view the elaborately painted walls and ceilings by torchlight. Nero might have been crazy, but he knew how to decorate, and Renaissance Italy was wowed by the discovery. Artists such as Ghirlandaio, Pinturicchio, Perugino, and Filippino Lippi, who had come to Rome to work on the Sistine Chapel at the request of Pope Sixtus IV, were among those who inspected the frescoes (sometimes leaving graffiti and their signatures behind), and Raphael was another frequent visitor. Around the margins of the paintings ran fantastic hybrid human, animal, and vegetable forms woven among garlands, flowers, and ornate geometrical designs. This style of ornamentation was labeled *grottesche* (from which we get our word "grotesque") because it had been found underground in what the discoverers thought were little caves or grottoes (but which were actually the rooms of Nero's palace).

Figure 8.1 *Ceiling of a passageway in the Golden House of Nero. When Renaissance explorers entered this lost, underground ruin, the paintings and decorations they found there initiated a craze for imitation Roman designs.*

This discovery sparked a fad for a new style of decoration that imitated what they found among the Roman ruins. *Grottesche* ornamentation became all the rage in interior decoration for the homes of the rich and famous, on interior walls, on outdoor loggias, edging tapestries, adorning metalwork, furniture, majolica ware, and jewelry. Its weirdness and exoticism appealed to people, and artists saw it as reflecting the free play of the imagination.

Over the next century, it remained popular, and this kind of pattern—often featuring monsters and creatures from myth, such as satyrs and sphinxes, and identified with the pagan world—decorated churches as well as palaces. Even that most Christian of edifices, the Vatican, and the apartments of the popes in the Castel Sant'Angelo, are painted with famous "grotesques"; Raphael created the designs for (and his workshop executed) the famous Loggia of the Apostolic Palace, in which scenes from the Bible are surrounded with fantastic "grotesque" patterns like the ones he saw in the Domus Aurea, and the Pompeian Corridor, the Library Hall, the Apollo Hall, and the bathroom of Pope Clement VII in the popes' apartments all imitate the decorations of Nero's apartments. Raphael's "grotesque" style (based on Nero's interior décor) is still imitated in Neo-classical government buildings today—even the U.S. Capitol. Over the years, "grotesque" evolved from its original meaning (linked to grottoes and Roman decorations) to suggest something exaggerated or distorted to the point of being either horrifying or humorous.

This story of a Roman palace and Renaissance painters offers an apt metaphor for how we use the past—reaching down and pulling out something that resonates with us and that we can use for our own purposes. This naturally means that the original meaning is sometimes transformed, misinterpreted, and altered either inadvertently or deliberately. Yet it still lives on in some form, and we can trace its lineage. We are also reminded of the great extent to which archaeological discoveries spark the contemporary imagination and lead to cultural developments that either imitate or reimagine the past.

Another notable time when the classical past resurfaced, the eighteenth century, still affects our public buildings (and our perceptions of the past) today. In 1755, the German writer Winckelmann published an influential interpretation of Greek art, which would soon fuel an important artistic and architectural trend known as Neo-classicism that sought to emulate the styles and subjects of the classical world. Many of Winckelmann's assumptions remained unchallenged for over a century and continue to affect popular conceptions about ancient art. We can trace to him the longstanding belief in the "noble simplicity" of pure white Greek statues, whereas they were in fact gaudily painted and gilded. The longstanding reputation of the ancient Greeks as being rather dignified and sober, which tended to blot out the livelier aspects of their culture, probably stems somewhat from Winckelmann's misinterpretation of their art.

A revival in Classical-style architecture had been pioneered by the Venetian architect Palladio in the sixteenth century, who based his "Palladian" villas on the writings of the Roman architect Vitruvius and on Greek and Roman architecture, but Neo-classical architecture now spread throughout the rest of Europe and to America, ensuring that nearly all of our state Capitols and government buildings were originally Neo-classical in style.

Figure 8.2 *The authors in front of the Supreme Court Building of the United States. Government buildings all over the world have been constructed in this sort of Neoclassical style emulating Greek and Roman models.*

While on a Grand Tour of Europe, an eighteenth-century Scottish architect named Robert Adam read Winckelmann, visited Palladio's villas, and went to Spalato (now Split, Croatia) to draw the ruins of the emperor Diocletian's palace. Adam's encounters with the Roman past profoundly affected the buildings that he and his brothers built after he returned to London. Even interior decoration of the era called for Greek, Roman, and Egyptian designs for furniture and wall paintings. Among the mentors he studied with was Giovanni Battista Piranesi, the Italian architect whose etchings of ancient Roman ruins and almost Escher-like fantastic, imaginary architectural environments exerted a great influence on the imagination of both his contemporaries and succeeding generations, perhaps still echoed in the current vogue for faux architectural fragments and pieces of ancient-looking reliefs in our own home décor.

The writings of Winckelmann and excavations at Herculaneum and Pompeii (started in 1748) inspired the late eighteenth- through early nineteenth-century artistic movement of Neo-classicism, which spread throughout Europe. Neo-classicism held a particular appeal for the advocates of the French Revolution, who looked to ancient Rome (an earlier Republic) as a model for their own Republic. The painter Jacques-Louis David in particular painted many Greek and Roman scenes encapsulating sacrifices made for the state, such as "Oath of the Horatii," "Brutus Receiving the Bodies of His Sons," "The Intervention of the Sabine Women," "Andromache Mourning Hector," "The Death of Patroclus," "The Death of Socrates," and "Leonidas at Thermopylae," and one of his sketches, "The Triumph of the French People," is clearly based on a Roman triumphal procession. The artist Canova sculpted Napoleon's sister as Venus as well as a famous statue of Cupid embracing Psyche. In England, Josiah Wedgwood named his country estate Etruria and began producing jasperware (based on the Portland Vase, a famous museum piece) made to resemble white cameo reliefs against solid color backgrounds and imitating Greek vases in shape and style. Women rejected corsets, hoop-skirts, and bustles in favor of the high-waisted Empire-style dress; loosely flowing layers of transparent white muslin were meant to imitate the clothing of ancient Greek and Roman women.

Thus we can see how the Classical world came to permeate all different aspects of society many centuries after its decay. Throughout this book, we have observed how antiquity has always exerted a powerful influence on culture and the arts, but also how every era has put its own unique stamp on the classical heritage. During the Renaissance, the two main areas artists could search for topics to paint and sculpt were the Bible and ancient history or mythology—although some of the gods and heroes depicted ended up looking more like contemporary Italians than ancient ones, in ahistorical costumes and armor. The works of the ancients were adapted to conform (in so far as it was possible) with Christianity, acquiring glosses and being transformed into allegories. Biblical exegesis interpreted various prophets and events in the Old Testament as prefiguring Christ and the events of the New Testament, and the same sort of process could be (and was) applied to classical mythology.

This sort of identification and absorption allowed pagan stories to coexist with Christianity, which meant that the classical world continued to provide artistic, literary, and cultural inspiration long after paganism as a religion had withered away. Ancient mythology and history offered a rich source of material for operas, such as Gluck's "Orfeo and Eurydice," Purcell's "Dido and Aeneas," Handel's "Giulio Cesare," Strauss' "Elektra" and "Ariadne auf Naxos," Stravinsky's "Oedipus Rex," and Berlioz' "Les troyens." But even rock and pop music still employ classical and mythological references. So, for example, Cream's classic rock song "Tales of Brave Ulysses" seeks to echo the cadence of epic poetry and Homeric epithets, and in the T-Rex song "Bang a Gong (Get It On)," Marc Bolan sings, "You have the teeth of the hydra upon you."

Later authors wrote their own versions of ancient stories and genres. As has been mentioned in Chapter 7, Shakespeare used Plutarch's *Parallel Lives* as an important source for several of his plays set in antiquity. The Elizabethan era also saw a revival of interest in pastoral and bucolic poetry, perhaps as an appealing alternative to the extravagance, excesses, labyrinthine complexities, and political intrigues of court life. Sir Philip Sydney's pastoral romance "Arcadia" employed many of the convoluted plot devices of ancient novels and included poems spoken by shepherds, such as "Ye Goatherd Gods"; Edmund Spenser organized his poem "The Shepheardes Calendar" into 12 pastoral eclogues representing the months of the year, in emulation of Vergil's ten *Eclogues*; Sir Walter Raleigh wrote "The Nymph's Reply to the Shepherd"; and, in "Queen and Huntress," Ben Jonson identified the virgin goddess Diana with the Virgin Queen, Elizabeth I.

Later, the Romantic poets imagined themselves as Classical ones: Shelley wrote the dramas "Prometheus Unbound" and "Hellas," and the poems "Song of Apollo," "Song of Pan," and "Adonais," while Keats wrote "On First Looking into Chapman's Homer" (a translation into English, so he could read it), "On Seeing the Elgin Marbles" (removed from the Parthenon by Lord Elgin and installed in the British Museum), "Ode on a Grecian Urn," "To Homer," "Ode to Psyche," "Endymion: A Poetic Romance," and "The Fall of Hyperion: A Dream."

When the Victorians came along, they filled their massive novels and poems with a plethora of classical and mythological allusions. Historical novels set in antiquity were smash bestsellers, such as Bulwer-Lytton's novel "The Last Days of Pompeii" (1834). This trend continued unabated into the early twentieth century. For example, the musical we know as "My Fair Lady" began as a George Bernard Shaw play, "Pygmalion" (1913), a title that refers to the Greek myth in which a sculptor falls in love with his statue, who then comes to life—an apt metaphor for the professor of phonetics who molds a Cockney flower girl into his vision of a "proper" lady.

Sometimes a division is drawn between "High" art and "Low" or "popular" art, but often one era's popular culture becomes another's "high art," with Shakespeare providing the most obvious example. While the ancient world clearly exerted an influence on "high" art, such as opera, architecture, classical music, and poetry, we have already seen how it has also affected more popular forms of literature such as romance novels, detective novels, celebrity biographies, and how-to manuals. Here, in the conclusion to our survey of the influence of the ancient world on the modern, it seems appropriate to end by considering what is perhaps the most quintessentially modern form of entertainment, a medium that is so dependent on technology that it has only been in existence for the last century: the motion picture, and its off-shoot, television.

Antiquity invades the silver screen: Film and television

Although they didn't have movies, the Greeks and Romans knew how to tell a good story, and have provided the inspiration for many movies; over 400 major films have been set in the ancient world. Thus, a totally new medium entirely unknown to the Greeks and Romans has chosen to tell their stories, over and over again. When cinema was born around the tail end of the nineteenth century, an interest in antiquity infused the cultural landscape. Students were still studying Latin and Greek at school; many bestselling novels, such as *The Last Days of Pompeii*, *Quo Vadis?*, and *Ben-Hur*, took place in antiquity; and stage plays set in the ancient world, such as Shakespeare's *Julius Caesar*, were routinely performed. It is therefore not surprising that some of the very earliest cinematic experiments dealt with ancient subject matter. Thomas Edison created a short film called "Cupid and Psyche," and the early films of the revolutionary French director Georges Méliès were peppered with classical references: "Cleopatra" (1899), "Neptune and Amphitrite" (1899), "Jupiter's Thunderbolts" (1903), and "Ulysses and the Giant Polyphemus" (1905), to name a few examples.

In the first three decades of the twentieth century, films about the ancients proliferated worldwide. In 1907, an American director shot the first (very small-scale) film version of Ben-Hur at Battery Park in Manhattan, using costumes borrowed from the Metropolitan Opera. The Italian film industry became a powerhouse, producing epic after epic showcasing elaborate sets and costumes that strove to bring the ancient world to life and leading the public to first associate antiquity with cinema on a grand scale; its version of "The Last Days of Pompeii" was a huge hit in 1908. The size of the sets constructed for historical epics is suggested by the remains of Cecil B. DeMille's 1923 film version of *The Ten Commandments*, discovered under a massive dune 150 miles north of Los Angeles. For this movie, 1,000 laborers worked for over a month to build the ten-acre set, including an entire city with 110-foot-high walls, four 20-ton statues of the Pharaoh Ramesses, 21 giant sphinxes, and 300 chariots that were shipped from Hollywood; after a month of filming, with 2,500 extras, the set was buried by bulldozers as a cost-saving measure. Early French cinema produced such charming titles as "Hercules and the Big Stick," "Jupiter Smitten" (both 1910), and "Back to Life after 2000 Years," in which a man from ancient Rome revives in the modern city (one of the earliest entries in the popular time-travel genre). Then interest in the genre waned for a time, before reviving with renewed life in the 1950s and 1960s.

The "sword-and-sandal" films of this era sought to pull people away from their TV sets and back into movie theaters by offering fantastic spectacles with huge sets and casts of thousands, as well as "high-tech" innovations like CinemaScope (first used in the 1953 epic of Christ and Rome, "The Robe"). Stories drawn from ancient history, mythology, and the Bible were especially popular; many of the Roman-era movies dealt with the theme of conversion to Christianity and the treatment of the early Christian community under the Roman empire. At that time, Hollywood was able to put on truly impressive spectacles—building massive sets, gathering and creating enormous, showy (and sometimes even accurate) costumes and props. At 1,312 ft. by 754 ft., the Roman Forum built for "The Fall of the Roman Empire" (1964) was the largest outdoor film set ever constructed, and 8,000 "soldiers," including 1,200 cavalry, took part in its huge battle.

Such large casts allowed the choreographing of scenes on a grand scale, such as Cleopatra's entry into Rome seated atop a giant sphinx being pulled by sweaty, half-naked men and surrounded by a gigantic crowd in Elizabeth Taylor's 1963 film of that name. The stratospheric expense of "Cleopatra" (originally clocking in at 6 hours) is legendary; it cost $44 million, a sum viewed as astronomical at the time, and which (when adjusted for inflation) still makes it one of the priciest films of all time. Memorable action scenes were another feature of these films, such as the impressive naval battle and the violent, death-dealing chariot race in "Ben-Hur" (in both the 1925 silent version and the 1959 one starring Charlton Heston) and the gladiatorial training and fighting scenes in "Spartacus" (1960).

Movies about powerful men, seductive women, and crazy rulers from antiquity have been perennially popular. The silent film "The Private Life

Figure 8.3 *Ruined giant head prop from Ben Hur. The remnants of some of the gigantic props made for the chariot race scene in Ben Hur now decay on the grounds of Cinecittà Studios at Rome.*

of Helen of Troy," based on a popular novel, came out in 1927, and 77 years later she once again sparked a war in "Troy" (2004). Over 50 films about Cleopatra have been made since the birth of cinema, from 1899 onward, including the 1917 film starring silent-era vamp Theda Bara, through Cecil B. DeMille's "Cleopatra" (1934) and Elizabeth Taylor's superlatively expensive 1963 version, to the sullen hashish pipe-smoking teenager in HBO's "Rome." Richard Burton got to play both "Alexander the Great" (1955) and Antony to Elizabeth Taylor's Cleopatra. Even William Shatner (pre-Captain Kirk) had the chance to portray a swaggering Alexander in a TV movie shot in 1964 (though not aired until 1968). On television, a 1981 mini-series, "The Search for Alexander the Great," and "In the Footsteps of Alexander the Great" (1998), a documentary series tracing his travels across a vast area that now consists of 16 countries, both reflected a continuing fascination with the man who conquered the known world by the time he was 30. The Roman emperor Nero has featured in at least ten major movies, including Peter Ustinov's lively portrayal in *Quo Vadis?* (1951), for which he was nominated for an Academy Award as Best Supporting Actor. More recently, Joaquin Phoenix memorably portrayed the unbalanced emperor Commodus opposite Russell Crowe in "Gladiator" (2000).

"Strong men" in the literal sense as well as the figurative one were also popular in such films. Movies set in antiquity offered bodybuilders the chance to show off their impressive physiques. Steve Reeves, the highest-paid actor in Europe at the height of his career, specialized in low budget sword-and-sandals movies made in Italy from the late 1950s through the 1960s. Most commonly identified with his role as Hercules, he actually only played the hero twice, but also got to portray Romulus, the first (perhaps mythical) marathon runner Pheidippides, and the Trojan prince Aeneas. Another bodybuilder turned actor, Arnold Schwarzenegger, had his film debut in "Hercules in New York" (1969), where, as the eponymous hero, he descends from Olympus to earth and experiences fish-out-of-water scenarios, driving a chariot around Central Park and becoming (naturally) a professional wrestler, until the gods decide that he is making them look silly (which indeed he was).

Reflections of Hercules can be detected in the yearly "World's Strongest Man" competition, in which massive muscled men from around the world pull semi-trucks with their teeth, lift cars, and carry a yoke with a refrigerator hanging from each side. These improbable feats of strength could be considered modern analogues to the legendary Twelve Labors of Hercules, which included such equally impressive acts as single-handedly cleaning out the muck from a vast stable of horses, strangling a lion, wrestling a bull into submission, and retrieving some fire-breathing mares. Angelo Siciliano, the father of modern bodybuilding and the first muscleman of the twentieth century, changed his name to Charles Atlas because a friend told him he looked like a statue of Atlas, the Greek Titan tasked with holding up the world on his shoulders.

Movies set in the ancient world have served as a legitimate excuse for showing off the female form as well. Scantily clad women, lascivious dancing, and sexually suggestive situations (such as the stereotypical Roman orgy scene) have appeared in films as long as they have been made, with historical accuracy sometimes sacrificed for effect. For the unfinished movie version of Robert Graves' novel "I, Claudius" (1937), the costume designer came up with authentic garb for six Vestal Virgins (the accurate number) based on a Roman statue, but the director rejected it, saying "I want 60 and I want them naked." He then submitted a design resembling a bikini with filmy fabric draped over it, so that the Vestal Virgins looked more like exotic dancers in a Vegas revue than fully clothed virgin priestesses. The famous scene of the Empress Poppaea (a naked Claudette Colbert) bathing in asses' milk in *The Sign of the Cross* (1932) could at least point to an actual ancient source, since Pliny the Elder claimed that Nero's wife "used to drag 500 she-asses with foals about with her everywhere and actually soaked her whole body in a bath-tub with ass's milk, believing that it also smoothed out wrinkles" (*Natural History* 11.96.238).

Directors could get away with a great deal, as long as they were depicting depraved pagans misbehaving. But suggestions of perversions and sexual excess gave way to very graphic depictions of them in Bob Guccione's X-rated "Caligula" (1979). In this case, adherence to Suetonius' biography of the emperor would inevitably result in a foray into pornography. Some hard-core porn films followed suit, such as "Cleopatra's Bondage Revenge" (1985) and "Rise of the Roman Empress" I and II (1987, 1990).

The popular film genre of heroes fighting monsters is best exemplified in the long and prolific career of Ray Harryhausen, whose stop-motion models brought all sorts of mythical creatures to life in a way that, before the advent of CGI, was positively unprecedented and stunning. His movies probably first introduced many of us to Greek mythology. "Jason and the Argonauts" (1963) and "Clash of the Titans" (1981) hewed most closely to story cycles from Greek myth (the latter dealing with the adventures of the hero Perseus), but his series of Sinbad movies also included lots of monsters either derived from (or at least somewhat inspired by) Greek myth.

"Jason and the Argonauts" retells the story of the hero's quest for the Golden Fleece, introducing mythological creatures such as the Hydra (with only seven heads instead of nine), the Harpies (the winged female monsters who prevent King Phineas from eating), the sea god Triton, the bronze giant Talos (created by the smith-god Hephaestus to guard the island of Crete by throwing rocks at intruders, with a single vulnerable spot in his ankle), and skeleton warriors who, generated from the hydra's buried teeth, rise out of the earth to fight the Argonauts (this last scenario actually echoes a myth about Cadmus, the founder of Thebes, who kills a dragon, sows its teeth in the ground, and watches armed men sprout up and fight one another). Some of these monsters were borrowed from other myths; others, like Talos, originally belonged to Jason's story.

In "Clash of the Titans," on his quest to kill the snake-haired Gorgon, Medusa, whose gaze turns men to stone, the hero Perseus encounters the winged horse Pegasus, the three "Stygian witches" who share one eye between them (known in Greek myth as the Graeae, or "Gray Ones"), a two-headed dog named Dioskilos (obviously based on the three-headed watchdog Cerberus) guarding Medusa's lair, and a sea monster who attacks the princess Andromeda. Jason receives the gift of a mechanical owl made by Hephaestus and modeled after the goddess Athena's pet owl—not actually part of Greek myth, but exactly the sort of thing the god would have created.

"The Seventh Voyage of Sinbad" (1958) borrows several elements from the story of Odysseus: Sinbad and his men seal their ears with wax so as not to be lured to drown by screaming demons (Odysseus' men do the same thing to escape the similarly murderous but seductively singing Sirens) and they meet a Cyclops who (like Polyphemus) tries to eat them, is blinded by Sinbad (standing in for Odysseus) with a torch, and throws rocks at their ship as they flee. In "The Golden Voyage of Sinbad" (1973), a griffin and a one-eyed centaur make an appearance, and "Sinbad and the Eye of the Tiger" (1977) introduces a mechanical bronze minotaur called a Minoton, an original creature pieced together from bits of Greek myth.

Movies have also retold ancient stories in a contemporary setting. In the *Anabasis*, the fourth-century B.C. Greek soldier–writer Xenophon wrote an account of his march with the Ten Thousand, a huge band of Greek mercenaries hired by Cyrus the Great, who was seeking to displace his brother as the Persian King of Kings. Cyrus was killed in battle, leaving his army of mercenaries stranded in the middle of enemy territory. Xenophon recounted their progress through scorching deserts and over snowy mountains, assailed by hostile locals as they headed for the coast where there were Greek cities; the moment when they first spotted the water and cried "The sea! The sea!" was thus an emotionally charged one. The cult film "The Warriors" (1979) transferred the *Anabasis* to the New York metropolitan area of the 1970s. Cyrus (referred to as "the one and only" rather than the King of Kings), who has been transformed into the leader of the most powerful gang in New York City, has called for a gathering of representatives from all the major area gangs at a park in the Bronx, where he is assassinated in the middle of a charismatic speech calling for all the gangs to unite. The gang "the Warriors," falsely accused of killing Cyrus, must make the long trip back from the Bronx to their home turf of Coney Island without being killed in revenge. Some of their names (Cleon, Ajax) suggest the classical connection. They ultimately reach Coney Island but must fight a final battle against a rival gang on the beach, by their own home "sea."

The latest upsurge in ancient-themed films has included everything from comic book adaptations to Oscar-winning films. "Gladiator" (2000), which won five Academy Awards, including Best Picture and Best Actor for Russell Crowe, has been credited with sparking renewed interest in historical epics. From the opening battle on the German frontier to the scenes set in the teeming city of Rome and the gladiatorial spectacles in the Colosseum, "Gladiator" dazzled the eyes—though it had help in fleshing out its "cast of thousands" through yet another technological innovation, CGI. This was followed by Oliver Stone's "Alexander" (2004) and "Troy" (2004), featuring a blonde, toned, pretty-boy Achilles (played by Brad Pitt) and Minoan-looking sets and costumes for the Trojans.

As a boy, the comic book writer/artist Frank Miller had seen the 1962 movie about the suicidally brave Spartan stand against the Persian Army at Thermopylae, "The 300 Spartans," and was so deeply impressed by it that he was reportedly inspired to create his own version in the comic book series, "300." In 2006, a movie adaptation (with Miller serving as executive producer and consultant) sought to recreate the comic's heightened, bloody, highly vivid sense of style, and fan-boys everywhere swooned with delight. As a measure of the film's success, Gerard Butler shouting "This is Sparta!" has been parodied countless times on the internet. In 2010, a remake of "Clash of the Titans" brought Ray Harryhausen's story to a new generation, but with slick CGI special effects replacing the charming stop-motion models of the original.

The "small screen" of television has also been invaded by the classical world. For children, there was the cartoon "The Mighty Hercules" (1963–6), which ran towards the end of the sword-and-sandals movie era, and was based (very loosely) on Greek mythology; the too-cute boy centaur and satyr duo, Newt and Tewt, were Hercules' companions. In 1976, a very adult take on the ancient world appeared, when the BBC adapted Robert Graves' chattily lurid novels *I, Claudius* and *Claudius the God* into an acclaimed (and sensationalistic) British mini-series featuring a veritable who's who of talented British actors; it proved extremely successful in both England and America, where it was shown on PBS's "Masterpiece Theatre."

More recently, HBO has produced a stratospherically expensive series called "Rome" for those who want gritty drama, while the History Channel likes to show documentaries about ancient Rome. For those who want campy fun rather than historical or mythological accuracy, "Hercules: The Legendary Journeys" (1995–9) and its spin-off, "Xena: Warrior Princess" (1995–2001), offered a combination of Greek heroes, gods, and monsters, light comedy, and lessons in self-improvement. The recent series "Spartacus: Blood and Sand" and its prequel, "Spartacus: Gods of the Arena," have taken a more lurid approach, with graphic, blood-drenched gladiatorial bouts and lots of sex. Different flavors of the ancient world are available for various tastes.

From awe to consumerism: The diminution and domestication of antiquity

In the ancient world, the gods and figures of mythology were genuinely frightening, dangerous, and awe-inspiring. But as they were recycled and reused over and over again by subsequent generations and cultures, they underwent a process of having their more menacing characteristics stripped away and their racier elements sanitized. This trend seems especially strong in pop culture, where a once-terrifying monster such as Cerberus can be reduced to a cuddly stuffed animal, and the Three Fates, who traditionally appeared at a child's birth to begin the process of measuring out his or her life on a piece of thread that would eventually be cut, have been transformed in fairy tales and Disney movies into the Fairy Godmother, a beneficent figure who functions as a sort of guardian angel.

Thus, in Hesiod's *Cosmogony*, Eros (Love) is a powerful, elemental force that comes into being at the very birth of the universe, just after Chaos and the earth and before night and day; a "loosener of limbs, [he] brings all immortals and mortals under his power and makes them unable to think as they should" (lines 121–2). In Classical Greece, he is a handsome, winged young man with a bow and arrows, but he is still a threat; if he shoots you with an arrow, you will not be able to control yourself, and while love can be sweet, it can also be painful. Then, in Renaissance art, he is gradually reduced to the chubby, smiling toddler with wings who now appears primarily on old-fashioned Valentine's Day cards.

Hercules was originally a demi-god with a dark side. In Greek mythology, he slays monsters and performs heroic acts, but he also goes mad and kills his family; strength, when uncontrolled, can do ill as well as good. During the Renaissance, he becomes an important symbolic figure in philosophy; as Hercules at the Crossroads, he must choose whether to follow the path of virtue or the path of vice. Whereas pagan heroes face and kill monsters,

Christian ones must face and defeat their own faults and sins. Today, Hercules inhabits pop culture primarily as a somewhat comedic strong-man, from the films starring Steve Reeves to cartoons, an animated Disney movie, and the campy, highly popular TV shows "The Adventures of Hercules" and its spin-off, "Xena, Warrior Princess."

In these shows, Hercules is your decent, average guy trying to do the right thing who just happens to possess superhuman strength. The gods appear as petty, childish figures meddling in the affairs of humans—which, ironically, is certainly an important aspect of how they are depicted in Homer's epics and Greek mythology in general. The 1997 animated Disney movie "Hercules" strung together bits and pieces of Greek mythology (erroneously making Pegasus his horse, for instance), and overlay his adventures with a Christian veneer; he achieves godhood through an act of self-sacrifice, descending into hell (actually, Hades' Underworld) to rescue his love interest, Meg (short for Megara, who, in Greek mythology, was indeed Hercules' first wife—the one he killed in a fit of madness). While Greek heroes did sometimes go to the Underworld to bring back dead people (Orpheus unsuccessfully sought his bride Eurydice, and the mythical Hercules himself tried to bring back the woman Alcestis, who had chosen to die in her husband's place), this could also be read as echoing Christ's harrowing of hell.

Aphrodite/Venus, the goddess of love, seductively naked in Hellenistic sculptures, becomes a serene, pale, detached beauty in Botticelli's famous Renaissance painting, "The Birth of Venus" and a saucy and slightly naughty aristocratic beauty in rococo art—still lovely, but no longer an awe-inspiring goddess. In the twentieth century she most often appears in pop songs, from Frankie Avalon's 1959 number one hit "Venus" (in which the singer implores her to send him a girl to love) to Shocking Blue's 1970 number one hit "Venus" (and Bananarama's 1986 remake and cheesy video, aired heavily by MTV). Woody Allen's lightweight 1995 comedy "Mighty Aphrodite" features a Greek chorus commenting on the romantic entanglements of hapless New Yorkers, but, as portrayed here, love seems somewhat less than "mighty."

Consider the figure of the Greek satyr (or Roman faun), a goat-legged, man-torsoed woodland creature originally symbolic of untrammeled sexuality (often showing off an erection), who spent all his time chasing nymphs. Elements of his untamed nature survive in Debussy's "Prelude to the Afternoon of a Faun," choreographed by the dancer Nijinsky into an erotically charged ballet that scandalized audiences in 1912 Paris; when nymphs run from him, he grabs one's veil and, lying down, thrusts at it lasciviously. A bit later, however, one can barely recognize Mr. Tumnus, the polite, proper, very English faun who befriends Lucy Pevensie in C. S. Lewis' *The Lion, the Witch, and the Wardrobe*, as the same sort of being.

Figure 8.4 *Mosaic of a satyr and a dryad (tree nymph). In modern stories such as The Chronicles of Narnia, many mythological figures, such as this lustful half-man/half-goat beast, have been reduced to much tamer versions of their original, more dangerous selves.*

Perhaps the ultimate form of diminution has occurred in advertising, where gods and heroes become the names of products. Nike, the Greek goddess of victory, with her own temple on the Acropolis at Athens and an iconic statue (known as the Winged Victory of Samothrace) dominating a grand staircase at the Louvre, has been transformed into a brand of sneakers; Ajax, the mighty if somewhat obtuse Greek hero who fought in the Trojan War, is now equated with an extra-strong cleanser; and "Little" Caesar has been reduced to a comic homunculus with a very limited vocabulary hawking pizza. From our childhood, some of us might recall a candy called Alexander the Grape, which transformed the hero into a smiling, big-footed grape wearing a helmet (now marketed under the less evocative name Grapehead). The Greek gods now sell a brand of Greek yogurt, with the various deities presiding over flavors rather than powers: Hermes for honey, Eros for vanilla honey, Athena for strawberry and honey, Apollo for pomegranate, Hera for fig, Aphrodite for vanilla/cinnamon/orange, Artemis for plain, and Poseidon for non-fat plain. (To be fair, their website slogan, "Experience the Myth," is at least accompanied by a family tree of the Olympian gods.)

The waning fortunes of the god of the forge, Hephaestus (Vulcan for the Romans), are reflected in the treatment of a giant statue of Vulcan erected atop a prominent hill in Birmingham, Alabama to celebrate the lucrative steel industry that once drove the local economy, and billed as "the world's largest iron man." Early on, he became a vehicle for advertisements. It was intended that he would hold a spear that he had just forged outstretched in his right hand, but the hand was put on wrong, making this impracticable. In its place, at various times, he held a giant ice cream cone, a bottle of Coca Cola, and a sign advertising pickles. At one point, he was clothed in a huge pair of overalls. A recent campaign to raise money for the statue's restoration sold T-shirts picturing the statue from behind with the caption of "The moon over Birmingham," because, naked except for his smith's apron, Vulcan flashes his buttocks at the city below. Classical nudity, once the standard in sculpture, had become a punch line.

Nowadays, toys and Halloween costumes are the primary means for getting in touch with your inner Greek or Roman. You can buy your own authentic head-to-toe Spartan King Leonidas costume as seen in the movie "300," including plumed helmet, wolf's tooth necklace, arm-guards, greaves, cape, shield, and red-leather briefs with codpiece for a mere $1,359, or perhaps you would prefer a blood-spattered, 12-inch action figure of King Leonidas that utters belligerent catch-phrases from the movie, such as "No retreat, no surrender" and "Tonight we dine in Hell." Finally, the ever-popular collegiate toga party offers an excuse for undergraduates wrapped in ill-fitting "togas" fashioned from bed sheets to get thoroughly drunk while allegedly emulating an atmosphere of Roman debauchery.

Figure 8.5 *The "World's Largest Iron Man," the giant statue of Hephaestus, the god of the forge. Erected on a hill above Birmingham, Alabama, this statue, seen in this photo from the main direction of approach, has been exploited to advertise everything from overalls to steak sauce.*

A day in the life: The ancient world lives on

Say you wake up in the morning and glance at the clock. It is 11 *ante meridiem*, and because it is Saturn's day, you didn't need to go to work at your office cubicle; instead you slept late in your *cubiculum*. You stop at an ATM to withdraw some money (named for the temple of Juno Moneta that once housed the Roman mint), and spend six quarters (stamped *e pluribus unum*, "Out of many, one," the Latin phrase found on the Seal of the United States) to buy a newspaper so that you can read about the current state of the Republic (modeled after the Roman one) and because, as a citizen and a "political animal," you want to know about what is going on in politics. You read about the interplay between the Republicans and the Democrats (the latter named for democracy, which was invented by the ancient Greeks). Then you head over to the gymnasium, "the naked place," and put on your Nike sneakers for a workout. Walking downtown, you pass by the city hall, adorned with a pediment and Doric columns, a domed Capitol building, a shrine of the Muses (or museum), the law court, and a library. In the afternoon, you watch a sporting event on TV that is being held in a big amphitheater-shaped stadium, where the fans wear their teams' colors and cheer in unison.

Every one of these actions, rituals, buildings, and institutions is either directly modeled upon or derived from ones found in the classical world, and whether you know it or not, you are constantly following in the footsteps of the ancients as you go through your daily routines. As we have seen in this book, we are all heirs to the legacy of the Greeks and Romans in a myriad of ways both large and small. We began this book by citing the Delphic Oracle's famous injunction to "Know Yourself," with its implication that it is essential for one to be aware of where one came from and the forces that have molded one's development. But "knowing oneself" is not just about gaining self-knowledge. It is only by understanding where we came from and how the current world has been shaped and created by the past that we can make informed decisions in the present. In order to choose the best future, we have to know our past. We hope that this book has helped you to appreciate, at least a little bit more, how the world around you got to be the way that it is. We are the product of our cultural heritage and there is no escaping the past, especially since so many of our familiar modern institutions and rituals actually have their roots in those supposedly long-dead Mediterranean cultures of 2,000 years ago.

Bibliography

This bibliography is organized by chapter. The first section, for the Introduction, contains both scholarly and popular books that directly discuss aspects of the influence of the ancient world on later eras. Many of these could obviously be placed under many, if not all, of the chapters, but to avoid redundancy we have grouped them all together under the bibliography for the Introduction. While acknowledging that much important scholarship about the ancient world is in languages other than English, for the convenience of an English-speaking audience we have limited the bibliography to works in that language.

Introduction

Cahill, Thomas. *Sailing the Wine-Dark Sea: Why the Greeks Matter*. New York: Doubleday, 2003.

Enenkel, Karl, Jan de Jong, and Jeanine de Landtsheer, (eds) *Recreating Ancient History: Episodes from the Greek and Roman Past in the Arts and Literature of the Early Modern Period*. Boston: Brill, 2002.

Finley. M. I., ed. *The Legacy of Greece: A New Appraisal*. New York: Oxford University Press, 1984.

Galinsky, Karl. *Classical and Modern Interactions: Postmodern Architecture, Multiculturalism, Decline, and Other Issues*. Austin: University of Texas Press, 1992.

Goldhill, Simon. *Love, Sex & Tragedy: How the Ancient World Shapes Our Lives*. Chicago: The University of Chicago Press, 2004.

Grafton, Anthony. *Commerce with the Classics: Ancient Books and Renaissance Readers*. Ann Arbor: The University of Michigan Press, 1997.

Highet, Gilbert. *The Classical Tradition: Greek and Roman Influences on Western Literature*. New York: Oxford University Press, 1949.

Jenkyns, Richard, ed. *The Legacy of Rome: A New Appraisal*. New York: Oxford University Press, 1992.

Knox, Bernard. *The Oldest Dead White European Males and Other Reflections on the Classics*. New York: W. W. Norton, 1993.
Richard, Carl. *Why We're All Romans: The Roman Contribution to the Western World*. New York: Rowman & Littlefield, 2010.
Wilkinson, Philip. *What the Romans Did For Us*. London: Boxtree, 2001.

Chapter 1: The bare necessities: Food and shelter

Beer, Michael. *Taste or Taboo: Dietary Choices in Antiquity*. Blackawton, Devon: Prospect Books, 2010.
Brothwell, Don, and Patricia Brothwell. *Food in Antiquity: A Survey of the Diet of Early Peoples*. Baltimore: The Johns Hopkins University Press, 1998.
Clarke, John. *The Houses of Roman Italy*. Berkeley: University of California Press, 1991.
Crawford, M. *Coinage and Money under the Roman Republic*. Berkeley: University of California Press, 1954.
Davidson, James. *Courtesans and Fishcakes: The Consuming Passions of Classical Athens*. New York: St. Martin's Press, 1997.
Garnsey, Peter. *Food and Society in Classical Antiquity*. New York: Cambridge University Press, 1999.
—*Famine and Food in the Graeco-Roman World: Responses to Risk and Crisis*. New York: Cambridge University Press, 1988.
Howgego, Christopher. *Ancient History from Coins*. New York: Routledge, 1995.
Packer, James. *The Insulae of Imperial Ostia*. Rome: American Academy in Rome, 1971.
Slater, William, ed. *Dining in a Classical Context*. Ann Arbor: The University of Michigan Press, 1991.
Wallace-Hadrill, A. *Houses and Society in Pompeii and Herculaneum*. Princeton: Princeton University Press, 1994.

Chapter 2: From the cradle to the grave: The family and the journey of life

Bickerman, E. J. *Chronology of the Ancient World*. London: Thames and Hudson, 1980.
Bonner, S. F. *Discovering the Roman Family*. New York: Oxford University Press, 1991.
—*Education in Ancient Rome*. Berkeley: University of California Press, 1977.
Dixon, S. *The Roman Family*. Baltimore: The Johns Hopkins University Press, 1992.
Eyben, E. *Restless Youth in Ancient Rome*. Trans. by Patrick Daly. New York: Routledge, 1993.
Fantham, Elaine, Helene Peet Foley, Natalie Boymel Kampen, Sarah B. Pomeroy, and H. Alan Shapiro. *Women in the Classical World*. New York: Oxford University Press, 1994.
Hallett, J., and M. Skinner, (eds) *Roman Sexualities*. Princeton: Princeton University Press, 1997.

Lefkowitz, Mary, and Maureen Fant. *Women's Life in Greece and Rome*. Baltimore: The Johns Hopkins University Press, 1982.
Scullard, H. H. *Festivals and Ceremonies of the Roman Republic*. Ithaca: Cornell University Press, 1981.
Toynbee, J. M. C. *Death and Burial in the Roman World*. Baltimore: The Johns Hopkins University Press, 1971.
Treggiari, S. *Roman Marriage*. Oxford: Clarendon Press, 1991.
Wiedemann, T. *Adults and Children in the Roman Empire*. New Haven: Yale University Press, 1989.

Chapter 3: Living the good life: Entertainments and leisure activities

Balsdon, J. P. V. D. *Life and Leisure in Ancient Rome*. New York: McGraw Hill, 1969.
Beacham, Richard. *Spectacle Entertainments of Early Imperial Rome*. New Haven: Yale University Press, 1999.
Cameron, Alan. *Circus Factions*. Oxford: Clarendon Press, 1976.
Casson, Lionel. *Travel in the Ancient World*. Baltimore: The Johns Hopkins University Press, 1994.
Fagan, Garrett. *Bathing in Public in the Roman World*. Ann Arbor: University of Michigan Press, 2002, reprint.
Harris, H. A. *Sport in Greece and Rome*. Ithaca: Cornell University Press, 1972.
—*Greek Athletes and Athletics*. Bloomington: Indiana University Press, 1964.
Köhne, E., and Cornelia Ewigleben, (eds) *Gladiators and Caesars*. Berkeley: University of California Press, 2000.
Kyle, Donald. *Sport and Spectacle in the Ancient World*. Malden: Blackwell, 2007.
Slater, William J., ed. *Roman Theater and Society*. Ann Arbor: University of Michigan Press, 1996.
Toner, J. P. *Leisure and Ancient Rome*. Malden: Blackwell, 1995.
Wiedemann, Thomas. *Emperors and Gladiators*. New York: Routledge, 1992.
Yegül, Fikret. *Baths and Bathing in Classical Antiquity*. Cambridge: The MIT Press, 1992.

Chapter 4: Power to the people: Systems of government

Hansen, Mogens Herman. *The Athenian Democracy in the Age of Demosthenes: Structure, Principles, and Ideology*. Norman: University of Oklahoma Press, 1991.
Nicolet, Claude. *The World of the Citizen in Republican Rome*. Berkeley: University of California Press, 1980.
Ober, Josiah. *Mass and Elite in Democratic Athens: Rhetoric, Ideology, and the Power of the People*. Princeton: Princeton University Press, 1989.

Painter, Borden, Jr. *Mussolini's Rome: Rebuilding the Eternal City*. New York: Palgrave Macmillan, 2005.

Pomeroy, Sarah, Stanley M. Burstein, Walter Donlan and Jennifer Tolbert Roberts. *Ancient Greece: A Political, Social, and Cultural History*. New York: Oxford University Press, 2007.

Rhodes, P. J., ed. *Athenian Democracy*. New York: Oxford University Press, 2004.

Richard, Carl. *Greeks and Romans Bearing Gifts: How the Ancients Inspired the Founding Fathers*. New York: Rowman & Littlefield, 2008.

—*The Founders and the Classics: Greece, Rome, and the American Enlightenment*. Cambridge: Harvard University Press, 1994.

Robinson, O. F. *Ancient Rome: City Planning and Administration*. New York: Routledge, 1992.

Sherwin-White, A. N. *The Roman Citizenship*. 2nd edition. New York: Oxford University Press, 1973.

Chapter 5: Understanding and shaping the material world: Architecture and science

Adam, Jean-Pierre. *Roman Buildings: Materials and Techniques*. Trans. by Anthony Mathews. Bloomington: Indiana University Press, 1994.

Aicher, P. J. *Guide to the Aqueducts of Ancient Rome*. Chicago: Chicago University Press, 1995.

Bomgardner, D. L. *The Story of the Roman Amphitheatre*. New York: Routledge, 2000.

Chevallier, Raymond. *Roman Roads*. Revised edition. London: Batsford, 1989.

Curd, Patricia, and Daniel Graham, (eds) *The Oxford Handbook of Presocratic Philosophy*. New York: Oxford University Press, 2008.

Dinsmoor, William Bell. *The Architecture of Ancient Greece*. New York: W. W. Norton and Company, 1975.

Edelstein, Ludwig. *Ancient Medicine: Selected Papers of Ludwig Edelstein*. Edited by Owsei Temkin and C. Lilian Temkin. Baltimore: The Johns Hopkins University Press, 1967.

Guthrie, W. K. C. *A History of Greek Philosophy*. 6 vols. New York: Cambridge University Press, 1962–81. Vols. 1, 2.

Hodge, A. Trevor. *Roman Aqueducts and Water Supply*. 2nd edition. London: Duckworth, 2002.

Lloyd, G. E. R. *Greek Science After Aristotle*. New York: W. W. Norton & Company, 1973.

Macdonald, W., and J. Pinto. *The Pantheon: Design, Meaning, and Progeny*. Cambridge: Harvard University Press, 2002.

Rykwert, Joseph. *The Idea of a Town: The Anthropology of Urban Form in Rome, Italy and the Ancient World*. Cambridge: The MIT Press, 1976.

Sear, Frank. *Roman Architecture*. Ithaca: Cornell University Press, 1982.

Ward-Perkins, J. B. *Cities of Ancient Greece and Italy: Planning in Classical Antiquity*. New York: George Braziller, 1974.

Warren, James. *Presocratics*. Berkeley: University of California Press, 2007.

Welch, Katherine. *The Roman Amphitheater from its Origins to the Colosseum*. New York: Cambridge University Press, 2009.
Wycherly, R. E. *How the Greeks Built Cities*. 2nd edition. New York: W. W. Norton & Company, 1962.

Chapter 6: Understanding and shaping the spiritual world: Superstition and religion

Adkins, Lesley, and Roy Adkins. *Dictionary of Roman Religion*. New York: Facts on File, 1996.
Beard, Mary, and John North, (eds) *Pagan Priests*. Ithaca: Cornell University Press, 1990.
Betz, Hans Dieter. *The Greek Magical Papyri in Translation*. Chicago: University of Chicago Press, 1986.
Burkert, Walter. *Greek Religion*. Cambridge: Harvard University Press, 1985.
Felton, D. *Haunted Greece and Rome: Ghost Stories from Classical Antiquity*. Austin: University of Texas Press, 1999.
Ferguson, J. *The Religions of the Roman Empire*. Ithaca: Cornell University Press, 1971.
Graf, Fritz. *Magic in the Ancient World*. Cambridge: Harvard University Press, 1997.
Luck, Georg. *Arcana Mundi: Magic and the Occult in the Greek and Roman Worlds*. Baltimore: The Johns Hopkins University Press, 1985.
MacMullen, Ramsay. *Christianizing the Roman Empire (A.D. 100–400)*. New Haven: Yale University Press, 1984.
—*Paganism in the Roman Empire*. New Haven: Yale University Press, 1981.
Ogden, Daniel. *Magic, Witchcraft, and Ghosts in the Greek and Roman Worlds: A Sourcebook*. New York: Oxford University Press, 2002.
Ogilvie, R. M. *The Romans and Their Gods in the Age of Augustus*. London: Chatto and Windus, 1969.
Turcan, Robert. *The Cults of the Roman Empire*. Malden: Blackwell, 1996.

Chapter 7: Words, ideas, and stories: Language, law, philosophy, and literature

Many of the books listed under the Introduction are also relevant to this chapter.

Aldrete, Gregory. *Gestures and Acclamations in Ancient Rome*. Baltimore: The Johns Hopkins University Press, 1999.
Benson, Hugh, ed. *A Companion to Plato*. Malden: Blackwell, 2006.
Crook, J. A. *Law and Life of Rome*. Ithaca: Cornell University Press, 1967.
Francese, Christopher. *Ancient Rome in So Many Words*. New York: Hippocrene Books, 2007.

Hansen, William. *Ariadne's Thread: A Guide to International Tales Found in Classical Literature*. Ithaca: Cornell University Press, 2002.

Humez, Alexander, and Nicholas Humez. *Alpha to Omega: The Life and Times of the Greek Alphabet*. Boston: David R. Godine, 1981.

Morstein-Marx, Robert. *Mass Oratory and Political Power in the Late Roman Republic*. New York: Cambridge University Press, 2004.

Nicholas, Barry. *An Introduction to Roman Law*. New York: Oxford University Press, 1962.

Ostler, Nicholas. *Empires of the Word: A Language History of the World*. New York: HarperCollins, 2005.

Powell, Barry. *Classical Myth*. Edgewood Cliffs: Prentice-Hall, 1995.

Conclusion: You can't escape the past: Popular culture and antiquity

Bondanella, Peter. *The Eternal City: Roman Images in the Modern World*. Chapel Hill: The University of North Carolina Press, 1987.

Cyrino, Monica Silveira. *Big Screen Rome*. Malden: Wiley-Blackwell, 2005.

Fraser, George MacDonald. *The Hollywood History of the World*. London: Michael Joseph, 1988.

Kovacs, George, and C. W. Marshall, (eds) *Classics and Comics: Classical Presences*. New York: Oxford University Press, 2011.

Solomon, Jon. *The Ancient World in the Cinema*. Revised edition. New Haven: Yale University Press, 2001.

Winkler, Martin. *Cinema and Classical Texts: Apollo's New Light*. New York: Cambridge University Press, 2009.

—*Classical Myth and Culture in the Cinema*. New York: Oxford University Press, 2001.

Wyke, Maria. *Projecting the Past: Ancient Rome, Cinema and History*. New York: Routledge, 1997.

Index